RED SERGE AND POLAR BEAR PANTS

W9-DCF-878

WILLIAM BARR

RED SERGE AND

POLAR BEAR PANTS

The Biography of
Harry Stallworthy, RCMP

The University of Alberta Press

Published by

The University of Alberta Press
Ring House 2
Edmonton, Alberta, Canada   T6G 2E1

Copyright © William Barr 2004

ISBN 0-88864-433-7

LIBRARY AND ARCHIVES CANADA
CATALOGUING IN PUBLICATION DATA

Barr, William, 1940–
   Red serge and polar bear pants : the
   biography of Harry Stallworthy, RCMP/
   William Barr.

Includes bibliographical references and index.
ISBN 0-88864-433-7

   1. Stallworthy, Harry. 2. Royal
Canadian Mounted Police—Biography.
3. Territory, National—Canada. 4. Canada,
Northern—Discovery and exploration.
5. Arctic regions—Discovery and explo-
ration—Canadian. 6. Canada, Northern—
Biography. 7. Explorers—Canada—
Biography. I. Title.

FC3216.3.S73B37 2004   971.9'02'092
C2004-906939-X

Printed and bound in Canada by Houghton
Boston Printers, Saskatoon, Saskatchewan.
First edition, first printing, 2004

The University of Alberta Press is
committed to protecting our natural environment. As part of our efforts, this book is
printed on stock produced by New Leaf
Paper: it contains 100% post-consumer
recycled fibres and is acid- and chlorine-free.

The University of Alberta Press gratefully
acknowledges the support received for its
publishing program from The Canada
Council for the Arts. The University of
Alberta Press also gratefully acknowledges
the financial support of the Government of
Canada through the Book Publishing
Industry Development Program (BPDIP)
and from the Alberta Foundation for the
Arts for our publishing activities.

CONTENTS

LIST OF MAPS

FOREWORD

THE SERVICE of the Royal Canadian Mounted Police in the country's north is one of the most dramatic and best-known chapters in the history of the force. Many of the more famous members of the RCMP made their reputations in the north: Sam Steele, who was in command of the Yukon detachments at the height of the gold rush, F.J. Fitzgerald of the "lost patrol," and W.J.D. Dempster, after whom the Yukon's Dempster Highway is named, are three examples. Surprisingly, Harry Stallworthy is much less well known, despite the fact that he was one of the most accomplished northern explorers in Canadian history and played a vital role in one of the RCMP's most important northern missions—the establishment of Canadian sovereignty over the Arctic.

The question of Canada's sovereignty in the northern reaches of the country is one that goes back to the late nineteenth century, and which seems still not to be finally settled. Rather ominously, the much-debated phenomenon of global warming seems likely, if the scientists on the pessimistic side are correct, to melt the Arctic ice to the extent that the Northwest Passage will become a practical shipping route. Since Canada's sovereignty over these waters is not universally accepted (the United States does not recognize it), the question is likely to remain contentious into the foreseeable future. Stallworthy's role belongs to an earlier period of the history of Arctic sovereignty, when Canada was concerned with establishing and demonstrating its control not over the waters, but over the land itself.

The mainland of Canada's north (and part of Baffin Island) was transferred to Canada as part of the 1870 transfer of Rupert's Land from the control of the Hudson's Bay Company, and it was always clear that this territory had been British and was now Canadian. The Arctic islands were a different matter. British title to these islands was a bit shaky, partly because some of them had been discovered and claimed by non-British explorers, and partly because at that time a number of them were still unknown.

After the islands were transferred to Canada in 1880, the government for several years did almost nothing to establish its title in fact. It was not until 1904 that Captain J-E Bernier was sent on a number of voyages to the eastern Arctic. He spent the winter of 1908–9 at Melville Island so that it could be said that a Canadian had actually lived in the north for that period of time. He fixed a plaque to a cairn on the island claming it for Canada.

However, the great northern explorers of that era—Peary, Amundsen, Sverdrup, Nansen, and Rasmussen—were not Canadians, and it was they who discovered most of the new islands in the archipelago. Vilhjalmur Stefansson, born in Canada and financed by the Canadian government to carry out an exploratory expedition during World War I, was the only Canadian actually to discover significant new land. The main reason why Canada's sovereignty in the Arctic was never in any real danger is that none of the countries whose citizens had made discoveries there had any interest in pressing claims to it.

It was for purposes of sovereignty that Canada began to establish RCMP detachments along the Arctic coast and on the Arctic islands after 1920. Bache Peninsula, where Stallworthy was sent in 1930, was the most northerly police post in Canada and in fact in the entire British Empire. Stallworthy's nearest neighbours were Inuit across the strait in Greenland. There was no one else within several hundred kilometers of the post. Nevertheless, Stallworthy and the two constables who served with him at Bache Peninsula were provided with the apparatus of a post office (though mail arrived only once a year), customs forms, and the other paraphernalia of officialdom. The point was to administer this territory in a day-to-day fashion, and thus emphasize the fact that it was Canadian.

Stallworthy not only fulfilled this function, but also carried out a remarkable series of patrols around Ellesmere Island that made his reputation as a skilled Arctic traveler, and for which he was later made a Fellow of the Royal Geographical Society. He spent a total of twenty years in the north and later was present at the historic meeting of Churchill and Franklin Roosevelt in Québec. Given the strenuous nature of his achievements, it is pleasant to note that he enjoyed a fairly long retirement, building and operating a small resort on Vancouver Island.

Red Serge and Polar Bear Pants is not a political or administrative history. It is a biography of a young man who like so many others of his era and background, came to Canada just before World War I, found a new and adventurous life, and spent the rest of his working life in the honourable service of his new country. Most of his career with the Mounted Police was spent in northern service, so the book is not only a history of a very interesting and likeable man, it is also a history of a region that was only then beginning to be incorporated into the Dominion.

This book is also a revealing portrait of a marriage, and what it meant to be married to a man who was stationed in the Arctic for months and years at a time—a marriage that was dependent to some degree on the whims of officials and superiors who were not always sympathetic. Much as one leaves this book admiring the toughness and character of Harry Stallworthy, the reader is bound to admire as much or more those qualities in his wife Hilda.

No one is better qualified than William Barr to write a biography of this important northern figure. Professor Emeritus of Geography at the University of Saskatchewan and a research associate at the Arctic Institute of North America, he has written on an impressive range of northern subjects, including books on Franz Boas, Peter Warren Dease, the Russian Northern Sea Route, and the First International Polar Year. He is also perhaps the best historical editor in Canada, having produced excellent editions of the letters and journals of several northern figures, notably Peter Warren Dease, Emile-Frédéric de Bray, James Anderson and Christopher Middleton. Here he finds a worthy subject in a man who should be much better known in this country, one who as a result of this book, no doubt will be.

WILLIAM R. MORRISON
University of Northern British Columbia

ACKNOWLEDGEMENTS

AFTER HARRY STALLWORTHY'S DEATH on Christmas Day 1976, his widow, Hilda, seriously contemplated writing his biography. Almost throughout his life Harry had written regularly to his brother Bill, who lived at Ampney Crucis in their home area of Gloucestershire, England. Fortunately, Bill had kept most of these letters and at Hilda's request he sent them back to her in January 1978 to provide details for the biography she was planning. When Hilda died her niece, Ms. Elaine Mellor of Edmonton, Alberta, inherited not only these letters but also a substantial volume of Harry's reports, photographs and documents, as well as several of Hilda's diaries. In the early 1990s Ms. Mellor donated all this material to the Arctic Institute of North America at the University of Calgary. These materials, augmented by Harry Stallworthy's RCMP service file and medical file, have provided the main sources for this biography.

I am grateful to the Arctic Institute of North America for giving me free access to the documents and photographs in the Stallworthy Collection. All the photos are from this collection with the exception of those on pp. 8, 13, and 20, for which I am indebted to Mrs. Barbara Stallworthy of Cirencester, and those on pp. 3 (lower photo), 4 and 323, which are from my own collection.

I am endlessly grateful to Ms. Mellor not only for making the Stallworthy Collection available to me and other researchers, but also for her ongoing interest, her valuable comments on a draft manuscript, and for her fascinating stories and her memories of Harry Stallworthy. As a high school student she spent several summers living and working at the Stallworthy's resort at Timberlane on Saratoga Beach, where she got to know both Harry and Hilda very well.

I am also indebted to Elaine for putting me in touch with Mrs. Barbara Stallworthy of Cirencester, Gloucestershire, daughter-in-law of Harry's brother, Bill. During a visit to Cirencester and area in the fall of 2002, Mrs. Stallworthy showed me, and allowed me to copy, a number of relevant letters and photos that I had not previously seen; her hospitality also extended to an excellent dinner. Through her I also met Mr. John Ward, a cousin of Harry's mother, who acted as my guide to various sites associated with Harry and his family, including Harry's birthplace at Village Farm in Winson, St. Mary's churchyard at Ampney St. Mary, where many of the family are buried, and where Harry's name has been added to his brother's tombstone. Mr. Ward also showed me The Mill at Ampney Crucis where Bill Stallworthy lived and worked and where Harry and Hilda were quite frequent visitors.

I also wish to thank Ole Gjerstad for providing me with a transcript of his interview with Ms. Elaine Mellor in connection with the preparation of a documentary film on the RCMP and Canadian sovereignty in the High Arctic and Ms. Sally Hamilton for allowing me to consult (and quote) relevant sections of the unpublished autobiography of her father, Paddy Hamilton.

My warmest thanks are also due to Dr. William Morrison for contributing the foreword, which very aptly places Harry Stallworthy's life and career in the context of the role of the RCMP in asserting Canadian sovereignty in the Arctic.

Finally, I wish to thank Mrs. Marilyn Croot for drafting the excellent maps of the various areas where Harry Stallworthy lived and worked.

The University of Alberta Press would like to acknowledge the editorial work of Peter Midgley and the design work of Alan Brownoff.

1

HARRY STALLWORTHY'S

Life of Adventure

ON A BRIGHT SUNNY DAY in late April 1931 Corporal Harry Stallworthy, dressed in just a mackinaw shirt and polar bear pants, was making his way cautiously along the top of the ice cliff at the snout of the Talbot Glacier on the east coast of Ellesmere Island.[1] He and his two Inuit companions, Nukappiannguaq and Inuatuk, were on their way back north to the Royal Canadian Mounted Police detachment at Bache Peninsula, the northern-most post ever occupied by the Force. The three men were returning from a patrol to the temporarily abandoned post at Craig Harbour in south-eastern Ellesmere Island. As they sledged across the sea ice they spotted a polar bear and Harry watched his companions approach and shoot the bear after their dogs had brought it to bay; he was now walking back to where they had left their sledges. He had tethered his team, leaving his parka slung over the upstanders of his sledge. Below him he could see the combined teams of his two companions towing the carcass of the bear across the sea ice back towards the sledges.

Suddenly the snow just ahead of him collapsed to reveal a crevasse about a metre wide. Carefully checking its width, he jumped across it but then, fearful that there might be more crevasses, he decided to follow the bear's tracks back to the sea ice, on the premise that the bear weighed considerably more than he did. Before he reached the line of big paw prints the snow beneath him suddenly gave way and he felt himself falling; he had found another invisible crevasse, barely 60 cm wide at the top. Suddenly his fall was arrested abruptly. The impact knocked the breath out of him. His chest was jammed in a narrow constriction in the crevasse, his legs and lower body dangling above a chasm of unknown depth. Harry's arms were free but there was nothing on the blue ice walls that he could grasp. Apart from the pain in his chest, he noticed that there was blood dripping from his chin, which he had banged against the ice during the fall.

The depths of an arctic glacier were a long way from Winson, the small village just northeast Cirencester in Gloucestershire, England, where Henry Webb Stallworthy was born on 20 January 1895. Throughout his life, he was known as Harry. His father, William James Webb Stallworthy lived as a gentleman farmer on a property called Village Farm after leaving his position as a solicitor in a firm of property managers. Harry's mother, Florence Fanny Stallworthy (née Cole), was one of a family of seven children born to a wealthy landowner who also owned a large mill in Cirencester.

Harry and his three brothers had a fairly privileged childhood.[2] After the death of their father in 1899, Florence took the children to live in Ampney Crucis, some five miles east of Cirencester. The four boys attended the village school in Winson before going to the Cirencester Grammar School on Victoria Road in Cirencester, where Harry became a Boy Scout. According to Harry's wife, Hilda, there was an expectation that he would go on to read law at Oxford, as his father had done. But the young Scout had other ideas. On leaving school, he was apprenticed to a company of auctioneers and fine furniture dealers, Messrs. Thomas Owen, whose premises were located in Dyer Street, Cirencester. Being a keen horseman he also served for 2½ years in the Royal Gloucestershire Hussars Yeomanry.[3]

Harry Stallworthy's mother, Florence Stallworthy.

Village Farm, Winson, Gloucestershire, Harry Stallworthy's birth place.

Cirencester Grammar School, which Harry and his brothers attended.

Harry was a young man with an adventuresome spirit. In 1913, he decided to visit his two older brothers, William and Archie, who had emigrated to Canada the previous year. The brothers had homesteaded on the thirsty prairie near Jenner in south-eastern Alberta, northeast of Brooks and northwest of Medicine Hat, just south of the Red Deer River. It appears that they were responsible for the name of the little town that was known as Websdale Post Office until 1913. One of the houses at the Cirencester Grammar School was Jenner House, named after Dr. Edward Jenner, the man who discovered a vaccination to prevent smallpox. The Stallworthy sons must have thought it appropriate to name their new home after a famous fellow alumnus.

The small, arid prairie town in Alberta that bore a famous name must have been a real challenge after the lush green countryside of the Cotswolds. And yet now, jammed in a crevasse, even the arid prairie may have seemed preferable to Harry. He blacked out temporarily from the shock of his fall. On regaining consciousness a few moments later, Harry felt the cold of the crevasse seeping into his body and he realized that being as lightly dressed as he was, death from hypothermia was a real danger. He started shouting in the hope that his companions were still close by, dragging the bear back to their sledges. They were indeed still within earshot, but their immediate reaction was one of surprised bewilderment, possibly mingled with apprehension. The crevasse in which Harry was jammed was connected to the ice cliff at the front of the glacier by a relatively narrow crack and to the two men on the sea ice it appeared as if his voice was emanating in ghostly fashion from the depths of the glacier. But their confusion was only momentary; years of experience had made both men familiar with the dangers of glacier travel and they realized that Harry must have dropped down a crevasse. While Inuatuk kept an eye on the dogs, Nukappiannguaq grabbed their harpoon lines, made from tough strips of bearded seal hide, and quickly clambered back onto the glacier. He soon found the place where Harry's tracks ended at the mouth of a sinister-looking hole. It was from this hole that Harry's muffled shouts still issued periodically.

To Harry's immense relief, Nukappiannguaq's grinning face appeared against the narrow strip of blue sky above him. Nukappiannguaq quickly made a loop in the end of his harpoon line and lowered it to where Harry could grab it. Very cautiously, Harry worked the loop over his head and shoulders and fixed the rope under his armpits. Then he gave Nukappiannguaq the signal to start hauling. Straddling the crevasse, Nukappiannguaq, whose relatively short stature and bulky fur clothing concealed a powerful physique, began hauling in the harpoon line hand over hand. Harry was unable to help as he could not get any purchase on the sheer blue walls of the crevasse until his head approached the surface. As soon as he was able to, he gripped the edges of the crevasse and hauled himself up. Amid shouts of relieved laughter, Nukappiannguaq helped Harry back to sunlight and safety.

With the help of his companion, Harry staggered down to where Inuatuk was waiting on the sea ice with the dogs and sledges. There, still shaking from his ordeal, he took several good slugs of brandy and rested while the Inuit built an igloo and cooked a large meal. They remained in camp the following day before resuming their journey back north to Bache Peninsula.

Between Bache Peninsula and the English countryside of Harry Stallworthy's youth lay two decades into which Harry had already packed a lifetime of experiences. On 5 December 1933, the northernmost tip of Axel Heiberg Island where Nansen Sound opens into the Arctic Ocean was officially named Cape Stallworthy by the Canadian Geographical Names Board. This was done in

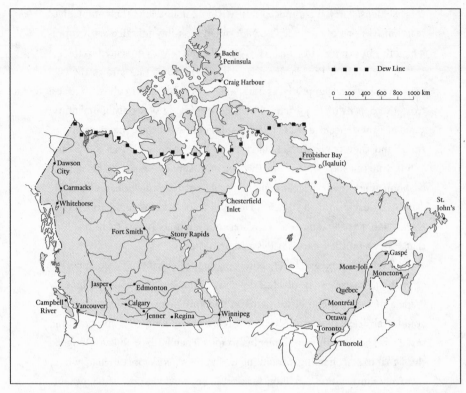

Harry Stallworthy's Canada.

recognition of Harry's contributions to the Royal Canadian Mounted Police and to Canada, especially Arctic Canada.

Harry's High Arctic sledge trips were not the only impressive trips he made during his career. While stationed at Chesterfield Inlet on Hudson Bay between 1923 and 1925, he travelled by dog team to Cape Fullerton and Baker Lake on two separate occasions. These trips were in addition to the numerous short trips he undertook to hunt for dog feed. Arctic trips held particular appeal for Harry because he always travelled with Inuit companions, men whom he admired and emulated and whose language he did his best to learn and whose beliefs and customs he respected. One of the reasons why he felt so attuned to the Inuit was that he was almost invariably calm and collected. His niece, Elaine, once remarked that for as long as she knew Harry she never saw him flustered or lose his temper. However, he could show displeasure—usually at somebody's thoughtlessness or carelessness.[4]

On Arctic trips he travelled with the long, heavy Inuit komatik, using the Inuit fan-hitch whereby each dog was on a separate trace. However, during his sojourns south of the tree-line, in the Yukon and while stationed at Stony Rapids, Northern Saskatchewan, he mastered equally well the use of a cariole or toboggan and of the tandem hitch as he travelled in deep snow and in forested country. Here, too, he made some very impressive sledge trips, such as the trip from Stony Rapids east to Nueltin Lake in 1929 and his near-disastrous trip from Carmacks to Ross River at the start of the melt in the spring of 1920. He also participated in the last of the patrols from Dawson City to Fort McPherson in 1921 with the legendary Corporal W. J. D. Dempster.

Harry Stallworthy was a man of many talents and the most remarkable feature of his career was its diversity. He travelled by horse-drawn post-sleigh during the Yukon winters, he guarded gold shipments waiting for the White Pass and Yukon Railway at Whitehorse, flew the length of the DEW Line as the person in charge of security in 1957, lay in wait for poachers at the mouth of the Oyster River on Vancouver Island, and stood guard as Winston Churchill greeted Franklin D. Roosevelt at their historic meeting at Quebec City in 1944. Despite the variety in his life, Harry was never happier than when travelling behind a good team of sledge dogs.

Travelling with Harry, or even just visiting at his home, was an experience, for Harry was a wonderful raconteur who could hold the attention of guests for hours with stories of his travels. He could converse with almost anyone, whether it be with his friend Naujaa in an overnight snow-house, using mostly mime or relying on their limited but growing command of each other's language, or with Queen Elizabeth at his investiture as an Officer of the Order of Canada. Harry's life unfolded like a storybook, beginning shortly before the outbreak of the first World War, during the Alberta winter of 1913.

2

A YOUNG MOUNTIE

and Prospector

WHEN HARRY STALLWORTHY ARRIVED in Canada in November 1913, his intention was to visit his brothers in Jenner, Alberta, and then to return to England. However, despite—or perhaps because of—the challenges of a prairie winter, he decided to stay and for several months he lived and worked in Alberta. For a while in the summer of 1914 he worked on a Canadian Pacific Railway survey crew before finding a job building pig pens at Donalda. Later, he stooked grain for a German farmer named Hillker near Stettler. If at this point Harry had any plans to return to England (as did his brother Bill), these plans were drastically disrupted by the outbreak of World War I.

William enlisted in a regular unit of the Canadian Expeditionary Force but Harry, who was a keen horseman, happened to see a handbill to the effect that the Royal North-West Mounted Police were looking for 500 recruits to

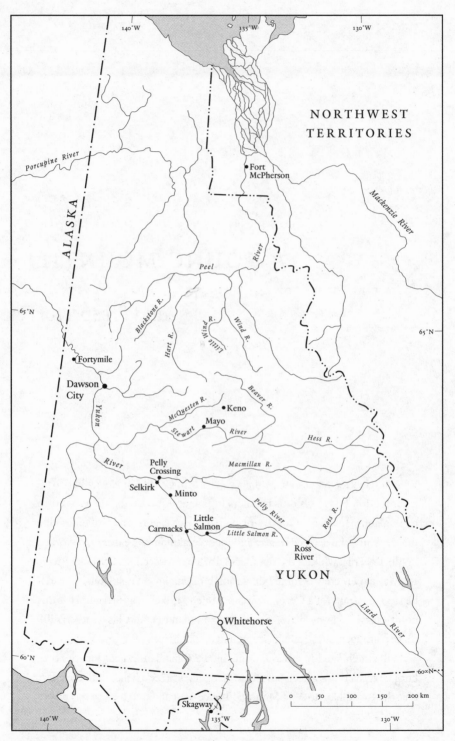

Yukon Territory, showing Harry Stallworthy's postings and travel routes.

form a cavalry detachment that would be heading for France with the Canadian Expeditionary Force. Harry travelled to Calgary where he was interviewed by Superintendent G. S. Worsley and joined the Royal North-West Mounted Police on 25 September 1914.[1]

Harry soon found himself at the Force's training depot in Regina where he underwent the standard training for a constable, which included a 40-mile route march across the prairie to Moose Jaw. By the time he had completed his training and had graduated as a member of the Force, the plan to send a cavalry detachment overseas had been shelved. To his disappointment, Harry was posted to Calgary instead. However, Harry wanted a more challenging posting and on 26 July 1915 he applied to be transferred to "B" Division for service in the Yukon.[2] The fever of the Klondike gold rush was over, but the Yukon still held a powerful allure for a young Englishman who was keen to see how he would measure up to the Yukon's severe environment. In August 1915 he travelled west to Vancouver, then north to Skagway aboard the Canadian Pacific steamer *Princess Sophia*. From Skagway he travelled via the White Pass and Yukon Railroad to Whitehorse, where he took up his new posting with the local detachment. Whitehorse's main function at this time was to serve as the transfer point from the railway to the river steamers that ran north down the Yukon River to Dawson City, which at the time was the capital of the Yukon.

Initially some of his duties were scarcely what he had been anticipating. During his first fall, Harry found himself engaged in such mundane duties as whitewashing the detachment buildings. On 10 September 1915, one of the scaffolding planks broke while he was working, sending Harry tumbling some ten feet to the ground. He sprained the arch of his right foot, but by 9 October he had recovered fully.[3] It must have been some consolation that he was receiving an extra 50¢ per day for this duty.[4]

The drudgery of whitewashing walls did not last long. In 1914 the White Pass and Yukon Railroad had employed Alexander Gagoff as a member of a section crew in the Whitehorse area. Gagoff's English was limited and he was reported to be of a "suspicious disposition." He would often refuse to eat with the other members of the crew at lunch, imagining that they were making fun of him because he could not understand their conversation.[5] Gagoff had been "outside" all summer and returned to Whitehorse in late September 1915. On 29 September he bought a 30–30 rifle and two boxes

Harry Stallworthy as a new recruit, RNWMP headquarters, Regina, 1914.

Harry Stallworthy guarding a shipment of gold bars, Whitehorse railroad station, 1915.

of cartridges from J.P. Whitney in Whitehorse. The following day he was seen carrying the rifle as he headed south along the railway towards where a section crew of five men was working about three miles out of town. One of the crewmen, Arthur Wilkinson, later reported that they had just finished their lunch when they saw Gagoff approaching with rifle in his hand. He fired between seven and ten shots at foreman Pat Kinslow, killing him and three other crew members, George Lane, Tom Boknovich and Henry Cook. The only remaining crew member, Arthur Wilkinson, managed to escape into the bush and lay low until after Gagoff had left.[6] After his shooting spree Gagoff took a handcar back to town, where he stopped at a house to ask for a drink of water. The owner reported that Gagoff "said he had killed three men who came at him like dogs."[7] Gagoff then called at the White Pass Hotel, where he had been staying and asked for his bill. He still had the gun in his hand and appeared to be very nervous, dropping several cartridges on the floor. From the hotel, Gagoff went to H.G. MacPherson's store where he again stated that he had killed three men. At MacPherson's request, Gagoff handed over his gun.

While Gagoff was making his way through Whitehorse, Dr. Clarke, the local physician, was alerted and went to the scene of the crime. He found three men dead and Cook still alive. He took Cook to the hospital, where he was able to make a statement before he died.

Gagoff was still at MacPherson's store when constable Fletcher of the Royal North-West Mounted Police arrested him. It is not known whether Harry Stallworthy was on duty at the time, but he certainly guarded Gagoff over the period leading up to the trial, and thereafter. At the trial, Russian interpreters translated the proceedings for Gagoff and on 10 November 1915 Gagoff was sentenced to death by hanging for killing Henry Cook, the only victim who had made a statement.

The execution was scheduled for 10 March the following year and during the intervening four months Harry Stallworthy was frequently the officer on duty for the so-called "death watch." For the task of guarding the condemned man he received an additional 50¢ per day.[8] Harry was also present at the hanging. It was a grim affair that was reported quite clinically in the newspapers:

> At 6.59, between two stalwart members of the Royal North-West Mounted Police, Gagoff mounted the scaffold stairs with unfaltering step, and was placed on the trap. The black cap was fitted by Official Hangman Ellis of Ottawa.... The trap was sprung at 7 o'clock sharp, and Gagoff dropped seven feet ten inches, and his soul was plunged into eternity. Death was instantaneous. The pulse ceased beating in fourteen minutes.[9]

Even a man much less sensitive than Harry must have been deeply affected by witnessing this event at close quarters.

There was an intriguing sequel to this hanging. Gagoff's cousin, Tom, arrived in Whitehorse a couple of days before the hanging.[10] Having been tipped off, the police met the train and found a loaded revolver and several extra shells on his person. He was arraigned in court on the 8 March for carrying a concealed weapon and was fined $105 and sentenced to three months in jail. It was presumed that his plan was to try to slip the gun to his cousin, who might then have tried to shoot his way out of jail. Alternatively Tom may have planned to shoot his way in to free his cousin. In either case,

Harry Stallworthy (left) at Whitehorse Rapids, 1915.

had Harry been on "death watch" at the time he would have been in grave danger.

Very soon after the Gagoff trial, still in March 1916, Harry was transferred to Pelly Crossing, situated at the point where the winter road that ran between Dawson and Whitehorse crossed the Pelly River. Winter passenger and mail service between the two towns, a distance of some 545 km, was provided by the British Yukon Navigation Company and later by the White Pass Company. From mid-October, after freeze-up on the Yukon, coaches drawn by six horses and capable of handling ten passengers were used until there was a good depth of snow. At that point, the coaches were replaced by sleighs drawn by four horses until spring break-up on the Yukon around mid-May. The sleighs could handle 17 passengers with their hand baggage.[11] The company used some 175 horses and some 60 coaches and sleighs. It maintained 15 road houses with sleeping accommodations and stabling for

12 to 24 horses. Passenger fares varied from $75 for most of the winter, when sleighing conditions were good, to $125 during the difficult conditions of the spring melt. Under optimal conditions the run from Whitehorse to Dawson took five full days, with three halts at road houses during the day and with overnight stops.[12]

Harry took the trip in the sleigh in his stride and soon settled into the routine of life at Pelly Crossing. Much of the officers' time was taken up with patrolling from roadhouse to roadhouse. Their duties were extremely varied and some tasks were quite mundane. In early November 1916, Harry received a request from Staff Sergeant G.B. Jod at Dawson to buy about 100 lbs of whitefish, have it frozen and see that it got to Dawson with one of the regular patrols.[13] In February he reported to his superiors in Dawson on a winter patrol he had just made to Minto in bitterly cold winter weather to investigate the ill-treatment of horses by crew members of a freighter.[14]

On 6 March 1917 Superintendent R.S. Knight, the commanding officer of the "B" Division in Dawson wrote to Harry with orders to ensure that he stopped a potlatch that was being organized at Selkirk, a small settlement about ten kilometres from Pelly Crossing at the confluence of the Yukon and the Pelly. Potlatches were a custom common to all the Indian groups of the Northwest Coast and involved the ceremonial distribution of gifts and feasting and dancing. The entire event sometimes lasted for several days and validated status and confirmed social structure. From 1884 to 1951, the Government of Canada banned the practice of potlatches, largely because of pressure from the churches, who saw potlatches as a pagan ritual. In addition to ensuring that the event did not take place, Harry had to acquaint the Indians concerned with the relevant clauses of the Indian Act.[15]

In early May 1917, Harry moved to Selkirk and soon thereafter Superintendent Knight asked him to ensure that a particular individual sign and submit a National Service Card.[16] Shortly after this Harry received orders to move north to Dawson. The instructions told him to

> report at Dawson for duty on the first boat that is able to bring you and your horse....
>
> Leave your cutter, which is condemned, also your harness and saddlery if in good repair but otherwise bring it in. Your forage you will store in some place where it will keep in good condition.[17]

Complying with these instructions, Harry then spent the summer of 1917 in the relatively civilized environment of Dawson City. By this time the population of Dawson had declined drastically from what it had been at the height of the gold rush at the turn of the century and there were numerous abandoned and dilapidated buildings in town.

Some measure of the changes that had occurred was the plebiscite on prohibition that had been held on 30 August 1916 throughout the Yukon Territory. After a prolonged and often heated campaign the voters of the Yukon had been asked: "Are you in favour of the sale, importation and manufacture of intoxicating liquor for beverage purposes in the Yukon Territory?" Harry had been employed as a scrutineer for the "Drys" in Pelly Crossing and area. Due to the problems of transport it was not until 5 September 1916 that all the ballots were in and the results could be announced. A total of 1745 votes were cast (over 90% of the electorate); the "drys" won by three ballots, 874 to 871![18] All the saloons in Dawson had been closed by the time Harry got to town and he found himself raiding poker games at which alcohol was being illegally consumed.

Soon after arriving in Dawson, Harry was put on "town patrol," a task that earned him an extra 25¢ per day.[19] Patrolling the streets of Dawson stood in strong contrast to some of Harry's sledge patrols, both in the Yukon and later in various parts of the Northwest Territories. However, being on town patrol was not always a routine task. At 5.30 A.M. on the night of 27/28 June 1917 Harry was standing at the corner of First Avenue and Church Street when he was approached by Rokuichi (Roy) Yoshioka. Yoshioka, who operated a fox farm across the Yukon River in West Dawson, was a well-known figure in town and had been in the Yukon since 1903. On this occasion Yoshioka appeared to be distraught and told Harry that his wife, Hisha, had been murdered and that he had just found her body near their property.[20] Harry accompanied Yoshioka back across the river to where his wife's body was lying. Hisha had what appeared to be a knife wound in the front of her body and a bullet wound in the back. Her skirts and petticoats were pulled up around her waist and she had on only one shoe. The other shoe was found some distance away on the trail back to Yoshioka's cabin, which might have indicated that she had lost it while being pursued.

Yoshioka also reported that an Indian named Percy James from the Peel River area [and hence probably Gwich'in], who had been working for

Yoshioka, was also missing, along with his three dogs and their dog-packs and Yoshioka's rifle. Yoshioka repeatedly suggested that James had murdered his wife. A post-mortem revealed that what Harry had mistaken for a knife wound was in fact the entrance wound from a bullet that had passed right through the body.[21] Hisha Yoshioka was also about four months pregnant.

When the police learned that Yoshioka was in financial difficulties and that he had taken out insurance policies for $2,000 for both himself and Hisha with New York Life, Harry's boss, Supt. Reginald Knight had Yoshioka arrested on suspicion of murder. On Sunday, 1 July, a search of the area near the fox farm revealed that a sandy area around an old tree stump appeared suspicious. It became clear that the stump had been placed there to disguise the fact that the area had been disturbed. When the police started digging, they found a 30–30 rifle at a depth of four feet and beneath it were the carcasses of two dogs and the body of a male Indian who had been shot from behind. He was clad only in his underwear and the bullet, which had passed through his body, was found caught in his underwear. Below him at a depth of seven feet was the carcass of a third dog and beneath it a pair of new leather boots without laces. In total the excavation was nine feet deep.[22] Two of the dogs had been shot with a shotgun and the third had been struck on the head, possibly with an axe. A shooting-stick that fired shotgun shells was found in the Yoshioka cabin with a shell jammed in it.[23] The search of the cabin also turned up a pair of rubber boots with brown canvas laces. On 22 June Percy James had bought a pair of leather boots from Leo Krause's general store in Dawson. Krause testified that they had had brown canvas laces of a type that could be bought in Dawson only along with a pair of boots such as those James had bought. He also testified that in April Yoshioka had bought a pair of rubber boots with rawhide laces. On the basis of a preliminary hearing on 17 July, Yoshioka was held for trial on charges of murder.

The trial began in Dawson on 6 August and lasted a week. Strangely, Yoshioka was tried only for the murder of his wife, but not for that of Percy James since it was felt that all the evidence covered both cases. Harry naturally had to give evidence on finding Hisha's body and on her husband's demeanour at the time. Yoshioka was found guilty of his wife's murder and was sentenced to be hanged.[24] The sentence was carried out on 23 November[25] and until the day of the execution Yoshioka was kept under a "death-watch" around the clock. Harry once again took his turn at this duty of keeping the prisoner under constant observation and was also one of the officers who attended the hanging—his second in only two years!

After the relative excitement of walking the streets of Dawson for the entire month of June 1917, Harry was employed as Pay Clerk for the Dawson detachment for three months. At least this job earned him and additional 50¢ per day.[26] After his spell as pay clerk, Harry made a few patrols out of town, on one occasion patrolling as far as Hunker Summit at the head of Hunker Creek. On these patrols he travelled either by horse and cutter in areas where there were winter roads, or else by dog team.

After his stint as Pay Clerk, Harry returned to Pelly Crossing and the range of duties associated with that detachment. In December 1917 he made a patrol to Selkirk to investigate an alleged assault and rape committed against Sarah McGinty, wife of the chief of the Selkirk band.[27] Early in the New Year he had to make travel arrangements to get a prospector who had frozen a foot to Dawson by stage coach. The prospector had no money for the stage fare or for accommodation at the road houses along the way.[28] A few days later, in response to an enquiry from Superintendent Knight in Dawson, Harry investigated allegations that sacks of mail had been thrown off the mail sleigh between Minto and Pelly Crossing.[29] Harry's report on this matter underscores the brutal nature of the Yukon winter climate:

On December 17th Driver Fiendle left Minto Post at 8 A.M. with R.M. Stage and about 1,800 lbs of mail and three passengers. Fiendle experienced considerable trouble that day; the temperature was between 64 and 73 degrees below zero all day. He had a team of four horses; one of these was sick and one became lame shortly after he left Minto. At mile 14 from Pelly the horses were played out and the passengers very cold. At this point the mail was unloaded and left on the trail; the party made a fire and got warm and recharged their foot-warmers and continued towards Pelly at about 4 P.M. At 6 P.M. they were at mile 8 from Pelly and the horses could not draw the stage any further. Here they made another fire and Fiendle and one of the passengers, H. Malmstrom, set out for Pelly and left the other passengers, W. Turnbull and Mrs. G. Brimston with the stage. Fiendle and Malmstrom reached Pelly at 9.30 P.M. and were very cold. I relieved Fiendle and assisted the stableman in taking out four fresh horses and bringing in the two

Trooper Stallworthy,
RNWMP Calvalry
Detachment, Canadian
Expeditionary Force,
1918.

passengers and the stage. It was 1.30 A.M. when we returned and the temperature was 73 degrees below zero.[30]

Towards the end of the month, at the request of the U.S. Commissioner at Nenana, Alaska, Harry investigated a Scotsman called Robert Dickson who was then working at the Pelly Farm, but who was known to the U.S. Commissioner as Tommy Trigger.[31]

In mid-March of 1918, in the light of rumours that the Selkirk band were again planning to hold a potlatch, Harry was ordered to warn chief Peter McGinty once again that doing so was illegal.[32] Soon after this Harry was ordered to investigate the alleged disappearance of an elderly prospector named Rose who had set off the previous November from Little Salmon for his cabin on the Pelly, 45 miles below Ross River, with only eight pounds of bacon, four pounds of flour, a blanket and an axe.[33]

Despite the plebiscite for total prohibition, the sale of liquor was permitted in licensed premises and within specific hours. Harry was obliged to prosecute Mrs. Schaeffer of the Pelly Crossing road house for selling alcohol outside of legal licensing hours.[34] Over a period of several months, Harry also investigated a series of drunken brawls between Indians at Selkirk.[35]

In the spring of 1918, the government decided to send a Royal North-West Mounted Police cavalry detachment overseas as part of the Canadian Expeditionary Force after all. Harry had no doubt let it be known that he wished to participate whenever such a decision was made and he therefore travelled south to Regina and on 9 May 1918 he applied to join the Canadian Expeditionary Force as a member of this detachment.[36] He was accepted and the detachment was immediately shipped overseas to England where it was stationed briefly for final training at Shorncliffe Barracks, located on a windswept site on the cliff top near Folkestone. In July Harry and the other members of the detachment crossed to France with their mounts. Here they were involved in pushing the Germans back from Arras to Cambrai and then across into Belgium. At the time of the Armistice they were at Mons.

Like most veterans of this and other wars, Harry rarely talked of his experiences in Flanders, although he did make mention of being involved with supplying remounts.[37] Harry must have seen some horrific sights associated with some of the fiercest fighting of the War. Harry's period of active duty coincided almost precisely with the Hundred Days, the final major Allied advance that began on 18 July 1918. The Canadian Corps played a critical role in this advance, starting with the Battle of Amiens that took place between 8 and 15 August.[38] After the Battle of Amiens, the Canadians attacked and took the five trench systems of the Drocourt-Quéant Line as far as the Canal du Nord (2–4 September) in an offence that is sometimes called the Battle of Arras. During this offensive, the Canadian Corps took 10,000 prisoners, 97 guns, over 100 machine guns and trench mortars and routed 18 enemy divisions. After crossing the Canal du Nord, the Canadian Corps attacked the formidable Hindenburg Line and captured Cambrai in a battle that lasted from 29 September to 3 October. In all, the Corps defeated 40 German divisions from early August to the beginning of October. In those two months it took 28,000 prisoners, 500 guns, 3,000 machine guns and vast quantities of stores, liberating 70 towns and villages and 175 square miles of territory.

For the final month of the War the Canadians were steadily on the move, although they still faced stiff resistance. For the first time they were in an area where there was still a significant civilian population and when they took the town of Denain on 20 October, they were given a rapturous welcome by the local population. Finally, in the early hours of Armistice Day, 11 November 1918, the Canadians took the town of Mons. Soon afterwards their commander, General Sir Arthur W. Currie, staged a triumphal entry led by the Royal Highlanders of Canada, the pipe-band of the 42nd Battalion.

This prosaic, almost clinical description of the Canadians' involvement in the Hundred Days gives little inkling of the horror, the terror, the din and the stench involved in each of the battles, nor can we ever know, at this remove, the details of Harry Stallworthy's involvement. The cavalry was seldom involved in these bitterly contested battles, but we know that horsemen of the Canadian Cavalry Brigade, of which the RNWMP Squadron was a part, took Beaucourt and Fresnoy during the first day of the Battle of Amiens. And on 8 October, during the final push from Cambrai to Mons, the Canadian Cavalry Brigade hastened the general advance by making a flank attack near Le Cateau. The attack cost them 168 men and 171 horses.[39] More often, the main duty of the cavalry was to escort prisoners to the rear. Still, even if escorting prisoners and supplying remounts were Harry's major contributions to the War, he was there, and though he never talked in detail of his experiences afterwards, he certainly never forgot them.

After the Armistice the RNWMP Cavalry Detachment moved on via Charleroi to Namur and were still there for Christmas; they returned to Britain only in January 1919 and were stationed at Rhyl in North Wales. Harry and his detachment sailed from Liverpool back to Halifax, from where they travelled by rail west to Regina. On 16 March Harry applied for leave and for a pass "to go to my farm near Medicine Hat to transact business for myself and a brother who is on active service at present, also to visit my relations in Vancouver."[40]

After his leave was over, Harry was assigned to "E" Division and posted to Vancouver. Harry, however, wanted to get back to the Yukon and made application for such a posting on 25 April 1919, soon after he got to Vancouver.[41] The challenges of the Yukon—the climate, the degree of independence, the challenges and the satisfaction of spending days and nights on the trail were now in his blood. In the meanwhile, he had to endure the Vancouver posting with all the concomitant irritations of an urban detachment. It must have been only a small consolation that from 1 May until 2 August 1919 he was awarded extra pay of 25¢ per day while employed as Quarter Master Storeman![42]

On 2 August Harry was granted his wish and was transferred to the "B" Division and headed back north to the Yukon. He was posted to Carmacks where he was in charge of the detachment. Much of his time was spent patrolling the stage route from roadhouse to roadhouse by dog team. It was during this period—in November 1919—that the Royal North-West Mounted Police became the Royal Canadian Mounted Police.

In April of the following year Harry received orders from Dawson to make a longer patrol to the detachment at Ross River at the confluence of the Ross and Pelly rivers, a round trip of some 388 miles (620 km). He left Carmacks on 5 April with a team of five dogs hauling a toboggan and, initially, a light load that consisted mainly of 40 lbs of mail bound for Ross River, since a cache had earlier been left at Little Salmon at the confluence of the Little Salmon and the Yukon, 35 miles (56 km) upriver from Carmacks.[43] At Little Salmon he picked up rations and dog feed for fourteen days and left there with about 300 lbs on his toboggan. That day and the next the weather was fair and the trail good. On the first day he made about 40 miles, camping about 5 miles below Little Salmon Lake and on the second he made 53 miles, travelling the full length of Little Salmon Lake and up the McCundy River to the foot of McCundy Canyon, riding on the toboggan all day. Next day he made a further 42 miles up the McCundy Canyon, over the portage to the Pelly and up the Pelly to the mouth of Orchay Creek. Getting under way at 6 A.M. on the morning of 8 April, he reached the Ross River detachment at 10 A.M., where he was welcomed by Constable McDonald. Next day he and McDonald visited the nearby trading posts, trappers' cabins and Indian cabins. While he was there a party of Indians arrived with furs to trade from the Liard River and Harry was informed that quite a number of Indians from the Mackenzie River came to trade at the Ross River Post, some coming from as far away as Fort Good Hope.

Since the weather had turned very mild, travel became increasingly difficult and Harry stayed at Ross River for only the one day before starting back for Carmacks at noon on the 11th. Initially, he made quite good time despite soft snow and difficult conditions and covered a fair distance each day (24,

47, 20 and 28 miles) as he retraced his route. However, from the lower end of Little Salmon Lake, the situation deteriorated drastically and the journey turned into a nightmare struggle for survival.

Water was flowing across the river ice to a depth of about two feet. On the 15th Harry left his dogs and snowshoed downstream about two miles to reconnoitre the situation before returning to where he had left the dogs. He noted the conditions in his report on the journey:

> Here I found travelling with dogs impossible, the snow on the hills being about three feet deep. The country is very rough in that part and there was no trail cut in the heavy brush. This overflow was caused by the heavy snow on the lake and river.
>
> On the following day [14th] I had to unharness the dogs and float the toboggan in some places. Owing to the fact that the weather continued to be very mild and I had only two days rations and dog feed I cached the toboggan, harness, robe, etc. and set out to walk the following morning with a pack of mail etc., snowshoes, parka and axe, my next cache of provisions being some thirty-five miles down the river.[44]

Harry turned his dogs loose to follow him but they were reluctant to follow where the water beneath the snow was particularly deep. On the 17th he lost his axe in deep water. The snow on the river banks was too wet and deep for snowshoeing and he was forced to stick to the river, despite the water and slush. For five days he struggled down the Little Salmon, making daily distances of only 5 to 6 miles. "Getting awfull [sic] hungry; looked at my last can of beans," he scribbled in the notes that were attached to his personal copy of the official report. "Looked at the beans again," he wrote on the 19th. And finally, on the 20th he wrote "Eat [sic] the beans in P.M."[45]

He reached his cache at Little Salmon on the morning of the 21st and borrowed some dry clothing from George Walker at the Little Salmon store. Harry's handwritten addendum for that day states simply: "Eat [sic] 3 days rations in about ½ hr."

Harry rested at Little Salmon Trading Post for two days, applying dressings to his feet and legs on the first day. The two days of easy travel back to Carmacks must have been a relief after the severe test of endurance and will power he had survived to reach Little Salmon. Yet the journey had taken its toll. Along the way back to Carmacks, Harry was puzzled by the fact that acquaintances he met either failed to recognize him, or, if they did, appeared quite shocked. He received the same sort of reaction from his fellow officers when he got back to the Carmacks detachment. "Good God, man, take a look at yourself!" one of the officers told him when he asked why everyone was looking at him oddly. On checking his reflection in a mirror, he found a sunburned cadaver staring back at him! For a moment, even he was shocked to see how his ordeal had affected him.[46]

Harry stayed at Carmacks until July and then moved to Dawson. He explained the move in a letter to his brother:

> I came down the river from Carmacks & got to Dawson on the 11th. Since that I have made a trip to Forty Mile, which is on the Yukon-Alaska boundary on the river. Dawson is by no means as good as when I left in the fall of 1917, only about half the people & there has been no new gold stampedes lately & with prohibition it's a pretty bum town now. However there is a little more life than at Carmacks. I am on the town patrol "days" now. Most of my time is taken up with work at the docks, inspecting trunks etc., & collecting taxes on gold & fur, that is export taxes. I have quite a lot of walking around town to do as well, but no specified beats. This is not such a bad job, 50¢ a day extra & a few dollars for Inspector's work & courts etc.
>
> I have the option of going back on my old job on Aug. 1st, Pay Clerk to "B" Division. I figure on taking that untill [sic] fall anyway & when the freeze-up comes I may apply for a Detachment again. That is if I am fed up with "city life."[47]

Dawson was only a shadow of its former self at the height of the Klondike Gold Rush. The population had dwindled to only 975 people. At the time, Whitehorse had only 331 citizens and there were only 4,157 people in the entire Territory.[48] Gold was still the mainstay of Dawson's economy, but the mining operations were a far cry from those of the Gold Rush era. The small-scale operations that worked a 250-foot claim had been replaced by the large-scale hydraulic mining introduced by the Yukon Gold Company soon after 1906.[49] To work the higher gravels, water was brought from the

Little Twelvemile River via a system of ditches, flumes and pipelines and was fired against the faces of frozen gravel under pressure from monitors and the gravel was then washed into sluice-boxes.

Another major new development was the introduction of dredges, which first came into use in 1901. By 1905 they were in general use, reworking the gravels that had already been worked over by the outdated placer methods. The resultant tailing ridges of sterile gravels are still the most striking feature of every valley bottom in the Dawson area and one of the monster dredges, Dredge No. 4, on Bonanza Creek is now a National Historic Site. While these new techniques meant that the gold output was still quite high at the time Harry was in Dawson, the manpower involved was only a fraction of what it had been at the height of the Gold Rush.

For the most part, Harry quite enjoyed the "city life" of Dawson. He was actively involved in the town's social life and became secretary of the Great War Veterans' Association. However, some of his duties did become rather irksome, as he remarked in another letter to Bill on 10 October:

Here I am in the guard room & a lunatic has been singing for about 3 hours…. He is a Slavonian & quite a case too, poor fellow. I have to releave [sic] the provost every other Sunday & unfortunately this is one of the other Sundays.

Gee, but a fellow sure gets fed up with his continual shouting etc. When I gave him his breakfast this morning he flopped the mush on his head before I had a chance to stop him. I'll have to hold him inside the cell while the escort feeds him through the bars. It is fortunate that we got him when we did because the ice is running heavy & the boat he is going on may be the last until next summer. Two of our boys are getting a transfer outside & going to take him to New Westminster Asylum. This is the 10th we have had this year & I hope that no one will go dippy in the winter as the travell [sic] is going to be pretty bum this winter. The White Pass Company are out of business & two fellows have got the winter mail contract. They will only drive single teams, one post a day, where the other company drove 4 & 6 horses, changing at every post & making sometimes 3 posts per day….

I guess I have to…pay more attention to this fellow. He is stamping & hitting the cell etc.

We have him strapped down in a straight [sic] jacket & he is praying now, quieter than usual.[50]

A couple of months later Harry did indeed get tired of "city life." On 6 December he was a member of a patrol heading out from Dawson to cache supplies at the Hart River, in preparation for the annual patrol to Fort McPherson that was set to leave in January.[51] The patrol was led by Staff Sergeant W.J.D. Dempster, who gained fame when he led a successful search for the patrol led by Inspector Francis J. Fitzgerald. Fitzgerald and the other members of his patrol perished while trying to reach Dawson from Fort McPherson in 1911.[52] Harry felt it was a real honour to be selected both for the preliminary patrol and for the later patrol to Fort McPherson by someone with a reputation as formidable as that of Dempster. Other members of the cache-laying patrol were Constable E. Pasley, Constable W.C. Tyack and Special Constable Sam Smith.

The preliminary patrol set off at 11 A.M. on 6 December with four dog teams. At first, they headed down the Yukon then turned up Twelvemile River (now the Chandindu) and reached the Power Plant, a hydro-electric plant that supplied electricity to the gold dredges, on the afternoon of the 7th. From Power Plant, they continued to the head of the Twelvemile River, over Seela Pass and down the Blackstone River to where it swings north-east. From there the route led them up a small tributary to the east, over a low pass to Lomond Lake and down Lomond Creek right up to its point of confluence with the Hart River. They reached this destination at noon on the 14th. Dempster's patrol report identifies the route by such place-names as Ryder's Camp, Big Glacier, Power's Cabin, and Calico Town, all of which are now defunct. The weather was quite tolerable by Yukon standards, dropping only to $-36°F$ on the morning of the 12th. Having cached 730 lbs of supplies for the later patrol, they started back for Dawson, arriving at 10 A.M. on 20 December after a journey of 304 miles.

On 6 January 1921, Staff-Sergeant Dempster led his fourteenth patrol along this route out of Dawson.[53] Harry's companions were Constables Pasley and Tyack—who had also taken part in the preliminary patrol—and Special Constables John Smith (also known as Johnny Walker) and Benjamin. They were driving four teams of five dogs each and the main function of the patrol was to deliver mail bound for Fort McPherson, Herschel Island and Rampart

Uphill through soft snow; on the Fort McPherson patrol, 1921.

House. The first part of the journey that took them to the cache at the Hart River was already familiar to Harry. When the patrol reached the cache, they travelled a short distance up the Hart River before striking northeast up Waugh Creek to its head, over the low divide and down Forrest Creek to its confluence with the Little Wind River.

It was the failure to identify the confluence with the Little Wind River that had led the Fitzgerald patrol astray on their fateful journey in 1911. Inspector Francis J. Fitzgerald, Constable George Kinney, Constable Richard Taylor and former Constable Sam Carter had set out from Fort McPherson on 21 December 1910 with three dog teams, the mailbags from Herschel and Fort McPherson, and enough provisions for 30 days. Sam Carter was the only member of the patrol who had travelled the route before—four years previously and in the opposite direction. From the start, the patrol encountered deep snow and bitterly cold weather. On 5 January 1911 the temperature dropped to –65°F, and it averaged –50°F for days at a time. The patrol made

slow progress in the inclement weather and as they headed up the Little Wind River on 12 January, they accidentally passed the mouth of Forrest Creek and continued south on the Little Wind River. For the next six days they struggled up and down the Little Wind River and it various tributaries, but could not find Forrest Creek. On 18 January, after 26 days on the trail and with only enough food left for another four days, Fitzgerald decided to head back north to Fort McPherson. None of the patrol members reached safety. Staff-Sergeant Dempster led the search patrol that eventually found the bodies of all four men. The last two bodies were found only 25 miles from Fort McPherson. Dempster also found the mailbags they had been carrying and in a cabin a little further south, he found Fitzgerald's journal.[54]

Under the experienced leadership of Dempster, the 1921 patrol did find the Little Wind River. They continued along this river until they reached the Wind River, which they then followed to its confluence with the Peel River. After a short haul down the Peel they cut north up Mountain Creek

Exercising the dogs, Dawson City, 1921; Stallworthy in the cariole.

Members of the Fort McPherson patrol; Dempster in centre in white anorak.

on a cut-off, thus avoiding the long eastward swing of the Peel. It was here on Mountain Creek that Harry celebrated his 26th birthday on 20 January. They had quite a celebration. Ben had shot a moose that day, so they had plenty of fresh meat and they even had a plum pudding! The cut-off took them over to the Trail River, then down to the Peel again. They followed the Peel River for the remainder of their journey and arrived at Fort McPherson on 28 January after an outbound trip of 22 days.

They stayed at Fort McPherson for 17 days while they waited for the patrol from Herschel Island, led by Inspector Stuart T. Wood.[55] The patrol from Rampart House, made up of Corporal Tidd and Constable Scott also arrived, as did the mail packet from Edmonton. Harry was particularly pleased to meet John Firth, who was the factor for the Hudson's Bay Company. Firth was a legend in his own right and the patriarch of the Firth clan of Fort McPherson. Harry and the other patrol members started their homeward journey on 13 February and reached Dawson safely on 5 March after a relatively uneventful trip[56] and in positively balmy weather compared to the bitterly cold temperatures they had endured on the outbound trip.[57]

The experience of this patrol stayed with Harry for the rest of his life and 40 years later he recalled it in an article:

I went on a thousand mile patrol with Jack Dempster in 1921. Dawson to Fort McPherson and return. Same trail that wiped out the Fitzgerald patrol. Jack had this down like a C.P.R. time-table. He made 14 round trips in his time. When I went along he had two Indians, four policemen and four dog teams. It was the mail run. An Indian by the name of Johnny Walker and I walked ahead of the dogs on trail-breaking snowshoes.

Dempster was a tough Welshman. We were up at four in the morning and after two plates of beans we hit the trail. Pemmican at noon. Bannock, beans, bacon and raisins at night. We all chewed tobacco. Too cold to smoke.[58]

This was the last police patrol made on this route. For the rest of his career Harry felt enormously privileged to have taken part in it and to have associated with such a tough wilderness traveller and almost legendary northerner as Dempster.

There was one nice surprise in store for Harry when he arrived back in Dawson. While he was away on this patrol, Superintendent R. E. Tucker, who was in charge of "B" Division, had written to the Commissioner in Ottawa recommending him for promotion to Corporal. Tucker characterized Harry as being "well-educated and of excellent character. He is a good man in any capacity...."[59] Harry was promoted to the rank of Corporal as of 2 February 1921. The promotion was appreciated, but Harry's three-year term of engagement with the Mounted Police was drawing to a close and he spent the summer working in the Pay Office in Dawson. During his last few months of service, Harry had a great deal of enjoyment hunting and photographing caribou. In early May he wrote to his brother:

> The caribou are positively thick (thousands). One may as well say they are invading the town. Two of our boys got 84 last fall when the run went south about 40 miles from here (west). We had caribou in the mess all winter, & feed our teams quite a lot too. Yesterday I was on the [Midnight] Dome, the big hill back of town & there was several bands of about 200 to 250. I got close enough to two bunches to take pictures of them within 18–20 yds. of one Bunch.[60]

Pending his discharge on 24 September, Harry took a month's leave starting 24 August.[61]

It had been years since Harry had seen his family and as he was about to become a civilian once more, he took the opportunity to do so. He travelled to England via Skagway, Vancouver and Montreal. He spent most of his time with his mother at Fairford and with his brother Bill and his family at Ampney Crucis. A highlight of the trip was undoubtedly the fact that his brother Wallis (Wallie) was home from Australia.

There is no record of when exactly Harry returned to Canada, but it must have been in the late fall of 1921 or perhaps even early in 1922. He was now a civilian, and he decided to return to the Yukon to try his hand at prospecting. The information on this period of his life is scanty and the only source of information of his whereabouts and activities is a heavily annotated map he appears to have sent to his brother Bill.

Harry's annotated map shows that from Vancouver he headed north by steamer to Skagway and from there he took the White Pass and Yukon

Caribou on slopes of Midnight Dome, above Dawson City, 1921.

Sternwheeler Casca, *one of the steamers on which Harry Stallworthy regularly travelled in the Yukon.*

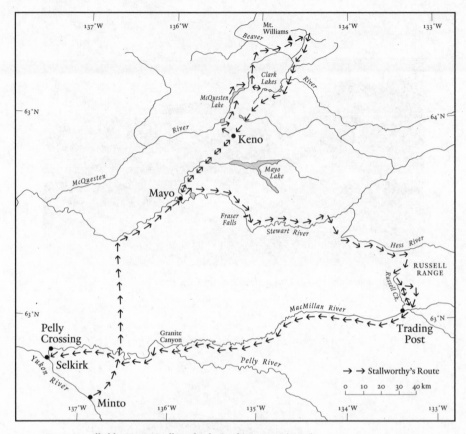

Route travelled by Harry Stallworthy during his prospecting trip, 1922.

Railroad to Whitehorse. At Whitehorse he caught the stage sleigh via Carmacks to Minto, which indicates that this journey happened well before spring break-up when steamers again became the mode of travel. At some point Harry teamed up with a "real prospector from Nevada."[62] At Minto they acquired a dog team and toboggan and headed northeast to Mayo and Keno where major silver mines were already in production. Their route ran north to the Stewart River, then north and east up the Mayo to Keno Hill. It was only two years previously, on 10 July 1919, that Louis Beauvette had staked his silver claim, Roulette, high on Keno Hill, sparking a small rush to Keno Hill the following year.[63]

By the time Harry and his partner reached Keno Hill, the major operator in the area was the Yukon Gold Company. The two prospectors spent some time in this area, staking two silver claims just north of the South McQuesten River and northwest of Keno Hill. They named their one claim the Douglas and the other they named the Winson Claim, after Harry's birthplace in Gloucestershire.

Having staked their claims, the two men headed north, crossing the narrows of McQuesten Lake, which probably indicates that the lake ice had not yet broken up. As they worked their way east through the labyrinth of swampy lakes between McQuesten Lake and the head of Scougale Creek, Harry scribbled "Swamp" and "Good Moose country" on his map, suggesting that by that time the snow was partially or completely gone and they may well have been using their team as pack dogs. From Scougale Creek their route cut north via a pass through the mountains to reach the Beaver River at the mouth of Williams Creek, then northeast along the southern slopes of Mt. Williams and through another pass to the mountains along the Beaver River/ Wind River divide south of Mt. Braine. Here, at a place located about a day's climb up the mountainside, they staked three more silver claims which they named Frontiersman, Optimist and Mountain Dew. Either on the basis of their own estimation, or on the basis of an assay of samples made later in Dawson, these claims ran at 14 to 20 oz per tonne. Heading back southwest to the Beaver River, they picked up their trail at Scougale Creek, past the Clark Lakes and McQuesten Lake back to Keno and Mayo.

Here they acquired a boat of some type and set off up the Stewart River, poling against the current. They either portaged past Fraser Falls, or abandoned the boat at that point and continued up the Stewart to an old cabin at the end of the trail, heading south to cut off the eastward loop on the lower Hess River. By this point they were certainly on foot and detoured around a number of lakes on this cut-off. Eventually, they reached the Hess River and headed southeast up it. Harry's annotation at this point reads "Beaucoup moose, trout, beaver." Turning south up a tributary, they climbed into the Russell Range where they had some good hunting, killing a moose and a bear. Then they headed south down Russell Creek and staked a placer gold claim near the mouth of Marion Creek before continuing south to a trading post at the confluence of Russell Creek and the Macmillan River.

At the trading post they probably replenished their supplies of such staples as beans, flour and coffee before starting back north up Russell Creek, making a swing east up George Creek (or the next creek to the south) and into the

Russell Range. Here they again had some hunting success, killing three caribou. Back at the trading post they acquired a moose-hide boat and started down the Macmillan River. They had the good fortune to get a moose within the first day and for the first few days they made excellent progress to the mouth of the Moose River in a swift current that had some white water. Here they entered a section of the Macmillan River, following it all the way to its confluence with the Pelly River. This section of the journey was marked by a slow current and exuberant meandering. "Very slow & some crooked!" Harry wrote on the map. Once they got onto the Pelly, the pace picked up—especially through Granite Canyon. The ride was clearly exhilarating, possibly even terrifying, for Harry's annotation reads: "Very swift; some ride in moose hide boat!"

When they reached Pelly Crossing, Harry and his companion caught the steamer downriver to Dawson, presumably to register their claims. Harry appears to have made no attempt to work any of the claims and may well have sold them, or simply allowed them to lapse. Much later he wrote: "We did not find enough gold 'to fill a humbing Bird's tooth' but I saw more bear, sheep, moose, big trout etc. on that trip to last for some time."[64] Nonetheless, he maintained his interest in Canadian mines and mining throughout his life. He often invested in mining shares—not always with his wife's approval, since these ventures did not always pay off—and he regularly subscribed to the magazine, *Northern Miner*.[65]

From Dawson, Harry headed south via Whitehorse and Skagway to Vancouver. There, he caught the train east and by 15 October 1922 he was in Calgary. Overall, it had been an impressive journey during which Harry proved that he was already an accomplished wilderness traveller. Travelling by dog team, on foot and by boat, Harry and his companion covered a distance very conservatively estimated at 600 miles (1,000 km). Although they took staple foods with them, they relied mostly on hunting and fishing to supplement of their diet. At this, they seem to have been quite successful since, in addition to fish, Harry noted at least one bear, two moose and three caribou on his map. Despite his successful hunting on the trip, the food on the steamer *Princess Mary* and the train made a very enjoyable change from staples of wilderness travel such as boiled moose meat and beans.

3

FROM THE CHOCOLATE TRADE

to Chesterfield Inlet

HARRY WAS ONLY PASSING THROUGH Calgary and he spent the time with an old Gloucestershire friend, Jim Bridgeman, and his wife. Some time before, Harry and Jim had discussed the idea of starting a chocolate-making business; however, at the time Jim was reluctant to take the plunge and give up his job at a harness-maker's. Now Jim and his wife were having difficulty in making ends meet and the proposal seemed more attractive.

On October 16, Harry left the Bridgemans to mull over their decision and caught the 1.25 A.M. train east to Moose Jaw, bound for Chicago,[1] where he had been invited to stay with friends. One of the friends was Ed Mackenzie, who had offered to help Harry find a job. As a natural sequel to his season as a prospector, and no doubt with hopes of further seasons in the northern bush, Harry was interested in taking a course in mining engineering, assaying, and other related courses, but for financial reasons could only work at such a course part-time.

Harry did not stay long in Chicago. He returned to Calgary well before Christmas, where, in collaboration with Jim Bridgeman, he went into the chocolate business. Of all Harry's varied career moves this seems most out of character. It is very hard to imagine that Harry ever saw it as the start of his life's work, especially since he had tasted and enjoyed the freedom and informality of life in the North. He never discussed his motives in his letters to his mother or brother, but one suspects that from the very start he saw it only as a stop-gap measure, his main aim being to help his friends, the Bridgemans, start a business that would provide them with a secure living.

Harry rented two rooms at the top of the apartment building where the Bridgemans lived. He paid $12 per month for his two rooms and paid the Bridgemans $5.50 per month for his board.[2] He lived in one room and devoted the other to making chocolates. Jim had already started making chocolates in his absence, but not very effectively. He bought his ingredients retail and worked at making chocolates only in the evenings after he came home from his regular job, and at weekends.[3] Harry promptly phoned every wholesaler in town and got the lowest prices for ingredients; thus whereas Jim as paying 15¢ per oz. for cocoa butter, Harry was able to get it at 90¢ per lb.

Working out of the apartment building was a temporary arrangement. Harry went to the appropriate authorities at City Hall and used the ex-soldier line to get permission to continue with what was essentially an illegal operation. Both the food inspector and the sanitary inspector visited their operation and gave them the necessary clearance to continue. "They were certainly pretty decent about it," he wrote to his brother William, "& said carry on for this year & then if we can make it go we have to move to suitable quarters (must have a shop) & pay taxes etc."[4] As it was, they had only to pay for a manufacturer's licence for the time being.

Even with their fairly primitive home operation, they were turning out eight different varieties of chocolate creams, such as maple walnut creams, coconut creams, peppermint creams, as well as ginger, almonds, brazil nuts and nougat dipped in chocolate. The two men soon worked out a routine: Harry would make the cream centres during the day, then after Jim got home from work, they would have supper. When the Bridgemans' young son, Philip, had been put to bed (usually by 8 o'clock), the two men would start dipping chocolates by hand, often continuing until after midnight. Their aim was to have enough ready to fill one hundred 2 lb boxes and five hundred 1 lb boxes for the Christmas market. They ordered the boxes from Winnipeg and Harry had 200 advertisement leaflets printed. He planned to distribute these himself to houses and apartment buildings in "the best districts" such as Elbow Park and Mount Royal, particularly the homes of doctors and other professional men. He also planned to put an advertisement in the *Calgary Herald* and had investigated the cost of placing advertisements on street cars and on movie theatre screens.

He had also investigated possible premises for their shop. One location that particularly appealed to him was in the 1200 block (the so-called Radio Block) of 1st St. West. For $85.00 per month they could rent a shop that measured 16' by 30' and had two bay windows and a central door.

Harry had also assessed the competition in Calgary and had compared their prices. There was the Greek-owned *Palace of Eats* at the lower end of the price-range and *Rochons* at the upper end. Harry's survey also extended to Winnipeg, where he had checked the prices of businesses such as *The Chocolate Shop*, *Picardy Chocolates* and *Commodore*. He had also assessed the prices of the products made by larger eastern (Ontario) companies such as *Neilson's*, *Pascall's*, *Moir's* and *Lowney's*.

Despite all their hard work, Harry and Jim missed the Christmas market, largely because the boxes did not arrive from Winnipeg on time.[5] Writing to his brother on New Year's Eve, Harry revealed that he and Jim were still making creams and dipping chocolate in their temporary premises, although Harry had taken an option on the store on 1st Street.[6] Despite the lack of premises, they had already sold over 100 lbs of chocolates. Harry had been out canvassing from door to door in Mount Royal and Scarboro districts and had received an encouraging response, even in the week between Christmas and New Year: "practically all the people I talked to were interested, & most of them who saw & tasted our famous product said it is really home-made."[7] On the basis of this response, he was planning to get a city canvassing licence.

By late May 1923 the business was on a much sounder footing. Harry and Jim had taken a lease on the shop on 1st Street and the business was officially named *The Chocolate Shop*, with its own letterhead.[8] They had set up a well-equipped candy kitchen in the back area and Mrs. Bridgeman, with the help of a girl, was running the shop, while Jim was in charge of production, marketing and administration. Their turnover between January 28 and May 20 was $2,700, and Harry felt extremely optimistic about the future of their business.

However, history was about to intervene in Harry's plans and drag him away from his mundane life as a chocolate merchant. In the spring of 1923 rumours of a gold strike at Stag Bay (between Makkovik and Cape Harrison) raised fears in St. John's of a gold-rush comparable to the Klondike Rush that had occurred 25 years earlier. The outcome was that the Government of Newfoundland (then still a separate British colony) had approached the Royal Canadian Mounted Police to select about a dozen men who could organize a police force that could control and regulate the anticipated rush, just as the RNWMP had done in the Yukon. The job appealed strongly to Harry who argued, correctly, that his experience in the Yukon qualified him perfectly for such a posting. On 5 May he applied to re-engage for one year, specifically with the Labrador assignment in mind:

> In event of some men being sent to Labrador for the Newfoundland Government I wish also to make further application for that service. During my service in the Yukon I served the greater part of the time on Detachment duty and became generally familiar with police duties and the conditions of the north, as dog driving, canoeing etc.[9]

He re-engaged with the Force with the rank of Constable on 18 May and was accepted for this special assignment. He caught the train for Ottawa on the evening of Monday 2 June 1923, having first made Jim Bridgeman an equal partner and manager in the chocolate business.[10]

As it happened, the Labrador gold rush did not materialize and instead of controlling another Klondike, Harry found himself in charge of 31 horses and eight men at the RCMP stables at Lansdowne Park in Ottawa. His main duty was to exercise and groom the horses,[11] a task that no doubt gave him some degree of satisfaction. It also reminded him of his service with the Gloucestershire Yeomanry as a youth and of his months of training at Regina. However, the North was still calling him. On discovering that there was a vacancy at the detachment at Chesterfield Inlet on the west shore of Hudson Bay, he submitted an application and was accepted. There was also a financial incentive, as the posting would allow Harry to do some fur trapping. He

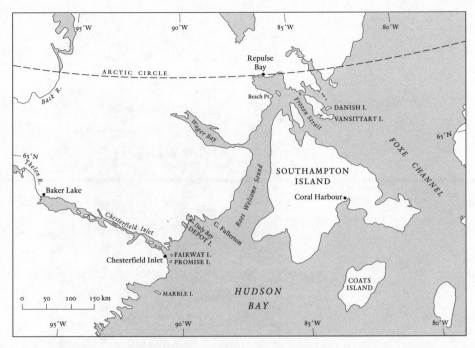

Northwestern Hudson Bay, showing area travelled by Harry Stallworthy.

was selected for this posting on 11 June[12] and travelled to Montreal by train on 12 July, along with Corporal Petty, who was also posted to Chesterfield Inlet.[13]

They sailed from Montreal on board the Hudson's Bay Company steamer, S. S. *Nascopie*, Captain G. E. Mack, on 14 July 1923. After a call at Port Burwell, the ship ran into heavy ice in Hudson Strait and was totally beset on several occasions for days at a time. Harry and others took the opportunity to stretch their legs on the ice. When a bear appeared about 270 m ahead of the ship, it was greeted by a fusillade of shots, killed, and hauled aboard. Harry was not involved since his rifle was stowed in his baggage. Having called at Wolstenholme on the south shore of Hudson Strait, the ship was again battling heavy ice in the western entrance to Hudson Strait on 29 July.

A few days later the *Nascopie* reached Chesterfield Inlet, their destination. Captain Mack anchored about 800 m offshore, but a southeast gale was raising a heavy surf and although there was great excitement on shore, with people running to and fro, they were unable to launch their boats because of

Harry Stallworthy and Naujaa, Chesterfield Inlet, 1923.

the pounding breakers. Scattered across the tundra, the entire settlement was visible from on board: the two neat white houses of the RCMP detachment with their distinctive red roofs, the buildings of the Hudson's Bay Company, the grey Roman Catholic Mission, and a scattering of Inuit tents. In the evening the gale slackened and two whaleboats were launched and sailed out to the anchored ship.[14] On board the first boat was a Qablunaq who stood over 6' tall, with a red bushy beard. It was the Dane, Peter Freuchen. He was a member of Knud Rasmussen's "Fifth Thule Expedition" that had wintered at Blaesebaelgen on Danish Island (east of Vansittart Island). Freuchen had frozen both his big toes and had travelled south to Chesterfield Inlet specifically so that the *Nascopie*'s doctor could amputate them. The journey had taken from 6 June until 9 July.[15] Having had the toes amputated, Freuchen started back north by schooner in early August.

Harry also met Constable Brown whom he was to relieve. The full RCMP complement at Chesterfield was four men. Inspector Munday was in charge of the detachment, but he and his wife were set to leave the following summer.

Constable Wiebe's two-year stint would also be up in the summer of 1924. Then came the two newcomers, Harry and Corporal Petty, who had travelled north to start their two-year stint.

Harry's first reaction was that the detachment was simply overstaffed and that there was nothing for him to do. In his view, he wrote, "this detachment is thot [sic] to be far more important by our own people 'outside' than I can see it.... I think this post is the biggest 'white elephant' the force has got," he added.[16] Nonetheless, he had contracted to stay for two years and for now he was stuck with this white elephant.

First impressions are not always accurate and the longer he stayed at Chesterfield Inlet, the more he changed his mind about the importance of the detachment—particularly as regards its impact on the Inuit. The detachment employed three Inuit on a permanent basis, which meant that their wives were also employed as seamstresses. Maria, wife of Parka, who had been brought up and educated in the home of an Anglican missionary, acted as interpreter for the police. Of the three men, Harry was particularly impressed by a man called Naujaa who had just arrived at Chesterfield from Southampton Island with his young wife, Manni, and their young daughter. Later, Harry would describe the moment he first saw Naujaa as he climbed aboard the *Nascopie*:

> He was bigger than the others, and had a dignity of face and manner. He was good looking, and a head of shining, coal-black hair, neatly braided. His hood was over his shoulders, and the long braids were tucked into the neck of his "kooletah."[17]

Inspector Munday had employed Naujaa on the basis of his excellent reputation as a hunter, traveller and igloo-builder; he also owned his own whaleboat.

Unfortunately, early in the fall Naujaa and his young wife Manni suffered a terrible blow. Their young daughter, Pedloo, died in the night as she lay between them in their sleeping bag. In accordance with traditional Inuit beliefs this meant that they had to abandon their tent (which Naujaa had just received from Inspector Munday as part of an advance on his pay) and everything that was in it at the time of Pedloo's death. This included the sleeping bag, clothes, harpoons and a primus stove. They even had to destroy a dog that had been in the tent. Naujaa asked Harry to shoot the dog, since he could not bring himself to do so. Naujaa and Manni were also obliged to respect a whole series of taboos. For Naujaa the most drastic of these was that he had to leave untouched the first two animals or birds of every species of game that he killed. This was particularly embarrassing to him since he had been hired as a hunter for the detachment.[18]

Harry was also greatly impressed by his new boss, Inspector Munday. Mrs. Munday was a different matter, however; he found her "rather too much of a High Brow" and referred to her as "the Commander-in-Chief," who was always telling her husband "to stand on his dignity." Since Brown and Wiebe were new recruits when they arrived at Chesterfield with the Mundays, she had been able to dominate them. They had not been able to go out on patrol and she had insisted that they polish their buttons and wear a uniform jacket at the meal table (they took their meals with the Mundays). However, Petty (with about nine years of service) and Harry (with seven years) were not about to tolerate such a situation. When Mrs. Munday tried to give them orders, they requested permission to cook for themselves. Permission was granted and thereafter Harry's relations with Mrs. Munday were much more amicable. In fact he felt quite sorry for her.

Harry quickly settled into the routine of the small white community of Chesterfield Inlet. There were three men at the Hudson's Bay Company post (Post Manager, District Manager and apprentice) and three Fathers and a Brother at the Roman Catholic Mission. Every Saturday evening the RCMP officers would visit the HBC post (about 1.5 km away), unless a blizzard made this impossible; on Tuesday evenings the HBC personnel would return the visit. A similar routine of mutual weekly visits was established with the Fathers and Brother of the RC Mission.

Early in the fall Harry went on his first trip away from the detachment, accompanied by two Inuit. They journeyed north to Cape Fullerton by sailboat, their mission being to dismantle an old blubber shed at the abandoned RNWMP post there. They were to retrieve the lumber and "recycle" a kitchen stove. Along the way Harry had his first experience of shooting seals in the water. Their tiny heads make an extremely difficult target, but Harry managed to kill two of the 25 he fired at. Whether a seal sinks or floats on being killed depends on how much blubber the creature has and on the salinity of the water. Both the seals Harry killed sank before he could retrieve them.

Harry was barely back from his trip to Cape Fullerton when he and the Inuit members of the detachment set off by dog team on a caribou hunt some 240 km up Chesterfield Inlet. They were gone for five weeks, during which it snowed quite frequently and wind blew almost constantly, making their tent, which was heated only with a primus stove, extremely cold. Naujaa was the most successful hunter, shooting all of the six caribou that were taken on this trip. Harry got a seal, a number of ptarmigan and two Arctic hares. "They are not unlike the Jenner jack rabbits, only shorter & finer fur & very white,"[19] Harry informed his brother, referring to their days together on the Alberta prairie. Since Harry did not speak Inuktitut and the Inuit did not speak English, communication between them was a challenge. While Harry had difficulty in communicating with the other two Inuit, he and Naujaa found it relatively easy to communicate by gestures and mime and the few words of each other's language that they quickly picked up.

The month of November was bitterly cold, yet there was no snow. When the snow did come the wind drifted it into the cracks or swept it into shallow drifts behind obstacles. This posed a particular problem in that, by tradition, the cutting and sewing of caribou-skin winter clothing could only be started in a snow house. Thus the Inuit found themselves shivering in their sealskin tents and still wearing their worn summer clothes. This restriction also affected Harry; the other members of the detachment still had warm caribou-skin clothing from the previous winter but he had just the clothes he had brought from the South.

To solve this dilemma some of the men and boys cut small blocks of snow from the scattered drifts in the cracks and gullies between the rocks, hauled them across the bare rocks to the settlement on sledges, and built a snow house barely larger than a dog kennel. One of the women then crawled inside with a caribou skin and cut and sewed the first garment. Thereafter all the women set to sewing winter clothing for their husbands, themselves and families, and also for the Police. Manni measured Harry using just her hands and soon presented him with a double suit of caribou skin. On 10 November he took a walk in his new winter clothes, scouting out the trapping potential within a radius of about five kilometres of the detachment. Apart from longer trap lines that he and Naujaa would set out and visit regularly, he intended setting about 10 traps near the settlement, which he would visit almost on a daily basis.[20]

Trapping Arctic foxes represented a major part of the winter activities of the detachment members. All of them, including Inspector Munday, saw fox trapping as an important way of supplementing their salaries. This applied not only to their own trapping efforts, but to those of the Inuit employees as well. It is not clear who had set these rules, but it was understood that the four officers would also share between them half the catch of the three Inuit employees. In addition they purchased the other half of the Inuit's furs at a price of $5.00 in trade goods (which actually represented $2.50 or $3.00 in actual value, in the light of the mark-up used). Writing to his brother, Harry candidly admitted that white fox fur had been fetching $35.35 at the London fur sales the previous summer.

Once Manni had finished their winter clothing there was an adequate snow cover for sledging and Harry and Naujaa set off to retrieve a cache of walrus meat (a total of nine animals) that had been killed and cached the previous summer. Once collected, this cache would supply dog food for a good part of the winter. The trip itself is best described by Harry himself in an unpublished essay:

The day was set, the sledges were loaded overnight with food, polar bear skins, guns, ammunition and spare footwear (the most important part of winter trail clothing). After a lazy summer the dogs were soft and eager for a long run. They would soon harden up. I was like a small boy looking forward to a long-promised outing.

When the morning at last came to start, a moderate blizzard was blowing. Nowya [Naujaa] came to the house with Maria. I waited while the long meaningless discussion went on. Then Maria told me that Nowya was unwilling to set out in such weather with the New White Man. It was too cold and the blizzard might increase. He did not think I would be able to stand the hardships.

I said: "Tell Nowya that I know it is only 32 below. I have lived far over there to the Northwest, when we have travelled when it was 60 below. It was a place of many trees. We travelled with dog teams there too, but not the same as here. Tell him I am not afraid of the cold. I have never had such clothing to wear as these double caribou skins and sleeping bags Manni made for me. I have confidence in him, if he is willing to go. Tell him I will help him and I don't intend to be a passenger on the trail."

Nowya had never seen a tree. He had not even seen a small, scrubby evergreen tree. He seemed to doubt that a country where trees would grow could be so difficult and cold as this. He knew only the barren, windswept wastes of rock and snow in the winter, and the low, green mosses of the barren lands. But he knew how to build an igloo and how to keep warm and comfortable under these grim conditions. I was young and filled with eagerness to set out on my first Arctic patrol.

So I convinced him. And we were off into the blizzard. And what a blizzard it turned out to be. This was my first long trip and to some men it would have been complete misery all the way. The drifting snow, fine, powdery, filled with frost particles, stung our faces and seeped into our clothes. We rode the sledge almost continually, for the dogs ran too fast downwind for us to keep up with them on foot. Occasionally I had to run to keep warm.

I was constantly entertained watching the manoeuvres of the dogs and the driver to avoid the outcroppings of rock where the snow had blown away. There seemed to be an instinct in the dogs, or perhaps training, to guide the heavily loaded sledge away from these rocky places, where the ice coatings on the frozen mud runners would have been broken to pieces. Nowya talked almost continually to the dogs in Eskimo and used the 40-foot-long whip, at which he was an expert, even in a blizzard.

Sometimes he would turn his head to me with a smile and ask "Ikii?" (cold?) and no matter how I felt I would shake my head, "Nauga." On the way south the wind drift was in our backs and my big hood kept my face warm.

Our travelling time was short because of the few hours of light. We couldn't stop to eat at midday. We made camp early because of the time needed to build an igloo. There was nothing I could do while Nowya was making our house for the night. I watched him, but had no skill to cut the snow blocks, nor to place them. When you are cold and hungry such a time seems long.

It was true that Nowya was a very fine igloo-builder. I discovered to my amazement that I could be really warm and comfortable after the furs were spread on the snow bench and the primus lamp was lit. I made bannock and heated beans previously cooked and frozen in slabs. The smell of the bacon frying and the coffee boiling was just as inviting as it is over an open fire in the woods. Nowya grinned and rubbed his stomach. That was a language we both understood.

It was fortunate that I had this accomplishment of trail cooking. It made up for the fact that I was no help in building and igloo or driving the dogs in the Eskimo fan-wise fashion. Back at the Inlet, Nowya reported that I was a good cook. When I cooked rice I slipped an extra portion of raisins into his dish. I loaded his bannock with the molasses which could almost be cut with a knife, because molasses, most of all the camp fare, hates the cold. I felt just a little important when I saw Nowya's enjoyment as he ate. He was unaccustomed to such food.

Our first night in the igloo set the pattern for all the nights which followed. We could not have the primus lamp going too long, or it would have melted a hole in the dome of our shelter. But after the meal was finished, we sat with our bodies warmly encased in our deerskin sleeping bags, and began to make ourselves known to each other. Two men of the same tongue would have no difficulty in this respect, but Nowya and I spoke different languages. We had a good understanding with gestures and facial expressions, but we were lost for words. So I started my pocket dictionary.

I would point at the articles in use on the trip and say their name in English. Nowya would give me his word for them. I had great difficulty with my tongue. The sounds were strange and difficult. He put his lips close to my ear and whispered the sound. This way I found that I could soon make the sounds without the crude imitation which most beginners use. It is a soft, musical tongue-and-throat-using language. It appealed to me. I think Nowya's personality helped make it so.

Then there was sign-language. Nowya took down his shining black braids every night. He had a big black comb in his duffel bag. I have seen women throw their long hair forward, carefully make the straight parting, then turn their heads to one side and plait the long, flowing locks into neat braids. Nowya used the same motions, and the result was the same. Somehow it fascinated me, but as none of the other men in the settlement had these long braids, I made motions to him with my fingers in a cutting movement. He laughed, shook his head, and said "Manni nauga," and I understood that his wife wanted him to keep the long braids.

I reached into my duffel bag for my harmonica and held it over the flickering candle flame to warm the metal before putting it to my mouth. As I had so often done on the trail in the Yukon, I began to play the popular tunes of the day. Nowya's eyes gleamed with delight. He might have been listening to an orchestra. When I stopped for breath, he expressed great pleasure and said, "Atiilu, atiilu" (Again, again). I tried him with a little classical music. He laughed with pleasure. I played "On the road to Mandalay." This became his favourite tune. He could hum it to show that he wanted it again.

Every night after this Nowya would get out my mouth organ and hand it to me, after first warming it over the candle flame, saying "Mandalay, atiilu." It became our theme song for the evening concerts. Sometimes after the candle was out and we were settled to sleep for the night Nowya would try the songs to himself. He had a deep melodious voice. It was pleasant to listen to him.

After four sleeps we reached the walrus cache. I marvelled that Nowya could find it. He might have had the name of the street and the number of the house in his pocket, so straight did he go to the snow-drifted mound of rocks which covered the meat cache. It was hard to believe that he could take us through a wilderness of rock and snow and say "This is the place." He had the directions from the natives who had been in on the kill and had made the cache. The address had been given in the number of sleeps, rocky promontories and inlets. As far as I was concerned I was lost when I left the buildings of the settlement behind.

Having reached our destination we decided to build a larger igloo and stay for a couple of days to see if the blizzard would blow itself out. While Nowya built it I cut into the snowdrift and removed the rocks which covered the tons of walrus meat. We had a crowbar, brought for the purpose, to pry and wedge off the chunks of stonily frozen meat. I hacked off chunks to feed the dogs, who gorged themselves, then lay down in a stupor to rest and digest their stupendous meal.

For two days we worked at the cache, ate our meals in leisure, had our evening concerts, and when it seemed the wind was dying down and the visibility was better, we made an excursion even further south. This appealed to Nowya, who was also on a pathfinding trip. We travelled for two more sleeps. There was nothing new, just more rocks, windswept ice and inlets. At last we turned north again.

This was a patrol with a purpose, which was to bring home the bacon, in this case one half ton of walrus meat, or as much as we could load on the sledge. Our problem was to dig down through the hard drifted snow to the main meat cache. We worked all the next day, prying, pounding, jarring loose the great unwieldy masses of frozen meat, blubber and tough hide. Imagine five or six large elephants butchered, piled up in a heap then frozen into one great mass.

Then we attempted to chop the tough pieces of hide with an axe; the sharp blade simply bounced back leaving no impression. I was baffled to know how we would ever pack the komotik with such an unhandy load. But my Man Friday had the answer. We tied sealskin lines to the slabs of hide, dragged them over the sea ice to a crack wide enough to allow us to push them through into the salt water. Next morning it was thawed enough to be cut into sledge-size pieces. It soon froze again and could be packed on the sledge, covered and tied in place. When all this was finished we started back.

The return was harder work and colder than the outgoing journey. Now we were facing the blizzard and as the December days were rapidly getting shorter, so was our travelling time. I had thought we would be able to use the igloos built on our way south. They were all drifted over with the continually moving snow and a new one had to be built every night. This did not seem to disappoint Nowya who took it all in the day's work.

I found too that as compared to the easy ride south, things were different with a full load. In many places the 14 dogs could not possibly pull up a steep grade. Then we both pushed from behind.

It is unbelievable how the real husky dogs will tie into the teeth of a blizzard. I found that the northern sledge dog knows what his job is. He has been trained for generations to work at the command, and the way those animals pulled and strained at their traces was wonderful. There were times when we literally could not see them, although they were only 20 or 30 feet ahead of us on their sealskin traces. Nowya shouted encouragement and directions and made the long whip crack like a pistol shot in the air over their backs. Like all animals they knew they were homeward bound and would swing away down a good slope after a hard uphill grind with their tails curled up over their backs.

One night I was awakened by the sound of Nowya singing to himself. I was surprised at what I heard. This was not the music of the harmonica. It was strange and weird, a native chant, full of melancholy and repetition. I thought "Old Nowya is thinking of his little girl." I fell asleep again, not wanting to let him know that I had listened to his private thoughts. Later I wakened and found that he was still singing the strange chant. Again I fell asleep.

Next morning Nowya was still asleep when I wakened. I left him alone until breakfast was ready. Then I shook him and called "Come, Nowya. Soup's on." After that he was strangely silent and morose.

We were just six sleeps from the walrus cache, with a blinding blizzard still shutting down our visibility when we suddenly bounded across a small rise. The Arctic twilight was shattered by the shrill barking of dogs and the answering yodels of our dogs. Lights showed up dimly through the mist. We were home.

The natives ran out of their igloos to take our dogs. We left them to unload the sledge and went into the warm house. Nowya had his meal with me. This was the custom after returning from a patrol.

Manni came in to look after the deerskins which I had taken off as soon as I got into the warm room. She turned each garment inside out near the bright light of the gas lamp and carefully examined every stitch to see if any repairs were necessary. She would mend any small parting of the seams, and return them to me in perfect condition for my next patrol.[21]

That evening Maria, the interpreter, came to say that Naujaa wanted to talk about the incident when he had been chanting during the night. He explained that he had heard Tornjak, the Evil Spirit of the Sea; she had come up out of the water at the floe edge and had kept walking around the igloo. She was a giant and Naujaa was convinced that she would lift the top off the igloo and carry Harry off in her hood.

Evidently he felt that he was being punished because he had kept the new tent, rather than abandoning it. He was quite emphatic, however, that he was scared for Harry and not for himself. His chanting had been intended to encourage his own good spirits to keep the Tornjak at bay. Harry listened sympathetically to Naujaa's story and explained that he thought he had been singing to his dead baby daughter, mourning her loss. Naujaa clearly felt more at ease that he had got the matter off his chest and that Harry's attitude had been sympathetic.

The trapping season began on 15 November and immediately Naujaa and Harry set off to establish a trap line some 60 kilometres in length. They had a team of 11 dogs and the load when they started weighed 1,500 lbs. Using chunks of walrus blubber for bait, they set a total of 43 traps—30 of them being Naujaa's and 13 Harry's. The trip took eight days, during three of which they were weather-bound in their igloos.

Their next trip took them northwards, with the aim of establishing a trap line as far as Cape Fullerton. They set off across Chesterfield Inlet on 7 December, but along the way their five-gallon kerosene can sprang a leak. Fortunately they were able to save some kerosene in their thermos bottles and thus did not have to abort the trip. Somehow they managed to get by on only nine quarts of kerosene on a trip that lasted nine days. Inevitably, their igloos were uncomfortably cold. Despite this mishap they managed to reach Depot Island, about 80 km north of Chesterfield and set 27 traps. They retrieved one fox from a trap on the day they turned back, while an Inuk who came in soon after Christmas found a fox and a wolverine in their traps and cached them on their behalf.

As was the case at most remote Arctic outposts, Christmas was cause for a major celebration. Harry described the festivities to his brother:

> We had quite a party. The entire population sat down to dinner at a reasonably small table. The Hudson's Bay fellows here are real good fellows, & brought four bottles of "Christmas Spirit." So we were able to drink to the King & other absent friends. My beard was the

source of entertainment for some reason; it was a funny one then. Sept. 21 saw my last shave. I've just had it trimmed now & it parts in the centre. We had an awful blizzard from Dec. 22–26 but we got our guests here by sending two Eskimos to guide them. It is impossible to try & describe how fierce the weather was. It averaged 40–45° below all the time.

Our ceremonious dinner was the funniest gathering of costumes I ever saw. Perhaps I had better state I actually put on my blue suit & a white collar & deer skin footwear, but my beard & long hair added a very aristocratic & perhaps sanctimonious touch. Petty wore his red tunic and his black beard and green civvy pants. Wiebe borrowed my dress clothes & with his sandy goatee he looked real cute. The O.C. was half uniform & half Eskimo. All of our visitors, of course, were in native clothing in order to get here in the weather, except Father [Turquetil] & he wore a short cassock with his fur pants. Really Mrs. Munday was the only one who looked civilized. All the others should have been under observation.[22]

Two days after Christmas Harry headed north again with Naujaa, driving a team of seven dogs.[23] This was in part an official patrol to visit Inuit camps and to hunt for caribou and in part a trapping trip. The two men started off by heading west along the south shore of Chesterfield Inlet for two days in search of suitable ice for crossing. Once they had reached the north side, they had to follow the shore back out to the open coast since the rocky terrain inland had been largely swept clear of snow. With occasional detours inland to search for caribou, they headed north to Depot Island where they were igloo-bound for four days due to a blizzard. Thereafter they spent several days hunting seals at the floe edge. In spite of losing several seals when they sank after being killed, Harry and Naujaa still succeeded in obtaining a substantial number for dog food.

Pushing north to Daly Bay they again made an unsuccessful hunt for caribou before continuing to Cape Fullerton where Harry inspected the police buildings built by Inspector J. D. Moodie when the *Neptune* had wintered there in 1903–04.[24] The post had been permanently closed in 1919, but Harry found the buildings still in good order. Since there was no fuel to heat the buildings, Naujaa built an igloo nearby as this was much more comfortable. Hunting trips in the immediate area were not particularly successful, although Harry saw thousands of eider ducks at the floe edge.

Two days' travel northwest of Fullerton they encountered an Inuit camp of three families. The Inuit were very short of food, having killed only two caribou since freeze-up, and had only a small supply of walrus blubber and seal oil which they had cached the previous summer. Harry gave them what little food he could spare and the Inuit presented him with *kamiks* and mitts in return. They reported that the caribou and fox were very scarce compared to other years.

On the return trip Harry and Naujaa followed a more direct route, mostly travelling on the sea ice and building their igloos on islands when this was possible. Where their return route coincided with the outgoing route, they used the old igloos if they could. One evening they arrived on a small rocky island where they had built an igloo on the out trip. However, the igloo was gone. Harry was convinced that they were on the wrong island, but Naujaa probed around with his snow-tester and eventually located the igloo. It was completely covered in snowdrifts and the two men had to dig a tunnel to the entrance. Soon, they were comfortably ensconced in their igloo, enjoying beans, bannock and tea.

Late one afternoon, Harry and Naujaa spotted a bear about three kilometres away. They quickly dumped the load off the sledge and raced after the animal with the empty sledge. Once the dogs spotted the bear they increased their speed. As they drew close to the bear, Naujaa cut four dogs loose but the bear managed to reach the floe edge and plunged in, heading straight out to sea. Naujaa indicated that it would probably swim right to Southampton Island, about 150 km away. Disappointed, the two men had to travel back about five kilometres, by which time it had grown dark and they had difficulty locating the sleeping bags and the provisions they had jettisoned. When they eventually found their belongings, they still had to drive for a further four hours to find suitable snow for building an igloo. Harry was particularly glad to crawl into his sleeping bag that night. They reached the detachment on 31 January.[25]

On this trip Harry checked all the fox traps he had set earlier and set a few more between Daly Bay and Cape Fullerton. In total, they collected 24

Manni and son, Chesterfield Inlet, 1924.

white foxes and one wolverine; they also shot three ringed seal as well as four caribou, of which they hauled three hind-quarters back to the detachment.

On a later sledge trip to Cape Fullerton in April the two men were accompanied by Manni; she thought that her mother might be there and wanted to see her, especially since she, Manni, was expecting a baby. A day out from Cape Fullerton they camped as usual and Manni prepared supper. Then Harry settled in to sleep, unaware of the excitement that was brewing around him:

Early the next morning I was rudely awakened. Nowya [Naujaa] was shaking me furiously and laughing in great excitement. He shouted "Huskie tikkiput" (A boy has arrived). I peeped into their sleeping bag and there I saw a tiny red face, two shining black eyes, and a pair of tiny hands. Although I had slept in the same igloo I couldn't have been more surprised. For all the fuss there had been, the baby might have been brought into the igloo by Old Lady Tornjak herself.

I have never seem such joy over the arrival of a baby. This was a delight impossible to describe. Both Nowya and Manni were like people released from a spell. This was the day so anxiously anticipated—the end of their taboos and the end of the power of the Evil Spirits in their lives. They had been rewarded beyond their wildest hopes. The spirit of their dead baby had come back to them in the form of a boy, so much better than a girl. He would grow to be a great hunter, who would provide meat for the young, the women and the aged. He will be a bank account for his parents. They had been under a great mental strain for months. Their troubles were now a nightmare of the past.

As I looked on at the little drama through the eyes of civilization, I thought how difficult it would be to convert these two happy people to any belief which did not offer such rich rewards as this gift from their Good Spirits.[26]

Around mid-February a party of Inuit was sent south to Churchill with the mail and were expected to arrive back around 10 April with incoming mail after a round trip of about 1,200 km. In one of the letters Harry sent to his brother with this mail, he remarked:

> It may seem a funny thing to say, but I feel that I am absolutely con-
> tented here. There is something about the North that appeals very
> strongly to me. I never thought that I would like this barren windswept
> country but I know that I should regret to leave it next summer if I
> had to.[27]

Most of June and the first half of July were spent hunting walrus for dog feed.[28] On 2 June a dog team hauled two whaleboats to the floe edge at Promise Island (about 10 km due east of the settlement). The following day, Harry headed out there with six Inuit (Nouvia, Naujaa, Parka, Atwin, Jimmy and Scotty) and their families, taking two sledges, 19 dogs and a canoe.

For the next four days ice conditions were uncooperative, so they spent the time hunting seals between Promise Island and Fairway Island (about 10 km south of Promise Island). Then on the 8th, both whaleboats were launched and sailed south to Fairway Island, continuing to Marble Island the following day. Over the next few days the party killed two walrus and two bearded seals, but in general walrus were quite scarce. On the advice of the Inuit it was decided to split up. Nouvia and his crew stayed to hunt around Marble Island while on 12 June Harry, Naujaa and Parka headed north to Depot Island, dropping off a load of meat at Promise Island en route and picking up the Inuit's families.

Soon after they reached Depot Island the ice closed in, preventing the men from using either the boat or the canoe. However, what appeared to be a misfortune worked in their favour as they found and killed a large number of seals on the ice between Depot Island and the mainland. On 29 June the ice broke up again and was driven out by a north-westerly gale that lasted for three days; after the storm there was no ice to be seen anywhere, not even with a telescope from a location about 16 km east of the island. The walrus, of course, had moved away along with the ice, but Harry and Naujaa were nonetheless able to kill one that they found sleeping in the water. Fortunately, however, seals were quite plentiful.

At Depot Island Harry hired another Inuk to help crew the whaleboat and his wife was employed scraping and drying sealskins. Two groups of Inuit stopped at Depot Island en route to Chesterfield Inlet. One group was from Repulse Bay and Wager Bay, and they were carrying the mail for the Hudson's Bay Company from Repulse to Chesterfield Inlet. The other group numbered about 30 individuals and was from Southampton Island. They were sailing to Chesterfield Inlet to trade their furs.

Harry and his party started back south on 6 July, rejoining Nouvia and his crew at Promise Island. Both whaleboats returned to Chesterfield Inlet on 16 July. Between them they had procured about 7,500 lbs of blubber and meat for dog feed, 125 gallons of seal oil (extracted from more than 50 seals) and a good supply of sealskins for summer clothing, footwear and dog harnesses. The seal oil was stored in steel barrels that were cached on the various islands for use as fuel on winter trips. During the trip, Harry and the other Inuit hunters had seen thousands of eiders flying north in June and found hundreds of them nesting on all the islands they visited. They had also spotted two bowhead whales off Depot Island and the occasional beluga.

Harry was witness to a very significant development in the summer of 1924: the Paris-based fur-trading company, Revillon Frères, arrived at Baker Lake and Repulse Bay to give the HBC the first competition it had ever experienced in this area.[29] Two large schooners arrived from Quebec City with the Revillon Frères personnel, buildings and trade goods. The Hudson's Bay Company had warned their staff in the area of this impending arrival in advance and had issued orders from London that their posts at these locations should outfit the Inuit hunters on credit and send them away to hunt so that the Revillon Frères should not get their furs. The new company's personnel were former HBC traders who knew the country and the Inuit and had a working command of Inuktitut. "They will soon make things quite interesting for the old HBC who think they own this country," Harry wrote to his brother,

> R.F. Co. have built a fine store & dwelling house at Repulse Bay & at Baker Lake & about 200 tons of cargo at each place, so they figure on staying & opening more branches next summer. They are making long sled trips this winter & trying to win over the Eskimo from the Company & find others & teach them to trap etc. For men & equipment they leave the HBC in the shade. They have good furniture, electric light, radio, pool tables, etc. in their dwelling houses & a line of substantial trading goods that beats the HBC.[30]

When the *Nascopie* called on her annual visit in July, Inspector Munday and his wife departed for the south and were replaced by Staff Sergeant Clay and his wife, Maggie. Soon afterwards, Clay ordered Harry to make a patrol to Southampton Island, taking advantage of the fact that the HBC's motor schooner *Fort Chesterfield* was heading for Coral Harbour to establish a trading post there.[31] The schooner was commanded by George Cleveland; the engineer was a Mr. H.E. Weller and her crew consisted of seven Inuit men and two boys. Apart from Harry, the passengers included Captain G.E. Mack, now Director of HBC Transport, two HBC employees, Messrs. Dudley Copeland and Bill Peters, and two Inuit families.

Fort Chesterfield put to sea on 2 August and they sighted the south coast of Southampton Island on the afternoon of the 4th. From there, Captain Cleveland followed the coastline to Coral Harbour. As a precaution he sent a small boat to sound ahead as he entered the harbour. They found a suitable site for the trading post and proceeded to land about 100 tonnes of building materials, fuel, food and trade goods.

A number of Aivilingmiut families was camped nearby, although the men were all away hunting caribou. The women and children were now moved to the site of the new trading post. Harry had met most of the families earlier at Depot Island when they were en route to Chesterfield Inlet with their furs. By his assessment they had abundant game resources on Southampton Island: caribou, hares, ducks and ptarmigan. They also had plenty of walrus and seal meat cached for the winter. There appeared to be more vegetation than on the mainland to the west and fresh caribou tracks were abundant.

Fort Chesterfield weighed anchor on 9 August, by which time the trading post was partly constructed: Peters, Copeland and the two Inuit families who were to man the post would finish the buildings. The schooner reached Chesterfield Inlet on the morning of 11 August having run under power and with a fair wind.

Copeland, Peters and their Inuit helpers were still putting finishing touches to the buildings at Coral Harbour when they were surprised by the arrival of another HBC steamer, the S.S. *Baychimo*.[32] On board were District Manager Ralph Parsons and about 20–25 Inuit families from Coates Island, originally from Cape Dorset. Parsons had closed a small post on Coates Island with the intention of relocating these families to Coral Harbour, where he was planning to open a post. Somewhere, the lines of communication had become badly crossed. It turned out that Mr. William Mitchell, sub-manager of the St. Lawrence-Labrador District, had taken the decision to despatch Copeland and Peters from Chesterfield Inlet to Coral Harbour after receiving a specific request from the Aivilingmiut of Southampton Island without clearing the matter with headquarters. Parsons had not only brought a prefabricated building and the Inuit from Coates Island, but also a new post manager, Sam Ford, his wife and three daughters. Copeland decided to stay on as a clerk under Ford, while Peters returned to the mainland.

Less than a week after his return, Harry started on another patrol aboard *Fort Chesterfield*, this time to Repulse Bay.[33] The schooner sailed from Chesterfield Inlet at 9.00 A.M. on 16 August; his fellow passengers on board were Captain Mack, Mr. W.R. Mitchell of the HBC and Father DuPlain of the Roman Catholic Mission at Chesterfield. The weather was fair and they made excellent progress. They passed Cape Fullerton at 6 P.M. that evening and anchored for the short hours of darkness in Roes Welcome Sound. Next night they anchored again off Beechy Point and reached the HBC post at Repulse Bay at noon on the 18th. Mr. Thom and Mr. W.O. Douglas who were running the post reported that the Inuit who traded there were mainly Iglulimiut and Netsilingmiut from further north. They also reported that some 20 Inuit had died in the past year. The dead were mainly old people and children who had died from illness and old age, rather than starvation. At the time of Harry's visit, most of the Inuit were out on the land hunting caribou for winter clothing. The HBC men were also able to give him an update on the Fifth Thule Expedition. Peter Freuchen and some of the expedition's Greenland Inughuit had set off north in February with the intention of sledging to Pond Inlet, Baffin Island, Cape Sabine on Pim Island, and then across to Greenland. Knud Rasmussen, the expedition leader, had passed through Repulse Bay on his long trek to Herschel Island, Point Barrow and the Bering Strait around 25 March,[34] while other members had dispersed to other destinations. Thus the expedition base on Danish Island was now abandoned.

As the *Fort Chesterfield* left Repulse Bay in the early hours of 22 August, she had to run through a long belt of ice about 16 km wide that Harry surmised had drifted through Frozen Strait from Foxe Channel. The next day they encountered very rough seas driven by a north-westerly gale. Most of the crew were seasick and Captain Cleveland hove-to off Cape Fullerton but let the schooner drift south-eastwards during the night. In the morning, Cleveland made use of the moderating conditions to run back to Cape Fullerton. Harry went ashore and supervised the dismantling of one of the outbuildings and the roof of an old carpenter's shop and the loading of all this lumber aboard the schooner. She sailed from Cape Fullerton at 7 A.M. on the 27th and with a fair wind reached Chesterfield Inlet at 5 P.M.

Just a few weeks later the small settlement was traumatised by an horrific incident. Staff-Sergeant S.G. Clay, who had arrived at Chesterfield Inlet only a couple of months earlier, had left aboard the *Fort Chesterfield* on a patrol to Baker Lake, accompanied by Captain Mack. His wife Maggie stayed at Chesterfield Inlet. This did not bother her unduly, as she had spent several years in the Western Arctic at Fort Norman, Fort McPherson and Herschel Island and was therefore no stranger to isolated outposts. In any case, Corporal Petty, Constable Robinson, and Harry were always available to help with any emergencies. Indeed she usually joined them for tea, prepared by the "cook of the week."[35]

Maggie really enjoyed Chesterfield Inlet and was very interested in the Inuit and their lifestyle. She enjoyed walking along the shore, playing with the children and the dogs. On the afternoon of 19 October Maggie set off for a walk along the beach as usual:

> She stopped at our door to say that she would be back for tea. I was cook of the week and was busy making a fresh batch of cookies for our teatime snack. So off she went to the beach, which was not far below the rise where our buildings were situated. A short time later Nouvia's wife came running towards the house, screaming incoherently. I gathered it was something about the "white woman and the dogs," as she pointed to the beach. I could see a tangle of dogs seeming to be engaged in a massive dog fight. I still didn't realize what her frantic screaming meant but took off like a March hare with the intention of stopping the fight before the dogs could cause each other too much damage.
>
> Before I actually reached the beach I was horrified to see that Maggie was in the centre of the snarling, snapping dogs, and that they were biting at her leg. She was on the ground in a sitting position and they were ripping at the flesh below her knee and biting at her arms and shoulders. By this time Petty was right on my heels and we quickly dispersed the dogs. We could then see the extent of the damage and were horrified and dismayed at the dreadful wounds and the amount of blood spurting from the severed arteries. When I picked her up to carry her to the house I placed my arm under her knee in such a position that I was able to check the spurting blood to some extent.
>
> All this happened in a matter of minutes and my thoughts were filled with dismay at the horrible situation which confronted us in the absence of Staff Sergeant Clay. This was no ordinary wound to be bound up and healed. It was a major catastrophe and we must make all decisions and take the responsibility.[36]

Back at the detachment, Harry tied off the arteries to stop the spurting blood and cut away the dangling shreds of flesh that extended from her ankle to above her knee. Using the first aid kit that was adequate for most normal accidents, he applied such bandages as he could. Maggie, meanwhile, was kept lightly sedated with some of the limited amount of ether (about a tumblerful) that was discovered at the HBC post.

Word of the crisis had quickly spread around the little community and the two priests, Norman Snow of the HBC, and Maria soon appeared on the scene. They quickly assessed the situation, but were probably reluctant to put their thoughts into words. It was Maggie herself who, on taking a look at the extent of damage to her leg, calmly faced up to the reality and said: "You will have to amputate my leg, and it will have to be done as soon as possible."[37] The calm bravery she displayed was quite remarkable.

Since St.-Sgt. Clay was not present to take responsibility or to authorize the operation, Harry, Petty, Norman Snow and Father DuPlain drew up a document stating that they intended to amputate the leg, since an operation was absolutely essential, and that they had every reason to believe that the operation would succeed. All four men, and Maggie herself, signed this document.

It was decided that Father DuPlain and Norman Snow would perform the operation while Harry looked after sterilization of the instruments and acted as anaesthetist. The detachment's medical kit contained a copy of Pye's *Surgery*, in which there were detailed and comprehensive instructions for performing amputations. Father DuPlain and Snow spent the night studying from this book and making diagrams and notes. Harry meanwhile looked after Maggie, explaining what they planned to do: "She wanted to be kept fully informed. Through it all she kept up her good spirits and apparent optimism. She was quite confident that she would survive. She was a very calm, well-adjusted person with good common sense."[38]

The operation was performed next morning on the dining-room table in the Clay's house. Harry administered the ether through a cone he had fabricated during the night. Working together, Father DuPlain and Snow tied off the arteries, cut back the flesh and sawed through the femur well above the knee. Towards the end of the operation, Harry noticed that Father DuPlain was becoming quite nervous and was turning pale. Maria gave him a stiff drink of brandy and Harry finished the surgery while Maria took over the anaesthetic cone. Harry then stitched up a flap of flesh to cover the severed bone. By this time there were only a few drops of ether left and Maggie came to almost as soon as she had been made comfortable in her bed. When Harry assured her that the operation was over and had been a success, she joked: "But I'll never be able to dance again, will I? Not with one leg."[39]

It was now decided to make every effort to get word of the accident to her husband in Baker Lake. Harry decided to try to launch the detachment's 25-foot sailboat and to sail up Chesterfield Inlet to Baker Lake. All the detachment's Inuit and Constable Robinson were away hunting walrus. Thus Harry had to call on all the Inuit women in the settlement to help him and Petty launch the heavy boat. Unfortunately, there was a heavy surf pounding on the rocky beach and the boat was repeatedly thrown back ashore before they could win clear of the breakers. Seeing that the boat was starting to suffer damage, Harry reluctantly decided to abandon the attempt and to wait till the seas moderated somewhat:

> We were now well into the second day after the operation and could see that Maggie was suffering from shock and loss of blood, and could not help seeing that she was losing ground, although she was quite comfortable and in no pain. Now we realized more than ever what a truly remarkable courageous person she was. Mentally she was alert and had been certain that she would recover. This attitude on her part helped all of us to recover our shaken spirits. She smiled and was able to eat a little and slept at times. We divided our time into shifts so that she would never be alone, day or night. She talked a lot about the dogs and the attack and which of the dogs had tasted blood. She hadn't been in the least afraid of them as they ran and jumped playfully around her. But it was the black dog Clay had brought from Labrador which had snatched at her coat, then took a nip at her leg. Then she knew she was in trouble. Talking it over with us, she became insistent on the subject that the dogs which had been involved in the attack must be destroyed; that this must be done at once to protect the women and especially the children, who were accustomed to playing with the dogs on the beach."[40]

Most of the dogs involved were from the Police teams. Harry had some chunks of meat scattered along the beach and while the dogs were feeding, he and Petty shot 19 of them with their .303 rifles. Norm Snow also shot some HBC dogs that had been involved. This was not done lightly, since it meant a crippling loss in terms of sledge travel during the impending winter. It was not until the following summer, when 12 dogs were shipped in from Labrador, that this loss to the detachment could be made good.

Two days after the operation Maggie began to talk about the possibility that she might not live, and gave Harry messages for her husband and for her family. As an Anglican, she was quite upset by Father DuPlain's attempts to persuade her to convert to the Roman Catholic faith and to be baptized so that he could give her the last rites of that Church. Clearly, from his remarks, Harry found this behaviour quite abhorrent. Maggie asked him to stay with her and she fell asleep holding his hand. "We had no further conversation," he wrote, "and she died quietly and without pain at midnight, just over two days after the accident."[41] Harry was exhausted by his almost constant vigil and the stress of dealing with the incident and he felt himself overcome with emotion:

> After Maggie died I had a complete letdown. I hadn't slept since the beginning of the ordeal and now that there was nothing more that I could do, the weight of responsibility was gone. I was completely exhausted, emotionally and physically. I crawled into my sleeping bag and fell into a sound sleep. Petty, who was a brave and reliable man, had gone to pieces before the operation and was in such a state of shock that he was ill and could do nothing but lie in misery in his sleeping bag. We all reacted differently.[42]

For the rest of his life, Harry never kept a dog as a pet. His niece, Elaine Mellor, surmised that this was in part because of the difference in the relationship between working dogs such as sledge dogs and their owner and that between a pet dog and its owner. However, she also thought that the trauma of seeing what the dogs had done to Maggie Clay may have influenced Harry's decision never to keep a pet dog.[43]

It was decided to bury Maggie the following day, since her husband would not be returning from Baker Lake for quite some time. Norman Snow made a coffin and lined it with soft white material from the HBC store. Since it was to be a Church of England funeral service, neither of the priests could conduct it, but they were invited as private mourners. Indeed, one of them acted as a pall-bearer, while Harry conducted the service:

> On the following day the strong southeast gale was still blowing full force. It was a small, pathetic group which bore Maggie up those barren rocks behind the detachment. Father DuPlain, Petty, Norman Snow and three Eskimo women carried her, leaning into the gale, up to the place we had prepared. My voice was lost in the howling gale as I read the burial service. Afterwards we built a great cairn of rocks over the coffin as it was impossible to do otherwise in the solid rock hillside.[44]

Harry and the rest of the little community still had one more difficult task awaiting them—they had to face the prospect of breaking the news to Staff-Sergeant Clay on his return from Baker Lake. Petty was the senior of the three RCMP men but could not face the task and asked Harry to do so. Finally it was decided that since Captain Mack and Clay were old friends, they would take the captain aside on the schooner's return, break the news to him, and ask him to break it to Clay as gently as he could. But even the best laid plans do not always pan out as intended:

> Ten days later, on a beautiful flat-calm, sunny afternoon, we sighted the schooner rounding the headland. All the settlement gathered on the beach as they always do in isolated places. The schooner anchored offshore and put out the small boats. The first boat ashore brought Clay, W. O. Douglas, the HB Factor, and two Eskimos. There was nothing for it, so I waded out to catch the prow of the little boat to pull it ashore. Clay called out: "Where's Maggie?" When I didn't answer he seemed to become immediately alarmed and shouted: "Where's Maggie? Where is she? She always meets me!" There was nothing I could say to help matters. I simply said, "She's not with us any more."
>
> I had heard of it, but I had never seen a big man struck down with shock. Clay stepped out of the boat and fell backwards into the shallow water. Douglas and I dragged him to his feet and half-supported, half-carried him to the Hudson's Bay post. He was in total physical collapse.

When he had recovered sufficiently, he demanded to hear the whole story. In the presence of Douglas and Capt. Mack I did my best to relate the sad events as well as I could. This was probably the worst part of the whole affair as far as I was concerned. How to tell the bare facts without any hope of comfort.[45]

Not surprisingly, this tragedy cast a dark shadow over the small community for the remainder of Harry's stay at Chesterfield and indeed to some degree affected the rest of his life.

With the coming of winter all the Mounties focussed their attention on trapping. Petty and one Inuk headed for the Baker Lake area with 45 traps, staying away for several months. Robinson made a five-week trip to the Cape Fullerton area. Meanwhile Clay and Harry stuck closer to home. Harry had made three trips of seven days each to the south by 27 January 1925, while Clay had made two trips over the same time. Between them they got 76 white foxes and 1 blue. Of these 19 were Harry's, while Naujaa got 28 white foxes and 1 blue. On one six-day trip they got 22 foxes between them despite the atrocious weather. As Harry described it in a letter to his brother:

> The weather is terrible this winter, Bill. There's just no use trying to describe it. This month (January) from 1st to 30th has averaged 35.6° below zero [F]. We have had some pretty thick drifts too. In fact the month has been one prolonged blizzard. 57° below was the lowest and 10° below the highest since Jan. 1st. The open flow is about 10 miles away now, but you can guess what an easterly Blizzard feels like. The Huskies can't begin to face the North and East heavy drifts. Snow blowing along the ground at 40 below would be termed a pretty decent day this month. This has made it pretty bad for trapping as it's next to impossible to find the traps (to say nothing of the night igloos) & the traps are blown under all the time and the bait usually taken away.[46]

The bad weather did have an upside, as it resulted in many hungry foxes. When they did manage to get to their traps, they were invariably full.

Bill Stallworthy must have been quite relieved to get this letter from Harry. On 1 December 1924 he had written to Inspector M.H. Vernon at

RCMP Headquarters in Ottawa to ask if the mails had come out from Chesterfield Inlet by sea the previous summer as usual:

> None of those to whom my Brother regularly writes have had any communication from him since the mail came out by dog team last winter, & I cannot credit that he has omitted to write, as he has important business outside, & is a good correspondent.[47]

Somehow Harry's other letters must have gone astray. Inspector Vernon was able to report that the ship had called at Chesterfield and had brought the mail from that post back south, where it was sorted at RCMP Headquarters, but there had been no letters from Harry. However, it must have set Bill's mind at rest to some degree to read that "The members of the Force who came down on the boat stated that Const. Stallworthy was in good health when they last saw him, and we have every reason to believe he is still the same."[48]

On 21 February Harry set off on a patrol to Baker Lake, accompanied by Parka and his wife, Maria. Parka drove a team of five dogs and Maria was their interpreter.[49] They reached Baker Lake on 14 March, only to find that there was no dog feed available there. They themselves had killed quite a few caribou on their way from Chesterfield Inlet but all this meat had been consumed. There were few Inuit at Baker Lake when they arrived, but various groups were expected in the near future. Harry and Parka set off eastwards on a hunting trip to the area north of Chesterfield Inlet and about halfway back to the Chesterfield Inlet settlement. Here they found numerous caribou and killed enough for their immediate needs and to create a cache for their return trip. On his return to Baker Lake, Harry found a group of Inuit from Shekoligyuak, about 320 km to the south. They reported that the game was plentiful and brought large numbers of white foxes to trade.

On 18 April Harry travelled west to the Revillon Frères trading post about 30 km away at the mouth of the Thelon River; it had been established only late the previous fall. The man in charge was M. Berthe and with him were four other white men, wintering there with the auxiliary schooner *Jean Revillon*. Here Harry heard second-hand rumours about a murder that had occurred somewhere on the Back River during the winter. Allegedly an Inuk had gone insane and had stabbed a woman, injuring her. Since he was a danger to the community, a man called Nouvia, who was a close relative of the deranged man, had very reluctantly killed him. Harry was unable to obtain the name of the man who had been killed, or to ascertain precisely where and when the killing had occurred. His conclusion was that since "No other natives or white men could give any further information, I thought it advisable to make no further investigation at the time."

Harry started back for Chesterfield Inlet on 16 April, arriving there on the 24th. He estimated that he had travelled about 880 km, including the hunting trips and the cache-laying trips. He reported that there were plenty of caribou along his route, and that some Inuit reported signs of a small herd of muskoxen north of Baker Lake. During his journey, Harry had encountered Inuit from a wide area of the Barren Lands and he could report that they were well clothed, that they had adequate supplies of caribou and fish, and that he had heard no reports of destitution or sickness.

Harry, and no doubt the rest of the small community, were glad to have the level-headed presence of Captain Mack at Chesterfield Inlet for the winter. Harry characterized him as "about as fine a man as one could meet." Mack had been captain of the HBC's steamer *Nascopie* for her first eight seasons, but he had more recently assumed a position as the Company's fleet commander. During his stay in Chesterfield, he bunked in with Clay and Harry and was an enormously steadying influence in terms of helping the latter handle his grief. But Harry was also impressed by the fact that he took his turn with the chores—baking bread, taking out the ashes from the stove, etc. Above all, he and Harry had a lot of fun brewing moonshine from raisins.

At the end of his posting, Harry boarded one of the Company vessels on 5 August. With him was Staff-Sergeant Clay, whom he and Petty had persuaded to go south for a break.[50] From York Factory, they travelled up the Nelson River by canoe to the head of steel on the Hudson Bay Railway, then caught the train via The Pas to Winnipeg. Inevitably, and to Harry's disgust, the press sensationalized the tragedy of Maggie Clay's death:

The *Tribune* last night and the *Free Press* today have terrible accounts of the tragedy of the North & the heroic work of Petty & myself clubbing bloodstained dogs to death. How these people can write up such rot without the least sign of sympathy for Clay or her people....[51]

After a brief stop in Ottawa, Harry accompanied Clay to Grimsby, Ontario, to visit Maggie's family, the Warners.[52] Harry had already received a sincere letter of thanks from Mr. Warner for his efforts to save Maggie's life,[53] and he and his wife greatly appreciated the gesture of this visit.

Mr. Warner was a fruit farmer and after two years on the barren tundra of Chesterfield Inlet, Harry revelled in the orchards of peaches, pears and plums, the vineyards and the fields of tomatoes. Nonetheless, the Warners insisted on knowing the details of Maggie's death. Watching her parents' anguish as he related to them the terrible moments when he heard Maggie's screams and discovered how severe her injuries were and the details of the operation and the heart-wrenching disappointment when she did not pull through, was almost as painful for Harry as the events themselves.

A subscription was started for a memorial for Maggie Clay. In total, it raised $450, sufficient to pay for a memorial tablet that was unveiled in the church at the RCMP Barracks in Regina on Easter Sunday 1926, and for a granite memorial that was erected at Chesterfield Inlet.[54]

4

FROM A NEAR-DEATH EXPERIENCE

to Jasper

After visiting the Warners in Ontario, Harry spent a short while attending to his own affairs before taking up his next posting at the Headquarters Division in Ottawa. After three months there (from 1 July– 1 October 1925),[1] Harry asked to be transferred to Edmonton's "G" Division, "with a view to being sent for duty in the Western Arctic at the first opportunity. I have now ten years service, of which over eight years have been spent in Northern service, and I feel that with my experience I shall be able to give better service under the conditions to which I have been accustomed."[2] The tundra, the Inuit and the challenges of dog sledge travel had clearly had a profound influence on him, and he had absolutely no doubt as to where his true métier lay.

Harry left Ottawa by train on the evening of 17 September.[3] He had been awarded six weeks' leave (from 2 September–4 November 1925) before he had to settle down to his duties in Edmonton and he took the opportunity to stop over in Calgary to visit the Bridgemans. From Calgary Harry made a trip to the Jenner area where he had spent time on Bill's homestead 13 years earlier. To his surprise, he found that Bill was still registered as the owner of one quarter section and their mother as the owner of a further two. One suspects that Archie, who had died of pneumonia in 1920,[4] had bequeathed his land to his mother. From the agent at Jenner, Harry learned that the municipal and school taxes due on the three quarter sections amounted to a staggering $992.09![5]

In 1917 Jenner had been a boomtown, riding on the bumper wheat crops of 1915 and 1916. According to A. D. Fidler of the Department of Municipal Affairs, it then boasted 28 businesses, including four general stores, four restaurants, three elevators, three livery stables, two lumber yards, a bank, a drug store and the barracks of the RNWMP.[6] But then came the drought and the boom went bust. Throughout southeastern Alberta, the years from 1917 to 1922 recorded below-average precipitation, often hitting record lows. At Suffield the average rainfall in the crop growing season in the decade before 1924 was only 6.36 inches and between 1917 and 1922 only 4.11 inches. These low precipitation amounts were accompanied by scorching temperatures. Whereas the mean daily maximum for July had been 77.7°F in the bumper year of 1915, in the following decade it averaged 86.6°, and reached a staggering 92° in 1917.[7] Crops failed year after year and homesteaders moved out in droves. In the wake of these lean years, Harry's visit to the "old homestead" was quite disconcerting. After years spent in outposts, Harry had become adept at recording his feelings and impressions in a letter to his brother:

> I got a horse from Bill Klink & rode out & believe me, even to me it
> seemed a very deserted place except for jack rabbits, badgers & gophers.
> It's no use me trying to tell you, Bill, how the whole district has gone
> to the dogs. I first struck Eddy Jones' place but I certainly did not know
> where I was, but I saw a puncher from Stapleton Ranch in the distance
> north of your place. He told me that [there] was not a soul in that part
> except Dan Abbey. Turner's & Klink's buildings have disappeared

completely. I found only a bunch of thistles where Turner was. Eventually I located your place. I know I was on your quarter because I found the gate posts we swiped from the CPR grade & I also went to the corner & found signs of the old well. The fences were of course all shot. I then found where Archie's shack was but there is only a bit of an impression where the cellar is. In 1923 a regular hurricane occurred. It even blew Klink's house out of existence. Your breaking & Archie's look as though a plow had never been on it but Turner, who left in '23 has a great crop of Russian thistles full of jack rabbits. I must have seen 20 during the day. I rode across the lake to Dan's. He was threshing for some trust company on Dick Kay's place. Dick's house was blown down towards the lake.

From there I went back to Jenner or what is left of it. A fire cleaned up the town; a Chink hotel, gen. store & Kemp's house and an odd building or two is all there is now. Going out around the old place reminded me of poor old Arch & then to see the country in such a condition fairly got my goat.... I understand that going from Jenner to Suffield there is, with the exception of Abbey's, only one place occupied. Con Topner is still at his place. I doubt whether the place they used to call Carlsbad's[8] is even a flag station. The Government have shipped all the people out. The Provincial policeman who was visiting Jenner said they had quite a lot of cases of destitution....

Yes, the only thing for you to do is to forget you ever had any land; it's too bad Mother paid up on that pre-emption. However my advice is, don't let it cost you another cent. When the trust companies & banks let it slide speaks for itself. By paying 2 & 3 years' taxes I could [acquire] any 3 quarters of a section close to Jenner along the C.P. for less than $1,000, so the only thing is to forget it. I don't know what it is assessed at, but it is of no consequence any way, because the actual value, as far as I can figure, is less than nothing to you or Mother.[9]

Having attended to his family affairs in the Jenner area, Harry returned to Calgary, where he still had some outstanding business to attend to. Throughout his time in Chesterfield Inlet and Ottawa, he had remained a silent partner in *The Chocolate Shop*. Jim Bridgeman and his wife still ran the place—with some success, it appears. In a letter to Bill, Harry reported that the Bridgemans had sold $18,000 of chocolates since he had left in May 1923, with over-heads of $241 per month.[10] Any profit after overheads and salaries was being ploughed back into the business. He estimated the stock in hand at $700 and they had $225 in the bank and no debts. The best day in terms of sales had been Christmas Eve 1924, when cash receipts had totalled $220.45, which represented the purchases of some 350 customers.

Before leaving Calgary, Harry spent a great deal of time making arrange-ments to rent a window for featuring a display of *The Chocolate Shop's* wares. After a great deal of negotiating he arranged to rent the window of a restau-rant run by Ed Kohl on 8th Avenue, just west of Centre Street. In exchange for allowing Mrs. Bridgeman to arrange displays in the window, the restau-rant would sell their products at a commission of 30 per cent.[11] Despite his pleasure at the success of the business, Harry admitted that he was already fed up with city life and that he longed to be back in the North and especially to see his Inuit friends. He reported for duty in Edmonton on 4 November 1925, but arranged to take five days' leave over Christmas. He spent the time in Calgary with the Bridgemans, relaxing and no doubt discussing business matters relating to the Chocolate Shop.[12]

The duties of city policing were a vast change from the sledge patrols of the North to which Harry had grown accustomed. Apart from such mundane, deskbound duties such as being in charge of stores, he made fairly frequent trips to outlying communities such as Vermilion, Viking and Dapp to inter-view applicants for naturalization, i.e., Canadian citizenship.[13] He investigated cases where individuals had allegedly been on a reserve at Saddle Lake ille-gally,[14] as well as incidents of domestic violence[15] and intoxication.[16] In one case, a person had been supplying intoxicating liquor to Treaty Indians.[17] The investigation eventually led to a conviction and the accused was sentenced to six months with hard labour in the Provincial Penitentiary at Fort Saskatchewan. In an unrelated case, Harry found himself in the company of a Customs and Excise Officer who had to search a farm (successfully) for an illicit still.[18]

Although Harry performed his duties in Edmonton without complaint, he was already making plans to get himself back North as soon as possible. By March 1926 he had received confirmation that he would be taking charge of the Tree River detachment in Coronation Gulf the following summer.[19] However, Harry also had a second string to his bow. He had arranged to become a partner in a fur-trading company along with two other "northerners," John Brockie and Redmond Brackett. Harry planned to invest $2,500 in the company (total capitalization $9,500). The three men already had their eyes on a suitable schooner, a 46' long new vessel with beam of 12', a draught of 3' and a 15 hp engine. The plan was for Brockie and Brackett to find a wintering site somewhere in the Queen Maud Gulf area and to operate as a trading post from there.[20] The agreement of partnership was signed on 13 March 1926,[21] by which time they had also signed a contract for building the schooner; she was to be taken down the Athabasca and Slave rivers, hauled across the portage past the Slave Rapids and launched at Fort Smith by 20 June.[22]

For Harry's part, these plans came to nought. On 31 March 1926 he was taken by ambulance to the Royal Alexandra Hospital in Edmonton with influenza at the recommendation of Dr. E.A. Braithwaite, the RCMP's Honorary Surgeon in Edmonton.[23] By 11 April Harry had developed pneumonia. Superintendent Ritchie arranged for him to have a special nurse and to be placed in a private ward where no expense was to be spared towards his recovery, since as he wrote in Harry's service file, "Constable Stallworthy… is a fine specimen of manhood, and I fervently hope that he will be able to withstand this insidious malady."[24] On the following day Commissioner C. Starnes sent a telegram to Mrs. Stallworthy in England:

Regret to inform you your son Henry Webb Stallworthy danger-ously ill with pneumonia at Edmonton STOP Receiving every care in hospital.[25]

For two or three days Harry's situation remained critical and he required morphine injections every four hours. He did not eat for five days, but by 17 April he had pulled through and although he was very weak his temperature was back to normal.[26] On that date Superintendent Ritchie cabled Mrs. Stallworthy: "Your son Henry out of danger making good progress."[27] Jim Bridgeman travelled from Calgary and spent two days with him until the crisis had passed.

But then Harry suffered a relapse. His temperature was high and his pulse rapid and he had a persistent cough. Fearing there was an abscess on one of his lungs Dr. Braithwaite decided to take an X-ray; this revealed fluid on the left lung that was pushing Harry's heart over to the side. After consultation with Dr. T.H. Prust and Colonel Dr. F.H. Mewburn, Dr. Braithwaite decided that an operation would be necessary[28] and scheduled a theatre for the next day, 1 May.[29] But Harry made a remarkable recovery overnight and it was decided not to operate after all.[30] A week later he was well enough to spend some time out on the verandah in his bed. Still, in view of his earlier relapses, he still had special nurses day and night.[31] Harry's recovery was slower than he had hoped. By 13 May Colonel Dr. Mewburn was advising that an operation might still be necessary to drain fluid from his lungs and the doctors felt that it was essential that the special nurses be retained for round the clock duty.[32] On several occasions Drs. Mewburn and Braithwaite attempted to drain any fluid or pus from Harry's chest by inserting needles, but little fluid or pus appeared.[33] On 19 May, in his first letter to his mother since he went into hospital, Harry mentioned these "minor operations."[34] At this point he was quite optimistic about going north in June, presumably to his new posting at Tree River.

Harry's recovery continued to be very slow and on 26 May Colonel Dr. Mewburn called in Dr. Egerton L. Pope from the University Hospital to get a further opinion.[35] Dr. Pope examined Harry on 26 May, 6 June and 9 June and had X-rays taken. From the X-rays, the doctors determined that there was an abscess of the lower lobe of the left lung. By the 6th of June there were definite signs of improvement "following upon the expectoration of a large quantity of pus during the previous twenty-four hours."[36] Nonetheless Dr. Pope considered it "probable that surgical intervention will soon become essential." By this stage Harry's appearance was quite alarming. Superintendent Ritchie reported that "he is so thin that if he places his thumb and first finger around his leg, the fingers will meet."[37] By late June Harry had lost 50 lbs in weight, and as a side effect he had lost his hearing temporarily.[38] A hearing specialist, Dr. W. Harold Brown, was called in and administered three treatments.[39]

Dr. Braithwaite and Dr. Pope recommended that if an operation became necessary it should be entrusted to Dr. W.A. Wilson of the University Hospital, who had an excellent reputation for lung surgery.[40] By 23 June Drs. Braithwaite, Pope and Wilson agreed that "his chances against an operation are gaining ground every day, and it was hoped that an operation would not be necessary."[41]

But then Harry had a further serious relapse; the diagnosis was that "the abscess had burst into the pleural cavity."[42] The trio of doctors decided to operate and on 7 July Dr. Wilson performed the operation successfully. By 4 August Harry was out of hospital and convalescing well enough that he felt able to include full details of his operation in a letter to his mother:

I have just received the very welcome letter you wrote on July 19th after you got the cables from Jim. I was very ill at the time & the doctors did not tell me about the operation I was to have untill [sic] late at night on the 6th of July & I was in the operating room at 8 o'clock the next morning. I was very weak at the time. Doctor Wilson who is a very clever surgeon, did the operation & 3 other doctors were there too. One injected germs into my chest to strengthen me. I was under gas for one hour & the cut was made in my back on the left side. It was for "abscess on the lung." Two small pieces of rib were taken out & a tube put right into the lung. At the time they pumped out 2 pints of puss. A tube was left in to drain the rest & 10 stitches below the tube. After six days Dr. Wilson took out the stitches and the tube. This left a hole 1 inch across and about 3½ inches deep. On the following day I got up for an hour & from that time on I began to walk & I got a piece of oiled silk put into the hole instead of the tube. My, but what an appetite I had. I could never seem to be satisfied though I had sandwiches in between my meals. From the second day after the operation I began to gain & every body, especially my own nurses were surprised at the way I improved so fast. I have still got an enormous appetite. I left the hospital on July 31st & I am now at the Barracks & I sleep in a tent. I go to the hospital once a day to have my back dressed. The lung healed inside on July 25th & today the outside is almost healed over, so I think I have a lot to be thankful for, considering the condition I was in when I was operated on. The cut in my back has been very healthy & no sign of infection. They have never put anything on it but plain gauze dressings. I am getting quite strong again but of course I am awfully thin. I lost 56 lbs. At the time of the operation I was 142 lbs or less than that; now I am 154 lbs, so you see I am picking up. Doctor Braithwaite, the police doctor, is going to recommend 2 months leave for me to go to England so I have decided to come home altho' I know I'll not like the weather in the late autumn, but I am so anxious to see my dear mother & Bill again that I feel it my duty to come home & see you when I know you have been so anxious about me. The trip home especially the sea air will do me good, but I am afraid I will be too late to have a bed on the lawn & the strawberries will be over for it will probably be Sept. 1st before I get there.[43]

Like many others who have had a near-death experience, Harry subsequently displayed a renewed zest for life and a thankfulness for being alive. Undoubtedly, the experience of having been so closely associated with Maggie Clay's death, reinforced his appreciation for his own good fortune.

Throughout his illness and recovery, Harry had received solid support from his colleagues at the Edmonton Detachment, including Sergeant-Major Spriggs who even sent his brother Bill in England a progress report.[44] Now however, instead of the Arctic posting he had been anticipating, Headquarters had posted him to the detachment at the mountain resort of Jasper, Alberta, where he would be in charge.[45] The very sensible rationale behind this decision was "that he would not be much use for Northern work for a year or two after his term of illness so that Jasper would be the logical place for him for a while."[46]

Before taking up his new appointment in Jasper, Harry had been awarded two months sick leave (16 August until 16 October) to assist his recovery.[47] Harry would later request an additional month's leave without pay.[48] As he had planned earlier, Harry took the time to visit his family in England. He spent most of his time visiting his mother in Fairford and his brother William and his family at the Mill in Ampney Crucis. He and his mother spent a brief vacation in Bournemouth, presumably for the beneficial effect of the sea air on his health.[49] He also met up with Corporal Petty in London, and together they visited some of Petty's relatives in West Wycombe where they went to cattle sales, bazaars, etc. Then Harry took Petty to Gloucestershire to meet his family. When they were not in the King's Head in Cirencester, they strolled around the Cirencester churchyard and climbed the church tower—churches and churchyards being one of Petty's interests.[50]

Corporal Stallworthy on Buster, Jasper, 1927.

While Harry was still in England his boss, Superintendent James Ritchie, wrote to the Commissioner to suggest that Harry should be promoted Corporal. On this occasion the Commissioner's response was that "your suggestion about his promotion will be considered after he has been on the job [in Jasper] and shown satisfactory work."[51]

Harry's posting to the Jasper, Alberta detachment was dated to 1 December. When Harry arrived there, the town was somewhat of an enigma as it was served by an excellent rail link, but it could not be reached by road. The only paved road led from the town to Jasper Park Lodge, 5 km away, then continued to Pyramid Lakes, Maligne Canyon and the eastern boundary of the Park. In 1928 a dirt road was pushed through from Edmonton to Jasper but it was often impassable for cars. This situation did not improve until the road was gravelled in 1937. It was finally paved in 1951.

The town site was the headquarters of Jasper National Park, which had been established in 1907 and originally encompassed most of the mountain watershed of the Athabasca River (some 5000 sq. miles). The Grand Trunk Pacific Railway reached the town site (which was originally named Fitzhugh, but later renamed Jasper) in 1911. In that year the Canadian Northern Railway also reached the town and the area of the Park was reduced to a swath 20 miles wide on either side of the railways. In response to protests from both the Alpine Club of Canada and the railways, the park was enlarged to roughly its original boundaries in 1914. Then in 1927 (during Harry's period of residence) the southern boundary was moved south to Bow Summit to incorporate most of the North Saskatchewan mountain watershed. However, in response to protests from the town of Banff, the southern boundary was moved back north to Sunwapta Pass in 1929.

Jasper was very much a rich man's mountain resort that was promoted by the Canadian National Railway. The major focus of the tourist trade was Jasper Park Lodge, which had opened only four years before Harry arrived. As Harry described it,[52] the Lodge consisted of a complex of 30–40 log buildings, dining rooms, dance-halls, swimming pools and a golf course that had cost $1.5 million to establish. It was open from 1 May until November, with rooms costing $15 and up—"mostly up" as Harry wryly noted. The Lodge employed a large staff and a fleet of taxis drove the tourists from the station to the Lodge or to local sights such as Maligne Canyon. Hundreds of saddle and pack horses were maintained for trail rides to the more remote parts of the Park. At the time of Harry's sojourn, Jasper had a permanent population of 1,200 to 1,500 but this was increasing rapidly. He estimated that in the summer of 1927 over 100 new houses were built and that the population was 1,000 greater than when he had arrived the previous November.[53] With the influx of people during the "season" at the Lodge, the town became quite hectic in summer and the Mounties were kept particularly busy then.

The RCMP Detachment consisted of Harry and two (later three) constables. One of the constables patrolled by motorbike and was mainly engaged in handing out speeding tickets; the other looked after the detachment's two horses. Initially Harry himself spent a lot of his time on paperwork producing the required nine copies of every crime report. Most of the cases were quite minor: intoxication, vagrancy and driving offences, but they all meant that Harry spent most of his mornings in court. Over the period stretching from 1 November 1926 to 30 September 1927, a total of 96 prisoners occupied the cells, 91 of them being convicted; in addition, of 27 summonses he handed out, Harry obtained 24 convictions (2 were withdrawn and 1 dismissed).[54] Occasionally Harry would have to attend the Alberta Supreme Court in Edmonton. He spent two weeks there in the fall of 1927, giving evidence in three cases and getting convictions on all of them. There was one case of seduction, one assault with intent, and one case of indecent assault.[55] For such trips, of course, he had to travel by train. If he caught the 10.30 P.M. train out of Jasper, he could go to bed and get up when the train reached Edmonton at 6.30 the following morning.

The majority of cases Harry dealt with during this time may have been minor, but occasionally even these relatively minor cases were cause for some soul-searching. During a dance Harry attended, a drunk C.N. engineer became a nuisance and when Harry asked him to leave he became obstreperous and made very derogatory remarks about the RCMP.[56] Harry arrested the man; he spent the night in jail and was fined $20 with costs. Harry's problem was that he was well aware that the conviction meant the man's instant dismissal from Canadian National Railways. But he felt that, especially in light of the opprobrious insults directed at the Force, he had no option. After his dismissal the man in question came to apologize to Harry and arranged for him to receive an invitation to the Engineers' Ball!

All this bustle was, of course, a far cry from life at Chesterfield Inlet! Even after only six months of this posting, Harry was ready to go back north again. As he wrote to his mother:

> I would rather go up north again. It's a healthier life & I like it better than being here and dressed up all the time & I get a lot of office work to do & a lot of court cases. We have men in jail here most of the time, & that means such a lot of office work and red tape to go through.[57]

Soon after moving to Jasper, Harry was promoted to the rank of Corporal (for the second time). Superintendent Ritchie had written again to the Commissioner on 9 December to recommend the promotion:

> Constable Stallworthy has served between ten and eleven years and prior to taking his discharge in 1921 served as a Corporal for seven

months. His past record is an excellent one, and he has now recovered from the serious illness which incapacitated him all summer. He is now in charge of the Jasper Detachment and is doing very well indeed.[58]

The promotion was approved and took effect from 15 December 1926.

Not all of Harry's official duties in Jasper were onerous or tedious, however. At the carnival to mark Canada's Diamond Jubilee on 1 July 1927 he judged the floats and sports. And on the following day he won the one mile race on one of the RCMP horses called Buster, winning by four lengths out of a field of seven. He received a case of pipes and a cup as his prizes.[59] Then on 22 April 1927 the Detachment held an official house-warming party for its new detachment building (which later became the town library). About 85 guests attended.[60] Work on the grounds (lawns, rockery, garage, sprinklers, etc.) continued well into the fall.[61]

Harry also took the opportunity to upgrade his qualifications, competing for the honour of "Marksmanship, Crossed Revolvers" in Edmonton in mid-September.[62] His score of 221 out of a possible 240 in the revolver section was the highest in "G" Division—he only required 200 to gain the "Crossed Revolvers." Understandably, Harry was quite pleased with himself, as he had not competed since 1919 when he was top scorer in the Yukon. Characteristically, he had some bets riding on the results and won a bottle of Haig's Dimple (Scotch), two boxes of cigars, and $7.00.

Whenever his duties allowed, Harry would get out into the fresh air, determined to get himself back into top physical condition. He went skiing quite often, even during his first winter in Jasper,[63] and by his second winter described himself as "a bit of a dasher on skis."[64] During that second winter he became proficient at the challenging sport of skijoring in which a person on skis is pulled behind a horse or a vehicle. In November 1927 he skijored the 5 km from town to the Lodge behind a Napier car travelling at 25–30 mph and participated in horse-drawn skijoring races during the Winter Carnival on 22/23 February 1928.[65] In winter he also found time for curling—on an outdoor rink and, on one occasion in November 1927, at a temperature of -14° F![66]

In summer Harry played golf and frequently went on trail rides. Once during the summer of 1927, he and some friends went on a trail ride to Maligne Lake and back, a distance of about 100 km.[67] Along the way they saw moose,

Harry and party on trail-ride from Jasper; Hilda Austin on extreme left, 1927.

bighorn sheep, Rocky Mountain goats, deer, elk, beaver and bear. The sight of so much game, all totally protected within the National Park, frustrated Harry whose hunting instincts had been honed after years as a hunter in the Yukon and Keewatin. "It sure gets my goat to see all the game looking at you," he wrote to his mother in September.[68] However, his frustration was somewhat relieved by their success in fishing in Jacques Lake: a rainbow and two lake trout.

By the fall of 1927 Harry was becoming increasingly friendly with one of the school teachers in Jasper, Hilda Austin. A native of Wetaskiwin, she was the daughter of Reverend Austin and had arrived in town in August 1926. She and her older sister Ethelind had spent several years teaching in remote country schools around Alberta before they both landed what were considered "plum" jobs teaching in Jasper. They were later joined by their younger sister Elaine, who was also a teacher.[69] Hilda first saw Harry in November of that year:

One Sunday afternoon in November, I was standing with my sister and her [future] husband on the edge of the open air ice rink watching the big boys of the town and school play a furious game of scrabble hockey. My brother-in-law pointed across the rink and said: "There's the new Corporal of the RCMP." I looked across at the tall, 6'2", blond, handsome man. He was bareheaded and wore the trench coat popular at that time; even at that distance I was struck by the sad, aloof, lonely expression on his face. I felt a strong attraction to a strange personality, without knowing anything at all about him.[70]

Harry and Hilda's future brother-in-law, Harry Mellor, became friends and through him he came to know Hilda. His first mention of her in his correspondence is in a letter to his mother dated 18 September 1927:

I have a very nice girl chum now who I take to dances etc., Miss Austin, a school teacher. I have met her people. Her father's a vicar but I don't think I'll ever need his services. No indication of getting married yet.[71]

A few weeks later, in a letter to Bill, he wrote: "I occasionally visit the school teachers & usually take a very snappy looking girl, Hilda Austin to dances. She is quite a good sport, Parson's daughter, College Graduate & all that sort of thing."[72] It is quite possible that she was a member of the party that went on the trail ride to Maligne Lake. The two of them enjoyed skiing together, as Hilda recalled much later:

When the winter came and the snow, we were part of the group that formed the first Jasper Ski Club. In fact in those days we were amongst the first little ski groups to form across Canada.... We all learned to ski after a fashion. It was all cross country trail skiing in those days.... We put on our skis at the back door and slid away down the snow covered streets to the surrounding hills where a ski trail had been carved out on the gentle ups and downs and in and out through the trees.[73]

Hilda and her sister got into the habit of inviting the two Harrys to Sunday dinner, leaving the two men to wash the dishes while the ladies went to church, where they were members of the choir.[74] These evenings meant a great deal to Harry: "It has made quite a difference to my life here knowing these young people. It is the first time I have known anything like a family

Hilda and Harry,
Jasper, 1927.

life since I have been in Canada."[75] By the following Easter the relationship
had clearly developed:

> I have had some great times here, especially with a couple of school
> teachers, the Austins. Hilda is a very fine girl. Description: 26, Canadian,
> pretty, slim, blond, blue eyes, good teeth. She is the youngest of three
> sister school teachers but is the senior & Assistant Principal at Jasper.
> She is talking of giving it up & going back to University. They are at
> home in Edmonton for Easter holidays. Harry Mellor (who is engaged
> to the oldest one, Ethelind) & I are arranging a party for their return.[76]

Hilda later characterized this as Harry's "police description" of her and noted
that her eyes were brown, not blue![77] Despite Harry poor observance skills
when it came to Hilda's eyes, this was the start of a life-long romance.

With a little persuasion Harry could be induced to talk at length about
his experiences in the north: the Inuit, sledge travel, hunting, etc. On one occa-

sion he related the tragic death of Maggie Clay—a moment that stood out in Hilda's memory:

> As he told the story a whole new side of his abilities and nature became visible. When he reached the end and her death, tears ran down his face and we knew why he had the remote sadness which was more than a concern for his own health. All this had happened, followed by his own illness the year before we met him.[78]

Initially Harry had hopes of going back north after only one winter in Jasper and in the spring of 1927 went to Edmonton for a medical examination. He made sure that every detail of his visit was taken care of and as he noted in his service file, he specifically had "a thorough examination by Dr. Pope and an X-ray photograph taken on my own account and expenses."[79] The reason why he specified Dr. Pope by name was that "Dr. T. O'Hagan of Jasper is not conversant with the details of my illness and an X-ray examination before going North was recommended by Doctors Pope and Wilson of Edmonton."[80]

Although Harry was pronounced medically fit, the Commissioner of the RCMP decided that he should wait for another year. Harry put on a nonchalant face in a letter to his brother: "I passed the Doctor OK & am feeling real fine but the commissioner said I am not to go north for another year. So that's that. I'm going to settle down at Jasper now & call it my home."[81] But he revealed his true feelings on the matter to Hilda:

> The night he returned to Jasper he asked me to go for a walk with him. We walked up the hill leading to Pyramid Mountain. It was sunset and the lights of the town were just coming on. We sat on the hillside and looked down at the town and the mountains rising all around. He said, "Would you know I have been crying all day?" I was astonished at such a remark, but that was the sort of sensitive, gentle person he was. I said "Why were you crying?" He said, "They won't let me go north this summer."[82]

It seems unlikely that Harry's remark about settling down in Jasper was ever a serious plan. As Harry later wrote to a friend back in England: "The chief reason I left there was that I don't like arresting and prosecuting people, or posing to be photographed & questioned by a flock of tourists, and I never felt comfortable in clean boots & buttons. However, this is an excuse after all, for going back north again."[83] In reality Harry still had hopes for a posting in the Western Arctic, such as Tree River, where he would have gone but for his illness. Early in 1928 he resubmitted his application for Northern Service and this time it was approved by the Commissioner, who wrote to Superintendent Ritchie on 17 February:

Reg. No. 6316, Corporal H.W. Stallworthy of Jasper is applying for Northern Service, and if selected by you I propose to place him in charge of the new Fond du Lac Detachment. I would like to have him in the Post in good time to keep in touch with the Buildings in course of construction, and also the Boat etc. I find this is a great help to the man who will eventually be in charge of them.[84]

Superintendent Ritchie then wrote to Harry saying that there were no vacancies for NCOs in the Western Arctic. He suggested that unless Harry wanted to stay at Jasper he should apply for a new detachment that was to be opened at Stony Rapids, Saskatchewan, at the east end of Lake Athabasca. Harry outlined this offer in a letter to Bill:

It means...a completely new outfit to which Ottawa has granted $8,700.00 & including NCO's quarters, Cnsts. Quarters & warehouse, i.e. 3 frame buildings, a 32 ft. Columbia River pattern boat (complete with 2 sails, fitted with a 25–30 hp Karmath medium-duty engine), 2 Peterboro canoes, one with a 3½ outboard motor, a fishing dory, 10 dogs etc. Also 6 tube Northern Electric radio outfit. I have to have an interpreter & guide at 75.00 per month & can take one or two constables.... It is just on the edge of the Barren Lands & quite a few Eskimo are starting to trade there.[85]

Harry mailed off an application immediately. He was going back north!

5

STONY RAPIDS

1928–1930

WHILE HARRY AND HILDA had become very fond of each other in the two years they spent together in Jasper and they enjoyed each other's company immensely, both were realistic individuals. They knew that the posting to Stony Rapids would be for two years, and that things could change in that time. But they could hope.

In early April 1928 Harry left Jasper and spent a few days in Edmonton to organize the supplies and lumber he would need for his new detachment. Since he was getting supplies for a new detachment, Harry's requisition for stores was extremely comprehensive and very detailed. His supply list included a wide range of items: a folding bath, a typewriter, four fire extinguishers, a tape measure, two pairs of waders, a dozen mouse traps, 48 gallons of kerosene, 6 Christmas puddings, 20,000 cartons of cigarettes (100 in each), a freighter canoe, two pairs of handcuffs, and two waste-paper baskets.[1] The lumber for the three buildings was all pre-cut and numbered, "but just the same there will probably be a few puzzles to solve," he told Bill in a letter.[2] By then the detachment's boat, the *Halifax*, was almost completed. The RCMP had arranged for the Northern Trading Company to haul most of the outfit (some 50 tonnes) down the Athabasca River and east to the head of Lake Athabasca, while the *Halifax* would carry a further seven or eight tonnes.[3] Having inspected the *Halifax*, Harry's assessment was that she was "a very fine craft for our work" and that the engine "works like a charm."[4]

Harry had hoped to be appointed as Justice of the Peace, which would have greatly facilitated law enforcement in such a remote location as Stony Rapids. Apparently the Commissioner discouraged the idea, much to Harry's disappointment:

> At present as far as enforcing law in a new country goes, I am going in with my hands more or less tied. It means a 400 mile trip to a Dominion J.P., so I'll hardly consider the time & expense of a trip of that kind unless it's a murder or something serious.[5]

Harry left Edmonton by train for Waterways on 19 June, accompanied by Constable W.R. Browne. The *Halifax* had gone ahead and was to be launched at Waterways. Harry took delivery of the boat from the Athabasca Shipping Co. and supervised the launch. The vessel was then rigged and the Karmath engine test-run for a few hours. At Waterways Harry was met by Special Constable F. Heron of the Fort Chipewyan detachment, who was to act as pilot on the trip down the Athabasca River.[6] Having loaded the boat and taken delivery of five dogs, Harry set off downriver on 20 or 21 June.[7] As Harry steered his boat down the wide, fast-flowing river and watched the spruce-clad banks slipping past, he felt in his element—he was back in the real wilderness once again.

At Fort McMurray he reported to Sergeant Ward, who was in charge of that detachment, and bought a further four dogs. Continuing downriver, *Halifax* crossed the west end of Lake Athabasca to Fort Chipewyan where Harry again reported to the officer in charge, Corporal Bryant. Bryant supplied Harry with a fishing skiff, two toboggans and 40 gallons of gasoline. Here, too, Harry bought another dog from an Indian.

The *Halifax* sailed from Fort Chipewyan on 24 June with Corporal Bryant as pilot and the skiff in tow and coasted along the north shore of Lake Athabasca. They called at the McGinnis camp and the Athabasca Fish Company's camp at Black Bay before reaching the Chipewyan village of Fond du Lac on the morning of the 26th.[8] In his report, Harry noted that his visit was well-timed in terms of making contact with most of the population of the area:

> I attended the Indian Treaty Payment with Const. Browne at Fond du Lac and spoke to the Chipewyan Chief and other Indians present through the treaty interpreter and told them in brief of the establishment of the new detachment. I also spoke on the matters of wanton slaughter of caribou, forest fires, wolf bounties and the new regulations governing dogs in the N.W.T. They appeared to have no complaints that would require police investigation. The chief stated that he was glad to know that the Mounted Police had come to stay.[9]

Harry also met with Mr. Card, the Indian Agent, who asked that Harry handle the issue of rations to destitute Indians; Harry anticipated that "it is probable that there will be some genuine cases of destitution during the winter as there has been in the past." He also visited all the traders and white trappers in Fond du Lac, "most of whom remarked that they were pleased to learn that the RCM Police were to establish a post."[10] He also received a number of applications for Hunting and Trapping Licences for both the NWT and Saskatchewan, the boundary lying only some 90 km north of Stony Rapids. Prior to this, having disbursed wolf bounty payments, Corporal Bryant had returned to Fort Chipewyan with the treaty party.

Before Harry left Fond du Lac he received a rather unusual request from a Saskatchewan Provincial Police officer, Constable F.G. Lowe. The Constable asked that Harry "report that he wished to stay at Fond du Lac and work under this detachment [i.e. Stony Rapids]."[11] What made this request unusual was that as of the beginning of June 1928 the RCMP had taken over responsibility for policing throughout the Province of Saskatchewan from the Saskatchewan Provincial Police (SPP), which had been disbanded. The SPP had had a detachment at Fond du Lac and while many officers from the SPP were absorbed into the RCMP across the province, this was only with official

Harry raising the flag at the new detachment, Stony Rapids, Saskatchewan, 1928.

The buildings that Harry erected for the new detachment, Stony Rapids, 1928.

approval from the RCMP. Quite correctly, Harry found Lowe's approach somewhat irregular: "As I did not consider that this arrangement would be in order, and that Corpl. Bryant was reporting the circumstances to the Officer Commanding, Great Slave Lake Sub-Dist., I did nothing in the matter."[12]

Harry's last item of business at Fond du Lac on the morning of 1 July was to hire Henri Laferté as interpreter and guide at a wage of $75 per month and a single ration. That same afternoon, Harry and Constable Browne left Fond du Lac for Stony Rapids, arriving the next day. On the following morning, 3 July, Harry hoisted the Union Jack and he and Constable Browne began the work of clearing brush, staking location lines and digging the basement for the NCO's quarters (the main office and living quarters), known as a C-type building.

The site Harry chose for the building was right by the Stony Rapids, the lowest rapids on the Fond du Lac River, where Black Lake drains into Lake Athabasca. In his own words:

We have a dandy site here, best in the country, at the foot of the Rapids overlooking the island & lake, which some call a river. The "Halifax" draws about 2' 6" loaded with about 3 tons. We can moor her to the bank 50 feet from the point. We are on a point & lots of good water & wood available. One could not wish for more.[13]

On 6 July the outfit (a carload of building lumber, general stores and rations for a year) arrived in a scow towed by a power boat in the care of Mr. Denholm, sub-contractor for the Athabasca Shipping Company. By the middle of August, Harry, Browne and Henri Laferté had erected two buildings. The main building (type C) measured 28' x 28', with a veranda 6' wide. The building contained a large office, a bedroom, a kitchen and a cell; on the outside it had cedar-bevel siding and the roof was shingled. The warehouse measured 18' x 22', with two windows and a shingled roof. Both buildings were painted white with red roofs. The detachment had also been allocated a third building (B-type, Constable's quarters) but the 18' floor joists had not arrived and so, since it was not needed immediately, Harry decided to leave the job of erecting it until the following summer.

Fishing for dog food was a high priority that occupied most of Laferté's time, although Harry and Browne also lent a hand. Laferté had the reputation of being the best fisherman in Fond du Lac and he certainly lived up to this reputation. By the end of September they had four nets in operation and on the morning of the 28th they netted 73 lake trout averaging about 14 lbs each. In two hours one afternoon Harry trolled a line and caught 33 fish. By the end of the month Harry was able to report that not only had they caught and dried 2,500 lake trout, but that since they had arrived the 10 dogs had been fed almost entirely on fresh fish, the imported dog food being used only occasionally to give them some variety. The fish weighed 7–10 lbs on average, although Harry had himself landed a fish weighing 33½ lbs.[14] The plan was to continue fishing after freeze-up using nets under the ice during the white fish run, and Harry was confident that they would supply enough dog food for the entire winter. On 28 September Harry wrote:

> The run is not really on yet. We have eight more nets ready to put in, then I guess it will keep the interpreter, Brown & I busy ripping & hanging the fish to dry. Our requirements (that is to save us cooking dog feed) will be about 4,500. I guess we will get them OK. The fish crop never seems to fail here. Stony Rapids is fast water at the end of 200 miles of lake & the trout all come east to spawn & of course they stick around the foot of the rapids.[15]

The only source of complaint about Stony Rapids that Harry saw fit to mention in his letters was the mosquitoes: "They were like tigers all the month of July. We used to have smudges all round the place in gasoline cans where we were working & we hid down the lake & slept on the 'Halifax' at night."[16]

The detachment was equipped with radio: a Northern Electric Victor with eight tubes and 21 wet-cell batteries and an antenna that stretched between two 60' towers. This was an important source of entertainment, since stations in Chicago, Winnipeg, Springfield, Boston and Pittsburgh transmitted concerts specifically to the North every Saturday night. In his official year-end report on the performance of the radio, Harry noted:

> Almost every night since November 15th reception has been good. Before winter set in we found reception best when the atmosphere was heavy with rain or fog. Since the freeze-up the volume has increased

The RCMP boat, Halifax, *Stony Rapids, 1928.*

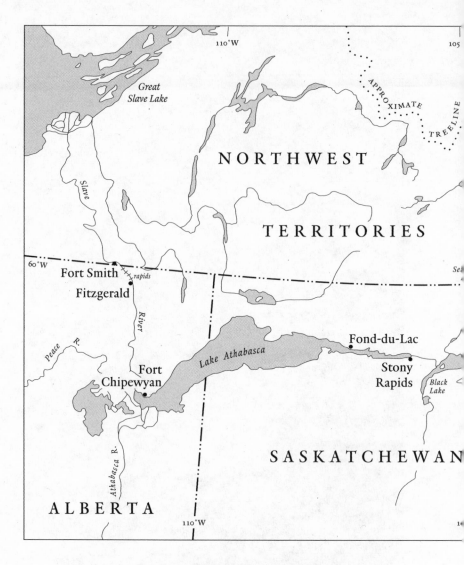

and at times the reception is very good in the daytime. On an average, in the winter evenings we can choose from 10 to 12 concert programmes.[17]

The best, most reliable reception was from CKY Winnipeg, but they also had clear signals from 19 Canadian and 66 American stations, ranging from Atlantic City to Long Beach, California. From time to time, the men stationed at Stony Rapids even received personal messages. On Christmas Eve 1927, Harry received messages from his brother in England, from Hilda in Jasper,

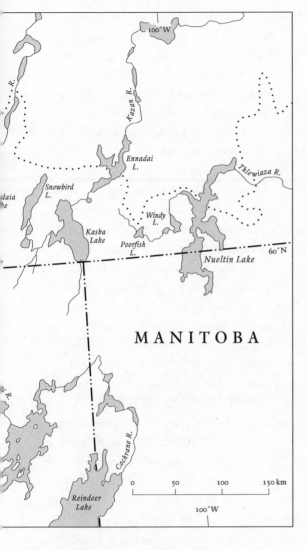

Area travelled by Harry Stallworthy from Stony Rapids, Saskatchewan.

and from Toronto.[18] In general, the radio was a very popular feature of the detachment's facilities:

> The personal [sic] of this detachment appreciate very much the Commissioner's kindness in supplying the set. We have been able to receive messages from friends and relatives and up to date news items. It has been very good company and a source of great pleasure especially during the long winter evenings.[19]

By the end of September Harry had already made two patrols in the *Halifax* to Fond du Lac and he planned to make this patrol on a monthly basis,[20] largely to take care of the business of applying the Saskatchewan and Northwest Territories Game Acts. The distance to Fond du Lac was about 88 km, which meant a trip of about 6 hours in *Halifax*. During the winter Harry made these monthly trips by dog team.[21] On instructions from the Great Slave Lake Sub-District, Harry used the former Saskatchewan Provincial Police buildings as his quarters when he was in Fond du Lac.

Harry had no doubt that of the two sites, the one at Stony Rapids was the better and he felt that moving the police detachment there was justified for a number of reasons. While there were four trading companies at Fond du Lac, three of them had premises at Stony Rapids as well, while a fourth company at Stony Rapids was not represented at Fond du Lac. Moreover, most of the Fond du Lac band (Chipewyans) hunted in the area north and east of Stony Rapids and were constantly passing through and did much of their trading at Stony Rapids. Indeed, except for Treaty Time, there were more Indians in and around Stony Rapids than there were at Fond du Lac.

There were also indications that Stony Rapids was to become an important base in terms of northern aviation. On 3 September Colonel C.D.H. MacAlpine of the Dominion Exploration Company landed at Stony Rapids, having flown from Baker Lake in seven hours. The plane, a Fokker Super Universal (G-CASK) that belonged to Western Canada Airways, was flown by the legendary flying ace from Alberta, C.H. (Punch) Dickins.[22] Harry gave the party a warm welcome, trying his best to "outdo the warmth of the hospitality the party had received at other points in the north."[23] MacAlpine informed Harry that Stony Rapids would be one of his supply bases for aerial mineral exploration in the Barren Lands for the next three years.[24] A rival company, Northern Aerial Mineral Exploration, had already established a fuel cache at Stony Rapids. It seemed probable that these companies might want to erect buildings at Stony Rapids in the future and since they all used float-planes, the buildings would have to be near water. Acting on instructions from his Commanding Officer, Harry staked an area around the RCMP buildings with a water frontage of 250 feet and running back 200 feet as the RCMP's exclusive domain.

At the invitation of Colonel MacAlpine, Harry took the opportunity to fly from Stony Rapids to Wholdaia Lake and back to see the terrain from the air and, if possible, to observe the caribou migration and check whether there was any indication of wasteful killing of the caribou.[25] Colonel MacAlpine's purpose in making the flight was to locate one of his field geologists, Mr. Carrol. Since those were the early days of air travel, it is quite possible that this was Harry Stallworthy's first flight.

They took off from Stony Rapids at 3 P.M. on 3 September and headed northeast at an average speed of 100 mph. When they reached Wholdaia Lake, they spotted a tent on the lake shore. Punch Dickins landed the plane and the men disembarked. Upon inquiry, they discovered that the tent belonged to the geologist they had set out to find. With him were Mr. O.K. Johnson, a trader from Stony Rapids, and a white trapper. Having found the person they were looking for, the aircraft took off again almost immediately and they were back at Stony Rapids by 5.30 P.M. Although Harry had not seen any caribou from the plane, he was informed on his return that the main mass of the caribou migration was at the north end of Wholdaia Lake, but that they were not thought to be as numerous as in previous years.

After more than a decade of service, it was second nature for Harry to file a report about the flight. "The visibility was very good; from an altitude of three thousand feet one could see a lot of territory which in no way resembles any of the maps that I have studied," he wrote. His experience of Arctic patrols in winter also led him to observe other useful features along the way:

> To observe that district from the air it appears to be about sixty per cent water. It resembles a large area of water filled with irregular shaped islands. The country is well timbered as far as I could see but trees are small and not thick. One should be able to travel without chopping out trails in winter. No caribou or other game were observed. The distance travelled was 211 miles, time two and one half hours.[26]

As airplanes did not stop at far-flung places such as Stony Rapids as a matter of course, Harry took the opportunity to scribble a note to his brother:

> An unexpected opportunity has occurred to send you a note by "Air Mail": a plane flew from Chesterfield Inlet a couple of days ago to a gasoline cache here. The fellow in charge, Col. McAlpine of the Dominion

Explorers Ltd. is a fine chap; brought us mail & presented us with 2 Imperial quarts of Dewars Special. I went for a little trip with them yesterday, that is the Col. and a geologist, pilot & mechanic. We went 109 miles northeast of here in 1 hr. 13 minutes. Spotted a camp, went down & picked up another geologist & brought him out with a bunch of samples of rocks. Today they fly to Fort Smith to report to Toronto by wireless also to their base just south of Chesterfield.[27]

While Harry undoubtedly enjoyed the challenges of a remote posting such as Fond du Lac, it was not where he really wanted to be. On 1 February 1929 he wrote to Superintendent Ritchie in Edmonton:

> I have the honour to request that I be relieved at this detachment with a view to being transferred to the Eastern or Western Arctic.
>
> My reasons for making this application are that I have served nine years in the north including two years at Chesterfield Inlet, that I am conversant with and would prefer the duties and conditions at a barren land detachment, I am interested in the Eskimo and wish to continue a study of their language.
>
> After my service at Chesterfield Inlet I was transferred to "G" Division and detailed to relieve the N.C.O. in charge of Tree River Detachment in 1925 but owing to illness the orders were cancelled. On making further application for arctic service in 1926 the Commissioner ordered that I would not be transferred to the far north for a year.[28]

However, Superintendent Ritchie did not seem to share the desire to get Harry to the Arctic. He wrote a letter to the Commissioner stating that Harry had been at Stony Rapids for less than a year and he felt that Harry needed to stay there a while longer. In addition, he wrote, there were currently no vacancies in the Western Arctic.[29] In the light of Ritchie's letter, it is not surprising that the Commissioner also refused Harry's request. For now, at least, Harry was stuck in Stony Rapids.

Even so, Harry managed to find a reason to travel north from Stony Rapids. In the spring of 1929, he made a major dog-sledge trip to Nueltin Lake, NWT—perhaps he simply wanted to get beyond the tree line and see once again the "barren land" and meet up with some of the Inuit whose language he wished to study further. However, his official reason for the patrol was

to visit traders, Indians and Eskimo to the east of this detachment where as far as I could ascertain there had not been a police patrol before, also to enquire into and observe the game conditions and in particular to visit Indian camps near the northern boundary of Saskatchewan in connection with the regulations governing the surrendering of beaver pelts and wolf pelts to the R.C.M.P. as many of the Fond du Lac and Reindeer Lake Indians did not know whether they were hunting in the N.W.T. or Sask., and could not understand the variance in the game laws.[30]

In preparation for the patrol, he set off on 18 March with a team of six dogs to lay a cache at Porcupine River. Since he was on a well-travelled trail he made good progress and was back at Stony Rapids by the late afternoon of the 20th, having travelled 98 miles (156 km).[31]

A week later, on 27 March, Harry left Stony Rapids. He was accompanied by a Chipewyan guide, Ross Cummings, who was headed to Nueltin Lake to trap there. Each man drove a team of 5 dogs hauling a toboggan. Harry's team was hauling a load of about 400 lbs, mainly dog food. Their route took them east to Black Lake, along the south shore of that lake, then up the Porcupine River. On the 29th they picked up the cache that Harry had deposited earlier, then they left the river and headed northeast across a whole series of small lakes and along a creek. On the evening of the 30th they spotted a herd of about 50 caribou; both teams of dogs ran off after the caribou but their drivers must have got them under control quite quickly, since Ross Cummings killed two caribou while Harry wounded one; unfortunately he was unable to track it down before it got dark.

The two men had been making open camps thus far, erecting a log windbreak with a fire placed in front of it. The logs radiated the heat back onto the men who slept on a layer of spruce boughs on top of the snow. For the night of the 30th Harry reported: "had to chop wood all night; too cold to sleep."[32] Next morning (Easter Sunday) they started off across a chain of small lakes with no trail, but then at noon hit a fresh toboggan trail and 5 km further on reached a camp of Chipewyan Indians on Poor Fish Lake. The 21 families in the camp came from Fond du Lac and Reindeer Lake. That afternoon they held a church service in one of the tents. The following day a Chipewyan guide led Harry south to a cabin that turned out to be that of C.M. Anderson, a licensed NWT trapper. They arrived back at Poor Fish Lake to a treat. A group of 11 Indians had been out hunting and had killed 23 caribou. This gave Harry the opportunity to give his dogs a good feed of fresh meat.

On the afternoon of 2 April Harry called a meeting of all the men present to discuss the game laws of Saskatchewan and the Northwest Territories, with particular reference to beaver and wolves. The following day he went out hunting with two Indians and from the numerous tracks they found, it was clear that the caribou had started their northward migration. Harry also reached an arrangement with the band counsellor, Toussaint, that one of the Chipewyan, John Azzi, would accompany him eastward from there to break trail. In preparation for pushing on again, Harry had some dog moccasins made (for use on prickly ice or crusty snow) and also bought some *babiche* (rawhide thongs) and dried meat.

After this welcome respite, Harry and Ross Cummings set off again on snowshoes on the morning of the 4th. John Azzi broke trail for them, heading in a northeasterly direction. Travelling conditions were tough and the men often had to negotiate deep, loose snow, very low temperatures, strong winds and drifting snow. On the 8th they reached Klokol Lake and on the 10th they made camp for the night on an island in the large bay on the west side of Kasba Lake. Next day they crossed the large expanse of Kasba Lake and started northeast down the Ennadai River to camp on an island in an expansion of the river. On the 12th Harry reported that it was "unusually cold"; still, they reached Ennadai Lake by 10 A.M. and made good progress north across the lake, camping at the second narrows at 9 P.M.; by now they were close to tree line or, as Harry remarked, "timber very scattered here."[33]

From Ennadai Lake they cut south across the tundra, seeing only scattered clumps of trees. At one point they found a cache of seven caribou carcasses and spotted two wounded caribou which they killed and fed to the dogs. Harry assumed that a hunter had run out of ammunition and had therefore not been able to catch and kill the animals. At their camp (an open camp) that night, they could find only enough firewood to make tea, and so they did not have the comfort of a fire to keep out the cold.

On the morning of the 14th Harry and his companion continued their journey southeast across the tundra on good snow. Some way into the day's journey, they encountered fresh Inuit sledge tracks heading south along a river. It was a long day for them. By 8 P.M. they had covered 45 miles (72 km) and the dogs were near exhaustion when they finally reached a trading post on Windy Lake. The post was operated by D. Simons Ltd. and managed by Wm. Buchholz.[34] Harry and his party stayed with Buchholz for one night. Nearby, a white trapper, A. Peterson, lived with an Inuit wife and two children. On the morning of the 15th, Ross Cummings continued eastwards to Nueltin Lake while Harry travelled the short distance (about 1.5 km) to the trading post of the French company, Revillon Frères, which was operated by George Yandle. He stayed there for the night, having given his dogs a good feed of caribou meat.

In the morning, Harry left his dogs to rest at the Revillon Frères post and travelled west with Buchholz to the Hudson's Bay Company's post at Poorfish (Sleigh) Lake, which was situated about 26 miles (41 km) west of Windy Lake and was operated by S. Keighley. On the way there they saw tracks of thousands of caribou, all heading north. The next day Harry and Buchholz travelled back to the Revillon Frères post, noting that thousands more caribou had crossed their tracks in the intervening 24 hours. That evening two Inuit arrived at the post and traded six white fox pelts.

On 18 April, driving his own dogs and accompanied by Buchholz, Harry set off from Windy Lake, called briefly at Simon's post and continued east some 23 miles (36 km) to the post of an independent trader, I. H. Smith, on the northwest shore of Nueltin Lake. Retracing his steps to Windy Lake the next day, he stayed with the trapper A. Peterson. By now the weather had warmed up to the point where there was some melting in the afternoons. Harry spent the whole day of the 20th at the Revillon Frères post preparing for his return trip to Stony Rapids, replacing his toboggan, fitting steel runners and generally getting ready for the return journey.

The concentration of four trading posts within such a small area was aimed at serving the needs (and harvesting the furs) of the Inuit from this southern area of the Keewatin. There were about 33 Inuit families who traded to one or other of the posts; very little trading was done with Indians or whites. Harry reported that 13 Inuit had died of what they termed "flu" in the early winter, two of them—Haki and Kongnolluk—being heads of families. On a brighter note, there had been no incidents of starvation for several years and the winter of 1928–29 was particularly good in terms of caribou and fish.[35]

The trading posts in this area received their supplies from The Pas, Manitoba via a water route along the Saskatchewan River, the Sturgeon Weir River, the Churchill River, Reindeer River and Lake, Cochrane River and Upper Thlewiaza River. However, as the railway line to Churchill had just been completed, it was anticipated that Churchill would become the supply base for this area via the Thlewiaza River, which drains Nueltin Lake to Hudson Bay.

At this point, Ross Cummings rejoined Harry. They were accompanied by John Azzi, who had now acquired a team of four dogs. Harry and his companions started on the homeward journey around noon on 21 April. Heading west and northwest, they reached the caribou cache near Ennadai Lake by the afternoon of the 22nd. Here they made camp and gave the dogs a good feed of caribou.

They left camp at 5 A.M. the following morning, crossed the narrows of Ennadai Lake and struck straight west, following a more northerly route than they had on the outward journey. As they were now back among some timber, they encountered some four feet (1.2 m) of snow with a crust, which slowed their progress badly. The conditions did not get any better. On the 24th they encountered some very rough, rocky country with little snow in an area of tundra, which was just as bad for hauling heavy loads of meat as the crusty snow had been. A warm south wind softened the snow, making travelling even more difficult. They reached a cabin just east of Snowbird Lake, owned by Ross Cummings, in the morning. Stopping only long enough to check the cabin, they continued southwest and crossed Snowbird Lake. By the evening, both Cummings and Azzi were suffering from snow-blindness.

On the 27th they continued west via a chain of lakes and camped at the narrows of Wholdaia Lake. Just as it got dark they saw a herd of some 40 caribou, but from the tracks they had been seeing all day it was clear that thousands had recently gone north. In the morning, they headed south along

Wholdaia Lake, killing two caribou for dog feed along the way. While Cummings and Azzi continued south to Selwyn Lake, Harry detoured to a police cache at a trapper's cabin on the west side of Wholdaia Lake. Finding it intact he had lunch, repaired his toboggan, then pushed on southwards. Throughout the day, he saw small herds of caribou. As it grew dark he made an open camp on his own.

Harry was up and on the road again by 5 A.M. on the 29th and he caught up with Cummings and Azzi at their camp by 7 A.M. They travelled south on Selwyn Lake all day. The ice was very prickly and the dogs' feet began to show signs of abrasion, so Harry had to stop and fit the animals with moccasins. Despite this delay, Harry covered 48 miles (76 km) before setting up camp at 10 P.M. at the south end of Selwyn Lake.

From the south end of Selwyn Lake, their route took them southwest via the Willow Lakes. In some places water had flooded the ice and the men had to carry their bedding to keep it dry while the dogs were wading for long distances. They encountered similar conditions on the chain of small lakes they crossed on the 31st. By the time they reached Stony Lake on the afternoon of 1 May, the lake ice was unsafe and they had to follow the south shore west to the detachment, which they reached at 8 P.M.[36]

It had been an impressive patrol, carried out with quiet efficiency. Harry had had to deal with bitter cold, deep soft snow, blizzards, rocky, almost snow-free terrain and melt-water that flooded the lake ice. He estimated that they had covered 984 miles (1575 km) in 32½ days of travelling. On several days he estimated that he had exceeded 40 miles (64 km), the maximum (on Selwyn Lake) being 48 miles (76 km).

In the summer of 1929 Superintendent James Ritchie made an inspection trip down the Mackenzie River, and on his way back south met Harry at Fort Chipewyan. Writing to the Commissioner afterwards, Ritchie noted:

This Non-Commissioned Officer is very anxious to go to the Eastern Arctic, and I promised to take the matter up with you. Corporal Stallworthy is an excellent Non-Commissioned Officer with a lot of Northern experience, and while I would be sorry to lose him, I recommend that his request be given consideration.[37]

This time the response from Ottawa was slightly more encouraging: "There are no vacancies in the Eastern arctic at the present time, but this N.C.O. will be given an opportunity to fill the first vacancy that occurs."[38]

There are few details available that can help us piece together a picture of Harry's second year at Stony Rapids. However, in a reply to a request from the Commanding Officer of the "N" Division (Ottawa) for advice on the possibility of making a patrol from Stony Rapids to Windy Lake in November 1933, Harry mentioned that in the spring of 1930 he had made a second patrol to Nueltin Lake but with dog-food running low, and with no success at hunting, he had had to turn back at Kasba Lake. He had been able to buy a limited amount of dried meat from the Indians, and this had allowed him to get back to Wholdaia Lake where he was able to get some caribou. It is interesting to note that on the basis of his own experience in the area, he recommended that the contemplated patrol should fly from Stony Rapids to Windy Lake, complete with a team of six dogs and a toboggan. Then, having patrolled in the Windy Lake/Nueltin Lake area, the party should return by dog team, using the more northerly route via Ennadai and Snowbird lakes to Wholdaia Lake that he had followed on his return to avoid the heavier timber and deep snow of the more southerly route he had followed on his way east.

During the winter Harry had once again submitted a request for a transfer to a detachment in the Eastern Arctic: "I am particularly desirous of serving in the Eastern Arctic and would ask that my application be considered for North Devon Island or Baffin Island, or for the establishment of a barren-land detachment should any vacancies occur."[39]

Harry's persistence was finally rewarded. The response from Ottawa was "that Corporal Stallworthy has now been selected for service in the Eastern Arctic, and should therefore be brought in to Edmonton in plenty of time to arrive at Ottawa at the end of June or early July."[40]

Harry left the detachment for good in early July 1930, handing it over to Constable Wood (who was about to be promoted), Constable English, who had been with Harry for a year, and a third man who had recently arrived from Jasper. On his way out, Harry first travelled aboard the *Halifax* to Fond du Lac where a series of 11 trials had been arranged to coincide with Treaty Time on 3 and 4 July.[41] Harry managed to get 10 convictions and the last case was withdrawn. From Fond du Lac Harry and Constable Purkis, who was also heading south, travelled as far as Fort McMurray on the Treaty party's boat, escorting two prisoners bound for the penitentiary at Prince Albert, Saskatchewan. Then in Fort McMurray Harry managed to hitch a ride by plane to Edmonton with Punch Dickins.

6

BACHE PENINSULA

SHORTLY BEFORE HE LEFT STONY RAPIDS, Harry had let Hilda know when he would be getting to Edmonton. To his delight, she agreed to meet him there, so that they could spend at least a few days together before he headed off on his next assignment in the North. Hilda arrived in Edmonton by train from Jasper on 13 July. While she was longing to see him again, she had very mixed feelings about his plans to head to the Arctic immediately. They had been separated for two years and now he was proposing to be away for another two years; as Harry put it in a letter to his brother, she was "giving me hell for going north."[1]

Harry's blissful few days with Hilda were marred only by a single incident that was to follow him for the rest of his career. On 19 July 1930, a single cryptic entry on the Defaulter Sheet appeared in Harry's Service Register:

S.S. Beothic, *Fram Havn, 1930.*

"Illegal possession of Alcohol." The remark says it all; it says nothing at all. Harry was fined $10. No further details of this offence are readily available but, trivial as the incident may seem, Harry would suffer serious repercussions for the rest of his career on account of it.

Harry left Edmonton by train on the same day, bound for Ottawa. There he spent two days tidying up loose ends before catching the train for Sydney, Cape Breton Island, where he was to board the S.S. *Beothic*, which was bound north on the annual Eastern Arctic Patrol on 31 July. He arrived in Sydney on 29 July, only to find himself rushed off his feet with last minute details. However, he did find time to dash off hurried notes to both his brother and his mother.[2] Although Harry makes no mention of it in his letters to Bill, the artists A.Y. Jackson and Lorne Harris were both on board.[3]

Harry's next assignment was to take charge of the remote detachment of Bache Peninsula at 79°08'N on eastern Ellesmere Island. When he heard that this position was vacant, he applied immediately. Apart from the fact that he would be separated from Hilda for a further two years, it seemed like his idea of an ideal posting. At 79°08'N on the east coast of Ellesmere Island, Bache Peninsula was the most northerly detachment in Canada and Harry knew that he and his fellow officers and a few Inuit assistants would be the sole inhabitants of this enormous Arctic island. It was just the sort of challenge for which he had been hoping and the prospect of working with Inuit again made it all the more appealing.

The presence of a detachment of the RCMP on this vast and otherwise uninhabited island resulted directly from Canadian sensitivities over its sovereignty over Ellesmere and adjacent islands. Ownership of these islands had formally been transferred from the United Kingdom to Canada in 1880,[4] but since the total extent of the islands remained unknown at that time and since what are now the Queen Elizabeth Islands (i.e., the islands north of Parry Channel) were totally uninhabited, Canada's claim to the islands remained less than secure. Canada's claim to the region was first challenged by the Norwegian Otto Sverdrup following his efficient exploration of a large part of the Queen Elizabeth Islands during his expedition on board *Fram* in 1898–1902. On the basis of this expedition, he had claimed all the area he had explored for Norway.[5] Initially Ottawa had not seen this as a particularly serious threat to its sovereignty over the area in question, but when an American expedition led by Donald Macmillan travelled extensively around the same area in 1913–1917, alarm bells began to ring in Ottawa.[6] The sound of those alarm bells became even louder when it was learned that Macmillan and his party had been killing muskoxen and that the Inughuit—the Inuit of Northwest Greenland—regularly crossed to Ellesmere Island to hunt muskoxen, a species that had been given total protection by the Canadian government since 1917.[7] As early as 31 July 1919 the Canadian government had sent a request to the Danish government via the governor-general, Lord Devonshire and the Secretary of State for the Colonies, Lord Milner, asking that it notify its subjects (the Inughuit hunters) "with respect to this Canadian law [protecting the muskox] and take whatever steps were necessary to prevent their subjects breaking this law."[8] The Canadian and British authorities were not to know it, but this placed the Danish authorities in something of a quandary, in that while Northwest Greenland (north of Melville Bay) was geographically part of Greenland, administratively (and even perhaps politically) it was not. The Danish government had repeatedly turned a deaf ear to requests by Knud Rasmusssen (owner and operator of the trading post at Thule) to take responsibility for law and order, health and education among the indigenous people of the area.[9] Effectively, Danish writ did not run beyond Melville Bay and Rasmussen, by default, had become the sole figure of authority in northwest Greenland since establishing his trading post at Thule in 1910.

Nonetheless, on 19 February 1920 the Danish "Administration of the Colonies of Greenland" relayed the Canadian message to Knud Rasmussen. His reply of 8 March 1920 caused a degree of consternation in Ottawa, in that he confirmed that the Inughuit regularly hunted musk oxen on Ellesmere Island. But perhaps even more alarming to the Canadian authorities was Rasmussen's statement:

It is well known that the territory of the Polar Esquimaux [i.e., that of the Inughuit, including their hunting territories on Ellesmere Island] falls within the region designated as "no man's land" and there is therefore no authority in the district except that which I exercise through my station.[10]

Perhaps even more disturbing was the indication in the covering letter from the Danish authorities that they thought Rasmussen's views were perfectly legitimate: "Having acquainted ourselves with the statement in question, my Government thinks that they can subscribe to what Mr. Rasmussen says therein."[11] The fact that the Danish government was thus condoning (or even encouraging) the killing of Canadian muskoxen probably rankled Ottawa just as much as the implication that the Danes refused to recognize Canadian sovereignty over Ellesmere Island.

Among his recommendations J.B. Harkin, director of the Dominion Parks Branch, Department of the Interior, proposed

That if Denmark will not immediately agree to entirely stop this slaughter, Canada should establish a Mounted Police post in Ellesmere Land for the purpose of stopping the slaughter and asserting Canadian authority.[12]

His proposal was accepted by the government and in 1922 the CGS *Arctic*, commanded by Captain Joseph-Elizar Bernier, transported a detachment of RCMP officers, consisting of Inspector C.E. Wilcox, Corporal B.C. Jakeman and constables E. Anstead, C.E. Fairman, L. Fielder, H.P. Lee and H. Must, north to Ellesmere Island. The intention had been to establish a post somewhere in the Bache Peninsula area, since this was the area most frequented by the Inughuit hunters on their annual visits to Ellesmere Island, but the ship was unable to penetrate Smith Sound due to heavy ice. Instead the detachment was landed at Craig Harbour on the southeast coast of Ellesmere Island, where they established the most northerly police post in Canada.[13]

A few years later, Canadians were apprised of a plan by the Americans Donald Macmillan and Richard Byrd to mount an aerial survey of Ellesmere and adjacent islands. They intended to establish a principal base at Etah and intermediate bases on Ellesmere and Axel Heiberg islands. Officials in Ottawa again saw this as a real threat to Canadian sovereignty. The response was to close the detachment at Craig Harbour and open a new base at Bache Peninsula, much closer to the Macmillan/Byrd expedition's area of operations. An attempt at establishing the Bache Peninsula detachment in 1925 had to be abandoned when *Arctic* was again unable to penetrate Smith Sound. So in the following year Staff-Sergeant A.H. Joy and two constables were transported north aboard the more powerful *Beothic*, and they established a post on the southern coast of Bache Peninsula.

This, in brief, is the history of the detachment Harry Stallworthy would be in command of for the next two years. As he pointed out to his mother: "You will be able to say now that one of your boys is in charge of the most northerly post in the British Empire."[14] As he also pointed out to his mother, he now had 14 years of service with the Force and in a further six years would qualify for a pension of $48.60 per month. His salary in 1930 was about $75.95 and since he had no living expenses when in the North, and the Force covered his insurance, he expected to be able to save most of his salary. In addition, he hoped to be able to make a significant supplement to his salary by fox-trapping at Bache Peninsula.

Harry's RCMP companions at the Bache Peninsula detachment were to be Constable M.F. Foster, who had travelled north with him and Constable W.P. Fraser, who had already been at Bache Peninsula for one year and was scheduled to stay for a further year. The Greenland Inughuit, Nukappiannguaq (commonly shortened to Nookap by Harry and his fellow officers), his father Akkamalingwah and the latter's wife Enalunguaq were already stationed at the post as hunters, dog drivers and general assistants, and were to remain there to work with Harry and his fellow officers.[15]

The *Beothic* crossed the Arctic Circle on the afternoon of 5 August after a rough passage from the Strait of Belle Isle; as Harry mentioned in a letter to his brother, "She can sure roll!"[16] He was looking forward to there being ice

RCMP officers (Harry in centre) with Greenlandic women, Godhavn, 1930.

between Greenland and Ellesmere since "if there is ice it's a cinch that the ship will not roll."[17] At the time of writing on 5 August Harry had had to discontinue his letter: "it's hard to hang on to the table & try to write too & she is rolling too much for me to think straight."[18]

He anticipated reaching Godhavn (now Qeqertarsuaq) around 10 P.M. on the 6th, where he expected "to visit the Governor of Greenland (& exchange the usual courtesies, mostly rum, I guess)."[19] Harry had with him 12 quarts of rum that he would take to Bache intact as well as a case of brandy from Headquarters. At Godhavn most of the local population flocked to the harbour to greet the Canadian visitors, the women wearing their striking traditional dress of heavily beaded tops and caribou skin or sealskin pants. They seemed to find the RCMP uniforms very appealing too, and gladly posed for photographs.

In his letter of 5/6 August Harry took the opportunity to give Bill the dates throughout the winter when the radio station KDKA Pittsburgh would relay messages to Bache Peninsula and encouraged him to send messages occasionally: "There is no charge for transmitting messages to Bache Peninsula; in fact KDKA seem to get quite a kick out of talking to us & there is no occasion to be too brief."[20] Just as he had done at Chesterfield Inlet, Harry was planning to do some trapping at Bache Peninsula:

I think I'm pretty lucky at getting this detachment; it is known to be an exceptionally good place for fox. P. S. Please don't mention foxes or fur over the radio, *but let me know if you want a polar bear hide* & how many. I hear there are lots of them here.

I have 5 doz. traps & a few useful trading supplies; but take it from me I'm not venturing too far from the house in the dark period from Oct. to February.[21]

Along with the letter to his brother also went 400 feet of movie film for developing. Harry had with him a movie camera and 2,900 feet of film and was hoping to produce some footage of activities at the detachment and on the trail.[22]

By 10 August the *Beothic* was battling heavy ice in Smith Sound and by Harry's estimate, they were still some 50–65 km from Bache Peninsula.[23] Between 11 and 16 August *Beothic* made several attempts to reach Bache Peninsula but all attempts were foiled by ice.[24] Instead, some 12 tonnes of coal were landed at a point just north of Cape Rutherford and all the rest of the supplies were dropped off in Rice Strait at Fram Havn, Otto Sverdrup's wintering site of 1898–99 situated some 50 km from Bache Peninsula. Constables McLean, Beatty and Fraser, as well as the two Inughuit assistants, Nukappiannguaq and his father Akkamalingwah, had travelled to Fram Havn to meet the ship; Akkamalingwah's wife Enalunguaq had stayed behind at the Bache Peninsula detachment.

At this point Harry learned that Fraser had been having trouble with his teeth, and it was decided that he should head south for treatment. Inspector Joy offered Harry the option of selecting one of the other nine constables on board who were destined for one of the more southerly detachments as a replacement for Fraser. However, since Harry had come to know Constable Foster quite well on the way north and felt he could get along with him, he declined the offer of a replacement for Fraser.[25] Foster was a man with 10 years of service, some of it in the Western Arctic.

Harry's first impressions of the two Inughuit were very positive. Inughuit men were the only people among the Inuit who normally wore polar bear pants as a mark of their prowess as hunters. Dressed in these distinctive pants, these two men seemed vigorous, healthy and supremely self-confident. These adjectives applied particularly to Nukappiannguaq, who had worked for the

RCMP detachment, Bache Peninsula, on occasion of visit by members of Oxford University Ellesmere Land Expedition, 1935.

RCMP at Bache Peninsula since 1925 and was one of the most widely travelled of the Inughuit. In 1929 he had accompanied Inspector Joy on one of the most impressive sledge trips ever achieved: from Dundas Harbour west to Winter Harbour on Melville Island, then north and east via King Christian, Ellef Ringnes and Axel Heiberg islands to Bache Peninsula—a total distance of over 2740 km.[26]

While the unloading was proceeding at Fram Havn, Harry made a trip to the detachment by whaleboat with Inspector Joy, Corporal Margetts, Constable McLean and Nukappiannguaq on 13 August. There he familiarized himself with the place and formally took over command from McLean before returning to Fram Havn. The round trip was accomplished despite quite difficult ice conditions that certainly would not have allowed the *Beothic* to reach the detachment.

The ship weighed anchor on 16 August. In the interim, some seven tonnes of supplies had been unloaded at Fram Havn. Harry and Constable Foster and the two Inughuit loaded perishable goods such as potatoes and fresh fruit, as well as a meteorological outfit into the whaleboat, which had been fitted with a Ford engine. Then, with a dory acquired from the ship and a

Butchering walrus, near Craig Harbour, 1931.

small ice boat in tow, they set off for the detachment. The distance they had to cover, including detours to follow leads and circumvent floes, was about 65 km. Several times the boats were jammed amidst fast-drifting ice floes but with hard work and patience and hauling the boats out onto floes at times, they managed to reach their goal. But this was only after leaving the ice boat on a small island about 1½ km from the detachment temporarily. Since the temperature was already dropping below zero at night, the fruit and vegetables were stowed in the living hut while Harry and his party went back to Fram Havn for another load. This time conditions were much better—almost no ice and a flat calm. Indeed, the *Beothic* could easily have reached the detachment during this period between 19 and 23 August.

The entire group then made a week-long hunting trip to the junction of Beitstad and Jokel fjords with the express purpose of catching narwhal for dog feed. They travelled in a whaleboat and an ice boat, but took a kayak with them as well.[27] They succeeded in procuring six narwhal, each weighing 1,000–2,000 lbs, as well as 20 seals. With a full load in both boats and towing two narwhal, they made it safely back to the detachment.

Harry and Inuatuk butchering walrus, Craig Harbour, 1931.

They had planned to make a further trip to Fram Havn the next day but an east wind got up, pushing the ice into the fjords and shoving it up on shore. A large iceberg shaped like a grandstand became grounded in the bay in front of the detachment, and indeed remained there throughout the winter. For a week no water was visible, but then the ice slackened somewhat and they set off on the postponed trip to Fram Havn. Even then, however, they had not gone far before the ice forced them to turn back. What appeared to be a calamitous journey did however have a positive outcome, as Harry noted in his annual report:

Fortunately we ran into three walrus. They were asleep on a small ice pan. There was not room for another one on the same pan. Fortunately we were approaching in a position to see their heads. I happened to be at the tiller and we stopped the engine & drifted up to them to about 10 yards. Jack [Foster] flattened one out & Noocap the other two. It was certainly lucky that they were killed instantaneously because if either of the outside ones had wiggled a flipper & slipped off the pan it would have tilted and at least 3 tons of dog feed would have gone into Davy Jones' locker. We towed two home and put the other on an island. We figured this was better than a load of groceries or coal, seeing that we had a year's supply at the detachment.[28]

In his letter to his brother Harry stressed that this was very different from recreational hunting: "This may sound to you like real sport, but not to me. It's all in the job of living & making out so to speak, and by the time this frozen meat is chopped & pried out of a frozen pile & chopped up & fed to the dogs during the dark period, there does not seem to be sport connected with it at all.[29]

It was extremely important to procure dog food (bear, narwhal, walrus or seal) before freeze-up since the detachment's dog teams were crucial for transport. Harry found that imported dog pemmican was a poor substitute. When he took over, the detachment had 21 dogs (a total of two dog teams), while Nukappiannguaq and Akkamalingwah probably each had about 10 or a dozen dogs. Initially the police dogs were not of very good quality, most of them being quite old; indeed there were only two young animals, one dog and one bitch. Harry made a conscientious effort to rectify this situation over the winter. He shot a total of eight old dogs and replaced them with eight younger dogs—six bought from visiting Greenland Inughuit and two from Nukappiannguaq or his father. He also improved the situation by breeding from the better bitches so that by the end of his first year (30 June 1931) he had 15 good pups from this source, plus a further six pups that came with one of the bitches he had bought. He was very optimistic that some of these would be ready for sledge patrols by the winter of 1931–32.[30]

On 1 September the radio equipment was hooked up and that same evening they managed to receive broadcasts from some southern stations. These broadcasts became a major source of entertainment throughout Harry's sojourn at Bache Peninsula. The detachment boasted a gramophone and 200 records but these were not in great demand, "for we get all the music we want on the air."[31] The radio was also a source of news, especially the evening newscast from KMOX in St. Louis that ran from 8.00–8.15 P.M. every night. They even managed to pull in news broadcasts from two English stations. But perhaps most importantly, they received personal messages either from CKY, Winnipeg (Northern Messages) or from KDKA, Pittsburgh.

The programme of meteorological observations was also started on 1 September. Jack Foster was mostly responsible for taking the readings three times a day. The statistics collected included temperature, clouds, pressure, precipitation and wind speed and direction.[32] The absolute minimum temperature for the period 1 September–31 July that winter was –49.2°F at 8 A.M. on 24 March; the absolute maximum was +58°F at 8 P.M. on 16 July. The mean minimum temperature from 10 January to 27 March was -35.9°F. Rainfall for the year was 0.32 inches and snowfall 23 inches.

Harry still had his caribou-skin parka (inner and outer) and pants from Chesterfield Inlet and he used these as his regular outerwear. But he was quite delighted when Enalunguaq took his measurements and shortly afterwards presented him with a pair of polar bear pants, as he felt that this was a sign that he had been elected an honorary member of the Inughuit.

By 4 October the sea ice on the fjords was thick enough to bear a dog sled and they could begin the work of hauling home the meat from outlying caches at Beitstad Fjord to the west and Cape Camperdown to the east. A round trip to either destination took two days and Harry was soon driving a full team of 12–14 dogs competently.

From early October onwards these meat-hauling trips were combined with trapping white fox. The foxes were prime from that time on and although the season did not officially open until 15 November, "Jack and I figured that necessity knows no seasons."[33] By 11 January, using 45 of his traps, Harry had taken 58 foxes, Akkamalingwah 56, Nukappiannguaq 39, Jack 36 and Enalunguaq 2. On one trip to Beitstad Fjord over the period 19–23 October, Harry produced a record haul of 10 foxes. By mid-January the foxes seemed to have disappeared; there were no fresh tracks and the Inughuit reported that the foxes usually left when the light came back.

Harry and his companions also made several trips to Fram Havn to fetch supplies from the cache there. This was not easy work, however, since there was a heavy fall of snow with little wind, which made for large areas of deep, soft snow that was quite unsuitable for freighting heavy loads. Another disadvantage was that it was difficult to find wind-packed drifts suitable for building an igloo.

Totally unbeknownst to Harry and the other officers at Bache Peninsula, their presence at the detachment had undoubtedly contributed to a significant event much further south. On 11 November 1930 the gently simmering dispute over the sovereignty of the Sverdrup Islands (as the islands visited by Sverdrup were known) was settled in a civilized fashion that salved national pride. On that date the Norwegian government formally recognized Canada's title to the lands Sverdrup had explored and in a related gesture that was covered in the same article in many Canadian newspapers, the Canadian government paid Sverdrup $67,000 for his original maps, diaries and documents relating to his expedition in 1898–1902.[34] The Norwegian government must have realized that the continued occupation of Ellesmere Island by officers of the RCMP from 1922 onwards greatly strengthened Canada's claim to it and the adjacent islands, when compared to Norway's total failure to maintain any sort of occupancy of these islands since Sverdrup's exploration of them 30 years previously.

During one of the trips to a cache in Hayes Fjord in early December, Harry suffered a minor accident. While carrying a heavy piece of narwhal meat from the cache to his komatik in the dark, he slipped on some wet ice and badly bruised his right elbow. Apart from the immediate pain, it gave him no further trouble but during the long trip he would make in spring the elbow became very painful from the stress of continually wielding his whip to control his team of dogs, which included three bitches that came into heat at different times.[35]

Harry and Jack Foster hit it off well together; in his annual report Harry noted that they had never had the slightest disagreement. His assessment was that Jack was "a practical man and always willing and has naturally adapted himself to the northern conditions having previously served for a year in the Western Arctic. One could not wish for a more amiable comrade to be stationed with at an isolated post."[36] Undoubtedly a major part of this harmony could be ascribed to the fact that these remarks of Harry's could equally well apply to himself.

Relations between Harry and Jack and the Inughuit were also generally harmonious. On 21 January 1931, when Harry had just started an instalment of an ongoing letter to his brother, he was interrupted when Nukappiannguaq and Enalunguaq came in for a visit. "So instead of writing we had a social evening & biscuits & cocoa & I tried to explain some of the advertising pictures in the Saturday Evening Post."[37] A month earlier the entire population of Ellesmere Island—a total of five people—had assembled for Christmas dinner. Gifts were exchanged; the Inughuit received gifts of tobacco etc., while they in turn presented Harry and Jack each with a narwhal tusk walking stick.

On 30 January Nukappiannguaq and Akkamalingwah set off across Smith Sound, bound for Etah and Robertson Fjord. Akkamalingwah was quite old and in poor health, although still very willing to participate in all the activities of the detachment. Even so, he had been discharged on the 28th and was now heading home and Nukappiannguaq was entrusted with the task of hiring a replacement for his father. Besides taking Akkamalingwah home, the other purpose of their trip concerned the missing German geologist Hans Krüger.[38] He and his party had passed through Bache Peninsula in March 1930, heading for Axel Heiberg Island and points beyond.

Born in Posen, Prussia (now Poznan, Poland) in 1886, Krüger had graduated from high school in Neustadt an der Weinstrasse in 1905.[39] He had subsequently studied law at Jena and Göttingen, but also attended lectures in the natural sciences, and had a deep interest in the arts and literature. In 1910 he emigrated to South West Africa (now Namibia), where he had worked at various occupations, including managing a game-farm. Krüger also spent some time prospecting and for three years between 1920 and 1923 he was manager of a vanadium mine. He returned to Germany in the fall of 1923, and from the summer of 1924 he worked as a volunteer assistant at the Geological and Mineralogical Institute of the Technische Hochschule in Darmstadt.

In the summer of 1925 he mounted what he referred to as the Hessian West Greenland Expedition, consisting of himself and one companion, the geographer Fritz Klute. They travelled quite extensively by boat in Umanaq Fjord and Disko Bugt, and also made an overland crossing of Nugsuaq Halvø. On his return to Germany, Krüger published a number of scientific papers on the basis of his fieldwork and also wrote and defended his Ph.D. dissertation at the Ruprecht-Karls-Universität in Heidelberg. The dissertation dealt with the geology he had studied in West Greenland and in November 1928 he was made a Fellow of the Royal Geographical Society.

In the summer of 1929 he headed back to West Greenland once again on board the Danish vessel *Hans Egede*. This time, he was accompanied by two other scientists and a Danish hunter/trapper, Åge Rose Bjare. Also on board was the young anthropologist Frederica de Laguna. The impression that Krüger made upon her was far from positive and she had premonitions as to how his expedition might end:

> I don't like Dr. Krüger. He thinks too much of himself and is always putting other people in the wrong. His mouth is that of a spoiled child, and he seems to cherish a sense of injury. I am glad that I do not have to spend the winter with him, as Bjare has to do.... I am afraid that he and Krüger will not get along well together, especially since Krüger knows nothing about the Arctic winter. I should not be surprised if there were serious trouble, and I would not blame Bjare too much, either. I tried to find out what he thought of Krüger, but he was tight-lipped, and I was afraid to question him directly. One never sees them together, and there does not seem to be any spirit and enthusiasm in their expedition as there is in ours.[40]

Krüger and party returned to the Umanaq area and, travelling by motor boat, investigated the geology of the area from there north to Svartenhuk Halvø. By pre-arrangement they were picked up at Godhavn by the Canadian government steamer, *Beothic*, on her annual run north. After she had called at Craig Harbour and Dundas Harbour, Krüger and Bjare were dropped at Nequi on Robertson Fjord, Northwest Greenland.

Having settled in with the Inughuit of Nequi, Krüger and Bjare made a fairly major sledge trip north-eastwards, to and possibly beyond the Humboldt Glacier. Caught by protracted blizzards on the return trip, they ran out of food and fuel and had to eat raw dog meat. Soon after their return to Nequi they both became seriously ill, possibly from trichinosis.

In the following March, accompanied by Akqioq, an extremely experienced traveller, Krüger and Bjare set off across Smith Sound with one dog team; with them went a support party of two Inughuit each driving his own dog team. When they reached the RCMP detachment at Bache Peninsula on 12 March 1930, Krüger was suffering from stomach cramps and persistent vomiting. When Constable N.M. McLean, the officer in charge of the detachment saw the condition not only of Krüger, but of the party's dogs, he invited them to stay to rest the dogs and themselves for a few days.

On the basis of the straightness of the northwest coasts of the Canadian Arctic Archipelago, Krüger postulated that this coastline was bounded by only a very narrow continental shelf, and that there was a steep drop-off to the abyssal depths of the Arctic Ocean. This being the case, it would preclude the existence of any further land to the northwest. He was proposing to prove his hypothesis by a study of the geology of Ellesmere and Axel Heiberg islands and by soundings from the sea ice. Krüger, Bjare and Akqioq left Bache Peninsula on 19 March with all three their sledges heavily laden. They crossed Ellesmere Island to Bay Fjord and the support party turned back at Depot Point on Eureka Sound.[41]

It was anticipated that Krüger and his party would return to Bache Peninsula before the summer of 1931. When there was still no sign of them by the end of the year, Harry surmised that they might have returned to the east coast by Makinson Inlet and had crossed to Etah, thus by-passing Bache Peninsula.[42] Harry wanted to investigate this possibility, but since he could speak neither Inuktitut nor Danish fluently and there would be nobody at Etah or Robertson Fjord who could speak English, he saw no point in going himself and was entirely happy to entrust this task to Nukappiannguaq.

The ice in the straits had been breaking up periodically until late January but towards the end of the month Nukappiannguaq reported that he could see unbroken ice all the way across to Greenland. After a rough trip, he returned on 1 March with another hunter, Inuatuk, and his wife, Natow. The temperature had averaged -30° to -40°F throughout the month they had been gone, and at one point they were adrift on some loose floes for "2 sleeps." As Harry commented wryly in his report, "but I don't think they slept much."[43] Both teams of dogs were very thin by the time they reached Bache Peninsula. They had found no sign of the Krüger party at Etah or elsewhere.

It was common practice among the Etah Inughuit for a hunting party to cross to Ellesmere Island in April and May to hunt polar bears. Four men were planning to do so in 1931 and they had agreed to head south along the east coast of the island and to keep an eye open for any sign of Krüger and his party. In the light of this Harry decided to focus his own efforts on searching the west coast of Ellesmere Island. Accompanied by Nukappiannguaq and Inuatuk, each man driving a team of 12 dogs, he set off from Bache Peninsula on 29 March 1931, leaving Jack with the two Inughuit women.[44] The sledges were quite heavily laden with rations for six weeks, 300 lbs of dog food and 20 gallons of kerosene. They followed a route west up Flagler Fjord to its head. Initially, they made good time on the sea ice and built an igloo for the night at the mouth of the valley. Along the way, they had come across two Arctic hares that became a good supper for the three men. But then their troubles began. Flagler Valley was almost devoid of snow and although the river was still ice-covered, it was a braided stream with numerous channels wandering over wide expanses of sand and gravel.[45] Unfortunately these channels were often too narrow for the sledges and the runners were often scraping over sand and gravel and some frozen waterfalls made travelling even more challenging. Nonetheless they managed to cover about 32 km in a very long day's travelling and even found enough snow to build a small igloo.

At that time, the glacier flowing north from the ice cap almost completely blocked Sverdrup Pass, although a west-flowing stream had cut a steep-sided gorge. In order to continue their journey, Harry and his companions had to find a way onto the ice cap. Harry and Nukappiannguaq reconnoitred a potential route immediately south of their campsite. The route up the ice-front looked extremely difficult to Harry and the 5 km between their camp and the ice-front was almost snow-free and was nothing but loose talus. The following morning, they continued west up the valley to a spot where Nukappiannguaq and Inspector Joy had earlier managed to get onto the icecap. But this time the situation here looked even worse than the site they had reconnoitred the previous day:

> There was absolutely no snow. On the west side of the valley we found a respectable size stream but it was away down. We had to walk around some cliffs for about a mile then climb down into it. It was some job getting down but it looked worth while. We thought we could walk up to the glacier on the small river & see if it was passable, then walk back downstream & find a way out & bring the dogs & loads up the next day. After walking up it narrowed in about a mile's distance & went under some overhanging ledges which seemed to me to tower about a thousand feet. Then we came to a sudden drop. There were frozen waterfalls hanging down the ledges, coming down from the mountains & a hundred yards further the water would have had to run the other way. We got to the top of this drop. Talk about a long, or I should say deep, precipice. It made me think of the pictures I've seen of Arizona Canyons…. A human fly might make it with a long, long rope. All this tough pulling & waste of time used up the bit of dog pemmican we took from home & we did not get to the glacier where we knew there was a tough climb & relaying for two days. So the only thing to do was to go back to Bache Peninsula & then south to Makinson Inlet.[46]

What made the situation more frustrating was that they were so close to Sverdrup Pass that they could plainly see the mountains of Axel Heiberg Island to the west.

The trip back to the detachment took two-and-a-half days; the sledge runners were badly scratched and scored and the dogs had sore feet. After resting for two days and adding two dogs to each team (bringing them to 14 dogs each) the three men set off again on 4 April, heading south. Reaching the depot at Fram Havn they camped for the night, dug out the cache and loaded 150 lbs of dog pemmican onto each sledge. The ice in Rice Strait gave good sledging but beyond that ice conditions were abominable. They travelled across rough, jumbled ice for the entire distance to Clarence Head. The stretch took them six days, in part due to repeated stops to repair broken runners and upstanders. The only consolation was that there was no open water. Off Paine Bluff they surprised two bears and immediately loosed all the dogs. One bear was brought to bay within a quarter mile and shot, but the other ran for about two miles through rough ice before the dogs bayed it. Before Inuatuk managed to shoot the bear, it had clawed four of his younger and more inexperienced dogs quite badly.[47] The meat was a useful addition to the dog food reserves.

By the afternoon of the 11th they were off Makinson Inlet and Clarence Head was in sight. Thus far there were no signs of the Inughuit who had said they would travel to Craig Harbour and keep an eye open for Krüger's party. In view of this, Harry decided to abandon his plans to head across to the west side of Ellesmere via Makinson Inlet and to go to Craig Harbour instead. Fortunately for them, sledging conditions improved greatly and they made better progress. Just beyond Cape Norton Shaw they spotted another bear and chased it for 10 km before releasing some of the dogs to stop him near the north end of Coburg Island. A blizzard started as they travelled southwest through Glacier Strait and the wind became so strong that the sledges began overtaking the dogs. At this point they took shelter for about four hours in the lee of a large berg and had a meal of boiled bear meat. Nukappiannguaq advised that they camp there for the night as he knew from past experience that there might be thin ice or open water off the snout of the Wilcox Glacier.

By next morning the wind was blowing strongly from the southwest. they passed the glacier snout without incident but soon afterwards, as they approached King Edward Point, they encountered open water and had to take to the ice-foot. In places they were soaked by spray from the waves breaking against the ice-foot; occasionally they had to lift the sledges over boulders. By the time they reached the detachment at Craig Harbour, one of the runners on one of the sledges was split for its entire length while the upstanders were broken off the other two.

They found the office and living room in the main building in good condition, but the kitchen door had been forced open, presumably by a bear, and the kitchen was drifted full of snow that had frozen hard. They lit a coal fire in the office heater and dried their fur clothing and their sleeping robes. Meanwhile the dogs were given a good feed of rancid bacon and dog biscuits from the store house.

The next day the wind from the east had strengthened again to the point that one could lean against it. When the kitchen table was disinterred, Harry found a note left by Constable McLean during his visit the previous year. The weather broke on the 18th and Nookap and Inuatuk went hunting and returned with two small bears that made one good feed for the dogs. The following day they spotted a herd of seven walruses on a floe and the three men were able to walk up to within 20 feet of the sleeping animals. While the Inughuit shot two animals (this being all that were needed) Harry filmed the hunt. As he himself reported: "Needless to say the walrus never did wake up. It was not much of a picture for action."[48]

After fastening all the doors and windows securely, they left the detachment around midnight on 21 April. On the first leg of their homeward journey they found that conditions had deteriorated: the ice-foot was even narrower now and in negotiating the rough ice and boulders two of the komatiks were again damaged. It took them until 9 A.M. to cover the 10 km to King Edward Point. From here Harry briefly considered crossing Jones Sound and Devon Island to the abandoned detachment at Dundas Harbour since there had been some suggestion that Krüger might head for there. On climbing to a vantage point they spotted a wide belt of open water and drifting ice in Jones Sound that extended past Belcher Point and Cape Sparbo on the south side of the sound and so Harry quickly abandoned that idea.

Retracing their steps through Glacier Strait and past Clarence Head, they killed another bear near Cape Norton Shaw and fed it to the dogs. As they started across Smith Bay they ran into deep, loose snow that greatly impeded their progress. They camped near an island in the mouth of Makinson Inlet. Then, leaving their loads and travelling light, they headed west up the inlet on hard, smooth snow that made for rapid progress. Reaching Swinnerton Peninsula, which separates the northern and southern branches of the upper inlet, they climbed to a vantage point from where all of the north branch and much of the south branch were visible, but spotted no sign of the missing expedition. In view of the long stretches of rough ice they still had to negotiate to get home and taking into account that there was still a great deal of coal and supplies to be hauled from Fram Havn and Cape Rutherford to Bache Peninsula, Harry now decided to temporarily abandon the search for Krüger and to head for home.

As they left Makinson Inlet and rounded Boger Point they encountered some more deep snow. Just beyond Boger Point they spotted a large male bear running off with a cub in its mouth. Male bears will readily kill and eat cubs (even their own offspring) if they get a chance, and this is clearly what had happened here. Not too long afterwards, they spotted the female bear.[49] Nukappiannguaq and Inuatuk started after the male bear, which had dropped the cub and was making for the nearby glacier. Harry picked up the badly mangled cub and put it out of its misery with a blow from his axe. About 400 m further, he spotted the remains of another cub. When Harry heard two shots, he knew that Nukappiannguaq and Inuatuk had killed their bear. Leaving his team where they had left their sledges, he turned their dogs loose to overtake the bear and followed the tracks north along the top of the glacier-front ice-cliff. The dogs caught the bear after about 900 m, just as it had left the glacier for the sea-ice again. While the Inughuit hitched up their 20 dogs to haul the bear back to the komatiks where they had decided to camp, Harry decided to follow the tracks back along the top of the low ice-cliff. It was at this point that he fell into the narrow crevasse and was rescued, shaken but unharmed, by Nukappiannguaq. Harry noted his reaction to the incident in his report:

> I felt a bit shaken for a while but after a drink of brandy and a good meal I was none the worse for the experience except minor bruises to the back and stomach and a small cut under the chin, which I felt was a lot to be thankful for.[50]

That was the official version. In a marginal note added later to his own copy of the report, Harry wrote, "This is not correct. I had more than 1 drink." Understandably, Harry made no mention of this terrifying incident in his ongoing letter to his brother. However, twenty years later he did submit an account of the incident to the *Blue Book* (which one suspects was "embroidered" by the editor).[51]

Since they had plenty of meat, and perhaps because Harry was still feeling somewhat shaken after his experience, they rested the whole of the next day before continuing northwards along the ice front. That night, they camped at a place Harry called Paine Bluff. He expressed surprise that what was shown on the map as a bluff was in fact a fair-sized island (Paine Island). Nukappiannguaq, however, was well aware it was an island. They climbed the east side of the island to look for bears, but without success. After another day's travel north they headed straight east to the floe edge; here they emerged from the rough ice and found a recently frozen lead, some 90 m wide, which they followed north for almost two days to Cape Sabine. From there, they swung west and travelled through Rice Strait to Fram Havn.

To Harry's pleasant surprise he discovered that all the stores had disappeared, but that there were numerous komatik tracks heading north. In his absence a large group of Inughuit had turned up at Bache Peninsula with 11 teams to go hunting in the area. Constable Foster had taken the initiative and had employed them to haul the remainder of the stores from Fram Havn. The task include chopping 14 drums of gasoline and kerosene from under about 90 cm of ice and hauling them to the detachment. The entire task had taken the group about a week. As nearly as possible they were paid at the same rates as they would have been paid by Knud Rasmussen at his trading post at Thule. Some of them had arrived at Fram Havn while Harry was still there, having been hunting in Buchanan Bay. Others were still at Bache Peninsula when he and his party got back there on 7 May. Some of the Inughuit asked to stay for the winter and Harry suggested they check with their own authorities on this point.

Harry's estimated that, including the initial trip to Sverdrup Pass, they had travelled 855 miles (1,370 km) on this patrol. He and his companions had covered this distance in 39 days, or about 30 days of actual travelling. While Harry was undoubtedly quite glad to find that all the supplies had been freighted from Fram Havn on his return, he reported that if he had known that this was to happen he would have crossed from Makinson Inlet to Stenkul Fjord and Baumann Fjord on the west side of Ellesmere Island to search that area for Krüger and party. At this point he speculated that Krüger must have crossed Jones Sound and Devon Island to Dundas Harbour and that Akqioq would have stayed there with the RCMP while Krüger and Bjare would have gone south on board the *Beothic*. However he did comment to his brother: "If they crossed to Devon Island last summer with a dog team in their pneumatic boat they did well."[52]

Soon after returning from his long patrol, Harry took advantage of the presence of all the Inughuit visitors to hire two new men, Kahkachoo and

Kahdi—the latter being Robert Peary's son. The two men were accompanied by their wives, Pedlunguaq and Alualunguaq. The summer passed very quickly, with barely enough time to get in some hunting for dog food and to undertake repairs and maintenance on the buildings. The emphasis on hunting was not as great as usual since the plan was to close the detachment and to move operations to Craig Harbour. Thus on 1 August Harry reported that they were planning to paint the kitchen before heading south to Fram Havn by boat on the 9th to meet the *Beothic*.[53] This was presumably in case the *Beothic* was again prevented by ice from reaching Bache Peninsula. Harry was very much hoping that the ship would bring news that Krüger and party had turned up safely at Dundas or perhaps Etah, in which case he would not have to mount a protracted search for them to the west. Instead, he had plans to make a major trip north via Lake Hazen to Fort Conger and Cape Columbia, the northern tip of Ellesmere Island. Both Nukappiannguaq and Inuatuk were enthusiastic about accompanying him on this trip, which would be the most northerly patrol ever undertaken by the RCMP.[54]

As always, a great deal of paper work had to be crowded into the last couple of weeks before the ship was due. As Harry ruefully reported:

> the never-ending flow of red tape, reports, returns etc. is required in Ottawa from Bache Peninsula, the same as from all our detachments from Dawson to Halifax. I am not stretching it when I relate that in the mail this year I received circulars re inspecting drug stores for narcotic drugs, list of escaped prisoners, stolen automobiles & what amuses me most is 4 copies of amendments to the Chinese Immigration Act. Of course these are all sent in for 'my information & necessary action.' I have to acknowledge all this sort of thing under the correct file numbers![55]

In handling all the paperwork at this time, Harry operated under an unusual handicap, as he reported somewhat apologetically to Headquarters:

> I have the honour to report in connection with the apparent neglect in the appearance of the reports and returns of this detachment, that I have had considerable trouble with my eyes, due I believe to the strong glare in the spring after so much artificial light during the winter. At

times I have been unable to use the typewriter on account of the keys becoming a blur, at other times I have been able to type for an hour or so without much trouble.[56]

The *Beothic*, with Captain Falk at the helm, had sailed from North Sydney on her regular Eastern Arctic patrol on 30 July with Major L.T. Burwash in overall command of the expedition; Inspector A.H. Joy was in charge of the RCMP party on board.[57] After calling at Godhavn, the steamer reached Fram Havn on 11 August to find Harry, Foster and the rest of the Bache Peninsula personnel waiting. Robertson, a writer on board the *Beothic*, described the scene:

There was a boat lying at the water's edge, and into it were climbing several men. It was the Police whaleboat with two Eskimo kayaks aboard. Out from shore it headed towards us. As soon as it came within hailing distance its occupants waved and shouted a greeting. We waved and shouted back. Presently, over the *Beothic*'s side climbed two Mounties and three Eskimos who had not seen a ship or a white man for a whole year. The policemen were Corporal H.W. Stallworthy, a blonde, stalwart young Englishman whose home is in Fairford, Gloucestershire; and Constable M.F. Foster, a strapping son of Fredericton, N.B., bubbling over with vitality and good humour.

What a picture they made, those five fine specimens of manhood, as they stepped on to our deck! They all wore knee-high white sealskin boots, banded at the tops with polar-bear fur. Above these came shaggy polar-bear pants, woolly as a cowboy's angora shapps [sic]. Sweaters, or kuletuks covered their bodies, and their heads of long, thick hair were capless."[58]

Since Harry reported that ice conditions were favourable for reaching Bache Peninsula, the steamer then proceeded to the detachment for the first time in three years.[59] While supplies were being unloaded, Robertson took the opportunity of going ashore and looking around the detachment:

It consisted of four little wooden houses, mere shacks in appearance. Off to one side were a group of Eskimo tents. This tiny settlement stood close to the beach on a narrow stretch of stony ground, sheltered from the north and its icy polar gales by a steep cliff of yellow rock some two hundred feet high.

Through the regulation porch which protects the front doors of all Police barracks in the Arctic, I entered the little structure.... Though it was mid-August a bit of fire was burning in the big kitchen cooking-heating stove which bore he name of Gurney, the pioneer Toronto firm. In winter there were auxiliary stoves in the adjoining rooms.

Looking about, I noticed that the outer sets of the double windows were off. It was amazing to see this little wooden house, seemingly no more substantial than a summer cottage, serving as a winter habitation up here. But the barrack building had double walls, whose intervening space was packed with excelsior, non-conductor of cold. Besides that, when winter comes the wind-driven, hard-packed Arctic snow is cut into blocks and the barracks encased in a solid wall, leaving a space between the blocks and the planks, which is filled with soft snow. The roof is also covered. This, with the further protection of a loft between the living quarters and the roof, proves most effective, I was told.... Policemen assured me that the house was comfortable in the coldest weather, though, due to condensation, one would see ice in the lower corners of the room, even when the stoves were going full blast.

The kitchen-dining room, as in all northern Police posts, occupied the centre of the building. Off to the left was a bedroom containing two iron cots, replete with thick mattresses and grey woollen blankets—summer bedding. Eiderdown canvas sleeping bags, made by the Woods Manufacturing Co. of Ottawa, were available for colder weather. But out on patrol and when sleeping in snow huts, everyone uses Eskimo sleeping bags of heavy fur.

To the right of the kitchen-dining room was a third room containing a bed for the senior Mounted Policeman, and a writing table for official business. Whatever his rank, this senior is vested with full powers as a magistrate and customs officer for the Dominion. Bache, like other posts, had its little jail—in this case a tiny lock-up in the adjacent storehouse.

Pictures and photographs of relatives and friends adorned the walls of the barrack rooms. Fur and woollen rugs on the floors, convenient tables for card-playing, well-filled book cases, and several easy chairs gave the place a cosy look. No wonder that Mounties longed to get back from their far patrols to this little garrison-home!

I noticed above each bed, arranged with military precision, the long boots and spurs and wide-brimmed hats of dress uniform, seldom used in this remote spot. Beside them hung the service carbines, revolvers and the belts-of-arms of the respective constables. The complete kits of Eskimo clothing worn by the Mounties in cold weather were stored away.[60]

Supplies were unloaded immediately and, leaving Inspector Joy at the detachment for the moment, *Beothic* returned to Fram Havn as a precaution against being beset at Bache Peninsula if the ice moved back in. Next day (12 August) Inspector Joy inspected the detachment. It had been his intention to close the Bache Peninsula detachment and move the personnel to Craig Harbour. In view of Krüger's non-appearance it was decided to postpone this plan for a year, since a search to the west could more effectively be mounted from Bache Peninsula.[61] Joy and Harry now sat down with Constables Paddy Hamilton and Art Munro, who were just joining the Bache Peninsula complement, and thrashed out the plan for a thorough search for the Krüger party in 1932. Harry was instructed to search the west coast of Ellesmere Island, Eureka Sound and the shores of Axel Heiberg Island and the Ringnes Islands as far as possible in March.[62] Joy proposed that two parties be dispatched, each consisting of an RCMP officer and two Inughuit with three dog teams and with a support party of a further two Inughuit. He arranged with Harry that since Bache Peninsula possessed a radio receiver (but no transmitter) any news as to whether Krüger and party had turned up at Craig Harbour, Dundas Harbour or Robertson Fjord would be relayed to Bache Peninsula by the radio stations KDKA, Pittsburgh and CKY in Winnipeg on particular dates in November and December. As Paddy Hamilton recalled this consultation:

Joy, who knew the country very well, realized this was going to be a most difficult and hazardous mission. He discussed all the plans and arrangements for the patrol at great length with Corporal Stallworthy. Then the itinerary and all the details were carefully put down on paper so there would be no mistakes. It was also decided to make arrangements with the Danish officials at Thule to send over extra Eskimos and dog teams early in the spring to assist in the search. It was after midnight before all the details were completed to everyone's satisfaction.[63]

A second motorboat had been delivered by the *Beothic*. Harry and his companions took both boats and escorted Joy back to Fram Havn, where the ship was preparing to sail on 14 August. Harry and his companions picked up two boatloads of coal and provisions at Cape Rutherford, then headed back to the detachment, where they settled down to the normal fall routine. Even more than usual, the stress was on hunting for dog feed as Harry and his companions had deliberately not done much hunting over the summer because of the anticipated move to Craig Harbour. But now they were faced with the prospect of having to feed not only their own teams, but those of the additional Inughuit who would be coming over from Greenland in the spring to assist in the search for Krüger. Even without that anticipated influx, the detachment maintained five dog teams throughout the winter— an average total of 100 dogs, since the Inughuit drove teams of 14–19 dogs.[64]

Leaving Constable Munro to look after the detachment, everybody else set off in the motor boats for two weeks to hunt walrus and narwhal. Paddy Hamilton was particularly impressed by Kahdi's prowess as a hunter. When they returned, Harry set off again with one of the motorboats to hunt in Flagler Fjord and elsewhere relatively close to home; he managed to get some more seals and three beluga.[65] By the time they had to pull the boats out of the water on 1 October, they had enough meat either at the detachment or cached at various places to last until the end of February.

Even by September 25 the sea ice was making fast and by 4 October it was strong enough for sledge travel. Harry then despatched Nukappianguaq and Kahkachoo to the west coast to hunt caribou for skins for winter clothing. Kahdi accompanied them as far as Flagler Valley to hunt hares, which were needed for making winter socks. Nukappianguaq and Kahkachoo returned on 25 October having killed seven caribou and one wolf. In preparation for the major patrols in the spring they had also hauled a cache of supplies to the west side of Sverdrup Pass. It consisted of items such as kerosene, ammunition, canned dog food and biscuits that could not be destroyed by wolves or bears.[66] Although the RCMP had a special dispensation to hunt a limited number of muskoxen (which had been generally protected by the Canadian government since 1917),[67] Harry had instructed Nukappiannguaq not to kill muskoxen if caribou were available since he suspected that muskox numbers were limited and that they might be of greater value during the extended patrols he had been ordered to make later when searching for Krüger.

During the dark period from 18 October to 23 February, all five men and the teams were kept busy hauling dog feed back to the detachment from the various caches of walrus, narwhal and seal meat accumulated in the fall. Most of them were within 20 miles (32 km) of the detachment, but the largest was at Cocked Hat Island (just north of Pim Island) and involved a round trip of about 70 miles (112 km). As usual, the snow was loose and deep, making for heavy sledging and/or fairly light loads. Harry put a positive spin on all this activity: "The two police and three native teams were all kept in good condition at this work which was also a benefit to the members of the detachment in that there was an objective and a good reason to get out and travel in the winter."[68] By Harry's estimate, hunting trips and meat-hauling trips accounted for a total mileage (by all five teams) of 7,000 miles (11,200 km) over the winter.

As always, the program of weather observations was maintained through-out "with very few exceptions when all members were on patrol." Cloud observations evidently remained something of a mystery:

> the observation of clouds, in which the height, kind and amount are recorded in code figures three times daily has been found rather difficult to carry out from the written instructions; while this duty has been carried out diligently I cannot vouch for the accuracy of this part of the returns.[69]

Christmas, as usual, was marked by a special dinner for the entire popula-tion of Ellesmere Island, and an exchange of personal presents. An innovation this year was a picnic trip on Boxing Day to Flagler Fjord, "where we played football and native games on the ice in the moonlight although the temper-ature was 29 degrees below zero with a breeze from the N.W. After a good meal provided by the natives and cooked on primus lamps we returned to the detachment.[70]

After the sun returned in late February, the weather turned very cold. Nonetheless since Harry wanted to reserve the remainder of the dog food accumulated in the fall for the planned search patrols, he sent Kahkachoo and Kahdi with their two teams, totalling 42 dogs, to hunt for dog feed in Smith Sound.[71] Inspector Joy had arranged that Ittukusuk, Quavigarsuaq and one other man would temporarily join the detachment to participate in the searches and that Kahkachoo and Kahdi were to assist them on the trip across from Greenland since it was assumed that they would be bringing their wives and children.

Kahkachoo and Kahdi reappeared on schedule by 15 March, accompanied by Ittukusuk, Quavigarsuaq, Inuatuk and their wives and seven children. During their crossing they had encountered very cold weather and the "North Water," the permanent polynya that occupies the north end of Baffin Bay with an arm extending into Smith Sound. This year, it had stretched unusually far north, necessitating a long detour. On arrival the 86 dogs that comprised the five teams were famished and nearly exhausted; indeed a fresh team had to be sent out to assist Ittukusuk and his family on the last lap, since his dogs were heavier and had lagged behind. With the addition of Inuatuk there were now enough dogs and drivers to allow Harry to field eight complete teams, three on each of the long patrols, plus two support teams that would relay supplies to Cape Southwest (the southwest tip of Axel Heiberg Island).

The next few days were spent in final preparations, which included building another komatik to replace Ittukusuk's which was in very poor condition. Meanwhile the women were kept busy until the last minute, sewing bearskin pants, socks, mittens and other clothing.

7

SEARCHING FOR KRÜGER

1932

THE CAVALCADE OF SLEDGES set off at noon on 20 March: 126 dogs making up eight teams, barking and yelping as they swung past Harry, who recorded the entire spectacle with his movie camera.[1] He himself was travelling with Kahdi, who was driving 18 dogs (three of which were police dogs); Paddy Hamilton drove a team of 14 police dogs; Nukappiannguaq had 19, Kahkachoo 14 (including two police dogs), Ittukasuk 14, Quavigarsuaq 17, Inuatuk 16 and Nukappiannguaq's son Seekeeunguaq 14 (six of them police dogs). The heavily loaded sledges carried supplies based on 60 days' rations for seven men (those on the main patrols) and 30 days' rations for two men (the support group). Most of the loads consisted of dog food, both canned meat in 48 lb cans and walrus meat cut and frozen in blocks.

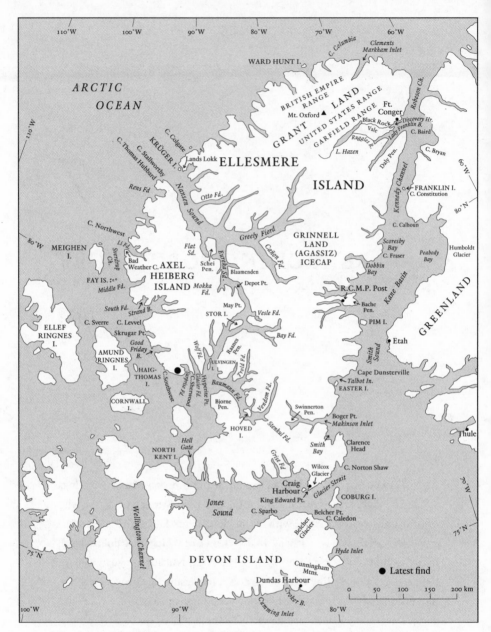

Ellesmere Island and area. "Latest find" refers to Krüger's campsite, discovered in 1999.

Paddy Hamilton's team, Bache Peninsula, 1932.

With fair weather and good ice the train of sledges made excellent progress up Flagler Fjord. They reached the head of the fjord at 10 P.M., where
they had to build a double snow house in which to house the big party for the
night. Early the following morning they started west up the valley, following
the ice of the braided river channels. There was much more snow and ice
than Harry had experienced the previous spring and only occasionally did
they have to cross strips of gravel. In places, however, the wind-polished ice
made it difficult for the dogs to gain any traction. They crossed the divide
around 6 P.M. and reached the depot that Nukappiannguaq and Kahkachoo
had left here in the fall. Since they were travelling well at the time, Harry
decided to negotiate the canyon beyond the depot before they built igloos
for the night.

In the morning of 22 March they ran into problems from the outset.
Their aim was to bypass the glacier snout that came from the south and
blocked the valley ahead entirely. The only option was to take to the hill
slopes to the north. It was difficult travelling: first they had to man-handle
their load 800 m up a hillside strewn with loose rocks. Each of them had to
make five or six trips before they could haul the empty sledges up the hill by
harnessing 25–30 dogs to each one. For the next two days they packed and
relayed along the rough, snow-free hillside for about six kilometres, ending
with a challenging descent to the river leading west to the head of Bay

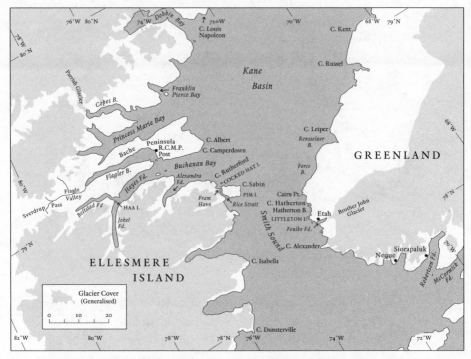

Smith Sound region, showing areas most commonly travelled from the RCMP's Bache Peninsula detachment and from the Oxford University Ellesmere Island Expedition's base at Etah.

Fjord. The descent involved negotiating a precipitous slope of about 1.2 km in length. Using harpoon lines, they let the sledges down in three stages, with one man guiding the sled while the rest of them paid out the line from above. The weather was unusually mild so everyone was sweating profusely by the end of the operation and their clothing was soaked, which made for considerable discomfort when the weather turned very cold a few days later. To quote Harry: "I think we all wore out a pair of mitts at this job. This was very strenuous work and necessitated a lot of climbing up and down on all fours. When the last sleigh reached the bottom safely after about 12 hours of effort there was a general cheer."[2]

Despite their fatigue, the day's travelling was not over yet. The men travelled a further three hours on hard-packed snow and river ice until they reached the sea ice of Bay Fjord. Here they unloaded the sledges, turned them over and filed and polished the steel runners with emery paper since they had been badly scored and gouged on the rocky terrain. Then they set off again. A few miles further on they built a large snow house that could accommodate all nine men. Then, having fed each of their dog teams about 60 lbs of canned meat, they had a well-earned sleep.

At this point the party split into two groups. Harry, Ittukasuk, Quavigarsuaq and Kahdi were to travel northwards to the northern tip of Axel Heiberg Island, then southwest to Meighen Island and on to Cape Southwest with three of the sledges and 49 dogs. Hamilton, meanwhile, accompanied by Nukappiannguaq and Kahkachoo, was to head directly for Cape Southwest, along with the two support teams driven by Inuatuk and Seekeeunguaq. The latter two were to cache their loads at Cape Southwest, then spend some time hunting in the area to augment the depot before heading for home. Meanwhile Hamilton, Nukappiannguaq and Kahkachoo were to search Cornwall Island and the Ringnes Islands before returning to Cape Southwest. Harry and Hamilton planned to rendezvous either at Cape Southwest or on Bjorne Peninsula, where they might plan further searches before returning home.

Both groups set off about noon on the 24th, Hamilton's party following the south shore of Bay Fjord and Harry's the north shore to improve each party's chances of hunting caribou. This was the start of a period of considerable frustration for Harry and his companions. Although it appears that RCMP officers had a special dispensation to shoot muskoxen for food in case of absolute necessity (Anstead later reported that the quota allowed the Bache Peninsula detachment was six animals per year[3]) Harry clearly felt that he could not avail himself of this dispensation except under extreme circumstances. That afternoon they spotted a total of eight muskoxen. The following day they went hunting inland to the north and encountered a herd of nine muskoxen, but only found the tracks of a caribou herd. Sparing the muskoxen, Harry pushed on reaching and crossing the head of Vesle Fjord before they finally spotted and killed three caribou. By then a blizzard had arisen and although the sledges were only lightly loaded, the deep soft snow exhausted the dogs on the return trip to the snow house on Bay Fjord.[4]

The blizzard confined them to the snow house for the whole of the next day, but by the morning of the 27th it had moderated to a ground drift and they were able to get under way again. When they reached Eureka Sound they turned north. Late in the day they ran across a fresh bear track. Leaving their loads, Kahdi and Quavigarsuaq set off along the track which led towards the mouth of Vesle Fjord. Meanwhile Harry and Ittukasuk built an igloo. The hunters returned about midnight with a team of exhausted dogs, but no bear.

On the 28th they made good progress north along Eureka Sound. At May Point they spotted a herd of 11 muskoxen and the next day they saw another herd of 19 asleep on a hillside across the sound. That night they built an igloo on land at Depot Point, where Krüger's support party had turned back. In the morning they checked the next three points to the west (as far as the mouth of Mokka Fjord) but found no sign of Krüger's party. During the day they saw three more herds of muskoxen, totalling 30 animals. Spotting a small cairn across the sound at Blaamenden through his binoculars, Harry and his companions crossed the sound to examine it but found it to be old and devoid of any messages. Having camped there for the night they crossed back to the west shore on 1 April, where they sighted two herds of muskoxen totalling 14 animals, either grazing quietly or sleeping, unconcerned by the dog teams passing only a few hundred metres away.

When Harry woke in the morning, he found that the muskoxen had moved closer to the igloo. Deciding that this was a good photo opportunity, Harry set out to film them. The two Inughuit and one dog came along to round them up, but to Harry's dismay, he "found on this and other occasions that muskoxen do not make very good subjects for motion pictures where action is concerned. They usually stood perfectly still or went on grazing sometimes within 25 feet of the camera."[5]

By now the dogs were starting to flag since, apart from the three small caribou in Bay Fjord, they had been eating only canned dog food and had been working hard in cold weather for about two weeks. On the evening of 2 April the Inughuit were building a snow house just south of Skraeling Point when four herds of muskoxen spread over both sides of the sound, came into sight. As they set off again in the morning, the dogs were clearly still hungry despite having consumed 48 lbs of canned meat the night before. Harry and his companions had expected to encounter bears in Eureka Sound and a good feed of bear meat would have solved the immediate critical problem of dog food. But such was not their luck and instead they saw herd upon herd of muskoxen. This frustrated the men and on several occasions, the Inughuit had asked for permission to shoot muskoxen, but Harry had

Muskox herd seen on patrol in search of Krüger, 1932.

refused. Now Quavigarsuaq and Kahdi asked if they would be reimbursed for any of their dogs that died of starvation.

As the party rounded Skraeling Point they were met by a northwesterly gale that was raising a high drift and their visibility was reduced to virtually zero. The dogs were in no condition to face into such a blizzard and when they also ran into an area of very rough ice, Harry decided to stop for the night even though they had covered less than 8 km. The blizzard died away in the evening and Kahdi and Quavigarsuaq went off to hunt caribou in a valley to the southwest. Ittukasuk stayed behind to rest his team, which was the smallest of the three. Harry took this opportunity to solicit his opinion as to how they should proceed. Ittukasuk had been one of the two Inughuit who had accompanied Dr. Frederick Cook on his alleged journey to the Pole and Donald Macmillan on his quest for "Crocker Land" to the north-west of Axel Heiberg Island. He was therefore very knowledgeable about the conditions that they might expected on the west side of Axel Heiberg Island. He was confident of finding caribou near the northern tip of the island or soon after they had started south down the west coast, but also reported that they were unlikely to encounter caribou or bears on the next leg through Nansen Sound.

After six hours the hunters returned empty-handed but reported that they had seen 17 muskoxen. Once again the dogs had to be fed canned meat, but there was enough left for only three more feeds. Bowing to the inevitable, Harry finally agreed to shoot some muskoxen. The following day they shot six bulls out of a herd of 13 and the dogs were given a generous feed and a day's rest since another blizzard had sprung up. Meanwhile the men spent the day drying their clothes. In his report Harry noted: "With regard to taking the muskox I regret having been in a position where it became necessary to do so; apart [from] the provisions of the Game Act this was directly against my personal feelings."[6] It is a measure of the man that he would admit to this technically illegal activity in his official report.

With the dogs greatly reinvigorated after a good feed and a rest, the party set off again in fine weather on 5 April. After checking several headlands west of Skraeling Point they crossed the very narrow isthmus of Schei Peninsula (which Otto Sverdrup had mistaken for an island). While the Inughuit filed the sledge runners that had been scored and gouged by travelling over rocks and gravel, Harry examined a small cairn on a high point on the isthmus but found no messages and deduced that it was an old Inuit cairn.

Continuing north down Flat Sound they camped on the southwest side of Nansen Sound. Since there seemed little prospect of finding any other source of dog food in the next few days and the Inughuit were still anxious about the welfare of their dogs, Harry decided to kill three more muskoxen from a herd close to camp. The ice close to the west shore of the sound ahead was extremely rough, but from a high vantage point above their igloo they spotted a way around it. About midnight on 6 April they set off again with three feeds of muskox meat and three of canned meat in hand. They had to swing almost right over to the mouth of Otto Fjord to avoid the area of rough ice and after camping for the night near a large iceberg off the mouth of that fjord, they headed back across Nansen Sound to the northernmost point of Axel Heiberg Island (now named Cape Stallworthy). The weather was clear and very cold but the going was good and they arrived there about 10 P.M. on the 8th.

Near the cape the snow was very soft and they had difficulty finding suitable snow for building an igloo. Even then the snow tried their patience since the blocks kept crumbling and breaking. After a long and frustrating struggle,

Ittukasuk finally placed the key-block in the top of the igloo and once they got the primus roaring, the partial melting and re-freezing of the inner surface of the igloo strengthened the structure.

Since this seemed an obvious place where Krüger might have left a message they searched the beach carefully over a distance of about 1.5 km, but to no avail; then they climbed to a conspicuous vantage point. Lands Lokk, the northeastern entrance cape of Nansen Sound appeared to be about 50 km away (in fact it is about 35 km away). Harry was keen to cross the sound to search that area too but when the Inughuit estimated that it would take "three sleeps" because of the rough ice, he abandoned the plan. A water sky— the dark reflection of water on the clouds—indicated a large area of open water out in the Arctic Ocean less than 80 km to the north.

The party headed west and by midnight on 9 April they were opposite Cape Thomas Hubbard but were unable to spot the cairn that they knew Robert Peary had left there in 1906.[7] Thinking that it might be on another cape a few kilometres further west, they continued in that direction but on looking back at Cape Thomas Hubbard through his binoculars, Harry spotted the elusive cairn. Turning back, Kahdi and Harry climbed to the cairn, each armed with a snow knife. Near the top they had to chop steps for about 100 m in the wind-packed snow. They found that the north side of the cairn was plastered with snow, making it invisible from the north and northeast. In a cylinder in the cairn they found a message left by Krüger, written in German. In translation it read as follows:

The German Arctic Expedition reached this cairn on 24 April 1930 and found notes by Peary and MacMillan, copies of which are attached.

We have come from Lands Lokk and are continuing to Meighen Island.

24 April 1930
Åge Rose Bjare   H. K. E. Krüger
Akqioq   Leader[8]

Although his command of German was limited, Harry was able to decipher the main gist of the message. Included with it were copies that Krüger had made of the messages left by Peary in 1906 and MacMillan in 1914. Harry made and left copies of all three documents and a record of his own visit, indicating its purpose and the names of the patrol members.

Harry was greatly encouraged by finding Krüger's message. Firstly, it clearly indicated that Krüger had abandoned his plans to head northwest onto the ice of the Arctic Ocean. Secondly, Krüger and his company had probably walked the whole distance and by reaching this point in 37 days and having also visited Lands Lokk along the way, Harry felt that his party must have made quite good progress. Thirdly, the information that they were next heading for Meighen Island gave Harry a solid objective. However the problem of dog food was still acute and they all agreed that they would need to accumulate a reasonable reserve of food before attempting to cross Sverdrup Channel to Meighen Island where Ittukasuk indicated from past experience that there were neither seals nor bears.

Harry and Kahdi descended to the shore by a safer route and followed the tracks of the other two sledges west to where Ittukasuk and Quavigarsuaq had built an igloo before going hunting. They returned around noon having managed to shoot only one Arctic hare, the first one seen on the patrol. While the Inughuit were feeding their dogs a large white wolf approached the igloo but then raced away again. Quavigarsuaq tried a long shot but missed. Initially both he and Kahdi had mistaken it for a bear and this was subsequently the source of much amusement and leg-pulling.[9]

On the 11th the party continued south on smooth, level ice and made good progress for the first 65 km across the mouth of Rens Fjord. The level ice ended the next day and as they approached Cape Northwest heavy pressure ice forced them to travel along the ice foot. Occasionally their path over the pressure ice was littered with boulders and they had to make a detour past the problem area. Also, by this time the dogs were becoming tired and were flagging. It was in this area near Cape Northwest that Ittukasuk, who had accompanied Frederick Cook on his trip in 1908–09, gave Harry convincing evidence that Cook's claim that he had reached the North Pole was a hoax: "It was in the vicinity of Cape North West that Cook took his famous picture of the 'North Pole True.' I recall Ittukasuk telling me they had to wait for the weather and a favourable position of the sun in order not to have any land in the picture."[10]

Having cut across the mouth of Li Ford and having passed Bad Weather Cape, Harry and his companions repeatedly climbed to vantage points on conspicuous headlands. Meighen Island was clearly visible and they estimated that it was about 100–115 km to the west (in fact the distance is about 45 km). As far as they could see from their vantage points, the rough ice extended right across Sverdrup Channel and so, not surprisingly, Harry was forced to abandon any idea of trying to reach Meighen Island, especially in view of their critical lack of dog food.

The rough ice continued past Middle Fjord and Strand Bay, all the way to Cape Levell, which they reached at about midnight on 16 April. Along the way they killed one small caribou, but it did not go far among the 49 famished dogs. The map that Harry was using bore little resemblance to reality and so it was in part to look for game and in part to get his bearings that Harry and his companions headed inland about five kilometres somewhere on the peninsula between Middle Fjord and South Fjord and climbed to a lookout point at about 475 m. Through the binoculars they could see the Fay Islands, both the Ringnes Islands and even what appeared to be Cornwall Island to the south.

By now the dog food was almost exhausted and they were feeding what was left mostly to the bitches since the Inughuit were anxious that at least their breeding stock would survive. The objective now was to reach either the cache at Cape Southwest or country where game was available before all the dogs died. Since leaving Cape Thomas Hubbard they had been travelling 18–20 hours per day and the dogs were very thin and towards the end of each day some dogs in each team had to be carried on the sledges.

On the 17th they were approaching Skrugar Point when Quavigarsuaq, who had exceptional eyesight, spotted what he thought were bear tracks on land about 6 km away. Taking 10 of the best dogs and an empty sledge he and Kahdi set off to investigate, but after about three hours they returned empty-handed to report that the tracks were those of three caribou being pursued by wolves and they were therefore likely to run far and fast. As they continued south almost all the dogs were staggering and after stopping frequently out of necessity, most of the dogs had to be lifted to their feet to get them started again.

On 20 April, after an almost continuous march of 43 hours the party was about 25 km short of Cape Southwest. During this march the dogs had been fed the last of the bacon, the remainder of the dog pemmican and all the spare sealskins, mitts and footwear. Although Cape Southwest was in plain sight, Harry decided to camp here since the dogs could go no further without a rest. They killed six dogs and fed them to the remainder. In the morning they cached the heavier items in the loads such as the tent, kerosene, and ammunition but even with lightened loads, the dogs could scarcely stagger along and it took them 16 hours to cover the 25 km. In a pencilled annotation to his own copy of his report Harry added the comment, "Worst day of all: thirsty, hungry." He could see that his Inughuit companions were getting noticeably thinner, and although he did not have a mirror, he realized that his cheeks were becoming sunken by feeling his own face.[11]

When they reaching Cape Southwest on the 21st, Harry found a note from Hamilton dated 12 April. He had experienced travelling conditions comparable to those experienced by Harry and his party and on his return from Cornwall Island had made only a short stay at Cape Southwest before starting back to Bache Peninsula, since he suspected that Harry's dogs might be in even greater need than his own of the dog food cached here. After caching the dog food they had hauled from Bache Peninsula, Inuatuk and Seekeeunguaq had managed to augment the depot with the meat of some bears they had killed in the area, but they too had found game scarce and had not stayed long, so as not to consume the supplies and dog food in the depot.

Harry and his companions camped at Cape Southwest for four days, feeding the dogs on canned meat and pemmican to let them regain their strength. Initially they were fed quite small amounts, but quite frequently. Then on the 25th, taking only enough supplies and kerosene for their immediate needs, the party started east on a hunting trip in an area where Paddy Hamilton had reported seeing caribou.[12]

During the four days at Cape Southwest, the dogs had revived considerably and actually broke into a trot with their tails curled over their backs. Just as they started off, Harry found a small cairn at the tip of the cape that had been built by Donald Macmillan in May 1916. It would have escaped his notice except that Ittukasuk, who had been with Macmillan when he built it, had mentioned it. In it they found messages left by Macmillan and by Inspector Joy during his patrol to Amund Ringnes Island in 1927. Harry had been watching carefully for cairns along the entire west coast of Axel Heiberg Island, but without success, and the fact that there was no note from Krüger in this cairn at this conspicuous headland, convinced him that Krüger and his party had not come this way.

Before leaving Cape Southwest Harry deposited his own message in the cairn. It read:

April 23rd
R.C.M. Police

Visited this point from Bache Peninsula having travelled around Axel Heiberg Island. Three natives, three dog teams. Dogs are practically [smudged]. Going to Glacier Fjord to hunt then to Bache Peninsula via Bay & Beitstad Fjord or Mackinson Inlet.

H. Stallworthy, *Corpl.*
German Arctic Expedition Search Patrol.

Harry's note was recovered on 24 April 1940 by Christian Vibe of the Danish Thule and Ellesmere Land Expedition of 1939–40. After wintering near Thule, Vibe and his companion, G. Thorlaksson, crossed Ellesmere Island to Bay Fjord and southwest to Cape Southwest, their turning point.[13]

As Harry and his companions headed east towards Cape Sherwood they again encountered fairly deep, soft snow and after only 20 km the dogs were labouring noticeably. At about midnight on the 25th they spotted four caribou on shore. While Harry looked after the teams, the Inughuit made a particularly successful stalk and shot those four animals plus another three. After building an igloo, the party remained here, resting and feeding the dogs, until early on the 28th. Three of the caribou were young and all were almost completely devoid of fat and so even when the caribou had been devoured, the dogs were still hungry. To make up for the critical deficiency of fat, the dogs were also fed some fat from the canned meat.[14]

Since the snow from this point onwards became even deeper, the dogs quickly became exhausted again even though the men helped by pushing the sledges. They built an igloo at the mouth of Glacier Fjord around midnight on the 29th and fed the dogs the last of the pemmican and of the caribou meat. Next day they travelled some distance up Glacier Fjord then climbed to a lookout point on its east side, from were they could see Wolf Fjord, Ulvingen

Island and Eureka Sound beyond. But there was no sign of game either on the land or on the sea ice.

On 1 May the sledges rounded Hyperite Point; in Wolf Fjord the going was better but the dogs were weakening again and could barely manage a walking pace even with Harry walking ahead, calling and encouraging them. He and Kahdi travelled down one side of Ulvingen Island while the other two teams travelled down the other side. When they met at the north end a blizzard blew up and they retreated some distance down the east side of the island to find a sheltered spot to build two igloos.

In the morning they had to kill five more dogs to feed the remainder. Then while Ittukasuk stayed in camp to prevent the dogs from eating their harnesses and traces, Kahdi and Quavigarsuaq went hunting in the hills across Wolf Fjord and Harry went to the north point of Ulvingen Island to look for seals or bears on the sea ice. When he got back empty-handed, Ittukasuk had killed another of his dogs and fed it to the rest. Fortunately the other two Inughuit returned at midnight packing the meat of two caribou. All four men then went to sleep in the open; the weather had turned so warm that the igloos had collapsed.

In warm, overcast weather the men kept a constant lookout for seals basking on the ice. When Harry spotted one about one-and-a-half km away on 4 May, Kahdi stalked it and killed it with a shot that broke its neck. It weighed about 140 kg and its blubber was over 6 cm thick. The following day Quavigarsuaq shot another seal, and when a bear approached the camp the dogs were loosed to try to bring it to bay. They had just finished a large meal of seal meat and most of them showed no interest in the bear, but fortunately two experienced bear dogs set off in hot pursuit and brought the bear to bay until it could be shot. On the 6th they killed another large seal. The men now felt that their troubles were over: the dogs were starting to show the effects of abundant feeds of fresh meat and they could anticipate finding plenty of seals basking on the ice from now on. Also, very importantly, the Inughuit were much more cheerful since they knew that they would not have to sacrifice any more dogs.

Harry and his companions now had a different problem to deal with. They had left their tent in the cache northwest of Cape Southwest, but now that the weather was warmer igloos were not a feasible option any longer and the men had to improvise a shelter from their sleeping robes and the sledges.

In addition, the supplies of kerosene and of food other than seal and bear meat were exhausted, although they still had plenty of bear meat and blubber to cook with. Since they had managed to procure another three seals by 8 May, Harry decided to send Ittukasuk and Kahdi back to retrieve the tent and supplies they had left at the depot northwest of Cape Southwest, as well as the remainder of the supplies from the cape.

The two men left with two sledges and the best of the dogs on 9 May. Although they only had to travel about 145 km, it took them nine days to make the round trip because the fresh deep snow forced them to detour far to the south. When they returned, Harry pitched the tent and the four men enjoyed a meal of bacon, hardtack and cocoa with sugar, although on his personal copy of his report Harry later added a pencilled annotation: "Damned little bacon!" The meal made a pleasant change after the straight diet of bear and seal meat washed down with cold water on which they had lived for the previous eight days.[15]

With three good feeds of seal meat on the sledges, the party left Ulvingen Island on 18 May and travelled north along Eureka Sound. They found the going in Bay Fjord excellent on the next day; the dogs were regaining their strength remarkably well, especially considering the hardships they had endured. On the north side of Bay Fjord they counted 23 muskoxen in three herds, while on the south side, on Raanes Peninsula, they spotted a large herd of at least 23. Harry stopped to photograph one of the herds on the north side but found that it was difficult to get a good view of the young calves "as they were hiding under the cows and were practically covered by the long hair."[16]

From the area of Augusta Bay, from where an alternate route cuts up and over the ice cap to Beitstad Fjord, they could see through the binoculars that there appeared to be a deep snow pack on the ice cap. Travelling by this route would have meant some 50 km of ploughing through deep snow to the other side of the ice cap and so, despite the relative lack of snow, they decided to return by the Sverdrup Pass route, as they had done on the outgoing journey.

Right from moment they reached the head of the fjord on 20 May, they found almost no snow in the river valley and had to sledge across mud and through water up to 25 cm deep. One of Harry's later marginal annotations reads: "Tailing piles; endless rows of ploughed furrows resembled A.Y. Jackson's paintings."[17] Having covered about 80 km that day, they pitched the tent for the night and the next day they backpacked the loads ahead in two trips for about 1.2 km and then brought the sledges along empty. After that there was enough snow left in snow drifts to allow them to travel with full loads in most places, although at one place they had to double the teams to haul the sledges across some gravel bars.

Prior to reaching the glacier, they travelled about 3 km up a narrow rock gorge; hard snow and ice made for good sledging but frozen waterfalls represented serious challenges:

> these falls were only six to ten feet deep but they presented quite an obstacle. At one place in particular where the walls were perpendicular and the canyon narrowed to approximately two feet we were delayed about three hours. The difficulty was in getting the first man up; after that the dogs were hauled up singly with a rope; most of the supplies and bedding were thrown up. The sleighs were then pulled up through the "gate" on edge after the handles were unfastened.[18]

At the summit of Sverdrup Pass they again had to backpack the loads across sand and gravel bars for a short distance before starting down Flagler Valley. The igloos they had built on the outward journey on 20 March had almost entirely melted. After some hard sledging over stretches of bare gravel they found good travelling conditions in the lower part of Flagler Valley. After a good night's sleep in the tent they made good time to the head of Flagler Fjord, where they stopped to repair the damage to the sledge runners and to give the dogs a rest.

Leaving there about midnight on 22 May they made rapid progress down the fjord, but were brought to a halt by a polynya at its mouth about 1.5 km from the post; there was not even an ice foot, just a sheer rock face rising from the water. Leaving the dogs staked out on the shore ice, the four men climbed up the rocks and walked the last lap to the detachment. They arrived home at about noon on 23 May. The Inughuit then ferried some food to the dogs by boat, but the dogs and sledges could not be ferried back to the post until the next night, when the sea was calmer.

Harry's search patrol had lasted 65 days. During that time he and his companions had travelled a distance which he estimated at not less than 2,250 km.

In this estimate he was taking into account hunting trips, the trip back from Ulvingen Island to Cape Southwest to retrieve the cached equipment and supplies and the very tortuous route dictated by the need to search as much of the irregular coastline as possible. It had been achieved at the expense of 12 dogs that had been killed to feed the others and of nine muskoxen, a species normally protected by Canadian law. Apart from the message found at Cape Thomas Hubbard, no trace of Krüger and his party had been found.

In the meanwhile, Paddy Hamilton had returned to Bache Peninsula from his patrol on 7 May. He and his companions, Nukappiannguaq and Kahkachoo, had parted from Harry's group near the head of Bay Fjord around noon on 24 March.[19] Paddy himself was driving a team of 14 dogs, Nukappiannguaq had 19 and Kahkachoo 14. They also had with them the support party of Inuatuk (with a team of 16 dogs) and Seekeeunguaq (with 14 dogs) who were transporting heavy loads of dog food and provisions to be cached at Cape Southwest.[20]

After Harry and his party had left, Paddy discovered an unpleasant surprise: by some oversight Inuatuk and Seekeeunguaq had no provisions for themselves—just the supplies intended for the cache at Cape Southwest.[21] This meant that he had to stretch the supplies intended for himself, Nukappiannguaq and Kahkachoo to feed two additional men. By the evening of the 25th they had reached Stor Island where they camped, feeding the dogs on pemmican and reserving the last of the walrus meat for later. On the 26th they crossed to Raanes Peninsula, where they cached a depot of pemmican for Inuatuk and Seekeeunguaq to use on their return journey. After travelling for only 25 miles, the party was forced to pitch camp because of a blizzard. Weatherbound, they were forced to stay in camp throughout the 27th, repairing harnesses and traces. On the 28th, the weather cleared and they crossed to Ulvingen Island, where they encountered and killed a small bear that was fed to the dogs. They reached the island at 10 P.M. and while the Inughuit built an igloo, Paddy visited a cairn about half a mile away which he later discovered had been erected by Donald Macmillan, but found no messages in it.

On the 29th the party split into two groups, each travelling along opposite sides of Ulvingen Island to improve their chances of hunting success. Inuatuk and Nukappiannguaq killed a small bear. That night the reunited group camped at Hyperite Point. Since there were abundant signs of both caribou and muskoxen in the area, the Inughuit went hunting the next morning while Paddy cached another small depot of pemmican and then spent the rest of the day unsuccessfully searching the coast for signs of Krüger. The hunters had only limited success, returning with only one small caribou. They had spotted a herd of nine caribou and were patiently stalking it a pack of six wolves caused the heard to stampede.[22] However, they did report seeing 10 muskoxen, mainly bulls. So far, the party had regularly seen herds of muskoxen along their route. Although they were only 10 days into their trip, Paddy remarked in his notes, "The dogs although being [fed] regularly on pemmican, were getting poorer through lack of fresh meat and subsequently [sic] becoming slower."[23]

After another fruitless day of hunting the party set off again on 1 April and reached Cape Southwest on the 3rd; for most of the distance they sledged along the fast ice despite deep, soft snow. Along the way, they constantly kept a lookout for cairns or any other signs of the Krüger party, but to no avail. Paddy and his companions searched the cape, but although they found some old cairns, there was no trace of the missing party there either. Paddy felt that since this was such a high and conspicuous cape, Krüger would certainly have left a cairn here, had he reached this point. The hunters killed two small bears at the cape and these were fed to the dogs. The depot of supplies that Inuatuk and Seekeeunguaq had been hauling was cached here. Leaving instructions for them to stay at the cape for a few days to try to accumulate some fresh meat as well, Paddy, Nukappiannguaq and Kahkachoo set off southwestwards on the evening of 4 April, aiming for Cornwall Island.

Rough ice and deep snow greatly slowed their progress and finally dense fog brought them to a halt after having covered only 32 km. By morning the fog had cleared and Cornwall Island was clearly visible and they were able to continue, but travelling conditions were as bad as ever and the dogs were slowing visibly. By evening some of the younger dogs were riding on the sledges; and that night they fed the dogs the last of the pemmican. When they emerged from their snow house in the morning on 7 April, the men found that several dogs had broken loose and had eaten some of their traces as well as Nukappiannguaq's *qulitaq* (parka). Paddy blamed much of their problems on the pemmican:

On this trip I was surely learning something about pemmican, which I had never used on any of my previous patrols. By this time I knew I would never again depend upon it as a source of dog feed if I should ever be called on to attempt another patrol of this kind. True, so far it had kept the dogs alive, but that was all that could be said in its favour. It had given them diarrhoea, and at times, had caused them to vomit. Now they were thin and unable to pull. It might have been all right provided we had had quantities of seal or walrus fat to mix with it. It could probably be used on local trips where you were only going to be absent from your base one or two nights, but here in the middle of the Arctic no man's land, where the dogs had to be on the move every day pulling heavy loads, it was absolutely useless. I felt the reason the dogs had broken loose and eaten up the koulitak and traces was that they were hungry for fat. Well, it didn't make much difference now, since all the pemmican was gone. The stark truth was that we had no dog feed of any kind, and the outlook was grim.[24]

That evening they reached Cornwall Island, again with a number of exhausted dogs riding on each sledge. The hunters set off inland but returned empty-handed. The ice to the northwest, towards Amund Ringnes Island, was a chaotic jumble of pressure ridges. After a short sleep Paddy decided to leave one sledge, most of the provisions and the dogs that were unfit to pull and to head west along the north coast of Cornwall Island to its northernmost point.

For eight hours they travelled through deep snow along the fast ice, with Nukappiannguaq breaking trail until they eventually reached the northern tip of the island. Nukappiannguaq and Kahkachoo again went inland to hunt. In their absence, Paddy found some cairns, one of which contained a message from Inspector Joy during one of his patrols. Paddy retrieved it, leaving a copy and a message of his own. There was no indication that Krüger and his party had reached this coast. "Had the Dr. passed this way," Paddy wrote, "he could not have failed to see these cairns as one is located on the summit of a high hill and anyone travelling from the north could see it for a long distance before reaching the island."[25]

After consultation with his companions, Paddy decided to head back to Cape Southwest the next day. He relied heavily on Nukappiannguaq's observation that bears rarely frequent multi-year pack ice such as that between Cornwall and Amund Ringnes islands and that from his experience there was no game on the Ringnes Islands. The most persuasive argument was his declaration that when the *Beothic* had called at Bache Peninsula the previous August, he "had received instructions from Insp. Joy...not to travel if he could not find game."[26] As if to underline the seriousness of their situation and to underscore the fact that the decision to turn back was the right one, they encountered a grim sight on their return to the cache. Four of the dogs they had left behind had died and one of them had been partly eaten by the others. After a quick cup of coffee, the party loaded the frozen carcasses of the dead dogs on the sledges and started back across the sea ice towards Cape Southwest.

They reached the cape at midnight on 12 April having killed only one small bear en route; the Inughuit had to stalk it on foot since the dogs no longer had the energy to pursue a bear and bring it to bay[27]; during the crossing, five more dogs died of starvation. Fortunately at Cape Southwest they found that Inuatuk and Seekeeunguaq had killed and cached enough bear meat before they started for home to give the remaining dogs a feed. Pushing on along the south coast of Axel Heiberg Island, it took the party 24 hours to cover the 50-odd miles to Glacier Fjord through deep snow. The men had to walk alongside the dogs to encourage them along the way. On spotting a herd of 18 muskoxen grazing on the west side of the fjord, Paddy reluctantly decided to shoot three of them to feed both dogs and men.

After a meal of muskox meat and after drinking some of the blood, the three men went to sleep; Paddy and Nukappiannguaq crawled into their sleeping bags, but Kahkachoo simply wrapped himself into one of the muskox hides, hair side inside. When he woke a few hours later, the raw hide had frozen solid and he was trapped. Even with the help of the other two he had difficulty extricating himself.[28]

Resuming their journey at noon on 14 April, they headed southeast to the northwestern tip of Bjorne Peninsula (Goose Point). Having pitched camp, they carefully searched the coastline and the conspicuous headland but found no trace of Krüger and party. On the 15th they headed east into the mouth of Baumann Fjord through deep snow and occasional belts of rough ice; a further five dogs died of starvation that day. The following day the dogs could barely move at a walking pace and they were able to cover only a short distance on account of the deep snow. That evening they spotted a herd of muskoxen on Bjorne Peninsula and again Paddy decided that he had no choice but to shoot four of them. They stayed in camp next day to let the dogs eat and rest and to dry clothing and footwear "which had become saturated with perspiration from so much walking. The outer covers of our mitts were frozen stiff as boards. The skin on our wrists had become frost bitten and through rubbing continuously against the frozen mitts, our wrists were now raw and bleeding."[29]

At midnight on the 18th the three sledges headed for Hoved Island, but a southeasterly blizzard brought them to a halt and pinned them down for the whole of the 19th and the 20th on a small, unnamed island. More than once the blizzard threatened to erode holes in the walls of the snow house and the men were repeatedly forced to bank the walls with snow and to build snow windbreaks to prevent disaster. When the storm abated on the evening of the 21st, they started off again and soon reached Hoved Island. A short distance beyond the island, Nukappiannguaq spotted a large bear approaching:

He immediately called a halt, took the best of the dogs from the three teams, and drove off in pursuit of the animal. After a long chase, he eventually caught up with the bear and shot him. However he waited until we came up, with the other dogs, before going up to where the animal was lying beside the ice pan. Luckily we all took our rifles along as we approached the bear, with Nukappiannguaq in the lead, for the bear, having only been wounded and momentarily stunned, now sprang up and charged. Before Nukappiannguaq could raise his rifle and fire the bear dealt him a slashing blow, knocking him down, tearing a long rent in his skin clothing and inflicting a deep gash in his hip. I think Kahkachoo and I must have fired at the bear at the same time. Anyway we killed him before he could recover and make a second lunge at Nukappiannguaq, or turn his attention to us. I had the tent set up at once and started to heat water to attend to Nukappiannguaq's wound. While the water was heating I rummaged through the gear on my sledge and found the medical kit. It was not extensive, but there were surgical dressings, iodine, surgical thread and needle. When the tent was warmed a bit and the water had been boiled and cooled, Nukappiannguaq removed his skin pants and I got to work. First I bathed the wound. Then I applied the iodine, a little more liberally than I should have to judge from the anguished yells and groans from the patient. Since it was my first sewing job it would be hard to say whether Nukappiannguaq or I suffered the most before the operation was finished. When it was all over Nukappiannguaq recovered very quickly and said that his being hurt did not matter as long as the bear was killed and we had lots of dog feed.[30]

Shortly before the party camped for the night, they managed to kill another small bear.

By morning, the snow was hard and the dogs were well fed and rested. Throughout the day they made good progress and the men were able to ride on the sledges again. The Inughuit even started joking and laughing again. They made camp about 16 km from the head of Stenkul Fjord, leading off Baumann Fjord. On 23 April the three sledges started up a river valley at the head of the fjord to start the overland crossing to Makinson Inlet, which was to take three days since the snow was soft and deep. They reached the summit of the pass only at noon on the 25th. Nukappiannguaq told Paddy that at Bache Peninsula he had shown Krüger this crossing on the map, but when they found a cairn built by an earlier RCMP patrol they did not find any message from Krüger, despite a careful search of the area. Having killed two caribou during the day, they had enough meat for to tide them over and so when they reached the head of Makinson Inlet on the morning of the 27th they stayed there for two days to let the dogs rest and eat and also to repair sledges and harnesses while a northerly blizzard blew itself out.

When the weather cleared on the morning of the 29th they headed east down Makinson Inlet on hard-packed snow and glare ice. They killed a bear later in the day and camped about 25 km west of Boger Point. The next day they crossed Talbot Inlet, which was bounded by a spectacular glacier front, through very rough ice and with open water not far to seaward. Passing through the narrow strait behind Paine Island, they were halted by open water lapping at the cliffs at Cape Dunsterville. After retracing their steps for eight kilometres they found a route overland across a glacier, thus bypassing the cape.

Further north, at Cape Isabella, open water again forced them to take to the land and to cross another glacier. The descent from the glacier back down to the sea ice was precipitous; they had to unharness the dogs and line the sledges down individually. At this point a further three dogs that had still not recovered from their protracted period of starvation on the west coast died. They eventually reached the depot at Fram Havn on 5 May. Paddy Hamilton later wrote that

We had long since finished all of our rations and had been living on a meat diet, so the biscuits and coffee we found in the cache tasted wonderful. There was also some bacon which, though several years old, was quite palatable when fried up, especially since we had not had any for several weeks. Anyway it was a most welcome change from our steady game diet.[31]

They camped for the night at Cape Rutherford and having spent the 6th hunting for seals on the sea ice, they covered the last lap to the detachment at Bache Peninsula on the morning of the 7th. They were warmly welcomed by Constable Munro, all the Inughuit women, and Dr. Holm, the doctor from Thule, who was visiting.

Hamilton's patrol had lasted 49 days, during which time he, Nukappiannguaq and Kahkachoo had covered approximately 1,510 km. Because of the paucity of game they had lost 17 dogs from starvation despite the fact that they had had recourse to killing seven muskoxen; in so doing Paddy had clearly experienced the same conflict of emotions and obligations as Harry.

In assessing the results of both searches, Harry wrote in his official report that "these patrols were most unfortunate in not finding game en route which would have enabled us to reach our objectives."[32] His own copy had a further note added in pencil: "but damned fortunate to be alive!" The report continued: "There was considerable anxiety at times chiefly concerning the dogs and how to provide for them. I am pleased to report that no serious hardships were experienced by any of the members of the patrols."[33] Here, Harry's pencilled emendation is more revealing of the trials the men suffered on their journey: "Good God!!!!"

Both RCMP officers included assessments of what they felt had been the most probable fate of Krüger and his companions in their official reports. Harry wrote:

In my opinion and that of the natives this party did not venture far out on the ice from the North West extremity of Axel Heiberg Island.

It is more likely that they hunted for dog food down the west coast and crossed to Meighen Island. It is in this district or further south in the vicinity of the Ringnes Islands that I believe the party perished in the winter of 1930 and 1931; as a result of their dogs starving they would have no means of transportation and probably no provisions. I think it would be impossible to exist in this district without having made adequate preparations.

...From the general ideas and theories advanced by the natives, all of whom were acquainted with the members of the missing expedition [they] are of the opinion that they perished in the winter of 1930–1931 during the dark period and would therefore be without heat or drinking water."[34]

In his report, Paddy Hamilton wrote:

It is my opinion that the missing Expedition...are [sic] north of the territory covered by this patrol, otherwise, had they visited any of the places at which we called during our journey, they could not have failed to see some of the cairns erected by previous patrols or explorers. And I think that Dr Krueger would have at least placed a record of his expedition in one of these.... The Natives who accompanied me on this trip are of the opinion that Dr. Krueger and his party perished in the year of 1930–1931.[35]

Harry and Paddy Hamilton were not the only RCMP patrols that searched for Krüger in the spring of 1932. Following instructions left by Inspector Joy the previous fall, Corporal P. Dersch, who was in charge of the Dundas Harbour detachment on the south coast of Devon Island, mounted a patrol aimed at searching the south coast of that island and the shores of Wellington Channel for any trace of Krüger's party.[36] Leaving the detachment in the care of Constable J.B. Currie, Dersch set off on 22 March. He travelled westwards with two Inuit, Kellekte and Keepoomee, driving two sledges pulled by 31 dogs. The party encountered problems almost immediately: a new fall of snow camouflaged thin ice and as they rounded the headland just west of Dundas Harbour, Keepoomee's sledge broke through; fortunately only the rear part of the load got wet.

Having crossed the mouth of Croker Bay, they pushed on westwards towards Cumming Inlet but detours around polynyas and wide leads consumed a great deal of time and involved chopping a trail through heavy pressure ice. The weather had improved by 27 March, but travelling conditions had deteriorated badly. Having crossed Cumming Inlet, some 200 km west of Dundas Harbour, they were forced to sledge across steep, hard-packed snowdrifts that sloped down from the coastal cliffs. At the foot of these drifts, brash ice and open water eliminated any possibility of coastwise travel on the sea ice. The drifts were so steep in places that they were forced to cut ruts in the surface for the runners to prevent the sledges from slipping sideways. Finally they reached an unusually steep snow slope some 400 m in width and with impassable brash ice below it. By cutting steps, Dersch was able to reach the top of the snow slope. There, he established that there were at least three more such drifts ahead, each more extensive than the one on which he stood. He decided to retrace his tracks to an inlet they had just passed, but even to achieve this they had to unload the sledges and tip them end-over-end to turn them on the steep slope. They next travelled north up the inlet to its head, a detour of about 15 km but found no break in the cliffs that would permit them to continue westwards overland.

Dersch now decided to camp and wait for the open water and brash ice to freeze solid, but over the next few days it showed no sign of doing so. Instead, large fields of ice kept breaking away and drifting eastwards. Reluctantly, Dersch was forced to admit defeat and he and his companions started back eastwards. They reached the detachment at Dundas Harbour on 1 April. This concluded the RCMP's searches for Krüger and his companions.

No further traces of Krüger and his party were found until 1954. In the spring of that year, Dr. Robert Christie and Dr. Geoffrey Hatterley-Smith travelled by dog team southwest along the coast of Ellesmere Island from a base camp that had been established by the Canadian Defence Research Board near Ward Hunt Island. At their turning point at a cape south of Cape Colgate and at the most westerly point on Ellesmere Island, just north of the small island since named Krüger Island at the north side of the entrance to Nansen Sound, they found a cairn built by Robert Peary in 1906. In it, soldered in an empty film canister that had been wrapped in old pieces of *kamik* tied with walrus hide thongs,[37] was a message left by Krüger on 22

April 1930, two days before he left the message found by Harry Stallworthy on Cape Thomas Hubbard. In translation this note read:

The German Arctic Expedition, coming from Nerke in Northern Greenland via Bay Fjord, reached this cairn built by Peary on 22 April 1930; no message found.

We are proceeding on to the northern tip of Heiberg Island. One sledge, 17 dogs and 3 men in good condition.

Åge Rose Bjare   H.K.E. Krüger
Akqioq   Leader[38]

Three years later in the spring of 1957, Dr. Ray Thorsteinsson of the Geological Survey of Canada led a party of four men and two dog teams on a visit to Meighen Island.[39] On 1 June, about 800 m inland from Anderson Point at the southwest corner of the island, he found the cairn built by Vilhjalmur Stefansson (or rather, by his companion Harold Noice) at their landfall on the island on 15 June 1916.[40] Stefansson had left a message inside two cans but instead of Stefansson's message, Thornsteinsson found a message written in German. In translation it read:

The German Arctic Expedition, coming from the northern tip of Heiberg Land, reached this point on 5 May 1930 and found Stefansson's note. A copy could not be made since the note is in such poor condition that it could not be opened without destroying it.

We are proceeding on to Cape Sverre on Amund Ringnes Island.

May 6, 1930
Åge Rose Bjare   H.K.E. Krüger
Akqioq   Leader[41]

On 17 August 1958 Thorsteinsson landed by light plane at Cape Sverre and made a careful search for traces of Krüger and his party, but found nothing to indicate that they had reached Amund Ringnes Island.[42] He has suggested two possible catastrophes that might have taken the lives of all three men at once. The explanation that he considered most likely is that all three men were killed by carbon monoxide poisoning inside a snow house (quite a common hazard in the Arctic), somewhere on the sea ice between Meighen and Amund Ringnes islands, in which case no trace will ever be found. Alternatively he has suggested that Krüger and party may have all broken through thin ice and drowned near the polynya in Hell Gate (between North Kent Island and southwestern Ellesmere Island).

Soon after his discovery on Meighen Island, Thornsteinsson wrote to Harry Stallworthy to tell him of his finding both Krüger's note and Stallworthy's note which he left on Cape Thomas Hubbard.[43] In his reply, Harry suggested:

In view of the increased exploration at the top of the Arctic, I believe that the remains of the party will be found. I believe their bones, remains of the Komatik and some of the equipment, probably including a heavy sounding line and weights will be discovered, probably on the Ringnes Islands or at least on land somewhere in the general direction of Southern Ellesmere Island.[44]

Up until very recently, however, no further traces of the missing expedition have been found. In 1999 Jerry Kobalenko had no luck searching the shores of Sand and Good Friday bays on the southwest coast of Axel Heiberg Island, where he felt there was a good chance of finding some traces of Krüger and party.[45] During that same summer, however, another group that was not specifically searching for traces of the Krüger expedition stumbled across artifacts that almost certainly belonged to that expedition.[46] On 3 July 1999, while surveying raised marine beaches, a party consisting of Dr. John England, Dr. Art Dyke and Ms. Michelle Laurie stumbled on an interesting collection of artifacts that indicated an abandoned campsite at a location to the east of Cape Southwest, halfway between that cape and Surprise Fjord. The site lies immediately inland of the present ice foot and about 0.5 m above high water mark. The site was on a knoll in an area subject to wind erosion and sand drifting and some of the artifacts were partially buried in sand.

The objects included a wooden box containing a small transit (with spare parts and tools), a small compass associated with the transit, an unopened tin of food, an enamelled metal cup and plate, a heavy metal canister with cork stopper of about 8-litre capacity, and a small pile of rock samples. Also emerging from the sand were what appeared to be tent canvas, some printed fabric, and a shirt or long underwear with wooden buttons and a German label. None of this partly buried material was disturbed, in anticipation of it being subjected to a proper archaeological investigation planned by the Nunavut government for the summer of 2004. There was no sign of firearms, a sledge, skeletal remains, tent poles or sleeping bags.

England and his party retrieved the transit and compass and sent them for identification and conservation to Dr. Randall Brooks, curator of scientific instruments at the Canada Science and Technology Museum in Ottawa. The latter was able to establish that the transit was manufactured by the Hildebrand-Wichmann-Werke in Freiberg between 1921 and 1925. It seems very probable that Krüger purchased the transit for his Hessian West Greenland Expedition in 1925 and again took it with him on his 1929-30 expedition.

Final interpretation of this campsite must await an archaeologist's report, but the provisional hypothesis advanced by Brooks and his co-authors seems very credible, namely that Krüger and party were camped at this site when a late spring snowstorm overwhelmed the tent. Unable to recover all their belongings due to deep snow, the men may then have been forced to abandon them and to flee onwards, presumably eastwards towards Bache Peninsula. If this hypothesis is correct, further traces of the expedition should be sought between this location and Bache Peninsula.

During the search for Krüger in 1932, sledge parties had travelled past the site of the abandoned camp on the sea ice a total of seven times. Paddy Hamilton and his companions had passed it both going and coming; the support party of Inuatuk and Seekeeunguaq had also passed it both going and coming; Harry had passed it once; and Kahdi and Ittukasuk had passed it twice on their journey from the north end of Ulvingen Island to retrieve the depot that had been left north of Cape Southwest. At least some of these parties would have been searching the coastline as they travelled, but given the scattered nature of the items and the fact that they were partially buried in sand, and possibly also hidden under snow, it is certainly not surprising that no one spotted them at the time.

Only the knoll on which the artifacts were found had emerged from the snow at the time of the visit by England and party. Further artifacts may well still lie beneath the snow in the adjacent snow-filled gullies. If so, the planned archaeological site-visit may recover any such items, in addition to what may be recovered from under the sand on the knoll.

8

MOVING TO CRAIG HARBOUR

THERE HAD BEEN SEVERAL DEVELOPMENTS at the detachment during Harry and Paddy Hamilton's absence from Bache Peninsula. When Paddy returned from his search patrol to Cornwall Island in May, he found Dr. M. Holm, the doctor from Thule, visiting the detachment.[1] Dr. Holm examined the Inughuit and their families at the detachment and gave useful advice on the medical supplies on hand. At his recommendation, it was decided that Kahdi's wife should return to Thule for an operation. Despite Kahdi's reluctance in this matter, he was discharged so that he could take his wife back to Greenland. Kahkachoo was also discharged at his own request on 24 May. Paddy Hamilton then engaged Ittukasuk and Seekeeunguaq in their places.

Much of the summer was spent preparing for the closure of the detachment at Bache Peninsula and the transfer to Craig Harbour. Paddy and Art

Munro were looking forward to the move since the hunting there was known to be better than at Bache Peninsula. It had become very evident that the number of narwhal and walrus visiting the fjords around Bache Peninsula had decreased since the detachment had been established in 1926. It was felt that the noise of motorboats and the smoke from the coal fires at the detachment were factors in this decline.

Unlike the other two, Harry was looking forward to heading home. While he had not had any chance to discuss his plans with Hilda, he undoubtedly was hoping to marry her as soon as possible. Still, he was keen also to leave Bache Peninsula in good order in case it were ever reoccupied. They cleaned and painted the buildings, overhauled the boat engines and painted the boats, and packed up all the stores, equipment and furniture. Then they hauled everything down to the shore in preparation for transferring it by sea to Craig Harbour. Even the massive cast-iron cook stove was hauled down to the beach[2] in anticipation of the arrival of the supply ship early in August.

As usual, the plan was to meet the supply ship at Fram Havn and so from late July onwards everyone was ready to head there by motorboat. Unfortunately, the ice in Buchanan Bay showed little sign of moving out. Every day, some of the group would climb to a vantage point to check on ice conditions, but day after day they returned with negative news. When a shore lead finally opened up, they decided to take a chance and to try to work the motorboat through to open water.

Leaving Seekeeunguaq and the two Inughuit wives at the detachment, Harry, Paddy, Art Munro, Nukappiannguaq and Kahkachoo set off at midnight on 26 July[3] (on 9 August, according to Harry[4]). Because of the floating ice, they started off poling the boat rather than using the engine. They were brought to a halt for several hours at a spot where massive pressure ice was jammed against sheer cliffs, but then a combination of the turn of the tide and a favourable wind opened a passage and they then had open water and a fair wind to Rice Strait.

The next 10 days were extremely frustrating. Smith Sound was still full of ice, although Harry felt that it would not have prevented the ship from reaching Fram Havn. Every day, he and his companions climbed to high points on the coast to the south of Pim Island and also Cape Sabine in hopes of spotting the ship, but the ship failed to appear. Nukappiannguaq had brought his kayak and spent some of his time hunting seals. Herds of walrus were often seen lying on floes, but no attempt was made to hunt them, since they did not anticipate needing any substantial amounts of dog food and because they could hunt walrus once they had reached Craig Harbour. Later, they were to regret this decision.[5]

Ultimately, and very reluctantly, Harry was forced to accept the fact that the ship was not going to arrive and that he and his companions would be spending another winter at Bache Peninsula. They built a cairn in which they placed a note with details of their long wait, then started back to the detachment. The ice had gone out from Buchanan Bay and they were able to reach the detachment by motorboat without difficulty.

Anticipating their practical requirements during a wintering, Harry started transporting coal to the detachment from Fram Havn and Cape Rutherford since there was almost no coal left at the detachment. During the rest of August and September, the motorboat made five round trips, transporting 5½ tonnes of coal and some provisions to the detachment. Throughout this period everyone kept a lookout for the supply ship and also missed no opportunity to hunt for dog food. On every trip they took a 19-foot dory in tow of the motorboat, on which they carried three kayaks so that the Inughuit could go after seal, walrus or narwhal if the opportunity offered. However, they only managed to take a few seals.

On the fourth trip in late August, ice delayed them for four days and completely prevented them from entering Rice Strait. They hauled the boats out at Cape Rutherford and walked to Fram Havn on 31 August. Their route took them high on a glacier and they had a good view of Smith Sound and even the Greenland coast. The range of vision, through binoculars, was estimated at about 100 km; the entire Sound was packed with ice and no water was visible. Not surprisingly, there was no sign of the supply ship, S.S. *Ungava*.[6]

Understandably, Hilda and Harry's family back in Gloucestershire became quite concerned when there was no news from him. Bill sent a telegram to Commissioner J.H. MacBrien on 6 November, asking for news. In his reply MacBrien reported:

> I beg to inform you that Corporal Stallworthy is still at Bache Peninsula. It had been planned to move the entire detachment from Bache Peninsula to Craig Harbour this summer, but owing to heavy ice conditions, it was not possible for the ship to get as far as Bache Peninsula.

The detachment will be moved next year, and I expect Corporal Stallworthy will be returning to civilization then.[7]

MacBrien then offered to arrange for any messages that Bill might have for Harry to be relayed to him by wireless. On December 3, Bill replied:

Dear Sir,

I thank you very much for your cable & for your letter explaining why my brother Corporal H.W. Stallworthy was unable to communicate with us in England. I fully understand the circumstances & as my Brother is such a good correspondent I knew that there must be some good reason why neither his Mother nor I had heard from him this Autumn.[8]

Bill also took advantage of the offer to have a message sent by radio:

Hello Harry.

Just heard you could not get your mail out this fall. Better luck next summer. Hope you are well. Cheer up. All the folks are O.K. at home. Mother living at Fairford now.

Love from all. Bill.[9]

Bill wrote to the Commissioner again on 3 and 13 December, asking that an almost identical message be transmitted to Bache Peninsula around Christmas or New Year's.[10] It was relayed for transmission to Station CKY in Winnipeg and Canadian Westinghouse in Montreal on 17 December 1932.[11]

Back at Bache Peninsula, the men received an indistinct radio message from the Commissioner via KDKA in Pittsburgh on 18 September. They were however able to decipher the fact that since *Ungava* had been unable to reach Bache Peninsula or even Fram Havn, the detachment's supplies had been landed at Craig Harbour. On reaching Smith Sound, *Ungava* had found it totally blocked by heavy ice. But it was only after 14 hours of searching for a route to Fram

Havn or Bache Peninsula that she had abandoned the attempt and made for Craig Harbour instead.[12] The message was repeated several times, more clearly, later.

This placed Harry in a real quandary. He felt it to be impracticable for the detachment personnel to attempt to sledge to Craig Harbour before the onset of winter, particularly since the two Inughuit women and three children would have to make the trip. However, staying at Bache Peninsula would involve some shortages: over the summer there had been little time for hunting since they had all been busy in preparing for the move or freighting coal or supplies. Thus they had little narwhal, walrus or seal meat on hand. And when they took stock of their own provisions and supplies, they realised that sugar, tea, coffee, tobacco and cigarettes would have be strictly rationed. They had run out of canned meat and bacon in June. Fortunately however, they had an abundance of flour.[13]

When the reserves of sugar were exhausted, they began using jams as sweeteners: they found that gooseberry jam went best in tea and raspberry jam in coffee. Later in life Harry would joke about imagining himself at an English tea party and seeing the reaction of the hostess when he requested gooseberry jam when asked, "And how do you take your tea?"[14]

Harry's past experience saved the day with regard to one critical shortage. Paddy Hamilton wrote that

by early winter we began to feel the pinch in some of the commodities used in cooking. Yeast was one of the first, when we found we had only two packets, or about eight cakes. In this case, it was Stallworthy, who had served in the Yukon and claimed to be a "sourdough," who came to the rescue. He took one cake of the yeast and made a batter to which he added some baking soda. Then he allowed the batter to ferment until it had filled the large crock in which he had made it. He then took half of the batter and proceeded to make bread in the usual way. To the remaining batter he added more flour, water and baking soda, allowed it to ferment again, and then put it out to freeze until next bread-making day. Munro and I were a bit sceptical that the batter would ever be any good after freezing, but we apologized handsomely to Stallworthy when the next bread-baking day came around, and the batter performed just as he had predicted it would. True, the bread had a somewhat sour taste, but it was bread, and definitely more palatable than a steady diet of bannock.[15]

The news that the ship would not be coming probably represented the hardest blow for Harry. He would have to wait another long year before he could marry Hilda. Paddy later suggested that it was in part to come to terms with this situation that Harry tried to keep himself busy in any way possible. When, after their fourth coal-hauling trip, ice conditions precluded any further trips to Rice Strait for a while, Harry went off to Jokel Fjord with the Inughuit to hunt narwhal. Unfortunately, the narwhal had already left the fjords, but the party did manage to get 13 ringed seals.

The final patrol by boat to Fram Havn on 19–21 September was quite an ordeal, but at least it greatly eased the situation with regard to dog food for the winter. On the way south, they found Buchanan Bay almost completely full of old ice, while new ice was forming on the leads. This greatly impeded their progress and on the evening of the 19th, a southwesterly gale blew up and the motorboat was driven quite some distance out to sea amidst heavy ice. They finally managed to get back ashore in the dark, but the boat had shipped a lot of water and everyone on board was soaked.

However, on the second day of their trip the weather was calm and clear and the ice had moved offshore. They spotted some 60 walrus in several groups, sleeping on floes off Cocked Hat Island. They managed to kill and retrieve 10 animals; three slipped off the floes but were harpooned and recovered. The other seven remained on their floes. To get these animals to shore, the Inughuit inflated the carcasses, which could then be towed behind the boat. New ice had started to form but by breaking the new ice ahead of the boat they managed to get ashore with all 10 animals, which represented some 7 tonnes of meat. Since there was a risk that freeze-up could prevent them from getting back to the detachment, cutting up the carcasses and caching some of the meat above high tide mark was a major task that could not be postponed.

On the way back to the detachment, they had to break new ice practically the whole way. To complicate the situation even further, one of the connecting rods in the boat's engine broke and they had to run on only one cylinder. The men took turns at breaking the ice ahead and on either side of the boat with axes and they hung fenders over the sides to protect the bilges, but even so the boat was still quite badly cut up and leaking before they reached the shores of the peninsula a few kilometres from the detachment. With the boat leaking quite alarmingly, they had to throw some meat and coal overboard and make for shore with the boat listing badly. They unloaded the rest of the cargo here, then headed for home. They had to break ice all the way and managed to get the boat ashore at the detachment with great difficulty.[16]

The 10 walrus were a real God-send, in that they ensured enough dog feed to last the winter. Walrus meat also appeared on the menu quite frequently at the detachment in lieu of canned meat and bacon, while walrus liver fried with dehydrated onions was a delicacy reserved especially for Wednesday dinners.

Harry and his men made numerous sledge patrols during the winter. Some were for the purpose of hauling dog feed (walrus and seal meat) to the detachment from various caches. These trips were usually only 50–65 km round-trip and involved only one night away from the detachment. They built snow houses at the caches and on these trips, Harry and his companions also established trap lines for white fox, checking their lines on the way out as well as on the way back with every trip. The bulk of the sledging was for the purpose of hauling stores from the detachment to Fram Havn so that they would be more accessible for shipment by sea to Craig Harbour. The trip was made 19 times during the winter, and involved a round trip of about 110 km with loaded sledges both ways. Anywhere from one to four teams would be involved in these trips. A heater was installed in the small building at Fram Havn so that the men could enjoy a comfortable night and walrus meat could be thawed out for feeding the dogs.

As usual at Christmas, the officers at Bache Peninsula hosted a dinner for the Inughuit and their families and exchanged gifts. Unfortunately, there was a lot of radio static that night and reception of the Christmas messages from the south was very disappointing. On 17 January Nukappiannguaq and Ittukasuk set off to cross to Greenland with a message to be relayed south by mail sledge to Godhavn and then by cable to the Commissioner in Ottawa. It was dated 10 January 1933:

> Expect carry out transfer to Craig in April. Nookapinguaq [Nukappiannguaq] and Ittukasuk leaving for Greenland. Arranging for former to return

with three other natives to assist in transfer. Dogs, present strength, twenty-three, and sufficient food, also two native teams. Provisions and trade stores very low. Have taken coal and provisions from NWT cache at Fram Havn. Particularly require three nought three (.303) soft and hard, also twenty two (.22) ammunition, large tarpaulin, radio peanut tubes and four B batteries. Connecting rod complete, number fifty three (53) and dry battery for Acadia engine, wet battery and coils for Ford, sleigh steel one and three quarters inches wide. Patrols last year, Hamilton, three sledges—west. My party, three sledges—north. Lifted Krueger's record from Peary's cairn at north west point of Axel Heigberg [sic] Island dated April twenty-fourth nineteen thirty signed by Krueger, Bjare and Akaioa [sic]. They had visited Lands Lock [sic] and intended proceeding to Meighen Island and had apparently decided against going further north on the Polar ice. Isachsen and Meighen islands not reached. Both patrols handicapped by bad ice and no game. Twenty-nine dogs died before return west coast Ellesmere. No trace of lost party seen on west coast Axel Heigberg [sic] or Cornwall Islands, Baumann Fjord or east coast Ellesmere. Mileage including Greenland Eskimos approx. three thousand. Temporarily employed natives returned Greenland paid. Heard and noted your message to NCO Dundas January First. Am endeavouring to place all important stores at Fram Havn this winter for shipment in case Bache inaccessible. Personnel well. Request parents be notified, also my friend Jasper, through Sergt. Bowen."[17]

The message reached Ottawa as a telegram on 4 May 1933 and the gist of it was relayed to Bill in England on 8 May.[18] Remarkably, he had already heard of Harry's message from coverage in the English newspapers of 6 May, as he reported in a letter of 7 June.[19]

Nukappiannguaq and Ittukasuk faced some very severe travelling conditions; the period of twilight around noon each day was still very short, and this was the coldest period of the year. On the outward journey they were held up by open water for nine days, but fortunately they managed to kill a bear and two walrus near the Greenland coast. They called at Etah, Robertson Fjord and Cape York where they handed Harry's message to the District Governor. On the return journey they were accompanied by two other Inughuit men and by Nukappiannguaq's new wife, formerly his step-mother, Enalunguaq, who had left Akkamalingwah in favour of his son; they got back to Bache Peninsula on 18 March. Harry was very impressed with this performance which he characterized as "a commendable trip."[20]

The reason why the two additional Inughuit had come over to Bache Peninsula was to help Ittukasuk travel back to Greenland with his wife, three children and their belongings for the sake of the children's education and at the request of the Danish authorities. They were to have travelled aboard *Ungava* the previous August, but now had to make the trip by dog sledge. They left on 22 March 1933.

The sun returned on 26 February and the next six weeks were spent hauling stores and equipment to Fram Havn and generally preparing for the move to Craig Harbour and for the closure of Bache Peninsula. Before the detachment was closed, they built a cairn in front of the living quarters and placed a Roll of Members who had served at the detachment in it. The information was extracted from previous Annual Reports and a copy of this record was also framed and hung in the house.[21] The detachment was officially closed on 12 April 1933 and Harry, Paddy and Art Munro set off by dog sledge for Fram Havn. Nukappiannguaq and Seekeeunguaq had been sent on there in advance with their wives and children to hunt in the area. The buildings of the detachment were left in a good state of repair with all doors and windows securely fastened. Harry felt that there was little likelihood of damage by bears, since they rarely visited the area.

On reaching Fram Havn, Harry found that the Inughuit had had no luck in hunting since blizzards had prevented them from going out to the floe edge. This meant that rations for the trip to Craig Harbour were rather slim. They had plenty of flour, lard and baking powder for making bannock, but only 1 lb each of tea and coffee and a 25 lb box of icing sugar. However, they did have two large sacks full of doughnuts, precooked and frozen.

After resting the dogs for one day, they headed south from Fram Havn, bound for Craig Harbour. On several occasions over the next few days, rough ice or open water forced them to head overland and/or across glaciers. One of these locations was at Cape Dunsterville[22] and on regaining the sea ice south of that cape they managed to kill a bear, the first fresh meat of the trip; men and dogs ate their fill. Crossing the mouth of Makinson Inlet, they spotted Clarence Head ahead of them, but before reaching it open water forced them to cross another glacier. They killed another bear on the sea ice southwest of Clarence Head and having passed through Glacier Strait they camped for the night just northeast of King Edward Point. On the following day, just beyond King Edward Point, they ran across the fresh tracks of two sledges heading in the opposite direction; the party had consisted of two white men and one Inuk. Over the winter, the men at Bache Peninsula had intercepted a message to Corporal Dersch and Constable Fraser at Dundas Harbour with orders that they should make a patrol to Craig Harbour in the spring to see if the party from Bache Peninsula had arrived. If they had not, Dersch and Fraser were to continue to Bache Peninsula to see whether the patrols in search of Krüger had returned safely. They therefore deduced that these tracks must be those of the patrol from Dundas Harbour.[23] Assuming that Dersch and his companions would run across their tracks fairly soon and turn back, Harry and his party continued to the Craig Harbour detachment, arriving on 23 April.

The buildings at Craig Harbour—a living hut, store hut, blubber house and outhouse—were found to be in relatively good repair, especially considering that they had been unoccupied since 1926. However, the kitchen door had again been smashed, presumably by a bear, and quite a few windows were broken and the stove pipes were nearly rusted through. Paddy Hamilton described the site as follows:

> Contrary to its name Craig Harbour can scarcely be classed as a harbour, inasmuch as the only shelter is Smith Island, which lies out to sea to the northwest a distance of nearly two miles. The post is located in a V-shaped valley with a large glacier at its head, the face of which is about a mile wide. In the summer time the glacier feeds a small river which empties into the harbour close to the detachment and supplies the fresh water during the months of July and August. The buildings themselves are built on a sandbar. During very high tides they are virtually on an island.[24]

Harry and his companions were not slow to make the most of the abundance of supplies. While the dogs gorged themselves on some ancient bacon mixed with walrus fat, the men regaled themselves with bacon, eggs, and fresh bread that Corporal Dersch had baked and left, washed down with vast quantities of tea and coffee.

A few days later, Dersch and his party returned. They had run across the Bache Peninsula party's tracks and followed them back to Craig Harbour. It was a real pleasure for both parties, having seen very few new faces for several years. When Dersch offered to supply such items as paint, putty and window glass that were needed to get the Craig Harbour buildings into first-class shape before ship time, it was decided to send a party back south to Dundas Harbour with him and his companions.[25] The route would take them across Jones Sound then over the Devon Island Ice Cap, this being the standard route used by RCMP patrols between the two detachments since it had been pioneered by Staff-Sergeant A.H. Joy in 1926. Harry took both Paddy and Art Munro with him. The combined party left Craig Harbour on the afternoon of 4 May 1933; the going on the ice of Jones Sound was excellent and the caravan of sledges reached Belcher Point (where they camped) in seven hours. Here they were joined by Nukappiannguaq and Seekeeunguaq who had been on a hunting trip and had killed a bear further west.

In the morning they started up the Belcher Glacier and made good progress across the summit of the ice cap, which rises to 1878 m. Visibility was excellent and they could use the *nunataks* of the Cunningham Mountains protruding from the southern edge of the ice cap as reference points. Guided by Dersch and by Nukappiannguaq (who had crossed the ice cap in both directions with Staff-Sergeant Joy in 1926) they easily located the Dundas Harbour Glacier and by fitting "rough locks" on the sledge runners they safely negotiated its steep front:

these [rough locks] were made with heavy manilla rope and had to be used under the runners for over a mile and turned occasionally to prevent the rope cutting through on the ice.

In descending the last 100 yards to the foot of the glacier where the snow was smooth and hard we rode on the komiticks to add pressure on the rough locks and dragged the teams behind; an accident might easily occur under these conditions if the dogs were not kept under proper control, as the foot of most glaciers, particularly the active ones, is usually a sheer drop where ice bergs have broken off, and it [is] difficult to get into a position to see the danger from above.[26]

RCMP detachment, Dundas Harbour, Devon Island, 1933.

They reached the bottom of the glacier in the late evening of 7 May and arrived at the detachment very shortly afterwards, having crossed the island in under 23 hours of actual travelling time (two-and-a-half days including stops).

After a pleasant week during which they enjoyed the hospitality of Dundas Harbour and loaded paint, putty, window glass, etc. on their sledges, Harry and his party started back north in the early morning of 14 May, planning to follow the same route in reverse. But by then the weather had changed. A heavy overcast, heavy snowfall and a headwind combined to slow progress drastically; since the sun was obscured for much of the time, maintaining a course on the featureless ice cap was difficult and by the time they reached the crest they were in fact several kilometres too far east. But at this point some clearing allowed Harry to make a correction. Fortunately, the visibility improved on the north side and a day of hard sledging through the new snow took them back down the Belcher Glacier to Jones Sound where they camped at Belcher Point. The weather in Jones Sound was calm and brilliant, in marked contrast to conditions on the ice cap where, as they could see on looking back, it was still blowing and snowing. However, open water dictated a substantial detour to the west to beyond Cape Sparbo, then north to the mouth of Grise Fjord.[27] The party finally reached Craig Harbour safely on the afternoon of 17 May.

This brief description of Harry's double-crossing of the Devon Ice Cap conceals or downplays the real hazards of this route. During Joy's initial crossing in 1926, two dog teams had fallen down crevasses; all the dogs were hauled out except one whose trace broke.[28] In 1932, Corporal Dersch had to abandon an attempt at crossing the ice cap from south to north because Jones Sound and the north coast of Devon Island were totally obscured by fog, but he managed to return safely to Dundas Harbour.[29] In 1935 Corporal H. Kearney was not even able to reach the ice cap on a trip from Craig Harbour to Dundas Harbour due to open water which prevented him from reaching the snout of the Belcher Glacier.[30] And in 1946, in an attempt to travel from Dundas Harbour to Craig Harbour, Constable H.M. MacLeod initially got so badly off course in very heavy weather that he reached the east coast above Hyde Inlet instead of the north coast. Having corrected his mistake, he and his party were descending the wrong outlet glacier on the north coast (one near Cape Caledon) when Special Constable Malla barely escaped death when the snow over a crevasse collapsed and he was left with the lower half of his body dangling over a drop of unknown depth. At this point MacLeod abandoned his trip and returned to Dundas Harbour.[31]

From his own experience of glacier-travel, Harry was fully cognizant of the very real hazards. In his patrol report he included very sage advice for any future patrols, who

> between Craig Harbour and Dundas Harbour would do well to be prepared for five days on the Ice Cap, as fair visibility is essential to make the crossing where wind and fog is prevalent; a party could easily travel in a wrong direction and get into a crevassed area. The distance is approximately 90 miles [144 km] and the crossing could be made in fair weather with good dogs in two days with one night camp on the top.[32]

One of the highest priorities now was to lay in a sufficient reserve of dog feed for the officers who would be relieving Harry, Paddy and Art Munro. There was some urgency here since there were no boats at Craig Harbour and the hunting would all have to be done before the ice went out. Consequently, Nukappiannguaq and Seekeeunguaq were dispatched to hunt at every oppor-

Some of Harry's team, Dundas Harbour, Devon Island 1933.

tunity. Harry accompanied them on one of these trips to Coburg Island only a couple of weeks after returning from the trip to Dundas Harbour.[33] The Inughuit set off on the early morning of 3 June with two teams; Harry started in the afternoon with 12 dogs. He secured a bearded seal at King Edward Point and returned with it to the detachment, starting out again around midnight. This time he covered only about 15 km before shooting another bearded seal in a pool of water near a large iceberg; this one he cached under the snow, but unfortunately a bear discovered it before he returned. The weather was fine and the dogs were pulling well and on reaching Smith Island he found a camp which the Inughuit had left only a few hours earlier. He gave his dogs a feed from a bear the Inughuit had killed and cached at the campsite. Then after a rest of two hours he crossed to the north end of Coburg Island.

Having travelled down the west coast of the island and having crossed the isthmus of Kent Peninsula, Harry found open water as far as he could see on the south side of the island. Nukappiannguaq and Seekeeunguaq had established a camp and had already killed two bears that they had found sleeping on the ice foot. On 6 June all three men travelled along the shore ice to the southwest point of the island where they found thousands of murres, gulls and a few eiders. That evening Nukappiannguaq killed a walrus on a floe that was then manoeuvred close to the ice foot so that the meat could be transported ashore at high tide. Harry noted that many walrus could easily be procured here, but in view of the large number of bears, caching them securely would be a problem. He therefore decided to wait to try to get dog feed for the winter closer to the detachment.

The three teams started back for Craig Harbour about midnight on 8 June and had to battle a headwind all the way. They reached the detachment safely on the afternoon of the 11th, having made a useful reconnaissance of the hunting prospects of the area covering about 400 km.

On 7 June, Bill Stallworthy had included a message to be sent by radio to Craig Harbour in his letter to the Commissioner:

Hello, Harry, old boy. Delighted to have confirmation of radio message from Godhaven & know that you are O.K. Hoping you will get out this summer, and that we may see you next Fall. All are well at the Mill. Mother very well and happy at Fairford. All send love and best wishes for your safe return. Your affectionate Brother, Bill.[34]

This message was forwarded on 19 June for transmission to Craig Harbour via Canadian Westinghouse in Montreal,[35] although it was recognized that the broadcasting season to the Far North was over for the season as reception tended to be very poor during the period of continuous daylight.

Over the remainder of the summer Harry and his companions spent a great deal of time sprucing up the buildings. They stripped the exteriors of the buildings with wire brushes and then applied a primer coat of linseed oil and two coats of paint; the interior of the living quarters was also given two coats of paint. The rubberoid roofing on both buildings was in quite good repair, but it too was given two coats of paint.[36] As Paddy Hamilton recalled, "Constable Munro added the finishing touch by making a new RCMP sign, which he placed to the left and in line with the top of the door. It made us feel part of the Force again, instead of the nomads we had become after leaving Bache."[37]

During her visit the previous fall, *Ungava* had landed lumber for building two huts for the Inughuit or Baffin Island Inuit employees and a blubber shed. The lumber had been unloaded on the beach near the store house, but unfortunately it had been buried under a deep, hard snowdrift. Initially it could not even be found and even when it was located, it was found that the lower part of the stack of lumber was encased in ice. Retrieving it was a very slow process and in the end, Harry discovered that they could not erect the buildings in any case since no nails had been delivered with it, and there were none on hand.

On the other hand, the *Ungava* had delivered a dog pen or "corral" as Harry termed it. He and his companions set about erecting it as soon as the snow had gone. Harry anticipated that it would be very useful for segregating bitches in heat at times of the year (fall and early winter) when it was inopportune for them to be bred since the pups would be born in the dead of winter.

During these final few months at Craig Harbour, Harry must have been very impatient waiting for the ship to arrive. By this time he had been on Ellesmere Island for three years and he was naturally longing to see Hilda again. He had made up his mind to propose to her and if this were not sufficient reason for wanting to get back south, he had been suffering acutely from haemorrhoids for most of the final year in the North.[38]

Around 4.00 A.M. one morning in late August the smoke from a ship was spotted out in Jones Sound. It was the Hudson's Bay Company's supply ship *Nascopie*, captained by Tom Smellie and chartered by the Canadian government for the Eastern Arctic Patrol. Initially her boats could not reach the detachment because of a wide belt of ice that had drifted into the bay. Harry solved this rather frustrating dilemma by taking a small skiff that had been found damaged but had been repaired for hunting and by hauling it over the ice and navigating leads to get past the ice barrier. Since there was not enough room in the boat for everyone, Harry took with him only Munro, Nukappiannguaq and Seekeeunguaq, leaving Paddy and the two Inughuit women at the detachment. As Paddy recalled the situation, when the skiff approached the ship this decision caused some consternation:

> While they were still quite a way from the ship those on board realized the party consisted of two white men and two Eskimo. They all knew there should be three white men at the detachment and therefore the question on everyone's tongue was what had happened to the missing man. As they drew closer some of the police on board recognized Stallworthy and Munro, and with the missing one identified there were all sorts of conjectures concerning my well-being or demise. Stallworthy told me afterwards he could not imagine why the greetings he received were rather subdued until Inspector Sandys-Wunsch

drew him aside almost at once and asked, "What happened to Hamilton?" Even after the explanation had been given everyone seemed to think I must be properly "bushed" not to have gotten out to the boat some way or other after being marooned for two years.[39]

The space in the boat was not the only reason why Paddy stayed behind. He was also reluctant to meet the strangers because that would mean having to explain to the Inspector why he was missing some of his front teeth. Paddy and Harry had generally got along extremely well together, although Paddy would irritate Harry with the mess he would make in the kitchen when baking or cooking, whereas Harry was known throughout his life as a particularly neat, tidy cook. But something Paddy had done or said one night shortly before *Nascopie* arrived had provoked Harry into hitting him: "I just decked him!" he would tell people afterwards, "Knuckle sandwich, right between the eyes. And knocked out a couple of teeth too."[40] And although Paddy's black eyes had faded by the time the ship arrived, the gap in his teeth was still very evident. Despite this, the two men remained the best of friends for the rest of their lives.

Once the ice opened sufficiently, *Nascopie*'s scows began ferrying supplies and equipment for the detachment ashore. Apart from the normal supplies for the year, all the equipment, supplies and furnishings from Dundas Harbour had also been brought north, since the latter detachment was being closed. Corporal Kearney, Constable Fisher and two Inuit from Pond Inlet would man the Craig Harbour detachment for the coming year. Having put them ashore, the *Nascopie* put to sea again. Harry, Paddy and Art Munro were fervently hoping that they would be able to retrieve their personal belongings from Fram Havn. According to Paddy, the *Nascopie* was unable to get there due to ice, but Harry placed the blame on Inspector Sandys-Wunsch. Harry was particularly keen to retrieve his personal belongings because they included almost 5,000 feet of cine film of everyday activities that he had shot during his three years in the High Arctic. But perhaps more importantly, they included 214 white fox pelts that he had trapped during the three winters. Setting and checking his traps could often be combined with trips to fetch meat from caches, but nonetheless the 214 pelts represented a considerable cost in terms of discomfort and hardship, in that the pelts are prime only in winter during the dark period when the temperatures are lowest and travelling conditions at their worst. Harry estimated variously that he should be able to recoup $2,000 or even $3,000 from these fox pelts[41] and he saw this as a useful amount on which to start married life.

But there was an even worse aspect to the issue of Harry's fox pelts. Inspector Joy had retired and his replacement, Inspector Sandys-Wunsch ("a perfect ass" in Harry's view) had issued a decree that fox-trapping activities by members of the northern detachments represented "a profitable business which is against R[ules] & R[egulations]"[42] and had confiscated all furs that other members had brought south, giving the proceeds to the Police Benefit Fund. As a sop to the northern officers, however they were to be allowed to trap and keep six pelts per man per year. Thus Harry would be entitled to only 18 of his 214 pelts!

Ironically, therefore, Harry's fur harvest was in fact safer where it was. In early June Inspector V.A.M. Kemp had written to the Officer Commanding "O" Division in Montreal to say that

in view of the fact that the personnel stationed at Bache Peninsula are being relieved this summer, I am directed to call your attention to the question of due investigation being made as to any activities in the matter of trading fur that may have been carried out by the men.

The Commissioner directs that if the circumstances warrant it, they are to be disciplined.[43]

Harry saw the proceeds from his fur-trapping as a useful "nest-egg" on which to get married, and it could not have been easy for him to break the news to Hilda:

The Force have (or are going to) taken all my fur away. And Hilda, dear, it was for our future that I worked hard at trapping and had many tough trips in the dark. I thought I was sitting pretty with my fur catch, when Wunsch upset everything. You see, my fur, worth about $3,000 at least, is a total loss, except for 18 pelts which I (according to the new regulations) am entitled to keep. The thought of it just burns me up. I don't want to moan to you, dear, in a letter. It has been hard for me, dear, to tell you this, before we can make our final plans for the future. We must have a serious talk.[44]

Is there even a hint in these last sentences that Harry felt that they might have to postpone or even cancel their wedding plans?

After calling at Thule, where Nukappiannguaq and Seekeeunguaq and their wives were put ashore,[45] and at Pangnirtung in Cumberland Sound, the *Nascopie* ran south to St. John's, Newfoundland, arriving there on 28 September. Returning to civilization presented a unique problem to the three officers from Bache Peninsula—their wardrobe. As Paddy explained the situation:

> Stallworthy, Munro and myself were thoroughly enjoying the trip out on the ship, which would have been perfect except for one thing. We had no decent clothes. When we had come aboard we were wearing the same clothes we had donned at Bache Peninsula to make the trip to Craig Harbour: heavy wool shirts, bearskin pants, skin boots and parkas. All our uniforms and civilian clothing were in our trunks at Fram Havn, where it now looked as though they would remain until the end of time. Meanwhile we went around amongst our fellow passengers looking like refugees from a destitute Eskimo camp. At last Constable Munro was fitted out by Corporal MacBeth in a civilian suit, and since they were about the same size and build he looked quite dapper again. Then Corporal Kerr dug down to the bottom of his trunk and came up with a civilian suit for me. However, we definitely were not the same size or build, and I now looked as though I had had a ducking. In spite of the fact my arms stuck out of the sleeves three or four inches, and the trousers barely covered the calves of my legs, and I was afraid to bend over to pick up anything from the floor, I felt as though I had shed an old skin. Poor Stallworthy, though, was so tall he could find nothing on board that would anywhere near fit him, and so he had to continue wearing his bearskin pants. Our first business after docking in St. John's was to visit a men's clothing store to purchase enough of an outfit so that we could arrive in Ottawa without being picked up for vagrancy.[46]

From St. John's, the three officers caught the train to Port aux Basques, then took the ferry to North Sydney and finally boarded the train to Ottawa.

9

MARRIAGE

and Honeymoon

THE PAST THREE YEARS on Ellesmere Island had been filled with adventure and Harry had been preoccupied with keeping himself and all the other people at the detachment alive. His initial plans for proposing to Hilda had been derailed when he had to spend an unintended additional year in the Arctic. Then the changed regulations regarding trapping in the Arctic threatened to swipe his nest egg from under his nose. It seemed as if his efforts to marry the girl of his dreams were doomed. Still, he did not give up and determined that this time he would to get it right. During the *Nascopie*'s slow progress south, Harry composed a wonderfully tender and sensitive letter of proposal to Hilda, who was still teaching in Jasper:

When the mail sacks were opened I found myself wanting to see your hand writing on an envelope. None of the others mattered, after two years of silence. But three years is a long time to hope that a young and desirable girl will still be free to say yes to a man with such a strange desire to see more and more of the Arctic.

I know now that, above all, you matter more to me than anything in my life and my future. I have crisscrossed Canada and the Arctic from the 49 parallel to near the North Pole, and from Halifax to Vancouver. Now I know that you are still there feeling as I do about our future together. I will have a lot of official business to attend to when I finally reach Ottawa—but when I am free I will take the first train west to see my dear little pal and to ask her parents (especially your mother) for their permission to marry you.[1]

...My thoughts are racing ahead of the slow progress of this ship. You are now 5 years older than you were when I said goodbye to you in Jasper. We both knew that we would have married then if our future had been more secure. But in the meantime my little pal has had time to grow up. I have always been so proud of your independent spirit and your ability to "paddle your own canoe." You have proved that and I am proud that you still want to join me in our future together. Darling, every time I took a fox out of a trap I thought: "There's another chair or something for our home. Maybe the wheel of a new car." There's almost too much pleasure in the years ahead of us. But most of all, I love you—just as much or more than when I left you in Edmonton 3 years ago. While I am held up in Ottawa we can write often and sort out our plans and feelings until we are free to meet and I can wrap you up in a big polar bear hug. Sweetheart, after so many years I can wait, but it's wonderful to know that you are waiting too. How can I be so lucky?

Harry anticipated that his official duties (writing reports, drafting maps, etc.) connected with his three years on Ellesmere Island would take some time. But as soon as this was done, he planned to travel out to Alberta to talk to Hilda's parents, get married and spend their honeymoon in Montreal or New York before travelling to England to introduce Hilda to his mother and family.

Hilda, however had other plans; she cabled Harry to say that she planned to resign from her job at Jasper and come east to Ottawa. This news was most welcome to Harry, but caught him completely by surprise. He cabled back: "Your wire almost broke me up. The idea that you would resign and come to me was a bit of a shock."[2]

If Hilda's decision to come to Ottawa had caught Harry off-guard, the news that waited for him in Ottawa would complicate matters considerably. As early as 18 July 1933, Acting Superintendent V.A.M. Kemp had written to the O.C. of "C" Division in Montreal to the effect that:

The Commissioner is desirous that Corporal Stallworthy, on his return to civilization, should communicate with Mr. Edward A.A. Shackleton, whose address is Hampton Court Palace, Middlesex, England, or Magdalen College, Oxford, England.

Mr. Shackleton is contemplating undertaking exploration work on the northern part of Ellesmere Island next year, and the Commissioner would like Corpl. Stallworthy to communicate with him, giving him any information which he may desire regarding conditions in that district. In the event of Corporal Stallworthy proceeding to England on leave Mr. Shackleton would be glad if he would call on him for a personal interview.[3]

However, once he had arrived in Ottawa, Harry discovered that his involvement might well be more than just a chat with Shackleton over a pint or two in an Oxford pub. He explained the situation as best he could in a letter to Hilda:

One thing the Comm. wanted to talk about was a proposed expedition to Northern Ellesmere next year. A bunch of Oxford men with a son of the late Sir Ernest Shackleton (explorer). The Comm. seems to have it cut and dried that I will take leave to England. He knew my home is near Oxford University and wants me to see Shackleton.

...When talking with George Hann (Sec. to the RCMP) he told me the Shackleton party has asked for a member of the Force to accompany the Exped. and that I am the most eligible for the job.[4]

While Harry was fully aware that this would mean a further 18 months or more of separation, the challenge of participating in such an expedition was simply too appealing and it is clear that Harry was already prepared to make this sacrifice: "I know that we must not put off our lives for another two years and yet I seem to be fated to spend another two years in the Arctic which will mean leaving you alone again."[5]

These personal problems aside, Harry was still dealing with a more immediate and pressing physical problem that needed attention. On 10 October he reported on Sick Parade at the RCMP Headquarters at Rockcliffe (Ottawa), complaining of haemorrhoids—an ailment which he reported had been troubling him for 15 years and that was getting progressively worse. The RCMP surgeon decided that an operation was necessary.[6] On 30 October he was admitted to Ottawa Civic Hospital for a haemorrhoid operation that was performed successfully the following day; Harry was discharged "cured" on 9 November.[7] As he admitted in a letter to Bill: "I had quite a time of it that last year up north....I think [the operation] was quite successful but, Gee, it was painful for a few days afterwards. The old btm. is getting quite comfortable again now & I'm going back to Rockcliffe [RCMP barracks] tomorrow."[8]

With that matter taken care of, Harry now had another matter on his mind. On 30 October he had written to Superintendent Tupper who was in charge of the "N" Division, requesting permission to get married.[9] Tupper forwarded the request to the Commissioner, who approved Harry's marriage plans.[10] At least one person besides the intended couple seemed to want to keep his plans intact!

Although Harry and Hilda would not learn of it until after their wedding, Commissioner James MacBrien also set the wheels in motion to honour Harry with a unique and enduring wedding gift. On 24 October 1933 he proposed that the northernmost cape of Axel Heiberg Island, where Nansen Sound opens into the Arctic Ocean and where Harry and his Inughuit companions had searched for traces of Krüger's expedition just before reaching Cape Thomas Hubbard in the spring of 1932, be named Cape Stallworthy. The name was officially approved by the Geographical Names Board on 5 December 1933.[11]

Despite Harry's news about the possibility of yet another protracted Arctic expedition, Hilda was not put off. She resigned her teaching position in Jasper on 29 October and caught the next train to Edson to see her parents.[12]

Hilda and Harry's wedding, St. Martin's in the Glebe, Ottawa, November 1933.

She did not tell them she was coming and may well not have discussed her plans with them. She arrived unannounced at Edson and walked up to the rectory alone through the snow. She spent two weeks at home and on the evening of 16 November, just before she was due to depart for Ottawa an old family friend, Canon Goulding, came to visit. The visit was probably prearranged, for as Hilda noted in her diary, he took the opportunity

> to give me a fatherly warning that I might be making an awful mistake as I hadn't seen "this fellow" for 3 years and might find that our feelings had changed. I said 'If our feelings have changed we'll know it and I'll come back. But, Canon dear, I won't be back. This man will *not* have changed.'[13]

Hilda caught the train from Edmonton on the evening of Friday 17 November and reached Ottawa early on Monday 20th. Her diary entry for that day reads: "At 6.30 I got off the train and there was Harry—just the same as though 3 years had been 3 days—through the tunnel to Château Laurier. We are both overcome at seeing each other."[14]

They were married at 11.30 that morning by Canon Jefferson at St Matthew's in the Glebe; the only others present were their two witnesses, Art Munro and Bob Bowen. That evening Hilda and Harry had an intimate dinner in a small French restaurant across the river in Hull, then spent the night at the Château Laurier.

On the 21st they rode the train to Montreal for a week's honeymoon, staying at the Windsor Hotel on Dominion Square. Hilda was entirely convinced that she had made the right choice: "We have started a wonderful honeymoon and a wonderful future together. It has all been worth our long separation to be together and so happy.... He's an unbelievable person. So real and so unreal."[15]

Although Harry did not know it at this stage, the wheels were already in motion to give him, Paddy Hamilton and Art Munro further recognition for their activities on Ellesmere Island. On 5 November 1933 the Commissioner Sir James MacBrien had written first to the Minister in Control of the RCMP and then to the Under-Secretary of State, recommending the three men for the King's Police Medal.[16] In his letters the Commissioner stressed their efforts in their searches for Krüger, their enforced unexpected wintering at

Harry on board Beringia *on his honeymoon, 1933.*

Bache Peninsula on short commons and the impressive way in which they had tackled the unscheduled move by dog team from Bache Peninsula to Craig Harbour. But apart from letters of acknowledgement there was no immediate reaction to the Commissioner's letters.

A while later, they also received official recognition for their efforts from Germany. In January, the German consul, L. Kempff, wrote to O.D. Skelton, Under-Secretary of State for External Affairs:

> I have been instructed to express to the Canadian Government and to the members of the expedition sent out to search for Dr. Krueger and his companions the sincere thanks of the German Government for their unselfish readiness and bravery in undertaking the search for the lost explorers.[17]

In the interim Harry and Hilda had caught the train from Montreal to New York on 28 November and had boarded the Cunard liner *Beringia* which

was due to sail the next day. The ship encountered some rough seas on 2 and 3 December and Hilda was very seasick. She was extremely glad to reach Southampton on the 5th. Her first impression of England were very positive:

> Everything is so exciting to me and so natural to Harry. He keeps my feet on the ground and we're so very happy—it's unbelievable that it is just as I expected it to be.[18]

On the 6th they took the train to Oxford and then on to Kemble, where Harry's brother Bill met them after dark and drove them to Fairford, where Harry's mother gave them a very warm welcome at "Milton Lodge, a neat comfortable 3 storey townhouse—heated with fireplaces in the living rooms—very cold bedrooms."[19]

Hilda spent much of the following day "getting acquainted" with Mrs. Stallworthy and vice-versa. That evening Rose, the cook, who had been with

Mrs. Stallworthy for 25 years, served "Harry's favourite dinner—a large leg of lamb—perfection."

On 8 December Edward Shackleton, son of the Antarctic explorer Sir Ernest Shackleton and the undergraduate organiser of the Oxford University Ellesmere Land Expedition, and A. W. Moore, the expedition's biologist and photographer, came to discuss things with Harry at Fairford. The Oxford University Exploration Club, which was mounting the expedition, was founded in 1927 with John Buchan (later Lord Tweedsmuir) as its president. In the intervening years it had mounted expeditions to West Greenland (1928), British Guiana (1929), Norwegian Lapland (1930), Hudson Strait (1931) and Sarawak (1932). In 1933 the Club mounted three expeditions: to Abyssinia, New Hebrides and Spitsbergen.[20] Both Shackleton and Moore had been members of the 1932 expedition to Sarawak and between them had conceived the idea of an expedition to the Arctic. Initially they had in mind a summer expedition to Spitsbergen, but when they heard that another expedition was heading there they switched their attention to Ellesmere Island at the suggestion of Professor J. M. Wordie who would himself be leading an expedition to Baffin Bay and Devon Island. Since the expedition would clearly involve work on glaciers, they invited the botanist Dr. G. Noel Humphreys to lead it. Although all his previous experience had been in the tropics, where he had discovered the source of the White Nile, he was also known for his mountain and glacier work in the Ruwenzori Mountains.

As early as 18 September 1933 (i.e., while Harry was still travelling south aboard the *Nascopie*) Eddie Shackleton had addressed a meeting of the Northwest Territories Council in Ottawa on the topic if his current plans for the expedition.[21] The main aim of the expedition was to explore and map Grant Land, the area of northern Ellesmere Island that lay between Lake Hazen and the Arctic Ocean and to conduct geological and biological research in that area. The expedition would consist of five members—Humphreys and Shackleton, a biologist, a geologist and, it was hoped, an RCMP officer who was familiar with the area.

As early as 5 July 1933 Eddie had received a promise of assistance "by word and deed" from the Greenland Administration[22] and his plan was to travel with their vessel from Copenhagen to Disko. From there Knud Rasmussen had provisionally offered to transport the expedition north to his trading post at Thule and possibly across to Bache Peninsula[23]; less realistically, if ice conditions permitted there were even hopes of establishing a wintering base at Fort Conger on Lady Franklin Bay. Failing this, the plan was to establish a temporary base at or near Etah and then to transport all the supplies and equipment across to Bache Peninsula by dog sledge after freeze-up. The expedition hoped to winter in the RCMP detachment buildings there while preparing for sledging in the spring. The main field party would set off in March, bound for Lake Hazen where a secondary base would be established. Two possible routes were proposed: one north across the Grinnell Land Ice Cap (now the Agassiz Ice Cap) to the northeast end of Greely Fjord and then north to Lake Hazen; the other up Flagler Fjord and across Sverdrup Pass to Bay Fjord and then north via Eureka Sound and Greely Fjord. From Lake Hazen the most competent mountaineers would locate a route across the United States Range; they would triangulate the main mountains and the coastline of Grant Land and investigate its geology. They planned to be back at Bache Peninsula by 1 June at the latest, hoping to beat the snowmelt. The total estimated budget of the expedition was £2,000. One item of the budget (£100) was listed as "Special expenses, possible wages to Eskimo"; at this stage it was not determined whether these might be from Greenland or from Baffin Island. It was felt that permission of the respective governments would be the deciding factor.

Eddie sent his proposed plan for the expedition to the RCMP Commissioner J.H. MacBrien on 28 October 1933. MacBrien forwarded the plan to the O.C. "N" Division on 13 November, asking that he pass it to Harry and asking the latter to comment on it.[24] Harry responded on 17 November with comments on many points raised in the plan.[25] He pointed out that if the expedition was hoping to cross Smith Sound aboard the Greenland supply ship, the crossing would have to happen no later than 20 August as ice would prevent any ship from reaching Bache Peninsula in September (which was when Shackleton proposed to make the trip). Harry also described the idea of hauling the expedition's supplies across to Bache Peninsula by dog sledge or boat as "*entirely impracticable*" since "the ice is usually very rough in this area; it is considered a difficult trip when hauling only dog food and Patrol equipment."[26] Harry felt that the Bache Peninsula buildings would make an excellent expedition base although "for five or six men it would be rather crowded." He also strongly supported the idea that a member of the force who had extensive Arctic experience be attached to the expedition, especially in view of the recent fate of the Krüger expedition.

Further, he recommended that two or three families of Inughuit winter with the expedition, including wives and children. The wives, he noted were indispensable in making and mending clothing. He felt that four dog teams of 12–16 dogs each would be needed for the major journey. As to the timing of the latter, he indicated that they would need about three months (15 March–15 June) and that if they planned to cross back to Greenland before break-up they should be back at Bache Peninsula by 1 June at the latest. As to the proposed route, he categorically vetoed the suggested route over the ice cap to Lake Hazen—in part because of the crevassed area the expedition would have to negotiate to reach the ice cap and the heavy snow that would be encountered on the ice cap, and in part because of the impossibility of procuring dog food on the ice cap. He strongly advocated the alternate route via Bay Fjord, Eureka Sound and Greely Fjord as being "as far as I know the best and perhaps the only practicable route into Lake Hazen with dog teams." The Inughuit had told him that large fish were abundant in Lake Hazen and that caribou were available in the area, hence these were potential sources of dog food there.

In his plan Shackleton had suggested that the geologist (he had a Canadian in mind at this point) and the RCMP officer might join the expedition at Disko or at Robertson Fjord; Harry did not see how this could be achieved since the Canadian Eastern Arctic supply ship did not usually call at Disko and when it did, it could be as late as 10 September—too late to catch the Danish government ship on its way north to Thule and Etah. Any Canadian members would have to join the expedition in England. Finally, Harry pointed out that he was heading for England on furlough in early December (for his honeymoon) and that he would then contact Shackleton. He would be happy to show him and other members of the expedition photos he had taken on Ellesmere Island and the movie film he had shot in 1930–31.

When Shackleton and Moore arrived at the Stallworthy's house in Fairford on 8 December to discuss their plans with Harry, he was intimately aware of every detail of the planning. While Harry may have been enthusiastic about the proposed endeavour, Hilda was more sober in her assessment of the visitors. She wrote in her diary: "They seem very young and make me think of Boy Scouts planning a summer hike into the wilderness. They have no idea what they are up against. If they ever do go on this arctic adventure."[27]

A week later, on 15 December, the entire family went into Cirencester to the cinema where, by special arrangement, they viewed the film that Harry had shot on Ellesmere Island in 1930–31 at the Picture House. Harry must have sent it out with the supply ship in 1931 "and because of age [the images] are very blurry and disappointing to Harry."[28]

They spent Christmas Day at "The Mill" in Ampney Crucis, home of Harry's brother Bill. Hilda's impressions were to the point: "Susy [Bill's wife] is very uptight and fussy. Roast beef dinner—no Christmas decorations or festivities—but lots of *talk* with Harry entertaining them. Quite an interesting uncle—home from the Arctic."[29] On Boxing Day Harry and Hilda went to see the start of a fox hunt at Eastington House, which was quite a novel spectacle for Hilda:

> Sherry and onlookers. Very exciting to see the riders in red coats, britches, boots. Dogs milling around—baying; the huntsmen keeping them under control. People walking around talking—patting horses' flanks. I kept myself clear of their heels. They look so huge. Then away they streamed across the road—over the wall; dogs baying; horses hoofs; flying red jackets.[30]

Hilda's nervousness in the presence of horses stemmed from the fact that she had been kicked in the forehead as a child in Wetaskiwin.[31] Despite her fear, she nevertheless accompanied Harry to another hunt meet at Fairford Park on 2 January 1934.

A few days later Harry attended the annual dinner of the Cirencester Old Grammarians in the King's Head Hotel Assembly Rooms in Cirencester. After dinner Harry was presented with a "handsome and modern eight-day striking clock, supplied by Mr. Leonard W. Jones of Cirencester" with the inscription on the back "Presented by the Cirencester Old Grammarians to Mr. H.W. Stallworthy on the occasion of his marriage, November 20, 1933."[32]

Then on 8 January Hilda and Harry travelled to London by bus for a week of sightseeing, shopping and shows. On 11 January, Hilda wrote in her diary: "Tried on all the coats on Oxford Street with Harry a bored and unwilling witness to the performance." She seemed to have made amends for letting him suffer in this way, for her entry on the following day reads: "Had a long hunt for a tweed cap for Harry." They also saw Fred Astaire in *The Gay Divorcée* and Mary Mills in *Man in the Air* at His Majesty's and dined and danced at the Kit-Kat Club. On 16 January they returned to Fairford.

On 28 January Eddie brought Dr. Noel Humphreys for his first meeting with Harry and on the 30th Moore turned up and escorted Harry to Oxford where he met the executive of the Oxford University Exploration Club and discussed plans for the expedition with them.

Their honeymoon was almost over and Harry and Hilda sailed from Southampton on board the *Beringia* on 3 February. Writing to Bill and Sue on the 8th, Hilda reported:

> We have had a perfectly *delightful* crossing, smooth sea and only one rough day—yesterday, when the ship performed every known heave, shudder, shimmy, side slip or nose-dive possible in such a large boat. I retired to my bunk at noon and stayed there. Harry continued to roam about, jeer at me and eat his way steadily through the menu—then lamented the increasing tightness of his waist band.[33]

They landed at New York on the 9th, where they stayed at the Hotel Pennsylvania and spent the following day sightseeing and going to a show. On the 13th they travelled by train to Montreal where they stayed at the Alexandra Hotel and on the 14th they travelled back to Ottawa where they took a room at 157 James St. Although his furlough was not over for another week, Harry went out to the RCMP Barracks at Rockcliffe in the morning to touch base and had dinner in the mess while Hilda unpacked. The next few days were spent meeting friends and going out to events such as the Motor Show at the Château Laurier. On 29 February Harry reported for duty at Rockcliffe.[34]

On his first day back at work, Harry wrote a confidential report to his O.C. on his discussions about the expedition while in England.[35] He noted the visits by Shackleton, Humphreys and Moore to Fairford when they had discussed their plans thoroughly. His overall assessment was, "I consider their plans quite practicable provided they have adequate supplies and transport," but that in view of the expedition members' total lack of polar experience "they should not venture on the Ice Cap of Northern Ellesmere Island unless accompanied by an experienced white man and some Greenland Eskimos." Harry also reported on his meeting with the Oxford University Exploration Club when he had given them all the information he could about living and travelling in the Arctic. At Shackleton's request, he had prepared an estimate of the cost of the supplies they would need, pointing out that it was greatly in excess of the expedition's own estimate (£2,000), largely because they had underestimated the amount and cost of dog pemmican.

He further reported that Shackleton had been to Denmark where he had met Captain Petersen of the Greenland supply ship and officials of the Greenland Administration; they had promised to transport the expedition to Robertson Fjord and, if possible, to Bache Peninsula, and to supply 60 dogs, sledges and harnesses, to be picked up at Disko. Finally Harry noted:

> In event of a member of the Force being attached to the expedition I wish to inform you that I am desirous of volunteering for this service, if it will not be to my disadvantage either financially or in regard to my future standing in the Force.[36]

Harry now found himself having to report to Rockcliffe every day except Sunday, and on every fifth day he was orderly officer for a period of 48 hours.[37] The first time this occurred was on 21 February, as Hilda noted in her diary: "Harry on night guard—won't be home tonight—feels funny and lonely without him—the big so and so."[38] As the second-senior NCO, his daily routine was as follows: ride from 8.45 A.M. to 10.30 A.M.; stables 11. A.M. to noon; lectures, drills and fatigues in the afternoon. A far cry from Bache Peninsula! He had about 65 men under him and while as NCO he did not have to groom his own horse, he found it tedious to patrol the stables for an hour at noon and for a further 45 minutes in the evening while the men groomed and fed the horses. However, he was able to get away by 5.00 P.M. and could be home by six.

On 1 March Harry and Hilda took a lease on a furnished apartment on the top floor at 305 Wilbrod Street. The apartment had a living room, dining room, bedroom, and bathroom and cost them $50 per month. This was to be their first home of their own. To celebrate this event they invited Paddy Hamilton and Art Munro for dinner on 7 March—"the Three Musketeers from Bache Peninsula" as Hilda referred to them,[39] and Hilda christened a new tea service.

A week later Harry had to face one of the worst ordeals of his career. The Imperial Order of the Daughters of the Empire had presented a portrait of King George V to every detachment in the Eastern Arctic and now to reciprocate the RCMP had decided to present the ladies with a polar bear skin—and Harry had been selected to make the presentation at a ceremony at the Mt. Royal Hotel in Montreal on 14 March. He candidly admitted in a letter to Bill: "Honestly I'm dead scared of the job already but I can't refuse to obey orders."[40] Hilda's perspective was slightly more practical: "Harry came in this afternoon...full of sorrow that he had to give a 15 min. speech at the I.O.D.E. Convention in Montreal to present the bear skin.... I wrote out a plan for Harry to follow for his speech while he polished his buttons, and so, much perturbed, to bed."[41] Next morning "Harry left for Montreal after eating a good breakfast—with manuscript in bag & heart in mouth."[42] And that night "Harry arrived after one—in that peculiar frame of mind that comes after a bad situation has been faced and conquered. He had not been a bit nervous—had in fact rather enjoyed himself when the experience actually faced him."[43] Or, as Harry reported the event to Bill: "It was a pretty tough job but I got away with it although I think my face was redder than my tunic. However I've broken the ice at speech making."[44]

In the meantime, Eddie Shackleton had written on 28 February to say that he had written to Commissioner MacBrien to indicate that Harry was his first choice as the RCMP officer attached to the expedition,[45] and asked Harry to cable him if he heard anything further. The bureaucratic wheels ground slowly, however. It was not until 17 May that MacBrien wrote a memo concerning the expedition to Ellesmere Island to Superintendent T.H. Irvine, the Commanding Officer of "G" Division and hence Harry's direct superior, to report that:

the Honourable the Minister in control of the R.C.M. Police has now approved of my recommendation that Reg. No. 6316 Cpl. H.W. Stallworthy of your Division be assigned to the above mentioned Expedition provided the Expedition authorities assume all expenses of his travelling and subsistence from Canada to England, and from there to Canada.[46]

He also approved of the expedition using the detachment buildings at Bache Peninsula and the cache of food and coal at Fram Havn.

On the following day Mr. J. Lorne Turner, acting Chairman of the Dominion Lands Board, wrote to Superintendent Irvine to inform him that since the Shackleton Expedition "has furnished satisfactory evidence that it is adequately equipped and financed and that it has the backing of the Oxford University Exploration Club and the Royal Geographical Society,"[47] and had assumed responsibility in case a relief expedition were required, the necessary permits had been issued. These included Scientists' and Explorers' Permits for Dr. Noel Humphreys, Edward Shackleton and A.W. Moore, and Archaeologist's and Ethnologist's Permits and a Sampling Permit for A.W. Moore (the latter authorizing Moore to capture up to 20 specimens of each mammal and non-migratory bird, but **not** buffalo, muskox or reindeer).

Following this, on 22 May the Secretary of State for External Affairs cabled the Canadian High Commissioner in London as follows:

Shackleton Arctic Expedition. Interior Department satisfied as to evidence regarding equipment and financial basis of Expedition. $1,000 to be included in supplementary estimates of Department by way of assistance. Stallworthy of Mounted Police available for Expedition, and awaits instructions from London. Government cannot meet his transportation expense, so Shackleton will have to make his own arrangements for getting Stallworthy to London. Permits follow by mail.[48]

On 28 May Shackleton wrote to General MacBrien to express his gratitude for the permits, the contribution of $1,000 and especially for Harry's secondment to the expedition, and to give him an update on developments. Since the arrangement with the Greenland Administration to travel from Denmark aboard its supply vessel had not proven satisfactory, he had chartered a Norwegian sealing vessel, the *Signalhorn*, to take them from London to Ellesmere Island for £1,000. This gave the expedition more freedom. In case they were not able to reach Bache Peninsula, they were taking a prefabricated hut in which they would winter at whatever point they were able to land. He now estimated the total cost of the expedition at £3,000, of which they had already raised £2,400 and hoped to raise more; however, they also had a further guarantee of £1,000 if it were needed. Regarding other matters concerning the expedition, he wrote:

As regards equipment and supplies we have been able to get practically all our food free, and at the moment we are getting together our equipment. Our deerskins have been despatched from Tromsoe and the sledges and the hut are being built in Denmark. Fifty dogs are being collected in West Greenland and we hope to get another twenty from the Cape York district. The Thule Administration, which are at present in rather a state of muddle owing to the death of Knud Rasmussen, has undertaken to let us bring an Eskimo family with us across to Ellesmere Land to help the Expedition.[49]

Meanwhile back in Ottawa, Harry and Hilda were mentally preparing themselves for another lengthy separation. Apart from running the household, Hilda was spending quite a lot of her time helping Harry write an article for the *RCMP Quarterly* on his northern experiences in the Yukon and at Chesterfield Inlet and Bache Peninsula. Harry finished the final draft on 17 May and it was published in the October 1934 issue of the *Quarterly*.[50] It was quite an unsettling winter, as they did not know exactly what Harry would be doing for the next two years. Eventually they received a cable from Eddie on 8 May to say that the expedition was definitely assured. Only two days before Eddie's cable arrived, Harry heard that they were to be posted to Chesterfield Inlet if he did not go the Ellesmere with the expedition. Hilda's comment on this news was quite understandable, since it meant they would not be separated: "Almost hope things will turn out this way."[51]

Naturally, how and where Hilda would spend the year or more while Harry was in the Arctic was a matter to which they gave considerable thought. For a time Hilda was making plans to take a summer cottage near Kingston with a Cousin Ruth, but was unsure as to what she would do thereafter: she was not keen on going to her parents' home in Edson.[52] They had discussed the possibility of her spending the year with Harry's mother at Fairford and on 13 May Hilda decided that this is what she wanted to do. They both wrote to Mrs. Stallworthy to suggest this, and when they had had no reply by 15 May Harry wrote to Bill asking him to get their mother to cable a reply. Hilda and Mrs. Stallworthy had found themselves to be mutually compatible during Hilda's visit during the previous winter and everyone felt this arrangement should work out well.

Inevitably this meant a considerable amount of preparation—at various levels. Hilda bought herself a new outfit and on 31 May "had a fashion parade for Harry's benefit. He liked everything—a white suit with long coat, a navy blue redingote with polka dot dress underneath and a sweet plaid silk organdie evening dress—all ruffles and very dainty."[53] Then on 7 June they threw a northern party:

Paddy and Art, MacBeath, Bolstad, Tyack, Joe Pepper, "Dubby" Kerr, Bobby Bowen, Zwicien, Duncan Martin, Gordie McLewin, Mrs. Stedman.... They drank a lot of beer and it was so hot that we all nearly expired—but the talk of the North continued in spite of the extremely tropical temperature.[54]

Meanwhile Harry was making arrangements to ensure that he would be properly equipped for the expedition. On 28 May he wrote to Irvine asking that he be issued two Mackinaw shirts, four tanned sheepskins for making stockings and a pair of prescription snow glasses, and asked whether he should take his service revolver and Sam Brown equipment on the expedition.[55] He had also negotiated with Major D.L. McKeand of the Northwest Territories Branch for the loan of a movie camera and 5,000 feet of film from that branch so that he could make a movie of the expedition.[56] He was to receive a positive copy of his own and suggested that the RCMP might like to have a copy made for the RCMP Museum in Regina.

Among their household effects, Harry and Hilda possessed two polar bear rugs that Harry had obtained in Chesterfield Inlet. He now suggested that he should take them back north with him so that he could have one or more pairs of polar bear pants made from them. Hilda, however, protested; she was very proud of them, and they made a great conversation piece.[57]

Since Eddie Shackleton was responsible for arranging the passage to England, Harry and Hilda still had no information as to their sailing date. While they waited, they went ahead with their preparations. On 12 June Hilda was washing, ironing and packing, while their furniture was being moved out, presumably to be put in storage. Finally, on the 13th they received a cable to say that they were sailing from Quebec City aboard *Empress of Britain* on the 16th.[58] Also on the 13th, Harry had a long meeting with Commissioner MacBrien in his office: "General MacBrien was very nice about everything," Hilda wrote. "[He] sent his personal wishes to the members of the Expedition through Harry—but nothing was said regarding another stripe."[59]

On 14 June, Harry received his final instructions from Superintendent Irvine: He was to be "a representative and observer of the Canadian Government" and was to see "that this expedition lives up to the permits which have been granted"; he was "expected to use tact and judgement and to uphold the traditions of the Force" and "when touching at ports of call" was to "wear uniform so that the Natives and other persons concerned may understand [his] position."[60] That same day, Hilda finished packing at home, while Harry cleared out the last things left in his office. They had a late supper at Carson's and walked to Union Station where Hilda fell asleep exhausted on a waiting room bench while Harry checked their considerable luggage.

They caught an early train to Montreal on the 15th and Harry spent the morning on expedition business. In the afternoon Superintendent Meade gave them tickets for the Blue Bonnets Race Course and lent them his car. The following morning they caught the train to Quebec City, boarded *Empress of Britain* about noon and headed down the St. Lawrence. It was only when they were already on board the ship that Harry received a telegram from MacBrien:

In view of your efficient service and importance of your new work it has been decided to give you the acting rank of Sergeant whilst with the Shackleton expedition to Ellesmere Island.[61]

10

THE OXFORD UNIVERSITY

Ellesmere Land Expedition 1934–1935

HARRY AND HILDA REACHED SOUTHAMPTON on board the *Empress of Britain* on 22 June 1934 and caught the train to London. Eddie Shackleton and Moore met them at Paddington Station and drove them first to their hotel, the Strand Palace, and then on to the Royal Geographical Society at 1 Kensington Gore for a quick lunch. They then drove to Aldershot to watch the Military Tattoo. Hilda was greatly impressed by the massed bands. Next morning they were driven back to Paddington Station where they caught the train to Fairford. Bill was waiting for them at the station in his cricket flannels. "Mummy Stallworthy very pleased to see us," Hilda noted in her diary that evening.[1]

On the following Monday, Harry caught the early train back up to London to join Eddie and the other members of the expedition at the expedition's office at the Royal Geographical Society. However, he also found himself travelling quite widely around England over the next few weeks. As Hilda reported, he went:

> all over England and from one centre to another. He is the "ambassador" for the Exped. to approve of and collect the donations to the cargo of the "Signalhorn." He travels alone as the only one who knows, "the Northern Expert."[2]

Harry's indispensable contribution was appreciated and acknowledged by Eddie in his account of the journey:

> [Harry Stallworthy's] knowledge of the necessities of life in the Arctic was of course invaluable, whether it was on a visit to Woolworths to buy dish-cloths, or a journey to Sheffield to see to the manufacture of special steel sledge runners.[3]

Despite his busy schedule, Harry did manage to get home to Fairford on weekends. On Friday 6 July he came home unexpectedly and very late. He had to walk home from the station and when he got there, he had to throw gravel at Hilda's window to gain access to the house. By the time he got into the house, Hilda commented, he was "very hot and tired, poor boy."[4]

In the morning, Bill took them to Bathurst Park, Cirencester, so that Hilda could watch her first cricket match. The note in her diary captures her sense of confusion about the game: "completely strange to me. I amused them by making stupid questions: 'Why did each man carry his bat with him?' People clapped politely and said, 'Well done' in low voices. How different from baseball. Tea in the Pavilion."[5]

During their time at Fairford, the reality of their impending separation began to hit Hilda:

> It's getting more and more imminent. Of course we knew all about this before we were married, but at that time it was a vague idea or an improbable possibility. Now it's right around the corner—ready to pounce upon us. I think we are beginning to realize how much we are in love, which makes parting very hard for both of us.[6]

Despite their anxiety over the separation, both Hilda and Harry felt that the arrangement for Hilda to spend the year with Mrs. Stallworthy was the best possible solution in the circumstances:

> It makes him feel so much better about leaving me. Fortunately his Mother is delighted. Says it is so wonderful to have a real daughter. I feel so welcome and at home. Harry says it will make our life together much better—that I will know all his family so well. They are all wonderful people. I am so very lucky.[7]

Meanwhile, on 8 July Harry received a very important telegram from Commissioner MacBrien: "Have received written communication from Department Interior informing me that Shackleton Expedition will not be permitted to kill muskoxen for any purpose stop Please inform Shackleton and acknowledge receipt this cable."[8] This absolute prohibition would have serious consequences during the following sledging season.

As an expression of the country's appreciation of the achievements of her late husband, Sir Ernest Shackleton, Lady Shackleton (and Eddie when he was at home) lived in a "grace and favour" apartment at Hampton Court Palace, and for the final few days before the expedition sailed Lady Shackleton arranged for Hilda and Harry to stay at the Hampton Court Hotel on the Thames, right across from the Palace. Harry could easily travel up to the Royal Geographical Society daily, while Hilda spent the days with Lady Shackleton and her daughter Cecily. They travelled up to London from Fairford on 10 August and the next morning before breakfast, Hilda, Harry, Eddie and Moore had a dip in the river. The 15th, a Sunday, was Eddie's birthday, and there was a birthday celebration at Hampton Court Palace. Later Hilda and Harry hired a canoe and drifted down the Thames past swans and luxury houseboats.[9]

By now the expedition's vessel, the Norwegian sealer, *Signalhorn* of Ålesund, had reached London and was moored in St. Katharine's Dock where the Port of London Authority had provided a free berth. The original departure date was set for 16 July, but it quickly became apparent that the amount of cargo that had accumulated on the dockside exceeded the vessel's cargo capacity. It fell to Harry to decide what was dispensable—mainly coal, oil and gasoline. However these materials did not go to waste, but were donated to John Rymill's Antarctic expedition that was due to leave from the same dock in September.[10] On the 16th Lady Shackleton and Hilda drove to the Royal Geographical Society and then on to St. Katharine's Dock, where they "found Harry working like a dock hand while the others at 4 o'clock had just arrived.... Harry seems to be the only one who knows anything."[11]

Harry hit it off well with *Signalhorn*'s captain, Captain E. With, and with the company representative and wireless operator, Captain Axnes. In view of this he devised a scheme to try to salvage something from the collapse of his fur-trapping enterprise. The furs that he had left at Fram Havn along with his personal belongings, had in the interim been brought across to Robertson Fjord by Nukappiannguaq, Quavigarsuaq, Kahkachoo and Seekeeunguaq. Harry now made arrangements with Captain With to bring the furs back to England on his return trip after landing the expedition. On 15 July he wrote to Bill to alert him of this plan and to give him instructions concerning the furs, including the name and address of the expedition's agents:

> I will leave them an order to turn over any personal luggage to you....
> Once that fur arrives in London it will be quite a relief to me to know
> that it will be saved after the disappointments for the last two years.
> So I shall certainly be tickled if you will take care of it for me.
>
> But please try to grab it as soon as you can. I'll have to leave the
> matter in your hands.... I'll ask the agents to wire you when (what
> time) the ship will dock in London, or I may be able to have the captain
> wireless you before he lands. I shall be glad to hear by radio if every-
> thing goes OK but please don't mention "Fur" or "Personal effects"
> on the air.[12]

From the final sentence of his letter, it is clear that Harry had no desire that word of his entrepreneurial activities reach RCMP headquarters in Ottawa.

The expedition members had arranged to rendezvous at St. Katharine's Dock in the late afternoon of the 17th, sailing time having been set for 6.30 P.M. Apart from Dr. Noel Humphreys, Eddie Shackleton and Harry, the members of the expedition were A.W. (Ev) Moore, biologist and photographer; David Haig-Thomas, ornithologist; and Robert Bentham, a geologist who had just received his B.Sc. from Nottingham University. In addition to

Signalhorn, *with the Oxford University Ellesmere Land Expedition on board, 1934.*

Members of the Oxford University Ellesmere Land Expedition and crew members on board Signalhorn, 1934. Nukappiannguaq front row centre; Harry front row right.

Inughuit in kayaks, Robertson Fjord, Northwest Greenland, 1934.

relatives and friends a number of dignitaries had gathered to see them off: they included Sir Percy Cox, President of the Royal Geographical Society, Admiral Sir William Goodenough, Colonel Vanier, representing the Canadian High Commissioner, and John Rymill, leader of the impending Antarctic Expedition.[13] There was something of a last-minute panic when it was discovered that to comply with dock regulations they would have to sail by 6.00 P.M., but they were able to accommodate this last-minute change.

Signalhorn's departure received wide coverage in the British press, especially a last-minute, unscheduled incident that was caught by a photographer. As the vessel had started to move away from the dock, Noel Humphreys was giving his wife a last-minute embrace, when on the spur of the moment, he said "Come to Gravesend with us." She stepped across the widening gap between ship and dock and was followed by several other relatives of expedition members.[14]

Hilda did not go to the docks to see the expedition off; she had said goodbye to Harry at the Hampton Court Hotel after they had sat in the garden by the Thames that morning. She took the train back to Fairford where Bill met her and took her home to Milton Lodge where, she wrote,

M[rs.] Stallworthy kissed me. I started to cry and she said "Now, now, none of that!" And that was that! I thought of the times when all 4 of her sons were in France [during World War I], and all the times she had said goodbye to Harry—going back to Canada. She is a really "stout fellow." I'm going to enjoy my time with her. She is determined to make my life as pleasant as possible in Harry's absence.[15]

The following day she picked up a typewriter that Harry had bought from the expedition so that Hilda could learn touch-typing. She planned to practice for two hours every morning so that she would be able to type up his reports for him on his return.

Signalhorn ran downriver to Gravesend where the various friends and relatives disembarked. Here she was supposed to pick up two motorboats, but was able to load only one of them because she was already overloaded, with her Plimsol line submerged. Having dropped the Thames estuary pilot, *Signalhorn* headed north; a mildly rough sea got up and some members of the expedition, including Shackleton, succumbed to seasickness.

The first stop was at Aberdeen to pick up some chronometers that had been forwarded by train from London. *Signalhorn* ran through the Pentland Firth on 21 July in calm misty weather and with a following tide that pushed her normal speed of 7 knots up to 14 knots. This was the last fine weather they experienced until they reached Greenland and the little sealer was battling a headwind and heavy seas all the way across the Atlantic. She took 11 days to reach Kap Farvel, with seas sweeping the decks most of the time. As a result there were fears that the deck cargo might be lost and it had to be relashed several times. Harry was laid low by seasickness for three days, but most of the others were totally incapacitated for the entire duration of the crossing. Fortunately, as soon as they rounded Kap Farvel and headed north, the weather improved and the seas abated and everyone enjoyed the superlative views of glaciers, mountains and icebergs.

The first scheduled port-of-call in Greenland was Sukkertoppen (now Manîtsoq) where the expedition was to pick up dried fish for dog food,[16] but a dense fog made it impossible to reach that settlement and *Signalhorn* continued north to Godhavn on Disko Island. The sun reappeared and so the crew was able to hang out to dry their clothing and bedding, which had been soaked during the foul weather. The vessel reached Godhavn on 5 August. They were welcomed by the Governor's assistant, who came aboard to check the ship's and the expedition's documents. Dr. Rosendahl, the Governor of Greenland, then extended an invitation to Dr. Humphreys, Eddie and Harry to visit him at his home. Rosendahl later travelled with the expedition as far as Jakobshavn (now Ilulissat). The prefabricated expedition hut had been shipped to Godhavn from Denmark and was now waiting to be loaded. Here the expedition took delivery of sealskin *kamiks* that had been ordered ahead of time.

Harry also purchased 50 sledge dogs. He had let it be known that he was looking for dogs and when he went ashore about 200 were presented for his inspection. Of these he chose the 50 that in his view "would compare favourably with some of the best average dogs in Northern Canada."[17] He did not take any bitches since he did not anticipate any need to raise pups for sledge work and was keen to avoid potential difficulties arising from bitches coming into heat during the spring sledge trips.

Once Dr. Rosendahl had come aboard, the *Signalhorn* weighed anchor around 2 P.M. next day and ran east across Disko Bugt to Jakobshavn, arriving about midnight. Here they found the Danish supply ship, *Dannebrog*; Harry, Humphreys and Eddie went aboard and met officers and officials. Among them were Captain Petersen; Mr. Knud Knudsen, the local administrator; Mr. Rudolf Sand, the late Knud Rasmussen's partner who had taken over the running of the Thule trading post since his partner's death; and Dr. Holm, the doctor for the Thule area. Amongst other things, they had a useful chat with Sand and Holm about employing some of the Inughuit.[18] On the 7th Harry selected and bought a further 20 dogs and a quantity of sealskin line. He also bought a 17-foot fishing dory, some lumber and 4½ tonnes of dried fish for dog food, while the others traded for parkas, *kamiks*, etc. That evening Mr. Knudsen entertained the expedition members at his home before the *Signalhorn* started back for Godhavn to pick up the dogs they had bought earlier and the lumber for the hut.

Signalhorn finally sailed from Godhavn on 8 August. Her decks were so cluttered with the lumber, dogs, the dory and dried fish that there was barely room to walk. Fortunately Melville Bay favoured them with atypically fine weather; moreover it was also unusually free of ice and although she had to push through brash ice occasionally, the little vessel made steady progress northwards, reaching Thule on North Star Bay on 11 August.[19] The local governor, Mr. Hans Nielsen, invited the expedition members to tea and Harry discussed with him the matter of employing a couple of Inughuit. Mr. Sand had suggested two individuals; however, one was not available and in any case Harry thought they were unsuitable. After only a short stay, the *Signalhorn* took advantage of the continuing fine weather to continue north to Robertson Fjord. They arrived around noon on the 12th and while the other members landed a cache of food, kerosene and ammunition, Harry made enquiries as to who might be willing to join the expedition. After consultation by radio with Mr. Sand, Harry hired his old friends Nukappiannguaq and Inuatuk. They soon moved aboard along with their wives Enalunguaq and Natow, sledges, dog teams (25 dogs apiece), kayaks, hunting gear and household effects, including a sewing machine and a portable gramophone.[20]

Signalhorn put to sea again on 13 August, but in the early hours of the 14th she was stopped by heavy pack ice that appeared to extend right across Smith Sound. Running west along the ice edge to within sight of the Ellesmere coast, Captain With could find no break in the ice barrier. Since the charter specified that in the event of the ship being frozen in the owners would be responsible for the expense incurred, the captain had strict orders *not* to allow his ship to be beset. As Shackleton ruefully commented, Captain With's ice navigation "could better be termed ice-evasion."[21]

There was absolutely no chance of reaching Bache Peninsula, let alone Fort Conger. As an alternative that was almost as convenient, it was decided to try to reach Refuge Harbour just south of Cairn Point on the Greenland coast, but even this was inaccessible. However *Signalhorn* did manage to put ashore just south of Cape Hatherton and a cache of food and ammunition was landed "on a grassy sward bright with flowers, and to the music of a babbling brook."[22]

It was decided to drop back south to Etah in Foulke Fjord and to wait for a couple of days. Then on the night of 15–16 August they reconnoitred the ice conditions in Smith Sound again in the hope that the spring tides might have opened up some leads, but found the conditions completely unchanged. *Signalhorn* penetrated as far north as the latitude of Cairn Point but here solid pack ice completely barred the way north. They again investigated the harbour at Hatherton Bay but it was now jammed with loose ice. Lifeboat Cove, where *Polaris* was beached in 1872, did not look at all promising and hence the ship ran back to Etah once again. Now a sometimes heated debate began. Captain With and Captain Axnes declared that it was pointless to make any further attempts at pushing north. Dr. Humphreys felt they should not give up yet, but Captain With refused to discuss the matter with him since the charter had been negotiated and signed by Shackleton and not the Doctor. Quite apart from the financial aspects, the ship's crew had neither adequate clothing nor provisions for a wintering, so the Captain's reluctance to make further attempts was understandable. Another consideration was that the charter expired on 20 August, but if ice conditions were favourable, and at the Captain's discretion, it could be extended for a further five days. Captain With had already notified the expedition members that unloading would take between four and five days. He then effectively delivered an ultimatum: the crew would start unloading next morning, 17 August.[23]

Reluctantly, Harry was forced to side with the captain as he felt that for the present it would be foolhardy to try to push north and that failing some extraordinary change, Bache Peninsula or even Fram Havn would be inaccessible. He was reluctant mostly because a base camp at Etah would be some 650 km south of their objective in Northern Ellesmere Island—but at least it was within striking distance by dog sledge. On the positive side, Etah was a good location for procuring walrus for dog food.[24]

While *Signalhorn* had been cruising amongst loose ice south of the main pack, groups of walrus had been sighted on ice floes. The expedition members, led by Humphreys and Haig-Thomas, blazed away at them at every opportunity. An unknown number slipped into the water, wounded, and escaped, but may well have subsequently drowned. The Greenland hunting regulations stipulated that walrus must first be harpooned then shot, so that an animal that escaped into the water could still be retrieved by the line attached to the harpoon. Nukappiannguaq and Inuatuk complained to Harry about the expedition members ignoring these stipulations. They themselves had tried shooting some of the wounded walrus to prevent them slipping off the floes and thus repair some of the damage, but they were quite upset by the whole situation. Harry found himself in a difficult situation, since he had no authority in these waters; all he could do to try to prevent any further breaches of the local laws in terms of this indiscriminate shooting was to hand Humphreys a copy of the Northern Greenland Game Laws that Mr. Hans Nielsen had given him.[25] Despite the strained atmosphere that resulted from this episode, the net result was that eight walrus, representing about five tonnes of meat and blubber, had been procured for dog feed.

Unloading *Signalhorn*'s cargo of some 65–70 tonnes was a slow process. The men used the ship's lifeboat, the expedition's motorboat and the small dory. The lumber for the house was floated ashore as a raft; this had the secondary benefit of cleaning the lumber of the dog faeces that had accumulated on it during the voyage.[26] Once on shore everything was temporarily stacked at the top of the beach, but then it had to be hauled up a steep bank, some 20 m high. This was achieved by forming a human chain and passing everything from hand to hand. A small village of tents sprang up around their workplace. While they offloaded the cargo, the dogs were put ashore on a nearby island where they could roam freely but could not easily escape. Once the unloading was complete, the *Signalhorn* departed on the evening of 22 August, after a farewell party on deck at which one of the crew played the accordion—much to the delight of the Inughuit.

Harry sent a letter to Bill with the departing *Signalhorn*. In it, he expressed his opinion of the other expedition members quite candidly:

The expedition is coming along fine but they don't realize what they are going to be up against in the winter. They all insist on driving their own teams of 12 dogs & half a ton of freight each. None of them have the remotest idea about carpentry, cooking or even washing dishes, but they are all game & figure that they can make records at almost everything. In fact I quite expect the North to be torn to pieces. The best in the crowd is Bob Bentham, quiet & hardworking & the only one who is not pestering me with foolish questions. Shackleton, Moore & Thomas are just like three kids & seem to be unhandy at every-thing. However we shall all get along O.K. Nookap is very much amused to hear of all the things the white men want to do & places they want to go.[27]

Naturally, Harry also wrote to Hilda and she received her letter on 19 September. In her diary she noted:

Had a letter from Harry—brought back on Signal Horn. They are on the Greenland side, Etah. Dr. Humphreys refers everything to Harry—and says the Expedition would have been impossible without him. So glad! Dear Harry, he deserves everything that this may bring him, because I fear he will have more than his share of work. I always said he was too nice to spend his life in the North where no one could enjoy him and I have let him go off again so soon after we were married. I hope when he comes back that we may go on as we have started. His life has been so unusual and may continue so. I miss him.[28]

At about the time that *Signalhorn* was heading down the Greenland coast, Mr. Rudolf Sand, Administrator for the Thule District, but presumably still further south at the time in question, sent a somewhat belated message to Hans Nielsen at Thule, asking him to relay the following information to Eddie Shackleton:

Permission to winter at Etah can only be given on the following terms stop the killing of bears and foxes is not allowed stop furs of animals being killed before this notice reaches you must later be handed over to the Thule station stop trading with the Eskimos and in the shops belonging to the Thule administration is only allowed in the case of emergency stop the employment of more Eskimos than mentioned in my note of 12 inst. is only allowed in the case of emergency stop as the district cannot feed 70 dogs extra it will be allowed only to kill 10 walruses in Danish waters all terms are put up in order to protect the vital interests of the Cape York Eskimos stop these terms will be transmitted to Oxford and RGS London making the society responsible in the case.[29]

It was not until 26 November that Nielsen forwarded this message to Eddie, but he was able to include encouraging news that in the interim he had been able to obtain permission for the expedition to take an additional 10 walrus.[30]

The site they used for their base camp had previously served as the base camp for Donald Macmillan, who had named it Borup Lodge.[31] The building at the site had long since been dismantled and removed by the Inughuit, but the level foundation made an ideal site on which to erect the expedition's base hut. Harry took charge of building the hut and was assisted mainly by Bob Bentham, "a practical man and a diligent worker."[32] The task took until the end of September.

Even before the ship left, Dr. Humphreys was contemplating moving everything further north using the expedition's motorboat and the dory. Both Harry and Nukappiannguaq advised him that this was totally impractical; however, Harry definitely saw merit in establishing a depot as far north as possible on the Greenland coast for the use of later sledge parties. On 4 September, accompanied by Nukappiannguaq, Bentham and Haig-Thomas, he set off in the motorboat, towing the dory loaded with about 2,500 lbs of provisions, dog food and about 40 gallons [c. 160 litres] of kerosene.[33] They hoped to reach Cape Calhoun north of the Humboldt Glacier, but after only some 40 km they ran into heavy ice near Cairn Point; climbing high on the cape they could see that the ice still stretched right across the Sound to Cape Sabine. Accepting the inevitable, Harry cached the supplies above high water mark near Cairn Point and returned to base, where he soon found himself in a rather difficult and irritating situation:

After receiving Haig-Thomas' report on our return the doctor [Humphreys] was given the impression that Nukappiannguaq and I were not keen enough and were afraid to take any chances. There then followed some long discussions in which some most extraordinary plans and theories were advanced in regard to getting more pemmican north. As far as possible Bentham and I avoided the discussions and carried on with the work of building the house, being assisted occasionally by the Eskimos.[34]

They made a further five cache-laying trips before freeze-up: a certain amount of supplies was moved some distance north, but at the cost of a series of mishaps that might have proved disastrous, even fatal. On one occasion in mid-September, plans had been made to take some supplies north using the motorboat and the dory. Since temperatures were dropping well below freezing at night, the inboard motor was extremely difficult to start in the morning. In an attempt to solve the problem, an oil stove was lighted and placed under a tarpaulin inside the motorboat. The boat had been hauled out of the water, but was propped up on its keel to keep it upright as the tide ebbed. However, the men forgot that the tide would also rise during the night. When the tide came in, the boat floated and the props fell away and so when the tide ebbed again the boat toppled over and the stove set fire to the tarpaulin. Fortunately, the entire boat did not catch fire and the damage was confined mainly to the spark-plug leads and the magneto.[35]

The outcome was that Shackleton and Moore set off in the dory, using its outboard motor. Next day they reached Cairn Point, where they unloaded their own food, fuel and sleeping bags to facilitate unloading the supplies they intended to leave at Cache Point, some 5 km further north. Having cached the supplies there, they started back for Cairn Point but in the evening new ice began to form and as they were unable to reach shore, they hauled the dory up on a floe and settled down for a rather uncomfortable night. They drifted south for some 18 hours, well past Cairn Point. Once the ice started to slacken and leads began to form, they launched and loaded the dory; fortunately the motor was functioning quite well and they headed south to near Littleton Island. But there the propeller hit a hard chunk of ice and the propeller shaft was bent. They managed to row the boat ashore and had started to walk the

16 km back to base when Humphreys, Bentham, Haig-Thomas and Inuatuk appeared in the motorboat, which they were rowing as Bentham had been unable to repair the fire-damaged engine. The wind had now dropped significantly so they started rowing both boats back to Etah, but when the wind picked up again in Foulke Fjord they were forced to put ashore again and walk the last few kilometres back to base.[36]

On a more positive note, they did manage to kill nine walrus during these boat trips and their meat was cached on the mainland or on islands. Once again the Inughuit repeatedly complained to Harry that the expedition members had wounded and failed to recover walruses. On one occasion Humphreys had even fired at a walrus in the water at close range with a 12-gauge shotgun! Nukappiannguaq and Inuatuk requested, through Harry, that they be allowed to hunt walrus in their kayaks, in order to take meat to the dogs on the island and to lay caches in the fjord. They insisted that they should both go, since it was too dangerous to hunt walrus alone by harpoon from a kayak. Instead, one of them was always involved in the cache-laying boat trips. Harry tried to intervene tactfully, but found himself in a difficult position:

> I made a number of friendly suggestions to the doctor with regard to the hunting, feeding the dogs, and general preparations for the winter, on which he always had the natives' views as well. On every occasion he was polite and outwardly agreeable, but he invariably did the opposite, usually under the influence of Thomas, whom he had previously placed in charge of the boats and hunting.[37]

The latter, meanwhile, was proposing "some of the most incredible plans" that would certainly have ended in disaster. Probably the most impractical was that, in late September he, Moore and Inuatuk should take both boats, loaded with supplies, north to Cape Calhoun on the other side of the Humboldt Glacier, stay there to hunt walrus until the boats were frozen in and then walk back to base in October. He suggested this plan despite the fact that the Inughuit had told him that walrus were not to be found off Cape Calhoun. Worst of all, the Humboldt Glacier, some 80 km wide, is extremely active and heavily crevassed. Haig-Thomas and Moore had worked out a special ration system, and were even packing the food into bags when they were forced to abandon their plan when Inuatuk refused to go with them. Nukappiannguaq had earlier refused to have anything to do with such suicidal jaunts.[38]

Harry and Bentham meanwhile had been working steadily at erecting the hut. It was a frame structure, 24' x 14', including a porch 4' x 14'. By reducing the area of the porch by half, they managed to obtain an extra small room that opened off the living room and was used as a pantry. The ceilings were 6' 6" high, and above them was an attic beneath the pitch of the roof, which sloped at an angle of about 60°.[39] The outer skin of the house consisted of ¾" tongue-and-groove planks, lined on the inside with either aluminum foil insulating paper or tar paper. Then, separated by a 2" air space, came the inner lining of ½" tongue-and-groove boards. The windows were double-glazed. The house had first been erected in Copenhagen, all the components numbered, and then disassembled again for shipping. Unfortunately some of the instructions for the reassembly were in Danish and hence the project was quite a challenge.[40] Harry would have been happier working to his own design using bulk lumber, although he admitted that the hut was very solid, well-planned and comfortable, if rather cramped for six men. The hut was all but finished by 16 September and some of the party moved into it from the tents immediately. In early October Harry and Bentham built a lean-to on the windward end of the building; it was lined with the boxes that had held kerosene and gasoline, stacked on top of each other to produce excellent shelves for storing provisions needed during the winter. It also increased the warmth of the living quarters and provided a place for recharging the radio batteries.

The various individuals also placed their own stamp on their own sections of the living area. Humphreys constructed "a most curious erection, also built of petrol boxes" for storing supplies; his bed was in the middle of this structure which also included a built-in desk. Harry's bunk was the envy of all the others; he even managed to "impart some sort of spring to the planking of which it was made."[41] The other four slept in the attic, three of them on the floor, while Bentham also built a bed.

In early October the dogs were brought ashore from the island by boat. It was expected that some would be missing, since the bones of four or five dogs had been found on the island, killed and eaten by the rest. They also knew that some of the dogs had gone adrift on ice floes when the wind broke up the newly-formed fast ice. On several occasions some of the dogs had been rescued by boat, but some had probably drifted out to sea unnoticed and had drowned. The net result was that 17 dogs were missing. Of the remainder, four were in such poor condition that they had to be killed,[42] leaving a total of 47 animals that were initially divided into six teams. Following the North Greenland custom (which had been adopted by the RCMP on Ellesmere Island) the dogs' molars were knocked out with the butt of an axe to discourage them from chewing through their sealskin harness and traces.

While the expedition was preparing to winter at Etah, Hilda received a phone call from Bill in Ampney Crucis on 2 October. Harry's trunk, which had been offloaded from *Signalhorn* at Newcastle, had arrived. She caught the bus to Ampney Crucis the next morning and they went through the trunk together: "Nothing had been touched at the Dock at Newcastle although the trunk had been opened. The 60 white fox were in perfect condition. Camera, binoculars, model kyacks and komatiks came."[43]

Back in Greenland, the base camp at Etah now settled down to a winter routine in which cooking and feeding and exercising the dogs played a major role. Each man took a turn as cook, a week at a time. Apart from Harry, none had previous cooking experience, but they soon learned. With some practice they all became quite proficient bakers too. The cook was usually assisted by one of the others, who fetched coal from the coal pile down by the shore about 100 m away and also fetched ice for water. Once the fjord had frozen solid after 15 October, ice was chopped from the Brother John Glacier that descended to the head of the fjord about 6 km away and was hauled back to the base by dog team.[44]

The sun disappeared below the horizon for the winter on 24 October, although there was still a short twilight period around noon for weeks afterwards, especially with a clear sky. However, the moon, especially a full moon in a clear sky, provided them with enough light for most outdoor activities. On 1 November Harry, Humph, Nukappiannguaq and Inuatuk set off to travel to Robertson Fjord and Thule, partly to arrange to hire more Inughuit for the major spring sledge trips and partly to communicate with England through the radio station at Thule. While the expedition was getting excellent radio reception and had received the messages that Hilda had sent to Harry on 30 October,[45] they had been unable to get the radio transmitter to work properly up to this point.[46]

The party set off with three dog teams. As was so often the case, the frequent easterly winds had blown the ice out, leaving a stretch of open water to the south of Foulke Fjord. As a result, they had to ascend the Brother John Glacier and cross the icecap. Shackleton, Bentham and Haig-Thomas accompanied them to the head of the fjord and helped them up the steep face of the glacier. This help was much appreciated since the glacier front was snow-free and they had to chop steps in the ice.

Continuing on their own, an hour later Harry, Nukappiannguaq and Inuatuk found themselves confronted with another steep, snow-free ice slope that would necessitate more step-cutting. Since it was getting dark and there was no snow for igloo-building, they dumped their loads and drove the empty sledges back to base. Overnight some snow fell and in the morning they had little trouble on the steep slopes of the lower glacier. They had climbed about 900 m over a distance of within 10 km when they ran into deep, loose snow and a strong wind. They had difficulty finding suitable hard-packed snow for an igloo, and even then had to drape a folded tent over the windward side to stop the wind from eroding the rather friable snow blocks.

The next day they headed across the ice cap in blinding drift, but they had the wind behind them. After a while Nukappiannguaq and Inuatuk suggested that the wind must have changed, since they were not travelling uphill as they should have been. They decided to turn back, but even over the short distance of no more than 3 km back to their last igloo, they had difficulty following their tracks. For two days they were weather-bound in the igloo, emerging only occasionally to dig the dogs out and repair a snow-block windbreak. Next morning they headed back down the Brother John Glacier to find the weather quite calm at sea level. Their colleagues at the base were quite surprised to hear that a blizzard had forced them to turn back.

Soon afterwards Humphreys, Harry, Inuatuk, Bentham and Shackleton set off in the noon twilight to fetch walrus meat that had been cached on an island in the fjord. Shackleton managed to get separated from the rest and his team ran away from him. As he wandered around looking for them, he heard what he thought was a bear quite close to him. He stood absolutely still in the gloom for a while. Then came a cautious voice out of the darkness: "Who's there?" This was Bentham who had also lost his team, had heard Shackleton's footsteps, and had thought *he* was a bear![47] They both found their teams, continued to the island and helped the others dig and chop out the frozen walrus meat; the caravan of sledges then headed home with Inuatuk leading the way, a hurricane lamp swinging from the back of his sledge.

On 27 November (4th according to Harry) during a calm period, Moore, Haig-Thomas, Nukappiannguaq and Inuatuk set off for Cairn Point to retrieve the sleeping bags and equipment that Shackleton and Moore had left there during their eventful boat trip in September.[48] There were stretches of open water along the coast and so they first had to travel up the steep hill behind the base and then overland as far as Lifeboat Cove. The moon was up, but there was also often heavy clouds and avoiding rocks was often a challenge. From Lifeboat Cove they were able to travel along the sea ice to Cape Hatherton, but then again had to head overland (and across a lake) to Refuge Harbour, from where the sea ice stretched away all the way to Cairn Point. The eider-down sleeping bags had suffered only some damage from the foxes, but initially they could not find two rucksacks containing scientific instruments, a camera, books, etc. A search revealed that they had been left below high tide mark and were now encased in the fast ice; they were recovered after some vigorous work with ice chisels and ice axes. Having started back, after a short distance they built an igloo for the night and returned to base by the same route the following day.

Meanwhile on the other side of the Atlantic, Hilda was compensated to some degree for missing Harry by the reception she got from his family. On 8 November she noted in her diary: "I am beginning to feel more and more a part of this large affectionate family of his."[49] And on 20 November, their first wedding anniversary, she wrote:

We were invited to Ashcroft for dinner and tea with Aunt Lill, Aunt Georgie and Uncle Tom. Betty and Joe came in for tea and we drank some cocktails in honor of the occasion, but somehow I did not feel very festive. Couldn't help thinking of my old sweetheart and wondering how he is feeling about it. I remember how had he held my hand when we were being married a year ago, and now we're thousands of miles apart again.[50]

On their anniversary Hilda wrote to KDKA in Pittsburgh with a request to broadcast a message to Harry on their next northern program. In it she mentioned that later that week she planned to go with Bill to see *Rose Marie* in

Cheltenham, and on 7 December she would be attending Harry's old Regimental Ball with Betty and Joe, Bill and Sue. She ended her message by reporting that she had had a cheerful letter from Mrs. Humphreys. "We are both very happy, but have a poor opinion of Arctic Expeditions."[51]

Once the sun had disappeared the daily routine at Etah tended to be dictated by the moon, or by the timing of radio program rather than by the clock.[52] The cook would get up about an hour before the others, light the lamps, stoke up the fire, sweep the floor and generally tidy up. He then made coffee and cooked breakfast, generally porridge and bacon and eggs (made from dried egg-powder). He would then encourage his colleagues to get up by playing a succession of increasingly loud and/or strident records on the gramophone.

Feeding, exercising and generally looking after the dogs took up much of each day. They were provided with windbreaks made of boxes and snow and even small igloos. With these shelters, the dogs would sleep through the most extreme cold or the worst blizzards, curled up with nose tucked into tail. Cutting up frozen walrus meat or fish provided the expedition members with some quite strenuous exercise, since they had to use an axe to chop the meat; each dog received about 1½ kg every other day. The expedition members also spent varying amounts of time learning to drive their own teams, with varying degrees of success. Initially they found themselves quite often in embarrassing predicaments but with time they all improved. They were using a fan-hitch and so they all had to learn to deal with the task of unravelling the tangled knot of frozen traces that resulted when the dogs jumped over each other's traces and wove to and fro as they ran along.

During leisure time they played card games and poker turned out the hot favourite. They kept scores religiously, but did not play for "real money." Harry was by far the best player and by the end of the expedition he was more than £140 ahead in theory. Besides cards, the men relied heavily on the radio for entertainment. The British Air Ministry had lent the expedition a transmitter and receiver, but the transmitter never functioned properly despite Bob Bentham's best efforts to improve its performance. Shackleton regretted this particularly because "Humph and Ev. [Moore] had been making night and day hideous by their diligent practice at Morse with a little buzzer."[53]

Reception, however, was a different matter, especially after the winter night set in. They were able to listen to music from Britain, the U.S. or

Canada almost every night and on 23 December even had a special concert performed and transmitted for their benefit by Harry Roy and his band from the Mayfair Hotel in London. Also, by courtesy of the Canadian Radio Commission and Westinghouse Station KDKA in Pittsburgh and later through CKY, Winnipeg, they regularly received personal messages from family and friends on Saturday nights.[54]

On Christmas Eve a special program of messages was relayed by KDKA to isolated posts throughout the North; this included hundreds of messages and the group at Etah sat up for most of the night listening for messages addressed to them. For Christmas dinner the house was lit by numerous candles and a tablecloth made from sheets also made an appearance. Everyone shaved and dressed in his best. Nukappiannguaq, Inuatuk and their wives appeared in their polar bear pants and their newest sealskin *kamiks*. Everyone exchanged gifts. Shackleton was particularly impressed by an intricately carved paper-knife made of walrus ivory that Nukappiannguaq gave him, the carving having been produced solely with a pen-knife. Christmas dinner was an enormous success. All the components had been provided by Lady Shackleton in the form of a hamper from Fortnum and Mason's and included turkey, wines and Christmas decorations. After-dinner speeches in English and Inuktitut and a number of toasts were followed by dancing, both English and Inuktitut. Here Harry displayed much more stamina than the others:

> Eventually everyone was safely in bed except for Harry who never succeeded in developing his party spirit to the full until everyone else had retired from the combat. In fact, in our rare waking moments during the long hours that followed we heard Harry dancing and singing away by himself, with periodical injunctions to some completely unresponsive person to have a drink.[55]

On New Year's Eve radio reception was excellent; not only did they hear the messages from home but they also heard Big Ben chime the New Year in.

Meanwhile in Ottawa the wheels were still grinding, though extremely slowly, on the issue of MacBrien's special recommendation for Harry, Hamilton and Munro to receive the King's Police Medal. On 7 January MacBrien tried to move things along with a follow-up letter to the under-secretary of state:

Base camp, Oxford University Ellesmere Land Expedition, Etah, spring 1935.

Sir,

May I refer to your letter of August 30th 1934, in which you kindly informed me that the recommendation for the award of the King's Police Medal to Corporal Stallworthy and Constables Hamilton and Munro had been forwarded for submission to His Majesty.

I have no idea of the appropriate time of the year that these medals are usually awarded, and I may be premature in asking at this date if you have received any further information respecting these cases, but it will be appreciated if you can give me some idea when the awards may be expected.

J. MacBrien, Commissioner.[56]

When nothing appeared to be happening, MacBrien repeated his enquiry on 8 May 1935.[57]

Back at Etah, the New Year brought with it the first serious health problem of the expedition. Late one night Humphreys was summoned to the Inughuit's snow house where Enalinguaq was coughing up blood. Humphreys diagnosed tuberculosis, but fortunately her condition did not appear to be critical and she soon appeared to recover her health.

For some time Humphreys had been planning a trip to Robertson Fjord to hire further Inughuit for the spring sledge trips. He also wanted to get to Thule to get permission for these hirings from Mr. Nielsen and to see the doctor, Dr. Holm.[58] Severe weather prevailed throughout most of January and it was not until the 28th, when they also had the benefit of more daylight, that he and his party set off. He was accompanied by Haig-Thomas and by Nukappiannguaq and Inuatuk, each driving a team of dogs. Harry stayed at the base to supervise the hauling of walrus meat from the various caches back to base.

Since the water was still open along the coast, Humphreys's party again headed up the fjord, up the Brother John Glacier and over the icecap, this time in excellent weather. They travelled via Nequi to Robertson Fjord, where Humphreys traded some of the provisions cached there in the fall for dog food and equipment. Then another icecap crossing took them to Thule which they reached at 3 A.M. on 2 or 3 February. They were welcomed warmly by the Governor, Hans Nielsen and by Dr. Holm. The latter insisted that Nukappiannguaq start back immediately for Etah to bring his wife to the Thule hospital for proper treatment.

One matter that must have strained relations somewhat was that Nukappiannguaq and Inuatuk informed the Governor of the breach of government regulations by the expedition members concerning the shooting of walrus without first harpooning them. Humphreys and Haig-Thomas were invited to appear before Nielsen and a Hunters' Council. Harry later heard that Humph claimed that he was unaware of this law, despite the fact that Harry had given him a copy of the regulations. For his part, Haig-Thomas told Harry that he had "defeated the charge" by explaining that shooting the walrus had been in an emergency situation in each case. Harry was well aware of the fact that at the time the incident occurred there was ample dog food, including about 5 tonnes of walrus meat at the base. After explaining the regulations Nielsen dismissed the case. Harry's assessment was that "Mr. Nielsen was most considerate towards the Expedition."[59]

To place this matter in perspective and to understand why the two Inughuit reacted in the way they did, it should be pointed out that the punishment for this infraction could be fairly severe. In the case of a first infraction, the perpetrator was liable to be summoned before the Hunters' Council and given a warning; for a second infraction a fine of 30 kroner for each animal was imposed; for a third infraction 40 kroner. For each infraction beyond that, the fine was increased by 15 kroner. If the fines could not be paid, they could be converted into imprisonment at a rate of 7 days for each 30 kroner, but not to exceed 8 weeks' imprisonment.[60] Since it is unclear how frequently the expedition members breached the regulations, it is difficult to tell what the fine might well have been had Mr. Nielsen decided to apply the full force of the law.

Back at Etah, Harry and the others celebrated the return of the sun on 20 February; it had been below the horizon for 118 days. It had not been a particularly cold winter but the constant strong winds and high humidity that resulted from the nearby presence of open water made for a very unpleasant climate—"a very cold and most undesirable place to winter"[61] in Harry's opinion. No sustained or regular meteorological observations were made, in part due to the lack of equipment, and in part because it was felt to be unproductive since a detailed set of meteorological records had been obtained over a period of four years during MacMillan's expedition at the same site. Irregular measurements were taken, however, and the lowest temperature recorded was -38°F (-39°C) on 4 February 1935, with a strong gale blowing.[62]

Humphreys, Haig-Thomas, Nukappiannguaq and Inuatuk started back from Thule on 14 February along with two other sledges. They were driven by a man who was hauling some of the extra goods for which they had traded at Thule, and a man taking his young son home from the Thule hospital. They travelled by Qanaq, Siorapaluk and Nequi. Here they were joined by Appellah (who was to replace Nukappiannguaq) and his wife and child, and Kahkachoo and his wife. Having obtained Nielsen's permission to hire additional Inughuit to assist with the spring sledge trips, Humphreys and Haig-Thomas were accompanied by a total of five additional Inughuit, each with his own team and some with their wives and children. They reached Etah safely on 24 February. Humphreys and Haig-Thomas reported that they had been in contact with England by radio and brought messages from friends and relatives of the expedition members who had stayed at Etah.

Nukappiannguaq had returned earlier with the instructions from Dr. Holm that he should bring Enalunguaq to the hospital at Thule for treatment. Neither of them was keen on the idea, since they did not want to be separated; however Humphreys had sent strict instructions that Nukappiannguaq be discharged from the expedition's service and Harry reluctantly complied with these instructions. Nukappiannguaq, Enalunguaq and their son left Etah, heading south. Apparently Inuatuk missed Nukappiannguaq and he also asked to leave the expedition, claiming that he had injured his hand. Since he was a willing worker who had acquired some knowledge of English and was popular with everyone, Harry and Eddie persuaded him to stay, at least for the present.[63]

When Humphreys and Haig-Thomas returned, Harry got the feeling that the expedition's plans were in a state of some disarray. First of all he had the impression that Haig-Thomas had to some degree assumed command. He had been discussing various plans with the Inughuit and partly because they had considerable difficulty communicating, the Inughuit were quite confused. They asked Harry who the leader of the expedition was and whether he knew that Haig-Thomas had asked some of them to go to Meighen Island with him to search for the missing Krüger party.[64] Being well aware of the disappearance of Krüger's party and of the dire situation of Harry's and Paddy Hamilton's parties during their searches in that same area, they were understandably concerned.

The plan for the main sledging season, as formulated by Humphreys, was as follows: The six parties previously envisaged would be reduced to three, the partners for these being himself and Eddie, Moore and Haig-Thomas, and Bentham and Harry. The Inughuit, Porsman and Inuatuk, would drive their own teams. The five teams would cross Smith Sound to Princess Marie Bay, then north across the Grinnell Land (now Agassiz) Ice Cap to the head of Greely Fjord, then northeast to Lake Hazen and Grant Land. Each unit of two men would draw separate rations and cook separately. A further eight Inughuit would make up one or more support parties, hauling dog pemmican, provisions and fuel.[65]

The Inughuit were strongly opposed to the proposed route. Apart from the hazards represented by crevasses and the probability of deep snow on the ice cap, they were very concerned that they might run out of dog food on the 100 km crossing of the ice cap, where clearly there was no chance of finding game. The plan also depended on all members of the expedition (or at least one member of each pair) being able to drive dogs competently and even Eddie admitted that they had not mastered the finer points.[66] Harry was somewhat more direct: "Up to the present time the doctor, Shackleton and Thomas had shown but little interest and no aptitude for driving dogs and handling sledges."[67]

The proposed sledging rations, Harry commented, had been devised "by some experts in Europe." The daily ration per man consisted of pemmican, biscuit, chocolate, sugar, tea, coffee, cocoa, 12 oz. of margarine, 4 oz. powdered milk, 26 candies, 30 malted milk tablets, 2 tablets each of vitamins A and D, 3 capsules of vitamin B and 2 tablets of vitamin C, for a total weight of 2 lbs 13 oz. Harry was not impressed: "While I did not question the food value and anti-scurvy properties of the above ration, it did appear to be a rather complicated and inconvenient ration, and not necessary for Eskimos."[68] At his suggestion adjustments were made: bacon was added; biscuit and sugar increased and margarine and powdered milk reduced.

The pemmican that was prepared by Bovril Ltd. in England proved to be very disappointing. The pemmican for the men was found to be too salty and quite unpalatable—so much so that the Inughuit requested that none be taken on the main sledge trips for them. Harry had tried experimenting by adding beef suet, oatmeal and raisins but even in generous amounts these did not seem to counteract the excess salt. "This item was more or less discarded from the ration, and most of the shipment, which was rather expensive, is being returned to the manufacturers in England," he wrote in his report.[69]

The problem with the dog pemmican was more serious in that it contained some unknown ingredient that caused chronic diarrhoea. At the start of the sledge journeys this was assumed to be the dogs' normal reaction to a change in diet (they were not fed the pemmican while at the base). But as time went on they did not improve and soon lost weight and began to flag when hauling heavy loads. In the end, this problem very nearly scuttled the expedition's plans completely.

In order to test the inexperienced drivers and the newly re-organized dog teams suggested by Humphreys, it was decided to make a trial sledging trip north to Cairn Point, where the pack ice began. There was a secondary and more important benefit to the proposed trip in that they would be able to move all the pemmican for the journey north by this distance. Since there was open water just north of Etah and since they therefore had to follow an overland route at the start of the journey, they first had to man-handle over a tonne of pemmican and other rations up a steep, rocky talus slope behind the base. This strenuous task was undertaken on 18 March with the help of the Inughuit, including two women, Natow and Koyipi. The two women greatly impressed the Englishmen with their strength, endurance and agility. Eddie Shackleton candidly admitted "that the Eskimo performed the lion's share of this work."[70]

The following morning, eight empty sledges were hauled up the hill by hitching two teams (22–25 dogs) to each sledge. At the top, the supplies were loaded and the teams set off up a ravine, each sledge carrying a load of 700–800 lbs. There were rocks protruding through the snow in places, making for delicate manoeuvring. Since they lacked experience at handling dog team, Humphreys and Eddie had to unlash their load and backpack it over a particularly rocky section.

The descent to the coast on the north was very steep and led to an accident that might well have been serious. Harry and Bentham's sledge failed to negotiate a bend and flew over a 15-foot drop into a wind scoop. Harry was driving, but was distracted because he was trying to get rough-locks ready to slip over the runners and therefore did not notice that the team had divided, one half going either side of the wind-scoop. Bentham managed to slide off the sledge in time but Harry was less fortunate: the sledge landed upside down with Harry beneath it and although the handlebars (upstanders) were destroyed, Harry was unhurt.[71] Harry made no mention of this incident in his official report or in his published article in the RCMP Quarterly.

Soon afterwards, they could see open water at Cape Hatherton to the north, with little or no icefoot present and so they decided to cache the loads and start back for base. Harry was very popular when he built a snow-block windbreak and brewed some tea, since many of the group were soaked with sweat and were starting to get chilled. It took only an hour to return to base, the sledges being left at the top of the steep hill behind the base.

There were now some 170 dogs at Etah, and keeping them fed was a major chore. On 20 March some of the Inughuit set off south to Robertson Fjord and on the 21st, Moore, Arkhio and Kahkachoo also set off with most of the expedition's dogs, bound for Peteravik to hunt for walrus or to buy walrus meat[72]—in part to give the dogs a good feed and in part to bring back meat for the first stages of the main trips. They visited Peteravik, Nequi and Robertson Fjord. Everywhere there was open water and hence no chance of hunting walrus; worse still, there was little or no walrus meat to be bought since the almost continuous offshore winds had kept the coast largely ice-free for most of the winter. When Moore and his party returned to Etah, the dogs were even in worse condition than when they started. However, Moore had been able to buy a good stock of *kamiks* and mitts from the women at the various camps.

Even some of the caches from the previous fall were a disappointment. Harry, Bentham and one of the Inughuit made a trip north to near Littleton Island where two walrus had been cached by one of the boat parties in September. However, all they found was 150 lbs of walrus hide beneath a snow drift; all the meat and blubber had been eaten by foxes. There were even three foxes under the snowdrift among the remains of the cache.[73]

Towards the end of March the various Inughuit who had committed to going on the spring sledge trips began to arrive at Etah, some with their wives and children. On 27 March Dr. Holm arrived from Thule for a short visit. The population of Etah, including wives and children, had risen to over 30, so the expedition members threw a party and dance. It was a great success, although the liquor stocks had by now been reduced to one bottle of Scotch, which did not go very far.[74]

If the alcoholic spirits were low by the time of the party, Harry's spirits at least were raised by one significant addition to their ranks. Among the Inughuit who arrived to help with spring sledge trips was Nukappiannguaq. He had not taken his wife to the Thule hospital and instead they had been travelling and hunting all winter and Enalunguaq appeared to have recovered completely without medical assistance. Harry and Inuatuk, probably more than anyone else, appreciated his presence and experience.

11

NORTH TO LAKE HAZEN

Spring 1935

THE PLANS FOR THE SPRING SLEDGING had been modified quite drastically yet again. Humphreys's plan to send a single, unwieldy party out in an attempt to reach Greely Fjord across the Grinnell Land Ice Cap was abandoned as it was clearly quite impractical. Instead, they decided that there would be three parties operating independently in separate areas. Harry and Moore, with Nukappiannguaq and Inuatuk and two supporting Inughuit would travel north up the west coast of Greenland, then head across to Lake Hazen via Lady Franklin Bay to explore Grant Land. Humphreys and Haig-Thomas would take four Inughuit with them and cross Ellesmere Island to Bay Fjord and then push north into the interior of Grinnell Land. And finally, Bentham and Shackleton would explore and study the geology of the east coast of Ellesmere Island from Bache Peninsula north to Scoresby Bay.[1] Nine Inughuit women would stay at Etah with their children and keep an eye on the base.

On 30 April Harry called a meeting of all the Inughuit and assigned them to the different parties. He particularly impressed on them that no muskoxen could be killed, not under any circumstances. Final preparations for the trip were now in full swing. These included a marathon doughnut-baking session to make up for abandoning the inedible pemmican and a shortage of bis-cuit. The doughnuts were made with plenty of powdered milk and sugar and were deep-fried in beef suet; together with sliced bacon they made a nourishing ration that was easy to prepare.[2] Once all the preparations had been completed, they staggered the departures of the three parties. Humphreys and Haig-Thomas left first on 2 April; Harry and Moore left on the 3rd and Bentham and Shackleton on the 4th, having tidied up the base.

The main objective of the expedition had always been to explore Grant Land, optimally from a base at Fort Conger, or failing that, Bache Peninsula. Although the expedition had been forced to winter some 650 km further south, this objective had still not changed, although they had realized by now that the best that could be achieved would be a brief visit to the area north of the United States Range and that there would be no time for scientific work. The strongest party, consisting of Harry and Moore, was selected for this chal-lenging task and they were accompanied by the most experienced Inughuit assistants, Nukappiannguaq and Inuatuk and the best dogs. They were also accompanied by two support teams driven by Rasmisi and Ilko.[3]

Harry, Moore and the Inughuit members of their party spent the day of 2 April portaging the provisions and equipment up the steep hill behind the base. On the morning of the 3rd they carried the last of the outfit up the hill, then took up the five sledges and 59 dogs and loaded the sledges in a cold wind accompanied by drifting snow.[4] Once the loading was complete, Harry and Moore set off across the rough country to Cape Hatherton, driving a team of 14 dogs and lifting the sledges over rocks in places.[5] They descended to the shore ice just north of Littleton Island and as they approached Cape Hatherton they saw that only a narrow icefoot clung precariously to the cliffs. They decided to wait for high tide since at low tide a slip would mean a fall of some 12 feet onto rocks in many places. The icefoot was also less likely to collapse at high tide. While they were waiting, Inuatuk shot a seal in the open water and retrieved it by using an ice-floe as a raft. They then enjoyed a welcome meal of boiled meat in the igloo that Humphreys's party had built and left here.

The narrow remnant of shore ice clinging to Cape Hatherton was very badly rafted with pressure ridges up to 25 feet high. Humphreys's party had done a sterling job of chopping a trail through the chaos but even so Harry and his group took the sledges through it one at a time. They reached the main depot at Cairn Point, where Humphreys's party were camped in two tents, in the early hours of the morning.

At noon on the following day, Humphreys's party set off across Smith Sound for Ellesmere Island while Harry and his party made their final preparations. They filed the sledge runners, which had been scored by scraping across rocks and gravel and completed their final loads. The total weight of their outfit approached 3,000 lbs—the largest item being dog pemmican at some 1,500 lbs. The men's own rations weighed 480 lbs; kerosene 240 lbs; robes, skins, spare clothes, camping equipment, cameras and film, scientific instruments, firearms, ammunition, hunting gear and other miscellaneous items came to approximately 750 lbs. The load on each of four of the sledges was about 650 lbs; the fifth sledge, driven by Rasmisi, who had only 8 dogs, was loaded with 400 lbs. At around noon on 5 April, they left a note for Eddie and Bentham and set off northwards with Nukappiannguaq and Ilko in the lead.

At first they made good time crossing Force Bay on hard-packed snow, but when they reached Rensselaer Bay they ran into deep, loose snow. Fortunately for them however, the fast ice between the tidal hummocks and the gigantic cliffs presented a smooth surface with only a recent light snow cover. Further on, as they got into Kane Basin, they could see that there was crusted snow out on the sea ice and extensive areas of rough ice. They felt fortunate to have good going on the icefoot, especially in view of their heavy loads, although it meant having to follow every indentation of the coast to Cape Russell.

On the 6th they ran across the sledge tracks of two Inughuit heading north on a bear-hunting trip. The following day Harry and his party had a brew-up of coffee in one of the bear hunters' old igloos.[6] Later in the day they met the two men who were heading south from their bear-hunt north of the Humboldt Glacier. They had seen no bears, had been unable to get any seals and their dogs were starving. They had already lost five out of 18 dogs, and had just killed two more to feed to the others. The men's faces were badly frostbitten. Harry and Moore gave them 1 lb of pemmican for each of their dogs, and a good meal for themselves.[7]

The two men reported that there was deep snow in Peabody Bay (off the front of the Humboldt Glacier) and hence when Harry and party started out in the early afternoon of the 8th, they struck well out from Cape Leiper, setting a course straight for Cape Calhoun, some 110 km away. Here the going was relatively easy, although they were still sledging through loose snow. Shortly after starting, they ran across an open lead where the dogs scented seals. Nukappiannguaq secured three seals in short order as they came up to breathe and Inuatuk got another soon after they had camped. The seals were a very welcome change for the dogs, since the diarrhoea caused by the pemmican showed no signs of abating and the dogs were already visibly losing condition. After a good night's sleep and eating their fill of seal meat, the dogs picked up noticeably, but by the 10th, Rasmisi's team was starting to flag again.

Having started out at about 1 P.M., they managed to cover some 25 km when, around 9 P.M., the dogs scented a bear near a large iceberg. Throwing off their loads, Nukappiannguaq, Inuatuk and Ilko set off after the bear with just their rifles, knives and a primus stove. While they were gone, Harry, Moore and Rasmisi pitched the tent as there was no suitable snow to build an igloo. The hunters returned with the bear about 6 hours later. Inuatuk had also pursued another one, but had been unable to overtake it.[8] The bear that Nukappiannguaq had shot gave the 59 dogs quite a respectable feed while the men enjoyed the heart, tongue and other delicacies.[9] The hunters had also brought back the skin, which was a very fine one and would be converted into two pairs of pants.

To rest the dogs, they stayed in camp the following day. The men spent the day drying *kamiks* and mitts on a line over the primus stove in the tent and checking and repairing dog harnesses. Before setting off again they "cached" the bearskin by suspending it on a rope about 9m above the sea ice off the vertical face of the nearby iceberg.

Travelling on the 13th of April the going was excellent and the dogs, well-fed and rested, covered the 60 km to Cape Calhoun at a steady trot. They had lunch at the cape and found some interesting fossil corals in the limestone that Lauge Koch had reported seeing earlier.[10] They cached some specimens to be picked up on their return. They spotted a large *ujjuk* (bearded seal) on the ice near Cape Calhoun, but it slid into the water before Nukappiannguaq could get a shot. After travelling another 13 km, they reached the northernmost cape of Morris Bay, where they camped for the night.

In the morning they established a small cache of provisions and dog feed for their return and rearranged the loads. Rasmisi and Ilko started back for base from here, taking with them enough supplies for the trip. Meanwhile, starting around 2 P.M., the three other sledges continued north with about 900 lbs on each sledge. They had with them 912 lbs of pemmican to feed the dogs, as well as a little seal blubber, and 9 gallons of kerosene to serve as fuel for the trip.[11] Once again the icefoot offered the best route, although huge piles of rafted ice pushed against the cliffs entailed a lot of chopping to produce a passable route at some of the capes. For a long distance north of Cape Constitution there was little or no snow on the new ice that had formed in Kennedy Channel. The ice was blue in colour and very rough, indicating that the water was open, but very choppy, when it froze in the fall. At Cape Constitution they examined a coal seam opposite the Franklin Islands that had been reported earlier by Lauge Koch; it was 5.1–7.5 m thick and ran parallel to the coast for at least 400 m just above high water mark.

On the evening of 16 April they camped in the tent on the icefoot at Cape Bryan. There had not been enough snow to build an igloo and they were windbound here for two days, but fortunately the tent stood up well. They used the time to make repairs to the sledges, as they had taken quite a beating on some of the rough ice and they all had broken upstanders and cross-slats and split runners.[12]

The weather was still bad on the third morning, but nonetheless they started across Kennedy Channel for Ellesmere Island. For the first few kilometres the ice was extremely rough, but then they emerged onto old, smooth, undulating ice that continued almost to Ellesmere Island. But then a thick fog rolled in, so that the other two teams were sometimes invisible. Nukappiannguaq was in the lead and in an impressive display of navigation managed to maintain a course straight to the other shore; when the fog lifted they were within about one mile of Ellesmere Island. Heading northeast along the coast, they pitched the tent not far from Cape Baird. This, like their previous few camps, was very uncomfortable for the dogs since they were exposed to cold winds and had little or no snow to insulate them as they lay on the bare ice. They were becoming quite thin and the only bitch in the teams was in such poor condition that she had to be shot.

They were now only about 30 km from Fort Conger, but this stretch across Lady Franklin Bay turned out to be the most strenuous day of the whole trip. The bay was filled with old polar pack and was covered with snow which was waist-deep in places. To avoid it as much as possible, they stayed outside this zone in Robeson Channel, but still had to cross about 25 km of it to reach Discovery Harbour. The deep snow between the rolling ridges of old ice was covered with a crust up to 15 cm thick. The heavy sledges kept breaking through this crust and then had to be dug out, slowing their progress considerably. It took them about 20 hours to cover 30 km.

They were understandably relieved to find the huts at Fort Conger intact. The original building erected by Lt. A.W. Greely's expedition for the First International Polar Year in 1881[13] had been disassembled by Robert Peary in 1900. Using the lumber, he and his men had built three smaller huts that were more energy-efficient.[14] Harry and Moore moved into what was known as "Peary's House" but was in fact that of T.S. Dedrick, Peary's medical officer.[15] The house contained a stove and they managed to get some coal from a nearby local outcrop, so the men were able to dry all their footwear, clothing and sleeping bags, which were becoming iced up. Nukappiannguaq and Inuatuk slept in the hut formerly occupied by Matthew Henson, Peary's black assistant; the third hut, which had been occupied by Peary's Inughuit helpers, was even then in poor repair. Despite a search, they were unable to find the tablets that had been erected to the memory of C.W. Paul and J.J. Hand of the HMS *Discovery*, who had died on G.S. Nares' British Arctic Expedition of 1875–76[16]—probably because they were covered with snow.

However, they did discover the cache left by Captain Godfred Hansen in 1920 in support of Roald Amundsen's planned return sledge trip from the Pole during his transpolar drift in the *Maud*. Hansen had sledged north from Thule to Cape Columbia, leaving several depots along the way.[17] Harry and Moore found most of the provisions spoiled, but 60 lbs of pemmican packed by Beauvais of Copenhagen were still in good condition and provided a welcome day's feed for the dogs. A tin of butter was found to be excellent, but some canned meat which they also tried was probably responsible for the stomach pains they experienced later. They found some cigars that had been

Harry and party on their return from Lake Hazen and the British Empire Range; left to right: Nukappiannguaq, Harry, Moore and Inuatuk.

somewhat spoiled by damp "and it must have been an amusing sight to see the Eskimos setting off the next day puffing at cigars as they cracked their whips."[18]

Before they left, Moore climbed to a cairn on a hilltop a short distance inland and deposited a record of their visit. On this and other short trips in the area they kept their eyes open for game. They had expected to find both hares and muskoxen but there were no signs of either.

They set off again early on 23 April, bound for Lake Hazen by way of Black Rock Vale rather than by the longer route via the Ruggles River. They crossed to Mt. Bell Island in very deep snow,[19] then travelled west along the north coast of that island and Sun Peninsula. They spotted the first muskoxen of the trip on the latter peninsula: four cows and three young calves. Harry thought it rather early to see calves at foot. They camped between two lakes

North to Lake Hazen, spring 1935.

in Black Rock Vale and found it bitterly cold. The thermometer read only -30°F at midnight, but they were in the middle of a windswept valley and the cold from the exposed gravel beneath their sleeping skins struck up through them. The dogs were now on a straight pemmican ration of 1½ lbs per day and were steadily losing condition and energy and Harry was anxious to get to Lake Hazen in hopes of getting plenty of fish for them there.[20]

Starting about midnight on the 24th, they travelled for 12 hours up Black Rock Vale and over a pass towards Lake Hazen, often over rocky and gravelly patches. Along the way they saw a herd of 16 adult muskoxen and a number of calves. Later they saw the tracks of an even larger herd. Given the severe shortage of dog food, the prohibition against shooting muskoxen must have been immensely frustrating to Harry and his companions.

They reached the east end of Lake Hazen on the 26th. Although the approach to the lake was downhill, the dogs could barely manage a walk, they were so weakened. There was a snow cover of about 35 cm on this part of the lake ice, which probably accounted for the fact that the ice was relatively thin—about 135 cm. They immediately chopped holes in the ice to start fishing. Their tools were ice chisels and a scoop improvised from a pemmican can attached to a bamboo pole for removing ice splinters.[21] Since the holes were about 37 cm in diameter, this involved some vigorous exercise. Eventually, they started jigging, using baited spoon hooks and were soon pulling out Arctic char from 15 cm to 90 cm in length, but the number of fish was quite disappointing. They cut more holes over deeper water and cleared the snow around them to let the sunlight penetrate, but this made little difference.[22] Occasionally, they cut new holes and fished more or less continuously for 24 hours, by which time they had only 34 lbs—in Harry's words, "only a small appetizer for the 37 dogs," and still had to feed them pemmican as well.

The four men jigged almost continuously for the next three days, stirring the water in the holes occasionally to prevent it from freezing. While the catch did improve to about 50 lbs a day, this was still not enough to build the dogs up again. Moore was impressed by his companions' unlimited patience: "Harry and the Eskimos displayed unbelievable patience at this fishing, and even slept on their sledges over the holes, occasionally waking up to 'jiggle.'"[23] But despite their best efforts, the quantity of fish taken did not improve and the dogs, rather than fattening up, continued to lose weight.

To their immense frustration, they could see two muskoxen grazing on the north side of the lake throughout their time on the lake. Their situation was becoming desperate, as Harry recorded in his report on the expedition:

We could see that the first part of the journey into Grant Land would be a hard climb through the Garfield Range, which skirts the north side of the lake, and the prospects of obtaining game, other than muskoxen, would be very small. We had left a small cache of dog-pemmican at Fort Conger, and the next cache on the homeward journey was across on the Greenland coast just to the south of Cape Bryan. On our return journey we could not rely on getting seal until nearing the south end of Kennedy Channel. We therefore found ourselves in a difficult if not a dangerous position with regard to making any further progress as a party.

I felt sure at this stage, that if our dogs had been subjected to absolute starvation for a few days, we would have found ourselves without any means of transportation. It was quite evident then, that the whole party could not venture into Grant Land for any length of time without starving a number of dogs (unless we resorted to killing muskoxen), which would make it very difficult, perhaps impossible, to get out of the country.[24]

The solution they agreed upon was that Moore and Nukappiannguaq would take one sledge and the pick of the best dogs and travel as far north into Grant Land as possible, while Harry and Inuatuk stayed at the lake fishing to try to get the thinner dogs into a good enough condition to make the return journey. Harry's rationale in staying at the lake was to allow Moore to get as far north as possible; also Moore was the official photographer and a more experienced surveyor than Harry. Even so, it was not an easy decision for Harry:

It was naturally a great disappointment to me not to travel further north from Lake Hazen, after our strenuous work in getting this far. I had every confidence in Noocapinguaq's [Nukappiannguag's] judgment and ability to take Moore as far north as possible under these adverse conditions, while I felt keenly my responsibility for the safe return of the party.[25]

To give him his due, Moore offered to toss a coin to see which of them should go north. He was fully conscious of the generosity of Harry's decision: "This was no mean sacrifice, and meant days of monotonous fishing, but Harry turned to this task with his ever-unfailing energy and enthusiasm."[26]

On the afternoon of 1 May, Moore and Nukappiannguaq set off northwards from Lake Hazen, heading for the Gilman Glacier via a valley through the Garfield Range. They had the 17 best dogs, a small quantity of fish and 136 lbs of pemmican which ought to provide eight feeds for the dogs. For fuel, they had about 6 litres of kerosene.

For the next four days, Harry and Inuatuk continued fishing, moving camp three times in hopes of finding a more productive spot. In total they cut 23 fishing holes since first reaching the lake, finally ending up at the northeast end of the lake. The results continued to be quite disappointing but by feeding the remaining dogs half rations (about 1 lb of fish per day) they were able to accumulate a reserve of 50–60 lbs of fish. With the 96 lbs of pemmican which they had kept, this should be enough to get the whole party back to Fort Conger.

This reserve was accumulated only at the cost of remarkable self-sacrifice by Harry and Inuatuk. While allocating 6 litres of kerosene to Moore and Nukappiannguaq, Harry had retained less than 1 litre for himself and Inuatuk, and their diet consisted almost solely of fish:

After a few meals of raw frozen fish, we found that the best of them were very unpalatable, being practically tasteless, but we could not afford to use our scanty supply of coal oil more than once a day to make cocoa, which we found very beneficial before turning into our sleeping bags, after the long cold days spent lying on the ice, "jigging" at the fishing holes.[27]

The solitary Arctic hare that Inuatuk shot on one of their days on the lake made a very welcome change of diet.

In the early hours of 5 May they saw Moore and Nukappiannguaq returning. Inuatuk had just returned with a further two hares, and assuming the travellers would be hungry, Harry used the last of the kerosene to prepare a hot meal for them. But to his surprise and delight, as Nukappiannguaq approached he announced that they had brought caribou meat, having shot three animals only the previous day. After several days of eating raw fish, Harry and Inuatuk undoubtedly appreciated a good portion of caribou meat.

Moore and Nukappiannguaq had reached the snout of the Gilman Glacier on the second day out, only to be faced with a sheer icewall.[28] After a search they found a spot with a gentle gradient and by cutting steps and portaging their load to the top and then driving the empty sledge up, they reached the more level surface of the glacier. They were then faced with a long, steady climb, fortunately with a good, hard snow surface. Once on the ice cap, under which most of United States Range is buried, they headed for a prominent peak to the northwest. They reached its foot and then waited a few hours for the clouds to lift before they left the dog team and climbed to its summit, cutting steps up a razor-sharp snow ridge for the last 90 m. The visibility was now excellent. From their vantage point, which they named Mt. Oxford, and whose height they estimated at 9,000 feet (in fact 2,210 m or c.7,200 feet) they surveyed an endless array of peaks protruding through the ice cap. The maze of peaks to the north they named the British Empire Range. Through the binoculars, Nukappiannguaq identified Clements Markham Inlet away to the northeast and the pack ice of the Arctic Ocean beyond. They had enough dog-pemmican left for only one more day of outward travel and their own food was practically exhausted. Sensibly, Moore decided to go no further. They descended to the sledge and slept.

The weather in the morning was superb and they climbed back to the summit in sunshine so that Moore cold sketch and photograph the panorama in every direction. Then, after hoisting the Union Jack that the expedition's patron, the Duke of York (later King George VI) had given the expedition, they started down again, hitched up the dogs and started on the back-trail to Lake Hazen. The descent of the steep ice-front of the Gilman Glacier was exhilarating and the sledge overtook the dogs, dragging them along behind; everything ended up in a heap at the bottom, Moore sprawled across the load and Nukappiannguaq flat on his back behind. Having spotted and killed the three caribou and having allowed the dogs to eat their fill of the first fresh meat they had had since Peabody Bay, they pushed on for Lake Hazen without sleeping.

After fishing without much success for one more day, the reunited party started on the homeward journey on 8 May, following a small river south from the east end of Lake Hazen. Initially the dogs started at a good pace after

Nukappiannguaq, summit of Mt. Oxford, Ellesmere Island, spring 1935.

Searching for best route among pressure ridges, Cape Bryan, Hall Basin, spring 1935.

the feed of caribou meat, but they soon lost energy and next day on the way to Fort Conger they could manage only a walking pace—so much so that on downgrades on hard-packed snow the men had to hold the sledges back.[29] By now the sun was quite warm and very bright, and Nukappiannguaq developed a severe headache from to the glare. Before reaching Fort Conger, Nukappiannguaq and Inuatuk each killed two of their dogs that were lagging behind, while four of Harry's dogs were simply staggering along. However he did not kill them since he hoped to obtain some seal fairly soon.

Since getting fresh meat was a primary concern at this point, they discarded one sledge and some equipment at Fort Conger and combined the dogs into two teams of 16 dogs each. Before leaving Fort Conger, they fed the dogs a small amount of the canned meat from Hansen's cache, along with some sealskin *kamiks* and harness, cut into small pieces. Harry also collected some samples of the coal from the nearby seam that had been used by both Nares' and Greely's expeditions.[30] Moore left a message about the expedition and the trip to Mt. Oxford in Henson's hut and since this was the most northerly patrol undertaken by any member of the RCMP, Harry also left a brief note with a request that the finder forward it to RCMP Headquarters in Ottawa.

They then set off southwards in the late afternoon of 11 May, deliberately travelling at night since it was then colder and the snow harder. They again had to cross the stretch of old polar pack with crusted snow and to ease the stress on the dogs they camped after only 11 km of this tough going. Progress was slow the next day, even with both Harry and Moore walking. At Cape Leiber, south of Cape Baird, they stopped to collect some rock specimens, then cut across Kennedy Channel to Cape Bryan. Going was generally good, but the dogs were still moving only at a crawl. At their old campsite at Cape Bryan, they found the cache of pemmican intact and the dogs bolted it down. Some sugar and tobacco were also very welcome.

Heading south after two long days of slow travel, they reached Cape Constitution on the morning of 13 May. Here they spotted some seals lying beside leads. The first two escaped, but the third one was killed and recovered. Unfortunately it was small and served as little more than an appetizer for 32 hungry dogs.

The next camp was at the cache south of the Franklin Islands, where the support party had turned back. They found the two cases of dog-pemmican and some food for themselves and spare clothing in good condition. On leaving their camp the next evening they found a large polynya off Cape Calhoun, caused in part by a large iceberg moving to and fro with wind and tide.[31] After making camp, they managed to shoot one small seal. Next morning an *ujjuk* surfaced near camp; Inuatuk shot and killed it but it floated towards the ice edge with the strong current. Inuatuk fortunately managed to harpoon it before it disappeared under the ice:

> We pulled it up on a floating ice-pan, cut it up, and quickly hoisted it up with ropes to the shore ice about ten feet above the water level, only just before the pan was turned up on its end by the current, and disappeared under the main pack.[32]

All the worries about dog food were now over since the meat and blubber totalled about 800 lbs and they were able to feed the dogs to repletion. "They ate and ate, and we could see them swelling up, until at last they curled themselves up and slept for a day with lumps of meat lying untouched beside them," Harry wrote of the incident.[33]

By now the kerosene was exhausted, so some of the *ujjuk* blubber was used for cooking, supplemented by some boards from the sledges. "It was a very slow and grimy job, and Harry, who generally cooked the meals, would get up black from the smoke."[34]

At Cape Calhoun and to the north of it they collected some very large fossil corals and photographed the largest ones. The corals included halysites, cephalopods and brachiopods. The dogs having recuperated somewhat after gorging themselves on the *ujjuk* meat, Harry and his companions started out late in the day on 19 May. They cut south across Peabody Bay, keeping well out from the front of the Humboldt Glacier to avoid the deep snow. As they left the land at Cape Calhoun, one of the sledges broke through some thin ice, but the dogs maintained the strain and the sledge rode up onto strong ice again without any of the gear being seriously soaked. The encountered some deep, heavy snow as they approached Cape Kent at the south end of Peabody Bay, but the dogs were now strong enough to cope with it. "One could hardly believe that these dogs were on the verge of staggering with weakness a week ago, as they strained at the traces with their bushy tails curled over their backs, apparently enjoying the work, while we rode on the sledges," Harry wrote.[35]

At Rensselaer Bay, Harry and Nukappiannguaq visited a small island where they found an arrow carved in the rock. This dated from Dr. E.K. Kane's expedition of 1853, and pointed to where his ship, *Advance* had been beset in the ice in 1853 and was ultimately abandoned in 1855.[36]

A wide belt of shore ice gave excellent going and the two sledges forged south. They killed several seals that lay hauled out along leads. On reaching the main pemmican cache north of Cairn Point, they found the tracks of the other two parties that had stopped here on their way back from Ellesmere Island. Nukappiannguaq and Inuatuk studied the tracks carefully and declared that they had all returned safely and that the dogs were wellfed.

On 25 May they reached Cape Hatherton to find a note from Shackleton to confirm that the other two parties had returned safely. Picking up two boxes of geological specimens and a field radio, they set off in stormy weather on 26 May. The overland crossing over the ice cap was tackled in a driving blizzard. The temperature was not particularly low but with a howling wind and wet, driving snow they found these the worst conditions of the entire trip. On the final steep descent to Foulke Fjord, Moore and Inuatuk descended first and were standing chatting on the sea ice while the rest of the party worked their way down. As Nukappiannguaq and Harry were letting their sledge down, they dislodged a large boulder. Realizing the danger to their companions, they started shouting. Moore later described the situation: "Inuatuk glanced upwards and then leapt aside, crying to me to do likewise. A few seconds later a huge boulder landed on the ice and swept past the sledge, missing it only by inches."[37]

Not long after this incident, they reached the base on the afternoon of 26 May to be greeted by Humph, Shackleton and Bentham; Haig-Thomas had already left for Robertson Fjord to pursue ornithological work. Harry, Moore, Nukappiannguaq and Inuatuk had been travelling for 55 days, during which time Harry estimated that they had covered some 900 miles [1440 km]. Despite being obliged to start from such a southerly base and despite the disastrous effect of the dog-pemmican on the dogs and the relative lack of game, they had achieved the expedition's objective of penetrating Grant Land. The place names of Mt. Oxford (the vantage point reached by Moore and Nukappiannguaq) and the British Empire Range are a fitting tribute to the party's endurance and perseverance. For Harry it was always a matter of great pride that he had attained the highest latitude ever attained by an RCMP patrol.

Humphreys and Haig-Thomas had set off from Etah, intending to cross the Grinnell (Agassiz) Ice Cap on 2 April. They were accompanied by Kooetigeto and Kakhachoo, and a support party comprised of Ootah and Kahkotchingwa. In total they were driving five dog teams as they crossed from the main depot north of Cairn Point to Pim Island. After picking up some provisions from the RCMP cache at Fram Havn, they continued to the detachment at Bache Peninsula,[38] arriving there on 8 April. They secured a substantial number of seals in the polynya at the mouth of Flagler Fjord and were able to give the dogs a good feed. Setting off again on 11 April, the party swung around the east end of Bache Peninsula and north across the mouth of Princess Marie Bay. They reconnoitred the valley at the head of Franklin Pierce Bay, since the Admiralty chart indicated a glacier flowing down to its head from the Grinnell Ice Cap. However, they discovered that this was not the case and so instead they headed west along the coast and along the full length of Copes Bay to the snout of the Parrish Glacier. This appeared to offer a promising route up onto the ice cap and at this point they sent Ootah and Kahkotchingwa back to Etah.

For several days they pushed north up the Parrish Glacier but were finally brought to a halt by deep, soft snow and were forced to retreat. They next contemplated crossing to Cañon Fjord from the head of Princess Marie Bay and to this end crossed the isthmus of Cook Peninsula. Then the plans were changed again and it was decided to cross from the head of Flagler Fjord to Bay Fjord. With this destination in mind, the party crossed the isthmus of Bache Peninsula to Flagler Fjord. However, at the insistence of the Inughuit, they headed back east to the Bache Peninsula detachment to dry their clothes before heading west.

Having dried their clothes, they started back west on 24 April. The party had now used much of their pemmican and so it was essential that they find game to allow them to continue their travels. They therefore decided to head west to Bay Fjord where there were good prospects of finding caribou. Their route west up Flagler Fjord and then over Sverdrup Pass was the same one Harry and his party had used three years earlier. The Oxford party, however, was able to navigate the river gorge where the glacier from they south almost abutted against the valley slope to the north. On reaching Bay Fjord, Moore tried to persuade the Inughuit to make an overland crossing to Cañon Fjord, but they demurred, wanting first to find enough game to give the dogs a good feed. They killed several caribou in Bay Fjord and rested the dogs for several days. On the following day they managed to shoot a bear as they continued their trip westwards. After camping opposite Grettna Island, they decided to head south to one of the fjords that branched off Baumann Fjord. Having encountered and killed some caribou, they continued south and southeast to the head of a fjord that Humphreys identified as Vendom Fjord, but which Haig-Thomas and Nukappiannguaq were convinced was Trolld Fjord.[39] Given the times and distances involved, it seems much more likely that it was Trolld Fjord.

Humphreys wanted to continue south down this fjord, but the Inughuit refused as they were afraid that a snowfall might make the return trip over the height of land difficult, if not impossible. As a result, they started back to Bay Fjord on the following day. Having headed east up Bay Fjord, Humphreys next tried to persuade the Inughuit once again to head north overland to Cañon Fjord, but they were concerned that an early break-up in Smith Sound might leave them cut off from their homes and families in Greenland. Humphreys and Haig-Thomas found this frustrating, since travelling conditions were good and the dogs were fit and well-fed. By the evening of 11

Negotiating a dangerous gap in the icefoot, Northwest Greenland, spring 1935.

May they were back at the Bache Peninsula detachment and from there Humphreys and Haig-Thomas made a brief trip of a couple of days to Haa Island at the junction of Jokel Fjord and to Beitstadt Fjord to investigate some ancient house sites. Since the ground was frozen hard, they were unable to excavate at all but they did manage to obtain some artifacts from the moss between the stones of some of the surviving walls.

Returning to Bache Peninsula, they started back for Etah. It took them just two days to reach the Greenland coast just north of Cache Point. Just south of Cache Point they barely escaped disaster when the icefoot collapsed under the weight of the first dog team. The sledge did not go with it but two dogs were killed by falling ice blocks and four were drowned.[40] They reached the base at Etah safely on 22 May. Reading between the lines of the various reports, it is evident that there were serious frictions between Humphreys and Haig-Thomas and their Inughuit companions. This was in striking contrast to the harmony that clearly prevailed on Harry and Moore's trip.

Eddie Shackleton and Bob Bentham led the last party to leave Etah on 4 April. They were accompanied by Porsman and Ahnowka and with Sakeus and Macheto in support. At the main depot north of Cairn Point they picked up the dog-pemmican that had been cached for them there before setting off across Smith Sound. They made good progress to the depot at Fram Havn, helped by the fact that the previous party had chopped a route through areas of rough ice. In the morning, Sakeus complained of a sore eye. Upon investigation, Shackleton found that an iron filing had entered his eye while filing his sledge runners. The priority now was to catch up with Humphreys, who was the expedition doctor and to this end they travelled non-stop all night. On reaching the Bache Peninsula detachment, they were relieved to find Humphreys still there. He immediately carried out a minor operation and removed the iron filing under local anaesthetic.

The plan from here was to travel up the east coast of Ellesmere Island as far as Scoresby Bay so that Bentham could investigate the geology of the area. However, the amount of pemmican they could carry was quite limited, partly because their loads included a radio receiver, a theodolite and other surveying equipment. They would therefore have to rely on hunting, but Ootah, who knew this coast well since he had travelled it with Peary, advised that it was still too early to expect to find seals on the ice. They therefore decided to postpone the trip for about ten days.[41] In the meanwhile, Bentham could search for Cambrian fossils around Bache Peninsula, while Eddie, Porsman and Sakeus crossed the isthmus of the peninsula to investigate the glaciers that were discharging into Princess Marie Bay as possible routes for Bentham to use on his geological field trips. Eddie examined the snout of the Sven Hedin Glacier but found that its 60-foot ice-cliff, seamed with crevasses, was totally impassable and so he returned to Bache Peninsula. On 18 April the support party from Humphreys's group called in at the detachment and then continued back to Etah. Eddie sent Macheto back with them, but retained Sakeus who was both a good hunter and a useful geological assistant.

Shackleton and Bentham set off on their trip to Scoresby Bay on the evening of 23 April with four sledges, the three Inughuit each driving a sledge and Shackleton and Bentham the fourth one; the latter arrangement allowed the two men to take photographs readily and Bob was also free to check outcrops when necessary. They crossed the mouth of Dobbin Bay to Cape Louis Napoleon, then headed along the coast of Daly Peninsula. On 30 April Bob examined the geology from Cape Fraser to Cape Norton Shaw, while Eddie and one of the Inughuit reconnoitred Scoresby Bay until Eddie fell ill and had to return to the camp at Cape Norton Shaw. Over the next three days (1–3 May) Bob investigated the geology of Scoressby Bay, but as the Inughuit had been unable to kill any seals and they had only three feeds of pemmican left for the dogs, they started back on 4 May. For two days, the party got a late start as Eddie Shackleton was still feeling very ill. During these two days, Eddie rode on Porsman's sledge, on the 6th he was again able to take his place as Bob's partner. Ahnowka shot a seal near the entrance to Dobbin Bay, but it did not go far among four starving teams. On the 8th they drove non-stop to Cape Albert, a distance of at least 50 miles—a stretch that had taken them three days to negotiate on the way north. Then on the evening of the 9th they completed the last lap west to the detachment. On their arrival, the Inughuit went out hunting immediately and got four seals for their famished dogs.

Humphreys and his party returned from their trip to Bay Fjord on 10 May. Once they were back, Bob and Porsman set off to investigate the geology of Princess Marie Bay, returning on the 17th. By now the Inughuit were keen to head for home before the ice in Smith Sound broke up. The group spent the 18th tidying up the buildings at Bache Peninsula then on the 19th they set off for Etah. To achieve greater speed, Eddie and Bob abandoned their sledge and added their dogs to the teams of the three Inughuit. Despite having to sit out a blizzard near the Greenland coast, they reached Etah in the early hours of 24 May. The Inughuit were keen to depart for their homes that same day, and so, rather reluctantly, Humphreys paid them off and they departed for home with gifts of all the tea, coffee, flour and other provisions that they could carry. Eddie was especially sad to see Porsman depart,

> for although they had all served us faithfully, we had a special affection for our kind, old friend. He had always shown that he took his responsibility for our safety very seriously, and I could never imagine him deserting a white man. It was his energy, endurance and cheerfulness, and that of his companions, that brought us such success as we attained.[42]

Soon after the last of the sledge parties had returned, the first signs of spring began to appear at Etah. The first running water was seen on 31 May and the first flowers (purple saxifrage) were seen on 9 June. Seals began to haul out along the leads to bask in the sun—although not in such large numbers at Etah as farther south at Robertson Fjord. The expedition members tried their luck at stalking them as there were no Inughuit left at Etah by this stage. Harry was the most successful and managed to kill quite a number.

On June 15 Harry, Moore and Bentham took the boat to Littleton Island to collect eider duck eggs.[43] They had to haul the boat for several miles by dog team to reach open water, with Humphreys and Eddie assisting. The ice was quite rotten and men and dogs were continually breaking through. Humphreys, Eddie and Moore took the dogs back to the base while Harry and Bentham camped for the night at the floe edge. When Moore joined them again next morning, they set off rowing in fine, warm weather, a calm sea and with practically no ice. Early on the 17th they reached a small islet (McGary Island) on the north side of Littleton Island where vast numbers of gulls and eiders were nesting. By law this was the last date on which they could collect eider eggs, and the party made the most of the few hours left at their disposal. By the end of the day they had amassed some 2,000 eggs.

While Harry, Bentham and Moore were collecting eggs, Humphreys and Eddie had returned to base since the were expecting to get wireless messages from Thule. Then they set off to walk the 13 km to a point opposite Littleton Island, where they intended to join the others at a prearranged point. There appears to have been some confusion about the prearranged time, since Humphreys and Eddie had left the rendezvous even before the boat party started back south. Not finding them, Humphreys and Eddie hiked back to Etah.

On McGary Island, the boat party was experiencing a minor drama. The line that moored the boat to shore was too short and as the tide ebbed, the boat was tilted up on the ice foot and the boat motor fell out into the sea. Fortunately, they managed to recover it.[44] Then the boat went adrift when the knot in the sealskin line slipped. Bentham spotted the boat drifting away and by racing along the icefoot they managed to hook the boat as it drifted past a headland by using an ice-axe tied to a line. This might have been a very unpleasant situation since the whaleboat was still embedded in ice at Etah, and there were no Inughuit to search for them in their kayaks. Also it was unlikely that Humphreys and Shackleton would have looked for them on the little McGary Island.

Before leaving the island, Harry and Bentham cached about 800 eggs under a rock to keep them cool, then loaded the rest in the boat and rowed back to Etah on 19 June. The bay was still ice-bound and they had to land some distance from the base; from here Moore and Bentham carried the eggs to the base in several trips. Since it was not safe to leave the boat unattended, Harry camped by the boat for three days, passing the time by shooting several seals for dog food until the ice cleared out of the bay.[45]

On 27 June, before the ice had gone out, Nukappiannguaq arrived back from Robertson Fjord with his wife, Enalunguaq, who now appeared to have recovered completely from her illness. They also brought with them Sakeus and two of Nukappiannguaq's daughters by an earlier marriage. Nukappiannguaq had decided to settle at Etah since he "was rather a solitary, backwoods sort of an Eskimo, and delighted not at all in the gay social life of Robertson Fjord with its large population of nearly thirty souls."[46]

During the previous fall, a high tide had overwhelmed the whaleboat and they had been unable to haul it out of the water, so the boat had been frozen in all winter. Now that it was spring again, they chopped it free from the ice and Bob and Nukappiannguaq managed to get the motor running again. Then, when the ice went out of the bay on 11 July they were able to refloat it. On the 12th, Bob and some of the Inughuit set off to hunt walrus and to retrieve some of the depots they had cached along the coast to the north. They completed their mission successfully, returning with all the recovered provisions and five walrus.

Meanwhile Haig-Thomas had been living with the Inughuit at Robertson Fjord, studying the birds and the flora. In anticipation of *Dannebrog* coming to pick them up on 30 July, Humphreys, Bentham, Eddie, Nukappiannguaq, Enalunguaq and Sakeus set off in the whaleboat to go to pick Haig-Thomas up, leaving Harry and Moore at Etah.[47] But at the first attempt, the motor quit and after drifting ignominiously around the fjord, they abandoned the trip for that day. They started out again on the evening of 1 August, but as they approached Cape Alexander the sleeve of Nukappiannguaq's anorak was caught in the engine's flywheel, and his arm hit the floor of the boat with a severe impact. Fortunately the sleeve tore just as he pulled the leads off the plugs to stop the engine. His wrist was very painful and Humphreys thought it might be broken, so they turned back to Etah so he could make a proper medical examination. Fortunately the wrist was not broken, although it was badly swollen the next day.

The party set off again on 5 August, leaving Nukappiannguaq behind. This time they reached Robertson Fjord safely despite recurring problems with the motor. They were pleasantly surprised, as they approached Siorapaluk, to see Haig-Thomas paddling out in a kayak. He had been as far south as McCormick Fjord and had started north by kayak, but none of the Inughuit would attempt to round Cape Alexander with him and so he had been forced to stop at Siorapaluk.

A few days later the entire party started back north for Etah, but after four or five hours, while they attempted a landing to let Bentham study the geology, the whaleboat was swamped and began pounding against rocks. They waited for a few hours until the sea had calmed before they tried to get the boat off the beach. They succeeded in doing so, but the boat was leaking badly and they decided to put back to Siorapaluk. Since the engine had now died completely and the *Dannebrog* was expected any day now, they decided to stay at Siorapaluk until she did arrive. While they began to get anxious about the ship's non-arrival, the expedition members quite enjoyed their stay in an Inughuit village despite the fact that they had to rely on the generosity of their hosts when their supplies were exhausted (except for coffee and sugar).

To show their appreciation, the expedition members organized a party and games for the children, although many of the adults also insisted in participating in races such as the three-legged race.

Finally, late on the evening of 21 August, on the anniversary of *Signalhorn*'s departure, *Dannebrog* arrived at Siorapaluk under the command of Captain Pedersen and with Hans Nielsen on board. Once the year's supplies for that settlement had been landed, she continued to Etah with the expedition members and a few Inughuit on board. They arrived there on the 23rd and while Harry and the other expedition members made final preparations for departure, the *Dannebrog* set off with all the Inughuit to hunt walrus. She returned 36 hours later with ten walrus. All the expedition's surplus provisions and coal were loaded aboard and taken to Thule as a gift to the North Greenland Administration. Nielsen took charge of the building, but only after it had been largely stripped of its interior lining, which Inuatuk had decided would be ideal for his house at McCormick Fjord.

The expedition members bid an emotional farewell to the Inughuit who had travelled with them and had shared so many of their experiences. Shackleton's parting from Nukappiannguaq was especially moving. He had been very perturbed by stories of the hazards of life in England, especially the incidence of road accidents. For ease of explanation, Shackleton had described cars as "motor-sledges." Now Nukappiannguaq begged him: "When you get back to England and take your own sledge out again, you must not go too fast, or perhaps you will hit another sledge and then you will be killed. That would be very sad."[48]

Dannebrog put to sea on the early morning of 25 August, but almost immediately ran into a severe gale and the vessel even had to heave-to for 12 hours, with loose deck cargo thundering about her decks. As a result it was late afternoon on the 27th before they reached Thule and even then they had to wait for two days for the sea to subside enough to allow the coal and supplies for Thule to be landed. The expedition members were entertained generously by Hans Nielsen and his wife, Dr. Holm, the District Nurse and Pastor Ohlsen, a Greenlander from Jakobshavn. At Thule, Harry also took delivery of the private belongings and RCMP property that had been left at Fram Havn in April 1933 and had subsequently been brought across by Nukappiannguaq.

Leaving Thule on 1 September, the *Dannebrog* experienced superb, calm weather and only scattered floes as she crossed Melville Bay. On 7 September she reached Umanaq, and then Jakobshavn, where she loaded rock ballast. Sailing again on the 12th, she next called at Godhavn on Disko, where she completed her load of 40 tonnes of rock ballast. Dr. Rosendahl and Dr. Porsild entertained them royally and the Greenlanders put on a dance in their honour.

On the 18th the *Dannebrog* reached Ivigtut, her final port of call in Greenland, where cryolite, which is used in the manufacture of aluminum, was mined until around 1975. The expedition members were given a very friendly reception by the officials at the cryolite mine and their invitation to take advantage of the baths was readily accepted.[49]

On 19 August, the *Dannebrog* put to sea, bound around Kap Farvel and back to Aberdeen. But even off Kap Farvel they ran into a vicious northeast gale that blew the ship a long way off course to the south; on the 23rd she made barely any progress in the right direction. But then the weather moderated and for five days she made good progress to about mid-Atlantic, about 700 miles west of Scotland. Evidently the propeller had been cracked while the ship was working in ice and now a blade dropped off; this caused severe vibration that resulted in turn in a serious leak in the propeller shaft housing. As a result, the diesel engine had to be shut off and the remainder of the voyage was completed under sail. For a time they had to heave-to again and were carried a long way south off their course. But then on 1 October the wind died and for a time *Dannebrog* was drifting stern-first towards Scotland.

Now a fresh north wind rose and the vessel began making good progress eastwards. But she was being set quite far south and it became clear that she would not be able to make the Pentland Firth round the north of Scotland. The captain then headed for Stornoway on Lewis, and later for Castlebay, Barra. On 6 October *Dannebrog* passed St. Kilda and on the 7th the ship reached Castlebay. Humphreys, Haig-Thomas and Moore caught the mail steamer to Oban that same day and Moore followed two days later. Harry, Eddie and Bentham stayed to help arrange for *Dannebrog* to be beached for repairs to her propeller and to keep an eye on the expedition stores and (in Harry's case) the RCMP effects from Bache Peninsula that were on board. Harry found this delay quite frustrating, as he explained in a letter to Hilda which Moore took south to mail for him:

Darling, I'm so anxious to see you again. It's been so long. A year and four months. I've been awfully fed-up on the last part of this expedition.

...We shall have a big dinner when I get in, darling. Four fat mutton chops for me. I'm awfully excited to actually be "coming back" darling. It's been a h—of a long year.[50]

In addition to venting his frustration, he also arranged for Hilda to travel up to London so that they could meet at the Cumberland Hotel.

Arranging to beach *Dannebrog* was a protracted business. The owners hired two local fishing boats and a lifeboat to help in the manoeuvre, but due to uncooperative weather and an insignificant tidal range, all these efforts were in vain and ultimately the owners arranged for *Dannebrog* to be towed to Oban where there were better facilities. But there was some compensation; in a postscript to his letter to Hilda, dated 6 P.M. on the 9th, Harry reported: "We had a lot of Scotch dances and whisky here last night. The people of the Isle of Barra are certainly very nice."[51]

Along with Eddie, Harry finally caught the mail boat to Oban on 11 October, while Bentham stayed with *Dannebrog* to see the expedition stores through customs at Oban. Harry and Eddie caught the train from Oban to Glasgow on the 12th, where they had an interview with the BBC concerning the expedition.

Having met in London as prearranged, Harry and Hilda returned to Fairford for a short holiday that Harry had cleared with RCMP Headquarters in Ottawa.[52] Writing to Eddie on 22 October, he discussed such things as bringing Eddie a white fox pelt he had promised him (from those he had trapped on Ellesmere Island) and the plans for a final party with all the expedition members when he and Hilda came up to London on the 30th. He also asked Eddie to select 12 of the best photos taken on the expedition and to have slides made, since he had received a request for a lecture to Cirencester Grammar School, "and if I do not get around to this I should never be forgiven by my brother's two boys."[53] To this letter Hilda added a postscript from "the stenographer," as she had typed the letter in one of her first efforts at taking dictation from Harry.

As early as 3 June, just after the sledge teams had returned to Etah, Eddie Shackleton's sister, Cecily, wrote him a letter that he received only after he had arrived back in Britain. She warned him against the type of manoeuvrings that she anticipated Dr. Humphreys would attempt on the expedition's return:

> ...This brings me to a matter about which I have been thinking a great deal—DR HUMPHREYS. Eddie, you must not stand down to him; once the Expedition is home he ceases to be leader. Charles Elton [treasurer and former chairman of the Oxford University Explorers' Club] tells me this is in a contract. Dr. H. did hardly a single thing before the Ex. Left, and there is no doubt that he is intentionally trying to do you down, and take all publicity and not even acknowledging you as having done anything. He has not once given a word of recognition to you as Organiser, and his articles do not show an unbiased spirit. You may be aware of all this, but I think that he plays up to you and pretends to be decent and the whole time is being a proper little "snake-in-the-grass." You must make allowances for any bitterness I may show, but do not put it all down to the feminine mind plus sisterly affection. I only write as strongly as I do, because C. Elton is very anxious that you should realise the true position. I am not saying anything has happened yet, but you must be prepared to stand absolutely firm and give way over nothing, in this you have the entire support of the Ex[plorers] Club, who I understand are very sick with H.
>
> Apart from purely the feeling of fair play, and honour going to whom honour is due, you must also remember the most important thing of all, which is, that YOU stand for something both with your supporters and the general public, and if we are to give a satisfactory account of the doings of the Ex. it should come from you, over the wireless and in any other ways, not from Dr. H. who means nothing to anyone, and who has no commercial qualities or selling value. This last sentence may sound very horrid and cynical, but truly it must be considered.
>
> To sum it all up, Dr. Humphreys will expect and will try to get (whatever else he may profess to you) the jam in the sandwich, having left you to work on the first slice of dull bread, i.e. preliminary plans, collecting money, etc., and will leave for you the other slice of bread, i.e. finishing up affairs and collecting of balance.

Darling, you are a most reasonable and sensible man; do not let a feeling of chivalry outweigh hard common-sense, and do not, from a feeling of personal generosity, disappoint those who have worked very hard for you and you alone. Several of us have been concentrating on holding the fort for your return, expecting YOU to benefit by our efforts and that is the only reward we ask, that you should sail in and take the place we have kept up for YOU. We are dashed proud of you and because of our belief in you, have loved to work for you, but we will be very, very disappointed if, on your return, you do not take your proper place as the Originator and entire Organiser of a very good show.

I can offer no advice on how you should deal with Dr. H. should he try and take the field too strongly on your return; the best method would be to use his own, of saying little unless forced to but firmly standing out for yourself without argument. Remember he can write and say nothing without the approval of the Explor. Club....

I am awfully sorry that Dr. H. and Harry do not get on and that the former is so incompetent as leader. I am not surprised to hear this and of course will discuss it with no one except Charles Elton as he, I feel, ought to know. You say that Dr. H. is kind and friendly; do not be too sure of this. I am certain that he is very jealous of you and his silly articles bear this out; it is disgraceful and most noticeable the way in which he entirely ignores you, both as Organiser and even as an ordinary member of the Ex; Haig-Thomas gets the most recognition all through. Several people have remarked about you not writing any of the articles and Gerald Christy, who rang up yesterday *re* lecture dates for you, remarked on any mention of you! I have referred him to Charles Elton (see enclosed letter). I am afraid that however unpleasant it may be, you will have to take a stand with Dr. H.; he has done for himself by the obviously biased articles which he has written and I believe that the originals which he sent to Elton were really pretty bad, as Charles Elton told me that he had had to cut out quite several bits, some because they were not too wise. Sorry to keep on about all this darling; it is only because I feel that you MUST be warned. You have your life in front of you and Dr. H. is well on in his and your future so depends on you taking your proper place on your return. It is a pity that Dr. H. cannot be unbiased.[54]

The situation evidently became even more acrimonious once the expedition was back in England, as is revealed by a remarkable document signed by all members, excepting Haig-Thomas and Humphreys:

We, the undersigned, hereby state that at no time was any attempt ever made, discussed or considered to depose Dr. Humphreys from Leader and substitute Edward Shackleton either by the Members of the Expedition in general, or Edward Shackleton in particular.

As proof of this we had always, when discussing the conduct of the Expedition [considered] Sergeant Stallworthy as the obvious leader, being the only member possessing the requisite knowledge of the country and the confidence of the natives and of the members of the Expedition. At no time was any attempt ever made to depose Dr. Humphreys from the leadership of the Expedition.

At all times in the opinion of the undersigned, Serg. Stallworthy carried out all orders and instructions given him by the leader of the Expedition, and endeavoured to help the expedition to the best of his ability both in giving advice and by his own personal example and work.

This also applies equally to Edward Shackleton, and other members of the Expedition. These statements are made in view of certain specific and unfounded charges made by Dr. Humphreys.

In the opinion of the undersigned the Expedition was successful.

> Edward A. A. Shackleton
> H.W. Stallworthy
> A.W. Moore
> R. Bentham
> Oct. 31, 1935.[55]

On the same day as this affidavit was compiled and signed, Eddie wrote to Commissioner MacBrien with a brief summary of the expedition's achievements, and to thank him

for the absolutely invaluable help rendered to us by the Royal Canadian Mounted Police. It is my opinion—and I think the opinion of the other members of the Expedition—that had it not been for Sergeant Stallworthy, our difficulties would have been so increased that it is probable we should have had very little success. He worked splendidly during the whole of the expedition, and it was natural therefore that he should be chosen, as the best Arctic traveller, to attempt the successful Grant Land journey.[56]

Once Harry and Hilda were back in Canada, General George Vanier, the Canadian High Commissioner in London, also wrote to General Sir James MacBrien, the RCMP Commissioner:

The Oxford University Ellesmere Land Expedition has now returned to this country—as you are no doubt aware. This expedition, as you will remember, was organized by the son of Sir Ernest Shackleton and led by Dr. Noel Humphreys and I gather from these gentlemen in recent conversations that they cannot praise too highly the services rendered to the expedition by Sgt. Stallworthy of the R.C.M.P.

They tell me that his knowledge of the country, of the customs of the Eskimos and of the dogs was simply remarkable to them and made a great deal of difference to the success of the expedition.

I think it only right to let you know how highly the services of Sgt. Stallworthy were appreciated.

Yours sincerely,

Gen. G. Vanier[57]

Harry and Hilda travelled up to London on Wednesday 30 November. The big party with all the expedition members had to be cancelled, in part because Eddie was ill and had been forbidden to celebrate by his doctor. Even if not officially, they did celebrate. Writing from the *Empress of Britain* on Sunday 3 November, Harry reported: "I've just got back to normal after a peach of a hangover from the London party."[58]

Harry, Hilda, Eddie and Moore went to see the show *Please, Teacher*, then visited Humphreys "and had a few"; then they went to the Mayfair and on to another nightclub. Harry and Hilda "got back to the hotel just about in time to change, pack & catch the boat train." Eddie and Moore came to see them off aboard the *Empress of Britain* at Southampton and they received telegrams (and flowers for Hilda) from Lady Shackleton and Humphreys. They sailed from Southampton on Friday 1 November 1935.

12

SOUTHERN MOUNTIE

AFTER CALLING AT CHERBOURG, the *Empress of Britain* experienced some rough weather and Hilda, once again, was laid low with sea sickness.[1] Harry threatened to "take her up on deck by force in the morning or I'm afraid she will be starved if I don't." Theirs was a relatively spacious cabin: "We've a dandy room with two bedsteads & about twice as much room as the six of us had on the Dannebrog."[2]

Two weeks later Harry and Hilda were ensconced in the Alexandra Hotel in Ottawa, waiting for details of Harry's next posting but "with nothing definite because Major-Gen. Sir James [MacBrien] has been judging horses at a New York show."[3] When they arrived back, Hilda had a bad cold but she soon recovered and was kept busy typing up Harry's official report on the Oxford University Ellesmere Land Expedition and as Harry wrote to his brother, she "made a good job of it."[4]

On 15 November Superintendent T.H. Irvine, Harry's boss at "G" Division, wrote to the Commissioner to recommend that Harry be able to retain the rank of Acting Sergeant, which he had been awarded for the term of the expedition.[5] MacBrien approved this recommendation in general but specified that Harry "be given a refresher course in police work as soon as opportunity affords."[6]

While he was in London, Harry had visited C.M. Lampson and Co., fur buyers. As a result, on 26 November he received a communication from them to the effect that they had sold on his behalf 60 white fox furs at 45/- each, netting him after commission £124.19.5.[7] This represented only part of Harry's profits from his Ellesmere Island fur; he had sold an earlier lot (the number unspecified) for an average of 48/9.[8] In total he made close to $1,000, but this represented only part of his harvest of furs. The remainder he turned in to the RCMP, some of them "just about falling to pieces." His assessment overall: "Well, that's the end of my trapping career. I guess I did not do too bad out of it. I didn't like to take any chances since I am near pension time & due for a raise."[9]

Shortly before Christmas Harry and Hilda experienced the worst crisis of their married life. On December 13 Hilda suffered the effects of a tubular pregnancy, with severe internal haemorrhaging. She was in the operating room within two hours and Harry provided the blood for a transfusion.[10] Late in her life, after Harry's death, Hilda recalled the circumstances:

Two months after his return I was in hospital dying—but I lived—and there was no longer any chance of having a son or a daughter to remember a wonderful father.

The first day after the operation he sat beside me holding my hand, tears in his eyes, and said, "Why have I done this to you?" I could barely speak. I said "We did this together because we love each other." I remember our words vividly after so many years. It was typical of him that he admired my acceptance of my dangerous condition.[11]

The trauma of the heart-wrenching outcome of Hilda's pregnancy was offset by another, happier event. At a meeting of its Council on 18 November

1935, Harry was elected a Fellow of the Royal Geographical Society.[12] The election was confirmed on 31 December, although Eddie had informed Harry unofficially as early as 21 November.[13] The Society also informed the RCMP Headquarters and his election was announced as item No. 567 in the RCMP "General Orders" for the week ending 22 February 1936.[14] Harry was undoubtedly quite proud of this honour, but pretended not to be. Writing to his brother he reported:

> The newspapers made quite a noise about my F.R.G.S. & my name came out in G.O.'s with a quotation from the Sec. of the R.G.S. Hq. in Ottawa "released the news" to the press, then the O.C. here had a photographer & reporter up to interview me in Regina so I was famous for a day. They seem to think that FRGS is in the dizzy heights somewhere & I did not tell the officers & others anything to lead them to think different (Why should I?). But confidentially I wonder if it was worth $15 bucks subscription.[15]

On 30 November Harry also received a Commissioner's Commendation "for his excellent conduct and deportment respecting his duties with the Oxford University Ellesmere Land Expedition."[16]

Another achievement that gave Harry considerable satisfaction was publication of his second article in the *Royal Canadian Mounted Police Quarterly*. His detailed account of the Oxford University Ellesmere Land Expedition appeared in the January 1936 issue under the heading, "An Arctic expedition."[17]

By Christmas Hilda was well enough to invite Harry to the hospital Christmas dinner, and was "on full rations" by then. Harry had received orders to report for the three-month refresher course in Regina on 5 January and it was unlikely that she would be well enough to stay in Ottawa on her own for that long after the operation. Hilda's sister Elaine came to Ottawa on 15 December and Hilda went back with her to her home in Windsor, Ontario.

Harry reported as scheduled for the 14th Instructional Class in Regina. He was the junior member in a class of 13, the rest all being well up in the Senior Sergeants' list, while Harry was still only 20th on the Acting Sergeant's List.[18] It was quite a gruelling three months, involving lectures and written or practical examinations that covered Foot and Arms Drill, Musketry, the RCMP Act, History of the RCMP, Criminal Law, Rules and Regulations,

Mechanical transport (including a driving test), Customs and Excise Acts, Constable's Manual, Federal Statutes, Financial Regulations and Physical Training & Ju Jitsu. They also had to present a lecture on a police-related subject and Harry chose "Patrols in the Arctic" as his subject. They also had to drill a squad of 24 men for 15 minutes. Harry's overall mark was 76.6%, placing him 10th out of the class of 13.[19]

Altogether it was a very rigorous course, and the only recreation Harry could find time for was a game of billiards every evening with an old friend, Staff Sergeant Healy. In a month he got "down town" only once, but then, he was not exactly enamoured of Regina: "Regina is a hell of a place in winter, 25–30–40 below & lots of wind. Thank goodness we don't have to ride. Only the mounted sections of the Force do that now."[20]

Throughout the period of his course in Regina (and for some time thereafter) Harry was mulling over a proposal from Eddie Shackleton that he might wish to participate in a much more ambitious expedition to Ellesmere Island in 1937–38. Eddie had first submitted an outline of this plan to General MacBrien on 31 January 1936.[21] In brief, he had proposed that a base be established by sea in the Robertson Fjord area in the summer of 1937 and that an advance party would winter there. Then in the spring of 1938 the main party would head north by sea, equipped with two 2- or 3-engined aircraft and two smaller planes. The party would include the necessary pilots, mechanics, etc. and Eddie had hopes of persuading either the RAF or the RCAF to lend him the planes and pilots. Once an airstrip had been prepared at Lake Hazen, the planes would operate out of a base there to conduct aerial surveys of northern Ellesmere, to search for new land masses in the Arctic Ocean northwest of Ellesmere Island, and to support sledge parties that would be investigating the geology and the ornithology of the area.[22] Eddie first broached the subject in a letter in January 1936 and asked Harry if he would be interested in the position of base camp manager. In Eddie's view, Harry was "unquestionably the only person who could do that job properly."[23] In his reply Harry indicated that he might be interested provided that it did not interfere with his career in the Force and provided that Hilda was fully recovered. But in a letter to his brother, Harry was less than enthusiastic: "I really don't want to go on a job like that again. So I told him that *I could not consider it* until the end of March.... I'm fed up with expeditions &

so is Hilda."[24] But as time went on the idea became more attractive. Writing to Eddie on 6 June, Harry indicated that:

> the more I think about another trip with you and Bob [Bentham], the more it appeals, but of course without knowing more about the plans and what my job would be I cannot decide whether I should go or not. Hilda is awfully good about it. She thinks that with all the time I've spent in the North it would be a pity to miss a really big expedition. The work of helping organize the expedition & establishing & taking care of the Base is a job I could handle alright with a few fellows of the right type & some Eskimos.[25]

Harry asked to see some detailed plans for the expedition and made some suggestions. Amongst other things, he suggested that Bache Peninsula might be a better location for the base than Robertson Fjord and that a landing strip could be established on the sea ice, either there or at Alexandra Fjord. Ultimately, however, Eddie's plans came to nought; the Northwest Territories Council referred his plan to an interdepartmental committee that rejected the proposal.[26]

Harry completed his course in Regina by 3 April and he and Hilda got back together in Ottawa around the 6th. Their pleasure at being together again was somewhat marred by the fact that a week later Harry was admitted to Ottawa Civic Hospital for an operation on varicose veins on both legs. His legs had been troubling him for at least six months and were giving him considerable pain; however, the operation was successful and Harry was discharged on the 27th.[27] He returned to duty in Ottawa on 1 May, but initially was "excused riding boots" in light of his recent operation to his lower legs.

Harry's next posting was to "J" Division, with headquarters in Fredericton. He first had to report to Shediac and he and Hilda left Ottawa for that destination on 4 May.[28] On arrival, Harry discovered that his duties would most certainly be very different from anything he had previously tackled. As of May 8 he was stationed at Gaspé, Quebec, in charge of aircraft observations in connection with smuggling prevention—mainly the smuggling of liquor.[29] Harry included quite a detailed outline of his new duties in a letter to Eddie:

One of the RCAF planes that Harry co-ordinated in searching for rum-runners,
Gaspé, 1936.

We have 2 RCAF airplanes attached and 2 pilots, 2 mechanics, 2 ground
men & 2 wireless operators & I have two constables to send out on
observation patrols. The work is in connection with observing the
activities of rum-running vessels chiefly from St. Pierre. My job really
is to determine when & where the air patrols are to be made daily &
wireless the positions of rum runners as soon as they are seen to
crews of our marine section & land detachments who patrol the roads.
It's rather an intense job but so far the rum runners seem to keep one
jump ahead of us. However we make it very difficult for them and
several motor boats & loads of liquor have been seized when trying
to get ashore from the vessels who of course don't take any chances in
coming inside the 12 mile limit. We have had no less than 7 rum schooners
laying off shore in the Gulf [of St. Lawrence] & Bay of Chaleur for
the last month & I don't think any of them have been able to unload
their wares. About the only thing in their favour is calm & foggy weather
when we lose their positions.[30]

News of his duties at Gaspé prompted Bob Bentham to remark: "Anyway,
what do you do with the rum you seize? I imagine that even you could not
consume it all."[31]

In August 1936 Harry and Hilda took the opportunity of a visit by some American friends, the Babers, to take a trip to Rocher Percé including a boat trip to Bonaventure Island. Hilda, always prone to seasickness, found that she still had a problem on the water.[32]

On 23 September, at the recommendation of Inspector F.A. Blake of the Campbellton Subdivision, who had just visited Harry at the Gaspé Detachment, and of Acting Superintendent E.C.P. Salt, who was in command of "J" Division, Harry was confirmed in the rank of Sergeant, backdated to the date of his promotion to Acting Sergeant on 15 June 1934.[33]

While he was no doubt pleased at this promotion, Harry seemed to have given up on ever receiving the King's Police Medal. Writing to Superintendent Sandys-Wunsch from Gaspé on 10 October 1936 he noted:

I very much appreciate your recommendation for the Police Medal, for my work of 1930 to 1933, which in the end was not approved, and I conclude that, since this recommendation was still pending, I was not mentioned for the Jubilee Medal.[34]

Evidently Harry's assessment was premature, for in an intriguingly ambiguous reply on 22 October 1936, Sandys-Wunsch stressed:

The question of the Police Medal is not yet settled. *Confidentially*, I saw Mr. Hann today, and the Commissioner has written about it again. I shall keep after it, and mention it to the Commissioner when I see him again....

Very confidentially, and I know I can write to you that way, your years of good service are well known and appreciated at HQ and I hope to see you fittingly rewarded before long. I have, of course, always done what I could but your own efforts have been so outstanding that you are a marked man.[35]

In mid-October Harry and Hilda moved from Gaspé to Moncton. Since Harry had learned to drive as part of his refresher course, they had acquired a Ford V8 and drove it from Gaspé to Moncton, a distance of 389 miles. "I collected 5¢ per mile instead of rail fare & when travelling we charge up

Sergeant Harry Stallworthy,
Moncton 1936.

75¢ per meal each and $4.00 for lodgings. So you see our travelling allowances are quite good,"[36] Harry commented in a letter to Bill.

At Moncton, Harry was in charge of Customs Preventive Work and Provincial Liquor Act Enforcement. This was his first plainclothes posting, with a plainclothes allowance of 25¢, making his salary $5.25 per day. As Harry remarked to his brother; "I guess the two bits will keep me in cigarettes!"[37] Provided with a large Buick, a constable, and a roving commission, he regularly visited five detachments within New Brunswick. He was in charge of road patrols and night-time road blocks where cars and trucks were searched. He was also in charge of three high-speed police patrol boats, based at Caraquet, Shippigan and Bactouche. Later, possibly also in conjunction with the duties outlined above, he was Patrol Sergeant for the subdivision, responsible for inspecting 13 detachments once per month. With memories of his own many years of being inspected, Harry found it quite entertaining to find himself in the role of inspector: "It's a bit amusing to me to have the detachment fellows meet the train with a car & clean buttons & office work rushed up to date at the last minute."[38]

In the spring of 1937 Harry was asked by his boss, Superintendent W.V. Bruce, to respond to a request that had come to him from R.A. Gibson, Deputy Commissioner of the Northwest Territories via Commissioner MacBrien. Harry was asked to comment on a proposal by David Haig-Thomas to mount a small expedition to Ellesmere Island in 1938.[39] Haig-Thomas, who had the support of the Royal Geographical Society, was to be accompanied by Mr. John Wright, of Trinity College, Cambridge as geologist and surveyor, and Bob Richard Hamilton who planned to study the ozone layer.[40] Harry pointed out some unstated assumptions in the report, but saved his really scathing comments for his assessment of Haig-Thomas and what he felt were probably the real intentions behind the proposed expedition:

The correspondence received does not disclose any detailed plans or objectives, nor where the party expects to spend the winter.... It is presumed that they propose to winter at the abandoned Police detachment on Bache Peninsula, and to travel by sledge on the Ellesmere Island ice cap....

I know Mr. Haig-Thomas intimately through our association on the 1934–35 Oxford University Ellesmere land expedition, when we wintered in North Greenland. I doubt very much whether his objective in the proposed expedition is entirely in the interests of science. His chief interest on the last expedition was undoubtedly big game hunting, which hobby he has pursued in other parts of the world. In this connection, I would suggest that reference be made to my general report covering the Oxford Ellesmere Land Expedition, in which it will be noted that a number of walrus were slaughtered and sunk in a manner contrary to the North Greenland Game Laws when they might have been saved, and as a result two members of the expedition were charged with this infraction. The two members in question being Dr. Humphreys and Mr. Haig-Thomas, who took a leading part in these hunting parties. They appeared before Mr. Hans Nielsen, District Governor, and a Council of Eskimo at Thule, and were given a warning. For this reason and because of his general attitudes towards any authority restricting his hunting activities, I am of the opinion that he would not have any scruples against the shooting of muskoxen nor any other wild life, and if Mr. Haig-Thomas takes some of the younger Eskimos with him from Greenland who have never seen muskoxen, I feel sure that his attitude in this respect would not be a good influence over them.

I was not impressed with his ability as a Northern man, particularly where manual labour, care of the dogs, cooking, etc., were concerned. He has exceptionally good physique but during the expedition he showed a decided lack of continuity of purpose. For these reasons I doubt very much whether he would be a responsible leader to be in charge of a small party wintering in the Arctic.

During the Dark Period and while making preparations for the Spring sledging journeys, Mr. Haig-Thomas often started discussions regarding the killing of muskoxen and generally criticised the Government's "action towards explorers." He stated to me on a number of occasions, "You couldn't do anything about it if a sledging party and their dogs were hungry," meaning, of course, the killing of muskoxen.[41]

Harry's suspicions about Haig-Thomas's intentions with regard to hunting muskoxen were more than just a hunch. Some nine months earlier, Haig-Thomas had written to him, outlining his plans:

I am trying to go back to Thule next year with a cinematograph camera to take photographs of birds, snow geese in particular, walrus, owls and Polar Bears if I am lucky enough. I also want to make a patrol of Ellesmereland taking with me old Noocap and Inuatak, and several others to come with us as far as Bache. If all goes well I hope to get cinematograph pictures of Musk-ox and do as much mapping as I can find time for. I am going to try very hard to get permission to shoot a limited number of Musk-ox—perhaps six....

Don't you think yourself that with the number of Musk-ox there are in West Ellesmereland, it could not do any harm if we shot, say, six old bulls? However, I expect it would do more good if we shot some cows, anyway old Noocap says so."[42]

Harry also checked the list of equipment, clothing and supplies that Haig-Thomas had submitted and working on the assumption that he was planning to winter at Bache Peninsula, commented: "I think it advisable to point out that a two years' supply of staple provisions and fuel should be planned on, and that the supply of fuel should be a minimum of 10 tons."[43]

In the book which Haig-Thomas later wrote about his expedition, he stated that the Canadian Government had insisted "that I must take at least twenty tons of coal to Ellesmere Land."[44] It is unclear why the suggested amount of coal had doubled. Haig-Thomas's reaction to this suggestion was that "some Mounted Policeman who had probably got a cold nose visiting Hudson Bay thought he must throw his weight about and tell us what it was necessary to take, though apparently nothing much else was needed except coal."[45] One has to assume that Haig-Thomas was unaware that the suggestion about fuel had come from Harry.

Despite Harry's misgivings, Haig-Thomas did mount his expedition and by all accounts he did so quite successfully. Having wintered at Thule in the spring of 1938, he was accompanied by Nukappiannguaq on a very impressive sledge journey. Having sledged north to Cape Hatherton they crossed Smith Sound and Ellesmere Island, then past Cape Southwest to the southwest corner of Amund Ringnes Island, his farthest point. On the return journey they crossed Amund Ringnes Island and to the east of it discovered a small island that has been named Haig-Thomas Island, although Haig-Thomas depicts it as about 35 km in length, instead of the actual length of 17 km. They then returned safely to Thule.[46]

But Haig-Thomas failed to mention in his writings that he killed muskoxen during this trip. Harry learned this from Paddy Hamilton in December 1938, when he wrote from Craig Harbour where he was then stationed, and where Nukappiannguaq was visiting:

Last year he [Haig-Thomas] and old Noocap made a trip to Axel Heiberg via Mackinson Inlet [actually Bay Fjord], and on that trip killed five Musk-oxen. He told Noocap not to mention it to the Police, anyhow old Noocap got a little too much grog one night and let the cat out of the bag to me. Enalunguaq tried to stop old Noocap from spilling the beans, so I packed her off home and got all the dope. Now I have a report in the mail and I am sure I have covered everything and I want to get that bird, just for the way he treated you when you were at Etah and talked about the force. He made a statement to you that he would kill Musk-ox when he wanted them. Bob [Bentham] told me everything that happened for that year.[47]

While Haig-Thomas himself added little to the knowledge of the area, the other expedition members, Wright and Hamilton, made a careful and meticulous survey of the east coast of Ellesmere Island from Alexandra Fjord to Makinson Inlet and produced the first accurate map of this coast.[48]

When they first arrived in Moncton, Harry and Hilda boarded at the Bon Accord House Hotel, which was quite close to his office, at a rate of $70 per month. For the time being, at least, it sufficed: "We have a nice room, 3 good meals a day & a garage for the Ford V8," Harry wrote to Bill.[49] But then on 1 August 1937 they either bought or rented a house of their own at 274 Mountain Rd., Moncton. To furnish it, they bought a full set of furniture—everything from a chesterfield suite to a refrigerator—at the Lounsbury Co. Ltd., Moncton for a total of $208.05 (after a discount of $55 for cash).[50]

Harry's health continued give him trouble and while they were in Moncton, he suffered regularly from stomach pains. His doctor diagnosed gastritis and Harry got some relief from taking baking soda, but when he started taking a preparation known as Amphogel, he felt even better.

Harry's duties at the detachment involved the usual range of activities handled by a Sergeant in a southern urban detachment, although little documentation appears to have survived. However one indication of what he was involved with comes from a letter written in May 1937. It was from the commander of the "J" Division, Superintendent W.V. Bruce, to Inspector J.D. Bird, Harry's commanding officer at the Moncton Sub-Division in which he commended Harry for his "excellent work in connection with the breaking into and theft from the Liquor Control Board Store at Memramcook."[51]

It soon became well known that Harry had considerable northern experience and he was often asked to give talks on the Arctic, as he did at the Moncton branch of the New Brunswick Fish and Game Protective Association's monthly meeting in Moncton on 3 May 1939. The possible topics he offered were: game conditions and the reserves in the NWT north of the timber limits; Eskimo methods of hunting sea mammals and land mammals; or the species of game found in the Arctic archipelago, including the habitat of the muskoxen, polar bear and walrus.[52]

Even at this stage Harry had not given up on getting the King's Police Medal, and in October 1938 he wrote to George Hann, secretary to the Commissioner on the subject.

Dear Mr. Hann,

I notice in the last issue of G.O.'s [General Orders] that there have apparently been some changes made regarding the regulations governing the King's Police Medal, where this Force is concerned. As you may remember, I was recommended for this award after making the Krueger Patrol and for "conspicuous devotion to duty in the Arctic." As a matter of fact the late Commissioner himself told me of his recommendation to the Minister. I have never heard anything official and naturally concluded that the matter had been disapproved or shelved in London. Since this notice appears in G.O.'s I can now understand that the award could not have been made in any case.

I have been thinking of making an official report to ask whether the application could be brought up again where I am concerned or whether the revised regulation refers only to "future performances." I should first like to have your opinion on the matter. I would appreciate it very much if you will drop me a line when you have time. Confidentially I have always entertained a hope that this medal would come along some day.[53]

George Hann's reply dashed any hopes that Harry may still have harboured of getting the medal and at the same time it did nothing to allay his fears that, as Superintendent Sandys-Wunsch remarked confidentially in previous correspondence, that he was "a marked man":

I was glad to get your note of October 20th, but I am sorry to tell you that I do not consider there is very much use of reopening your case for the Police Medal.

If anyone tried hard to get it for you it was the late Commissioner [Sir James MacBrien], and personally I believe the fault was in our Ottawa end of the business. I do not think it was shelved in London at all.

Your case was one of three which were persistently and consistently brought to the attention of the Department of External Affairs, and I feel certain the late Commissioner, as well as others, including myself, were sincerely disappointed at your not receiving the recognition you deserved.

You please yourself as to whether you reopen the subject, but to be perfectly candid to you, I now think it is too late to do anything about it, but I can give you this satisfaction that the department never let up on reminding the External Affairs about it.

I am sincerely sorry that the late Commissioner's recommendations did not bear fruit, but no doubt you already know that there are others who are in the same boat, and who did outstanding work and were strongly recommended for the King's Police Medal but yet never received it.[54]

One cannot help but speculate on the circumstances surrounding the continued failure of Harry's application. And in doing so, the thought naturally arises as to whether there was any correlation between this incident and the long delay he experienced in getting Force's Long Service Medal. Harry had first applied for the Long Service Medal on 10 April 1937—after he had completed 20 years and 18 days of service.[55] The response to this application can be found in a memo in his Service file, dated 18 June 1937. It is from G.L. Jennings, the Deputy Commissioner:

In view of the fact that this N.C.O. was convicted in 1930 of having intoxicating liquor in his possession contrary to regulations, his application for the Long Service Medal is not approved, but in view of his meritorious work in the far North, should be reconsidered in a year's time.[56]

This information was relayed by the Adjutant, Superintendent V.A.M. Kemp to Harry's immediate superior, the O/C, "J" Division in Fredericton several months later.[57] Almost 50 years later, long after Harry's death, Hilda stumbled across this last memo, and was moved to write a scathing note:

To my amazement I found this memo dated Sept. 8/37 in Harry's papers. Knowing the long meritorious service which Harry had completed I wonder that this extraordinary reason for denying him the L.S. Medal at that time should have been given.

The "liquor" in his possession was being taken to Bache Peninsula where he spent 3 years in complete isolation. It was used in moderation for such limited occasions as Christmas dinners—returning from difficult, dark, cold patrols or returns from the extensive patrols—hundreds of miles—which he made, risking his life in some cases.

In 1930 he was about to leave Sidney, N.S. for this furthest North human habitation of white man in the world.

It makes one wonder who—in Ottawa—sitting at a desk—could have been responsible for such a scathing and senseless punishment of a respected gentleman of Harry's known stature.[58]

The misdemeanour of possession of alcohol continued to haunt Harry for several years more. In a memo in his file, dated 29 February 1940, when Harry had presumably again raised the matter of the Long Service Medal, the adjutant, Superintendent F.A. Blake simply states that "The Commissioner will not consider awarding the Long Service Medal in this case at the present time."[59] No explanation was given.

For quite some time during his posting in Moncton, Harry had been contemplating going back north, but to a detachment where Hilda could accompany him. On 28 January 1938 and again on 28 February 1939 he applied for northern service, specifying that:

As Mrs. Stallworthy is desirous of accompanying me, I would prefer to be stationed at Chesterfield Inlet, or in the Yukon Territory, or at Aklavik, where suitable quarters and medical attention are available.[60]

The outcome was that he was offered what was almost certainly the most southerly posting that qualified as "Northern Service," namely Fort Smith.[61] Located precisely on the 60th parallel on the border between Alberta and the Northwest Territories. Fort Smith had grown up at the northern end of the major portage that bypassed the impressive rapids on the Slave River. Although it had no road access from the south, in 1941 it was the seat of the Administration of the Northwest Territories and had a population of 241

Members of RCMP detachment, Fort Smith, 1940; Harry at left.

(of whom 46 were whites and most of the remainder Métis⁶²), it was relatively civilized and, as Hilda would find, certain of the ladies of the community
went to considerable lengths to maintain the trappings of "civilization."
Whatever misgivings he may have had, Harry indicated his interest and his
appointment as Sub-Division Sergeant and in charge of the Detachment at
Fort Smith was confirmed as of 4 May 1939.⁶³ Harry was to report in Ottawa
on or about 22 May before heading north. At that time one reached Fort
Smith by taking the train to Waterways, then taking a sternwheeler down the
Athabasca and Slave rivers to Fort Fitzgerald and finally taking a taxi for the
short distance (by-passing the rapids on the Slave) to Fort Smith. New furniture was being provided for the married NCOs quarters at Fort Smith, and
would be going north on the first boat downriver from Waterways to Fort
Fitzgerald.

Harry headed north first, with Hilda following in September. Although
she had travelled well, the crowded conditions in the taxi at the end of the
journey made her nauseous. Soon after her arrival, however, Hilda had more
serious problems to worry about. On 20 September Harry was struck by a
bout of flu. When there was no sign of it clearing he was admitted to Fort
Smith hospital on 25 September. Both he and Hilda (probably even more so)
must have been very worried in the light of Harry's brush with death in the

Royal Alexandra Hospital in Edmonton 14 years previously. Treatments in the Fort Smith hospital were effective, however, and he was discharged as convalescent on 3 October and returned to duty on the 7th.[64]

Being in charge of a sub-division with 11 detachments under his control (including his own detachment), Harry found that his duties were almost entirely administrative and clerical. In one of his regular letters to Bill, he complained: "I have a full time job and keep a pretty fast steno[grapher] fully occupied from 9 to 12 & 1.30–5. I have to wear glasses all the time now. Consequently I don't read much and seldom write at night."[65] On occasion he would even go back to the office in the evenings to put in a further two or three hours. Much to his disgust, Harry found that he spent a considerable amount of time on domestic disputes. Hilda noted that the Indians and Métis

pester him continually with their family affairs. A breed woman with a face as long as a sick horse will talk to the married sergeant and no one else. He will find out that her husband has been beating her and after much gentle prodding or straight rough handling, she will admit that she has been gambling, neglecting her children or, apparently least crime of all, has been sleeping with some other Indian. I don't think the fact of sleeping with the other Indian is the crime, but neglecting her own home and family to do it. Then an injured husband will put in an appearance, and will try to get the law to see that his wife looks after the brats, bastards and family roof tree while he is out on his trap-line. Harry would be only too happy to have less business-dealings with them. He handles them pretty roughly, by all accounts. We have many a laugh over his Court of Human Relations.[66]

To make up for the lack of official outdoor activity such as sledge patrols, Harry and Hilda did their best to get out on an informal basis as often as possible. One of the first of these outings was down the Slave River:

Last Thursday, October 12th, we had a little trip down the river in the Police boat, *Fort Smith*. It had just come back from a month on Great Slave [Lake], fishing for the winter supply of dog feed, so it didn't look like a thing of beauty, nor did it smell like a rose garden. However, it was quite an interesting trip: Harry and I, the native interpreter and the Junior Constable. It was snowing when we left, after snowing all night, and it was a pretty dreary, miserable early-morning start, but it cleared up a bit and the sun tried to struggle through several times during the day. We had a series of mishaps, which ended in running out of gas. Carburettor trouble, the steering wheel slipped its cable, the exhaust parted company from the boat from being stuck in a mud bank while we were tied up and finally, on the way home, when the engine had sputtered and choked and coughed, we found that we were out of gas, and I had visions of rowing the darned 32-foot boat home, but we managed to limp back to Bell Rock where the H.B. Co. boats are beached for the winter, where we borrowed a drum of gas. I was thankful to get home and into bed that night.[67]

The location of the RCMP detachment was ideal for strolling in the woods, lying as it did to the east of the HBC establishment, between the portage road and the steep bank dropping to the river. The water here foamed over the rocky outcrops of the Rapids of the Drowned. But walking in the woods, even near town, also involved its own peculiar hazards:

Harry and I went for a hike in the woods today. We have spent our Sundays out of doors ever since I have been here. It is the only day Harry is free from the office and so far is the only day I have been free from the house. If we walk through the woods along the river bank above the rapids, we come out at the village dump, which is right on the 60th parallel. A trail from the dump to the Fitzgerald portage road follows the 60th, and the walk home is along the portage road. It's a bit dangerous walking in the woods at this time of year, because every man, woman and child in the settlement is wandering around with a .22 or shotgun, looking for birds, spruce hen and partridge. I'm not afraid of looking like a spruce hen or partridge, but I might be mistaken for a fool-hen.[68]

Once the snow arrived in early November, their horizons expanded somewhat, and they were able to go on toboggan trips that must have brought back memories of his years in the Yukon and at Stony Rapids for Harry:

Last Sunday Harry and I went off on a dog-and-toboggan trip to Seven-mile Lake. It was my first time to ride in this sort of Rolls Royce. Unfortunately the trail was very rough. A trapper with a much shorter toboggan had made the trail. The result was that our toboggan rode up over the ends of every turn in the trail and tipped over, throwing me out into the deep snow. Harry rode on the little platform at the back, and tried to keep the thing from tipping. The next day I was covered with bruises from being thrown against tree trunks and Harry was sore across his back and arms from straining at the handles of the cariole. But we had a lovely time. We crossed the lake but found that the marshy sides were not frozen although the lake was frozen solid, so we came back to this side and made camp. We cleared away the snow and pulled down the standing dead trees for firewood and cut spruce branches for our couch by the fire. By this time it was dark—about four o'clock—so we decided to stay until the moon rose. We cooked canned sausages and bacon and munched bran muffins. Harry wanted to bring hard tack—but I could see no reason for being so awfully Northern as that. We lay by the roaring fire until the moon came up, then packed up camp and started home.... We shouted at the dogs at the tops of our voices—sang and yodelled all the way home. The dogs were eager to get home and buzzed along at top speed, and I lay flat in the bottom of the toboggan, which made it ride much better than it had in the afternoon, although I was still spilled out several times.[69]

With snow on the ground Hilda had also started skiing again. Initially she borrowed a pair of skis from Barbara Conibear, but then she heard of a pair at the store that had been ordered by somebody from Yellowknife who had then cancelled the order:

I went in to try them on and found the whole thing a perfect fit, skis, boots and poles, so I walked—or I should say ski'd—out of the store complete—for $14.... There was enough snow for easy falling, although I found that I had not forgotten how to push off on skis.[70]

From then on skiing became an important form of recreation for Hilda, and by mid-November she could report:

I've been doing quite a lot of skiing. The snow is very deep this year, much deeper than usual they say. There are some good ski trails cut through the woods over towards the 60th parallel. The woods are lovely. There is very little wind here and when the snow falls on the spruce boughs it hangs there for a long time. It is like a picture of all the pictures of Canadian winter scenes.[71]

While Hilda skied, Harry was looking forward to going hunting. When Harry heard that the caribou migration had begun, he and Constable Stevens, the most junior member of the detachment, went on an overnight hunting trip. They went about 25 miles to the east across the Slave River, but did not see any caribou.

With a few notable exceptions, such as Leonore Urquhart, the doctor's wife, with whom Hilda had attended Normal School [Teacher's Training College] and Mrs. Ken Conibear, Hilda found she had little in common with most of the other white women in the settlement, in part because they seemed so pretentious:

I'm beginning to think that this place is more South than North anyway. Last Tuesday I was invited out for tea. All the white women were there in their best bib and tucker. Mrs Bettaney (wife of Inspector Bettaney, Harry's boss) POURED, in a black georgette model with a little black hat tipped over one eye. She confessed to me that she bought it for Gov. Gen MacLaren's reception—I suppose she whispered it to everyone else too. There were little hot biscuits, two kinds of sandwiches, four kinds of cake, olives, fudge and two kinds of sticky Turkish delight, and about 15 kinds of sticky, silly afternoon-tea lines of conversation just the same as here, there or anywhere.[72]

Hilda managed to find more useful activities to fill her time. She played the organ in the Anglican church and assisted the schoolteacher, Mrs. Link, with the Christmas concert, teaching the children an Irish dance and playing the organ.[73] She also took French lessons from Barbara Conibear, who had a degree from the University of Alberta, had studied in France and had taught school in Weston-super-Mare; Hilda had studied French earlier and found that she could still read quite well.[74] Much to her later regret Hilda was also recruited for the organizing committee for the annual Masquerade Dance. As a result she found herself embroiled in a bitter "civil war" over a proposal to prohibit or limit attendance at this event by Indian women accompanied by young offspring![75]

One rather novel aspect of the Stallworthy household was that prisoners were employed as handymen. In October the RCMP plane brought three prisoners down from Yellowknife, having spent the summer building new detachment buildings there. They were recommended to Hilda as being "very decent boys" and good workers.

One of the prisoners, named Bascheault, first built a set of shelves for Hilda in a corner of the living room then removed an interior walkway and archway to make a spacious living room from two rather cramped rooms. He then made a dressing table for Hilda.

Despite Harry's misgivings about his boss, Inspector R. Bettaney, he recommended him for promotion to Sergeant-Major on 3 April 1941, specifying that Harry was:

well educated and has a very good knowledge of both Police and clerical work. I have found him to be conscientious and hard working. He has the best interests of the Force at heart, is well respected and exercises a good influence over junior ranks.[76]

But for the moment this recommendation came to nought since a Sergeant senior to Harry, who was stationed at Dawson was next in line for promotion to Sergeant-Major.[77]

It must have been some consolation to Harry that on 23 April 1941, three days before hearing that he was not going to be promoted, he received his Long Service Medal at a parade of all ranks—more than four years after he was first eligible and had first applied for it. Although they had expected most of the townspeople to turn up for presentation ceremony, the inclement weather produce only a few die-hards.[78] Hilda and Harry recalled the occasion with disapproval and years later, Hilda wrote:

It was an occasion which lacked everything in dignity. I remember the occasion well and Harry's complete disgust after the proceedings:

"To be decorated for Long Service by a man who had been a city policeman of the Fredericton Police Force!!"[79]

Although they were kept abreast of the latest war news by radio, Harry and Hilda felt strangely isolated and even insulated from events in Europe. While they were very happy to find themselves in the remote security of Fort Smith, they naturally sympathized intensely with Harry's family in England and sent regular care packages. One of these packages was to have unexpected repercussions when Harry's mother found herself in court for attempting to obtain extra amounts of rationed butter and sugar. In one of her letters to Harry, she enclosed a £1 note to help pay for the cost of postage on some butter and sugar that Harry had sent her, but the letter was intercepted and so Mrs. Stallworthy had her day in court. She pleaded that "she had not the slightest idea there was anything wrong in so obtaining the sugar and butter."[80]

On 17 October 1941 Harry was walking from the detachment kitchen to his office and was about to walk over a trapdoor to the basement when the detachment cook, Special Constable S.A. Bigelow, pushed the trapdoor open from below. Harry fell down through the trapdoor and hit the edge of the door, fracturing the cartilages of two of his lower ribs. He was in great pain and after having had his ribs strapped up with an adhesive bandage, Harry was booked off for ten days and given only light duty for a further four days.[81]

Harry's engagement at Fort Smith was for only three years and on 12 February 1942 he wrote to Inspector D.J. Martin, commanding "G" Division, expressing interest in another term in the North, but requesting a change from Fort Smith. He specifically asked whether there might be a vacancy at Dawson.[82] His request for another year in the North was approved, but he was also informed that there would be no vacancies for a married N.C.O. in the Dawson Sub-Division.[83] If he wished he could stay at Fort Smith for a further year. But apparently Harry and Hilda had had enough of Fort Smith, and Harry asked to be relieved from Northern Service.[84]

Harry and Hilda left Fort Smith on 2 June 1942 and they therefore missed most of the turmoil that resulted from the influx of American troops that passed through Fort Smith with vast amounts of equipment bound downriver to Norman Wells.[85] The equipment was required for the construction of the CANOL pipeline across the Mackenzie Mountains to Whitehorse and the first troops (some 200 men) arrived with the first boat from Waterways in the spring of 1942.

Throughout their stay in Fort Smith, Harry's stomach complaints were an ongoing source of distress for him. As soon as they reached Edmonton, he went to the hospital to have X-rays taken. The diagnosis was a duodenal ulcer of long standing[86] and the doctors recommended a bland diet and rest in hospital. Since he had been granted a two-month leave prior to his next posting, he skipped on the hospital bed and opted instead for a holiday and a bland diet. For part of the time, at least, they visited Hilda's parents, who had by now retired and had moved from Edson to Gibson's Landing on the Sunshine Coast of British Columbia.

There was a possibility that Harry would be asked to return to the North in connection with the building of the pipeline and the construction of the Alaska Highway. Inspector Martin, Harry's former boss at Fort Smith, had contacted Headquarters in Ottawa and the Commissioner's immediate response was to cable Edmonton to hold Harry there "until a decision is made regarding personnel for the Fitzgerald-Fort Smith portage, additional strength for Norman, etc."[87] However, the powers-that-be then decided that his services would not be required after all and he was officially per-mitted to proceed on his leave.[88] Then someone higher up in the chain of command had a change of heart and on 15 June the Commissioner's office wrote to the Officer Commanding "E" Division, Vancouver, to instruct Harry to contact the Commissioner of "G" Division at the end of his leave, since he might still be needed in the Mackenzie Valley. He was also informed that "he will have to make arrangements to leave Mrs. Stallworthy outside as he would probably not be stationed at any definite point but would be travelling."[89]

For whatever reason, this northern posting did not materialize[90] and instead, Harry was posted to Thorold, Ontario, a small town immediately south of St. Catharine's on the Welland Canal.[91] Harry reported in Toronto on 17 August and proceeded straight on to Thorold.[92] Here a major part of Harry's duties was inspection patrols to the various detachments in the Niagara Peninsula and further afield, including London.[93] Hilda managed to get a job as teller in the Canadian Bank of Commerce in Thorold. It was also during their sojourn in Thorold that Harry joined the Freemasons, becoming a member of Mountain Lodge, No. 221. In what was to become a recurring pattern for the remainder of his life, Harry found himself in demand as a guest speaker at various organizations. On 26 October 1942 he gave a slide presentation at the meeting of the Thorold Kiwanis Club on the subject of the duties of the RCMP in the North, the Oxford University Ellesmere Land Expedition, and arctic game animals.[94]

The stomach ailment that had been hounding Harry since Moncton refused to go away and once again Harry was given strict instructions to stick to a bland diet. Even worse, this time the doctor recommended that he stop smoking. For a while at least, the Stallworthy household struggled to adjust to the new regimen—as did Harry's waistline as his weight rose from 195 lbs in 1942 to 216 lbs:

> Hilda kept me on milk, dry toast, soft boiled eggs & it was some time before I graduated to chicken & lamb. I gradually got better but no smoking nearly sent me "nuts." It was certainly hard on the nerves. After a light supper & every time I craved a smoke I found myself eating a dish of grape nuts or corn flakes several times between supper and bed time. No smoking certainly gave me an appetite."[95]

It was not only withdrawal symptoms that contributed to Harry's increasing waistline. As of 1 September 1943, Harry was posted to Toronto, where he and Hilda took an apartment at 22 Woodlawn Ave., but they later moved to an apartment at 458 Brunswick St. Harry's duties in Toronto were almost entirely administrative. He was in charge of the RCMP Barracks on Beverley Street, where he was in charge of 65 single men and even 6 women in the canteen. He also had charge of 51 cars, 2 trucks and 3 motor cycles, with all the paperwork that their maintenance involved. As he lamented in a letter to his brother: "None of this work gives me any exercise or real weight lifting, like throwing 250 lb sacks of barley around, perhaps, and I've no doubt that's why I weigh so much, I seem to keep growing out of my clothes."[96]

Another major part of Harry's work in Toronto (even more so than his duties at Thorold) was inspecting detachments scattered over a wide area of southern Ontario. This inevitably meant a great deal of travelling and on occasion in July 1945 he even had to travel as far as Sault-Ste-Marie to inspect the detachment there. It was not all work, though. Harry drove from Toronto by way of Manitoulin Island and managed to find time for a spot of fishing, catching some black bass weighing 1½–2 lbs.[97] Once he had completed the inspection, he even found time for nine holes of golf. Despite these periods of relaxation, Harry had a recurrence of his gastric problems and again he had X-rays taken. Now the doctors could find no sign of any ulcer and indicated that if he had had an ulcer it had cleared up. He was still not smoking and once again by watching his diet, Harry (with Hilda's help) managed to combat the problem.

In Toronto, Hilda got a job as cashier at the Guarantee Trust Company. She and Harry rode the street car together for the five miles to downtown every morning and Harry jokingly referred to Hilda as "the Old Lady of Threadneedle Street." Later she was employed at Simpson's Mail Order Department. For the next few years, Harry and Hilda spent their summers on Toronto Island, renting a house at 614 Lakeshore Ave., Hanlan's Point; they cycled around the island and commuted across to Toronto by ferry.

Soon after the move to Toronto, on 1 November 1943, Harry was promoted to the rank of Acting Sergeant-Major. Almost a year later, on 10 October 1944, he was confirmed in the rank of Sergeant-Major, retroactive to the date of his promotion to acting rank.[98]

Harry and Hilda had entertained the well-known Arctic expert, Vilhjalmur Stefansson, when he and his wife, Evelyn, were in Toronto. Afterwards, Hilda had sent Evelyn a manuscript and a letter and not long after, she received a letter from Vilhjalmur thanking her for the evening. He also mentioned that he had lunched with Commissioner Wood of the RCMP, who had informed him of Harry's promotion:

I told him it was a move in the right direction but that my idea was an Inspectorship. He was full of admiration for Sergeant Stallworthy, and let us hope he finds a way of translating that into another promotion.[99]

Some months later, writing to Lieutenant Colonel W. Hurst Brown, RCAMC, Stef noted:

Stallworthy is one of the best men in the RCMP and I think Commissioner Wood realizes that his promotion has not been quite as rapid as his merits call for. Therefore it might do some real good, for you or whoever is most strategically placed, to write the Commissioner telling him

Security for meeting of Prime Minister Winston Churchill and President Franklin Roosevelt, Quebec City, 1944; Harry at extreme left.

Meeting of Prime Minister Winston Churchill and President Franklin Roosevelt, Quebec City, 1944; Harry is in the corner at extreme left.

that Stallworthy has been valuable and saying whatever you feel justified in saying about his ability and his suitability for promotion.[100]

Although he would undoubtedly have appreciated getting a commission, Harry himself had no illusions as to his chances, and was reasonably resigned to remaining an NCO. In a letter to his brother, he offered his take on the matter:

It is quite evident that my chances for a commission have been buried by so many young applicants from R.M.C. & others with political strings and the overwhelming number of officers' sons who are getting their pips. I am now one of the Senior NCO's & should soon be in the first 12 who get 5¢ per diem extra.[101]

Despite this show of bravado, Harry's constant battle to receive recognition for what everyone seemed to describe as his sterling contribution to the RCMP left its mark on him. Later, after his retirement, he confided to his brother:

It was a great disappointment not getting a commission which I certainly would have had in 1935 or 6 if Comr. Gen. MacBrien had not died, but that is a long story. My chief reason for wanting a commission was to make Hilda's future more secure. You see an NCO's pension does not carry on for the wives, which is the case with officers.[102]

In the fall of 1944 Harry had a pleasant break from his normal routine when he was assigned to the security forces stationed in Quebec City on the occasion of the second meeting in that city between President Franklin Roosevelt and Prime Minister Winston Churchill, hosted by Prime Minister Mackenzie King. In a postcard to Hilda from Quebec City, he noted: "I had a close up at the officials conferring degrees today and the main press conferences."[103] He also took the opportunity to catch up with the news and have a few drinks with friends and fellow officers who had been seconded to Quebec from all over Canada. His later recollections of Churchill at Quebec City were that "He (they say) downed a bottle and a half of Scotch a day, wore blue clothes aged with green, and usually forgot to do the front of his pants up."[104]

During their sojourn in Toronto, Harry again had trouble with the haemorrhoids that had been such a torment to him on Ellesmere Island. And to add to his discomfort, he again began suffering from varicose veins in his left leg. At the recommendation of the Division Surgeon, he was even permitted to wear slacks instead of breeches on parade because of the varicose veins in his legs.[105] During the winter of 1944–45 he decided to do something about these medical conditions. He was in Christie Street Hospital from 7 March until 5 April, during which time his varicose veins were again operated on and he received treatment for haemorrhoids. Afterwards, he convalesced at home and returned to duty on 15 May.[106] While he was convalescing, his Commanding Officer, Superintendent F.A. Blake, wrote to the Commissioner, suggesting that Harry might be considered for a transfer for reasons of health:

> I know that Sergeant-Major Stallworthy upon his retirement to pension hopes to reside on the Pacific Coast. Under these circumstances, and in view of his long and faithful service, I wonder if the Commissioner might consider transferring him to the West where the change might be of great benefit to his health.[107]

Unfortunately this rather benevolent suggestion was refused "in view of the fact that there is no need of an N.C.O. of senior rank in 'E' Division."[108]

At the time, both Hilda and Harry were dealing with concerns about their respective parents. Some time previously the Reverend Austin had to be placed in a home in Vancouver; he had completely lost his memory and recognized nobody. Then in the late fall of 1944 Mrs. Austin had an operation on one eye that resulted in a general breakdown. Betty, Hilda's younger sister, had to go out to Gibson's Landing from Ontario for three months to look after her.[109]

Mrs. Florence Stallworthy, Harry's mother, was also becoming very forgetful, and was no longer able to live on her own at Fairford. Late in 1944, she moved in with Bill and Susie at the Mill in Ampney Crucis, but she evidently did not adjust well to the move, as is clear from a letter Harry wrote to his brother:

We know it must be very trying to live with her after she has paddled her own canoe for so long. Our sympathies are with you & Susie. I wish I could help share the responsibility. I know Mother is very apt to want to bend everything to her will & I suppose her deafness makes matters worse.[110]

Although it was a small consolation for being so far from his mother as her health deteriorated, he at least knew that she was being taken care of living as she did with Bill's family. Hilda's parents were a different matter. Although Betty had been able to stay with her mother for a while, this was not a permanent solution and Harry and Hilda wished to be closer to them.

13

TIMBERLANE

On 5 December 1945, Harry received notification that the Commissioner had approved his retirement from the Force as of 28 February 1946, prior to which he was granted two months' leave as of 1 January 1946.[1] At the Toronto Division Christmas party in the Sergeant's Mess, he was presented with a waterproof watch by the Division and with a pen-and-pencil set from the Sergeants, both suitably engraved. As he later described the event to his brother:

> They tell me I made quite a speech and reviewed my life & travels in the great outdoors and that I never enjoyed being an S/M, especially Orderly room cases, of which I had quite a few. One of my best friends, Sgt. McElhone said (of course he had packed away a few beers) "You

almost brought tears to my eyes in your parting speech in the Sergeants' Mess. I could hear the roots coming out."[2]

On the same occasion Hilda received a bouquet of red roses. Then soon after New Year's they were the guests of honour at a party thrown by their neighbours on Toronto Island, when they were presented with an oil painting of a northern scene.[3]

Harry and Hilda left Toronto by train on the evening of 9 January, bound for Vancouver. Initially they stayed with Hilda's mother in Gibson's Landing, but shortly afterwards they took a six month lease on a small cottage "with running water but no bathroom" at Saltair, about 3½ miles out of Ladysmith on Vancouver Island.[4] Harry, who was now at last able to indulge his keen interest in gardening, planted a garden that provided them with peas, celery, potatoes, carrots, turnips, raspberries, cherries and other fruit.[5]

In early July Harry and Hilda made a bicycle trip over to Saltspring Island. They crossed from Crofton to Vesuvius Bay and cycled south to Ganges. From there they visited a property on a lake that was set among the hills of Saltspring Island about three miles from Ganges. The property belonged to a couple from Lethbridge and the house and property (160 acres) were available for rent. After thinking the matter over, Harry suggested that he and Hilda take the place rent-free in return for maintenance and renovations. The owners agreed to this proposal, on condition that the Stallworthy's paid the taxes of $19.50 per year. The 3-bedroomed house and the garage were both of log construction. There was also a separate building that contained four separate bedrooms. Harry felt they would be able to take in summer visitors, especially since there was good trout fishing on the private lake. But whatever the reason, these very appealing plans did not materialize. When he wrote to his brother the following May, Harry and Hilda were still in the cottage near Ladysmith.

In the spring of 1947, Hilda's mother became seriously ill and Hilda travelled to Gibson's Landing to be with her, as did her sister, Betty McLellan, and her daughter Barbara. In early May Harry planned to go over to join them, rent a bicycle and cycle around the Sunshine Coast on the lookout for a place to settle, as they anticipated that Mrs. Austin might have to move in with them because neither Harry nor Hilda thought that she should remain on her own for the winter.[6] Harry's health troubles had flared up again and in addition to his gastric complaint, he had a recurrence of his haemorrhoids. He went onto a strict diet again and stopped smoking. Predictably, his nerves were on edge.

Hilda and Harry stayed in the cottage at Saltair for another year or two. Writing to his mother in October 1948, Harry reported that they were living quietly and that he was spending most of his time fishing for salmon. He had a 14-foot open boat with an inboard engine, which he christened the *Blue Goose*. He would go off on trips lasting four to five days. At night he would pull up on a remote beach, build a fire, enjoy a quiet meal, roll into his sleeping bag, which he covered with a tarpaulin to keep the dew or rain off, and sleep soundly.[7] Much as he enjoyed Hilda's company, he also enjoyed these solitary fishing trips. On his return to Saltair with his catch, Hilda would can the fish for future use.[8]

Harry was still determined to find a suitable location for a small tourist resort. He was still very concerned about the fact that, as the wife of a former NCO, Hilda would not receive a pension after Harry's death. She was 11 years younger than Harry and could anticipate being on her own for a considerable time after his death. He wanted to find a way to build up a decent amount of savings for Hilda's old age and a tourist resort seemed to be the ideal solution, given Harry's background and skills, and their gregarious natures. One day while driving up-island, they had stopped to eat a picnic lunch near Saratoga Beach at the mouth of the Oyster River, just south of Campbell River. As they later described the incident:

They joined a bulldozer operator who was having his lunch. They told him what they were looking for and he suggested they follow him as he broke a trail down a survey line. The bush was being opened for development. They followed the clanking machine as it crashed through the bush and came upon a wonderful sandy beach. Harry conceived the idea of a resort on this spot and Hilda visualized it completed. The man with the explorer's eyes chose his place well.[9]

It was (and is) a magnificent beach, lined with a bulwark of driftwood at high water mark, and backed by some magnificent old Douglas fir trees. On a clear day the mountains of the Coast Range on the mainland appear to be only a few miles away across the Strait of Georgia. It was just the ideal spot for the modest tourist lodge that Harry and Hilda had in mind.

In the summer of 1949, in partnership with another retired RCMP officer and his wife, they bought a property of some 2½ acres, covered with mature Douglas fir trees and extending from the road down to the beach. The property in fact consisted of three lots: the main part of it zoned for commercial use, but with separate lots for residences at both north and south ends. The partnership did not last, however, and the partner and his wife, who hailed from the prairies, sold out to Harry and Hilda even before the winter and moved away. As of 30 June Harry was in the Campbell River area trying to finalize the purchase of the property, while Hilda was still back at the cottage at Saltair; some hitch concerning title to the land was delaying the proceedings.[10] As Hilda outlined their plans, they

hoped to have a quiet type of camp where our guests could enjoy the fishing and hunting and out of door life without too much of the frill and fuss, but a little solid comfort—such as indoor plumbing and, we hope, a fireplace in each cabin.

The property we are interested in is on the sea-front within a stone's throw of Oyster River, famous for steel-head trout fishing. It is halfway between Campbell River and Courtenay. The whole of that district is famous for its big salmon fishing.[11]

By the late fall of 1950, with only limited professional input in areas such as plumbing and electrical wiring, they had built the first elements of their resort, which they named Timberlane. Although the interiors were still not complete, Harry and Hilda moved into one of the units for the winter of 1949/50. Hilda arranged two Adirondack lawn chairs in front of the fireplace and draped one of Harry's polar bear rugs over each. Their niece, Elaine Mellor, recalls Hilda's description of that first winter:

Ensconced in front of a roaring fire with dinner on his knee & a hot drink on the arm of the chair [Harry] would announce, as he as known to do when everything was most satisfactory: "I wouldn't call the Queen my aunt!"

There was a particularly heavy snowfall that winter, but they had an ample supply of firewood. At first Harry would haul driftwood logs from the beach and cut them up, but the sand that had made its way into some of the logs tended to dull the chainsaw very quickly and it was some distance from the beach to the duplex. So when a large dead Douglas fir had to be cut down at the end of the driveway, it became the firewood source of choice for the rest of the winter. Having cut it into manageable logs, Harry (and Elaine when she arrived the following summer) would split them using a sledge hammer and wedges.

By the spring of 1950 the interiors of the two units of the duplex as well as a separate cottage were finished. The units of the duplex and the cottage were self-contained holiday units, each with a kitchen, bathroom, living room and bedrooms. For that first summer Harry and Hilda occupied two large tents, a sleeping tent and a cook tent cum dining tent at the back of the property so that both duplex units and the cottage could be rented. Harry had erected a sign (painted by Hilda) advertising the resort on the Island Highway just south of the Oyster River bridge; then, when everything was ready for occupation, they drove out to the highway in their old Fargo truck and hung up the vacancy sign—and waited for the first tourists to arrive. They did not have long to wait. News of this comfortable rustic resort, with its superb fishing and genial hosts soon spread and slowly but surely, Harry and Hilda built up a very loyal clientele, with many clients returning year after year.

Particularly during the early years of operating Timberlane, Harry and Hilda maintained an ongoing correspondence (which had begun at least as early as 1933) with Bruce Carruthers, who had made a career for himself as technical adviser to the Hollywood movie industry on all aspects of the RCMP and the Canadian North. He went to enormous lengths to ensure that uniforms, behaviour, and general style of RCMP officers as portrayed by Hollywood were as authentic as possible; indeed he was something of a thorn in the side of scriptwriters and producers.[12] He functioned as an unofficial liaison between the RCMP and Hollywood and had a good working relationship with successive Commissioners, especially MacBrien and Wood, who generally approved of his attempts to portray the Force accurately. He advised on films such as *Heart of the North*, *Susannah of the Mounties*, *Barrier* and *Mrs. Mike*, and even had a bit-part in the last of these. He himself had been a member of the Force from 1919 until 1923, reaching the rank of Corporal, and had served with Harry in Dawson City during Harry's second spell of duty in the Yukon.

Carruthers quite often relied on Harry for detailed information about more obscure aspects of RCMP uniforms, equipment and activities. Thus in 1937 he asked: "Could you draw me a diagram and give me the exact dimensions of the badge worn by our men when on plainclothes duty?"[13] Then, also in 1937, shortly after Harry had been involved at Gaspé with the aerial operations against rum-runners, Carruthers sent Harry a list of questions starting with: "Has the Force got any aeroplanes permanently attached to the Force?" and ending with "Could you draw me a rough sketch of a communications tube which is used by planes on Police duty for dropping messages at sea? What are they made of and what are the approximate measurements?"[14] In a postscript Carruthers added another unrelated question: "Don't we use rifle-boots on saddles any more? If not, how is the rifle carried?"[15]

On a later occasion, Carruthers sent Harry a whole page of questions about gold mines and gold smuggling in connection with a script he had been asked to critique.[16] Later still, he enquired where one might find six or eight wolf-like dogs (huskies) that could play the part of a pack of wolves.[17] Thus, through his contact with Bruce Carruthers, Harry played a small part in keeping Hollywood's portrayal of the RCMP and of the Canadian North slightly more authentic than it might otherwise have been.

To augment his income Harry obtained a part-time job as Fisheries Warden with the Federal Department of Fisheries. Writing to his brother, he reported:

I am working for the Fisheries Dept. again this fall for Sept., Oct. & Nov. We estimate the run of pinks (humpbacked salmon) which have now spawned in the Oyster River at 130,000. A very heavy run of (Coho) Silver salmon are starting upstream now. I was checking them this A.M. It is quite a sight. In some pools they are 10 & 12 deep where they rest before making it over the next riffle. They go above 14 miles upstream.[18]

His duties included estimating the numbers of fish in the spawning runs in the Oyster River and Black Creek. With a couple of friends he also blew up beaver dams on the Little Oyster River and French Creek in November 1953 to allow salmon to get up those streams to spawn.[19] He was also empow-

The "duplex", Timberlane Resort, Vancouver Island, built by Harry and Hilda, 1954.

ered to apprehend poachers. His niece Elaine, who from 1950 until 1958 spent the summers with them helping Hilda during the busy tourist season, recalls that Harry took great satisfaction in quietly running into the mouth of the Oyster River from seawards and catching poachers by surprise as they poached salmon in nets that they had stretched right across the river mouth.[20]

On at least one occasion, in March 1954, Hilda worked as a substitute teacher in the elementary school in Campbell River, thus making her contribution to their supplementary income.[21]

In the spring of 1952 Harry began work on a further building that would house both the office and their home. This would allow them to rent out both sides of the duplex and the cottage, not only for summer tourists but also for long-term occupants in winter. Thus over the winter of 1951–52 they had two of the units rented for most of the winter, at $50 and $60 per month.

The house was located on the residential lot at the north end of the property and the long-term plan was that once they felt like retiring they would sell Timberlane, but retain the house, which had its own beach frontage.[22] By late March 1952 Harry had cleared the site for their house and had constructed the forms for its foundations. But in part due to Harry's poor health it was not until the early summer of 1954 that it was completed and they were able to move into it from the cottage. It measured 48' x 24' with an open car port on the end, for a total length of 60'. Designed by Hilda, it contained the office, laundry room, two bedrooms, bathroom, cabinet, kitchen and an L-shaped living room with a dressed stone fireplace. Particularly prominent in the living room were the two polar bear rugs, which tended to draw young visitors like magnets. With its cedar siding and a shingled roof, the house matched the rustic style of the two earlier buildings.

Finally, in the spring of 1956 Harry and Hilda began work on building a further two units (units 4 and 5). As with all the buildings, Hilda designed their house and the new units and drew up the plans. Then, apart from electrical wiring and plumbing, all other aspects of building were tackled by Harry and Hilda themselves, with a certain amount of assistance from various volunteers. They levelled the site, poured footings, framed the walls, raised and shingled the roof, applied cedar siding, installed windows, hung doors, built shelves, cupboards, counters, drawers and closets, put up ceiling tiles, installed electric fixtures, built fireplaces and chimneys, painted inside and out, hung wallpaper and drapes, varnished floors, and poured cement patios and walkways. Hilda with her artist's eye for colour and balance was responsible for the interior decorating and for selecting the furniture, drapes and wall coverings. Some of her own oil paintings were hung in their own house and in the guest units. Furnishing the various units was quite a challenge, since invariably most of their available funds had been expended on building materials. The Stallworthys became experts at picking up treasures at country auctions.[23]

Each summer the grounds also demanded a great deal of time and energy, and this work largely devolved on Hilda and their niece Elaine. Together, the two of them raked and burned leaves and branches, mowed grass, and planted and weeded flower beds. Other major outdoor jobs were usually a group effort, such as excavating gravel for cement, digging and enlarging a well, laying waterlines, installing septic tanks, and laying cement paths and stepping stones.

Unless a unit was to be rented over the winter, they were "winterized" late in the fall; the most important task was to drain the water tanks and toilets to prevent damage. On one occasion in the spring of 1955, the water heater in the tank in Unit 2 was accidentally switched on before the tank had been refilled. The result was a fire that caused quite a lot of smoke damage, but it could have been much more serious.

In addition to the challenging work of building the resort, the chores of operating it, especially in summer, were never-ending, and again these tended to fall on Hilda's shoulders. She handled cleaning, dusting, changing beds and doing laundry each time a new party moved into one of the units; for several summers in the 1950s, Elaine assisted her with these chores. Hilda also handled the considerable correspondence associated with enquiries and reservations and, of course, she handled the cooking, cleaning and general upkeep of their own home. In her spare time, she also painted and read.

Apart from the multi-facetted tasks of building and running the resort, Harry (often assisted by Elaine) would act as a fishing guide for their guests, and would handle the rental of boats and motors. He had two 10-foot clinker-built boats each with a 3 hp motor and also later a 12 foot boat with a 5 hp motor. Harry's preferred fishing tackle was a spoon flasher with a number 7 hook and a 40 lb test line. If Harry was out on his own, his aim was not the sport of playing a fish, but simply a pleasant outing, and, if he were lucky, to catch a decent-sized salmon for dinner.

Harry's polar bear rugs now became a useful resource. Bucktail flies had become a favourite lure for salmon fishermen. Harry would trim some of the hair from the edges of the rugs and give them to a friend who was an expert at tying these flies. In return Harry would receive several examples of the finished product.[24]

Early in their residence at Timberlane, Harry had had a caterpillar tractor clear an access path to the beach. On reaching the bulwark of driftwood at the head of the beach, the cat driver had simply pushed through it, leaving the logs on either side of the entrance leaning in every direction. When seen from seaward the tops of two steeply angled logs, one on either side of the entrance, appeared to cross. Harry whitewashed the tops of these logs to give himself a useful navigational aid when coming back to Timberlane, and if it was getting dark before he returned, Hilda would hang a lantern on each of them.

Harry's "navigation beacon" was also useful for guiding him around the end of a gravel bar at the mouth of the Oyster River that could present a hazard at low tide. Inside this bar was a kelp bed that gave refuge to small fish that tended to attract salmon and it represented one of the most popular and safe fishing spots for Timberlane guests. Harry, Hilda and Elaine frequently joined their guests (many of whom became close friends) at barbecues or clam-bakes on the beach.

In late April 1952, leaving Harry to look after Timberlane for a few days, Hilda travelled to Gibson's Landing on the occasion of her mother's death. She had been generally in good health, and her death came as quite a surprise to everyone: "Just dropped out of the picture without notice," Harry wrote to Bill.[25] Harry drove Hilda down to Nanaimo to catch the ferry to Vancouver, then picked her up again on her return.

Despite the fact that the paved highway ended at Courtenay, some 30 km to the south, many of their clients were Americans. With a little encouragement, Harry could quite easily be persuaded to tell stories of his years in the Arctic, which must have added a fascinating element to a vacation at Timberlane. Unfortunately Harry's retirement years were quite often bedevilled by ill-health. In the springs of both 1953 and 1954, for example, he was bedridden for weeks at a time with lumbago and, more seriously, with stomach ulcers. To combat the latter he had to suffer a diet of milk and arrowroot biscuits. Then in the spring of 1956 he suffered from a painful attack of hives.

Both Harry and Hilda clearly loved the resort they had created, even in winter, as is evident from the entries in Hilda's diaries. Thus after a record snowfall in late January 1954 Hilda wrote:

We had a wonderful winter until this snow came—mild rains and plenty of sunshine. Then who-o-o-osh! Down it came overnight, and in the morning the place was a fairyland—so still that the fluffy snow clung to the trees and bowed them down. The wires & smallest twigs were like white chenille ropes. The trees were tall white ladies wrapped in ermine, standing silently about, holding their cloaks around them. And the steel grey sea was quiet too. The air felt spellbound. We couldn't get out, so we just shovelled paths to the wood pile and the oil barrel, and stayed inside and gazed out at the beauty. Our world closed in to a small white circle of cozy enchantment. We had late, large breakfasts in front of the fireplace, listened to the radio and felt sorry for all the people who had to go to offices and schools and hospitals. When the snow plow came to dig us out, we felt like telling them to go away. Then it snowed again and our private white world was back again.[26]

The beach, Timberlane, 1950s.

By late June 1956 Unit 4 of the two new units was almost ready to rent, but Unit 5 was in a very unfinished state. Then on 28 June Harry received a letter from his brother-in-law, George McClellan, who was by then an Assistant Commissioner in the RCMP, to alert him to the fact that the Federal Electric Corporation, which was responsible for the DEW Line, the system of early-warning radar sites extending from East Greenland across Greenland, Arctic Canada and northern Alaska, had a vacancy for which Harry appeared ideally suited, particularly in the light of his police experience and his experience of living and travelling with the Inuit.[27] Hilda recorded their reaction in her diary:

On Thursday Harry drove up to the mail box and brought back the letter from George.

In all our summers in the past since arriving here in 1949 this has been the most hectic. Here we are into June and facing our summer season—almost fully booked—and we are still up to our necks in the building—No. 4 almost ready to rent, and already booked—No. 5 in a very unfinished state. We don't expect it to be ready until well into the mid-summer. We work from early A.M. until we drop into bed at night.

We sat on the hearth eating our lunch and tried to forecast what it would mean to us—our life here—and our plans for the future. But there was this promise of a big addition to our very slim financial resources. It appealed to Harry, who had never entertained the idea of returning to the North. And to me—it would mean being alone again with a rather large unfinished project.

The biggest appeal was the salary. It was so tempting. We finally ran out of arguments for and against. I got up from the hearth and said "Well, in the meantime—back to the varnish pots! And hanging out that washing!" And Harry—back to No. 5.

It is very hard to go on with the work, with our minds pre-occupied with the surprising D.E.W. offer. We work in different cottages then get together for meals and the talk goes on. I have made up my mind to say nothing that will influence Harry one way or the other. It must be his own decision. I have only said that he must not consider me. I can manage with summer help. The three cottages are running smoothly. We are beginning to be well known and have good return business.

If this offer hadn't come up, we would have gone on and managed financially. So the discussion goes back and forth. Harry is tempted. His health is so much more stable now after all his miseries.[28]

With all the usual hustle and bustle of running the resort in summer, the DEW Line job had almost faded from their minds. But then, over a month later, on 5 August, Harry received a follow-up letter from Thomas Lawrence, Air Vice Marshal RCAF (Retd.), then Regional Manager for the Federal Electric Corporation that operated the DEW Line.[29] He offered Harry a position as "Morale, Security and Safety Representative" for the DEW Line at a salary of $800 (U.S.) per month.[30] As Hilda recorded in her diary:

We are stunned with this unexpected offer of a high income job for Harry—coming in the midst of our involvement with our summer. The letters from George had been almost forgotten in the continual coming and going of our summer visitors, and the unfinished cottage, No. 5.[31]

In fact once Harry received a job description, it was to find that his title would be *Assistant* Supervisor Morale, Safety and Security. His duties included:

a. Assist the Supervisor Morale, Safety and Security in the maintenance of a high standard of morale among personnel on the Line.
b. Assist in the training of FEC Personnel on Arctic conditions and how to live "with" the country and its conditions.
c. Indoctrinate FEC Personnel on the Eskimo, his character, his way of life and how to maintain friendly and good working relations with him.
d. Maintain a liaison with Department of Northern Affairs Representatives in the Eastern Arctic in respect to employment of Eskimo labour by FEC."[32]

For almost another two weeks Harry and Hilda agonized over the job offer, then, on 18 August they received a telegram: "Please advise immediately if interested position offered our letter August 2, 1956, Frediani."[33] The next day Harry cabled back: "Will accept position. Letter follows."[34]

Inevitably it took Harry a few months to tie up all the loose ends connected with running Timberlane and with his position as Fisheries Warden, and it was not until 5 October 1956 that he started the journey east to Federal Electric's DEW Line headquarters in Mont-Joli, Quebec. That morning Hilda drove him to Nanaimo to catch the ferry: "Back home alone and not feeling too good about the whole thing and home to Timberlane—feeling very lost & quiet and alone. Gee—this house is too big for me!"[35]

But in fact this was a false alarm. On reaching Vancouver airport Harry found that his airline ticket was not waiting for him, as he had been advised. He arrived back at Timberlane by bus on the 7th and finally departed on the 9th.[36] He was stationed at Mont-Joli for some time and his title soon changed to Security Supervisor. Soon after his appointment, he toured all the DEW Line sites in the Eastern Arctic.[37] In February 1957 he managed to take advantage of a conference in Lodi, New Jersey, to get together with Hilda for a short break in New York and Ottawa.

In Harry's absence Hilda, with Elaine's help during the summer, had been coping with the never-ending tasks of running Timberlane, even to the extent of building the forms and pouring the cement for the patio for the units of the new "duplex." But in mid-December she had travelled to Edmonton to visit her sister Betty and her husband George McClellan. It was from there that she flew to New York on 17/18 February to see Harry.

Their rendezvous was at the New Yorker Hotel on 18 February.[38] The following day, while Harry headed for Lodi, Hilda took the subway to the Chase Manhattan Bank at 73rd and Broadway, then took the bus to Times Square, from where she walked back down Broadway to the New Yorker. Then Harry phoned to say that the conference had been called off and moved to Ottawa. They were able to spend the evening together but Harry headed for Ottawa next day, while Hilda spent a further two days seeing the sights in New York with friends. Then on the evening of the 21st she flew via Montreal to Ottawa, where she and Harry stayed in the Château Laurier. They visited numerous old friends over the next couple of days, including Paddy Hamilton, who was now married. On the 24th Harry returned to his duties in Mont-Joli, and on the 27th Hilda flew to Toronto, then on to Stratford to visit her sister Elaine Joyce. On 11 March she flew back to Edmonton to visit Betty and George again, as well as Ethelind and Elaine Mellor, and was home at Timberlane by 21 March.[39]

In the spring of 1957, FEC's head office for its DEW Line operation (including Harry) was moved from Mont-Joli to Frobisher Bay (now Iqaluit). Writing in the fall, Harry described his office facilities as follows:

We have quite a large staff now occupying two double Atwells, and many desks. More chiefs than Indians! There is a connecting room between the Atwells to house the teletype and crypto staff. You would not know the old mess hall now, with all the separate bedrooms, a large reading lounge and a large cocktail lounge. Canned beer is all along the Line now and the Main and Aux. Sites will soon be stocked with liquor."[40]

Harry's duties were varied and included attending to security requirements for visitors, fire prevention, authorizing security clearances, and distributing rifles and ammunition at DEW Line sites. He was not stuck behind a desk for the entire period of his employment with FEC, however. In August 1957 he visited many of the sites to organize fire brigades.[41] On that trip he was weather-bound for a week at Fox 5 (east coast of Baffin Island). While there he investigated a rumour of an illicit still, but found that it was simply a wine-making operation, exaggerated into a still by an employee who had a chip on his shoulder because he had been fired.

In early September Harry flew west to Fox Main (now Hall Beach) and worked his way west along the line to Cam Main (Cambridge Bay). From there he flew south to Edmonton to confer with Henry Kearney (Security Supervisor—Western Region). As he was relatively close to home, Harry took the opportunity to fly to Vancouver and home to Timberlane "for a few days on R & R."[42] Hilda and Elaine picked him up at Comox airport in scorching hot weather on 10 September: "We wore sleeveless cotton dresses and to Harry, just down from Baffinland and fur parkas and blizzards it was quite an impact."[43] Harry left again on the long trip back to Frobisher Bay on the 17th.

After a year of mainly bureaucratic work and, one suspects, much less contact with the Inuit than he had anticipated, Harry had had enough and tendered his resignation. A number of things about the operation of the DEW Line had irritated him, one of them being the enormous waste of food in the kitchens and messhalls at the sites he visited, particularly when he saw the living conditions of the Inuit and recalled some of the starvation conditions he himself had endured in the Arctic.[44] On 6 December Hilda noted in her diary: "Heard from Harry after nearly 6 weeks silence. Coming home for good—and expects to be home before Christmas."[45] But before this he had to deal with the fallout from quite a serious fire at Fox 4 on 18 November. Lunch was being prepared on a kerosene stove in an Atwell building when the stove exploded, spewing flaming fuel across the room. The two occupants, a civilian working for Crawley McCracken Company and a U.S. Navy man, received second and third degree burns to head, face, neck, arms and hands. The building and its contents were totally destroyed. The severity of the burns that the men suffered was exacerbated by the fact that the door was jammed by the explosion, impeding their escape. The men were flown to Frobisher Bay and then south; one man was treated in hospital in Montreal, the other man in the United States. The cause of the explosion was the improper use of a highly flammable fuel called "Blazo" instead of kerosene.

Hilda, Harry and their niece, Elaine Mellor, Timberlane.

Elaine Mellor and Harry on fishing trip from Timberlane.

Having tendered his resignation, Harry was back home at Timberlane by Christmas—much to Hilda's delight. He would never visit the Arctic again. As he said to Hilda: "I'm through with the North for ever. I want to go as far south as I've been North."[46] Acting on this sentiment, Harry and Hilda spent three months during the winter of 1958 in Manzanillo, as Hilda later recalled very fondly:

So we spent an idyllic winter in Manzanillo, in a heavenly spot, which is now a millionaires' retreat. We did nothing but swim in the warm Pacific, lie in the shade of the palm umbrellas, and cook all our meals in the electric frying pan. We would go up to the totally primitive ancient seaport of Manzanillo to buy our food and poke around and talk [1] to the Mexicans in my pigeon [sic] Spanish. Such charming, gay, responsive people. Poor, uneducated, victims of their social system, but always gay and responsive. No wonder I love Mexico.

We were the only guests at Las Hadas. The other half of the resort was under construction and it was only because I had acquired some Spanish that we heard about it and were allowed to stay there. One of the most enjoyable times we have ever had—no golf—no tourists—just sun, and beauty, the warm Pacific and each other. We lived in shorts, shirts, bare legs, and ate fruit, tropical vegetables and whatever we could scrounge in the native market and cook in the electric frying pan. Three months of that—then back to Timberlane.[47]

Thereafter life for Harry and Hilda settled back into the comfortable routine they had established over the years. For the summers they were the congenial hosts at Timberlane. Then during the winters they headed south to Mazatlan, Mexico, to Laguna Beach, to Manzanillo and even Guadalajara—wherever their desire took them.

In 1970 Harry suffered a heart attack and was taken to St. Joseph's Hospital in Comox; when he was discharged he was wearing a pacemaker.[48] Because of Harry's health they sold Timberlane and bought a house at 1842 Queen's Ave., Comox, within easy reach of the hospital. Over the years they had made numerous friends in Comox, and so they felt quite at home almost immediately. The house was also within walking distance of Comox Golf Club where they both became members.

Soon after their move, Harry went back to England to visit his brother Bill and other family members. Then in the fall of 1972 he and Hilda again returned to England and also toured parts of Europe. This was the first time Harry had been on the continent since his experiences in Flanders in 1918–19.[49] They took the opportunity to visit Elaine, who was then living in Baden-Baden and teaching at the Canadian Army base at Bad-Solingen. Harry was given a tour of the base and was greatly impressed by the fighter aircraft, armoured personnel carriers and tanks, all a far cry from the horse-drawn technology of World War I. They also visited the casino where Harry played at the tables, quite successfully.[50]

On 11 September 1973 Hilda and Harry set off by car for a trip to Jasper, sharing the driving and travelling by way of Powell River, Gibsons, Vancouver and Kamloops.[51] At Jasper they stayed at the Pine Cabins and on the 16th Hilda wrote in her diary:

Drove to Maligne Lake—a beautiful day. Had lunch on the hillside looking up the Lake at the gorgeous view. Crowds of people, cars, campers, boats. Nothing left of the peace and beauty of 1933—my last sight of Maligne Lake with Phoebe Young, cook and guide, courtesy of Fred Brewster.[52]

In the afternoon they took a boat trip up the lake "in a crowded bus boat, complete with microphoned commentary by driver." Evidently Hilda was not greatly impressed, comparing this experience, no doubt, with her visit in 1933. Undoubtedly, she and Harry must have reminisced at length about their horseback trip to Maligne Lake in 1928.

They had planned to continue east to visit various family members in Edmonton, but when Harry started feeling unwell, Hilda decided they should run for home, which they did, arriving in Comox on the 24th. Throughout the trip Hilda had kept a careful eye on their finances and recorded the daily expenses of the trip in her diary. This was quite an ambitious road-trip for a man of 76 who was in poor health. However, seeing Jasper again, with all its pleasant memories, must have made it well worthwhile for both Harry and Hilda.

Some time thereafter, with increasing traffic on the island roads moving at ever-greater speeds, Harry felt he was no longer competent to drive. He

Harry receiving Order of Canada from Queen Elizabeth, Ottawa, August 1973.

had Hilda drive him to the RCMP detachment in Comox and relinquished his driver's licence.[53] On 2 August 1973 Harry was made an Officer of the Order of Canada for his contributions in the Canadian Arctic at a special investiture at Government House in Ottawa.[54] It was special in that the medals were presented by Her Majesty Queen Elizabeth II. The honour was enhanced by the fact that Harry was only one of five people to receive this order from the Queen herself out of 16 Officers who were so honoured that summer. During a brief chat with Queen Elizabeth, Harry commented that the ceremony was much more of an ordeal than even the worst of his sledge trips in the Arctic.[55] At the same investiture, Jules Léger, who held the office of Governor-General of Canada from 1974 until 1979, was made a Companion of the Order of Canada. Hilda accompanied Harry to Ottawa for the investiture, and taking advantage of the fact that they were in Ontario, they travelled as far as Thorold to visit old friends there before heading back to Comox.

When they returned home, Harry's health deteriorated. On 27 August 1976 he developed intermittent minor nosebleeds and when the problem became more severe, he was taken to St. Joseph's Hospital in Comox in the early hours of the 28th. He was given blood transfusions and was kept in hospital so that the staff could monitor his heart. Hilda visited him daily, but then, on 21 September she was taken to hospital on the advice of her doctor to have an operation on a hernia and her gall bladder. On the 26th Hilda's elder sister, Ethelind, arrived from Edmonton to look after her and Harry. Once Hilda was allowed home on the 30th, Ethelind stayed to keep her company and to prepare meals for her, since she was spending every day sitting with Harry. He was allowed home on 12 October and was well enough on Saturday 15 October to be sitting up, watching the hockey game on television.[56]

Then on the 19th he had a relapse and was taken back to hospital. From then on his condition steadily deteriorated. On 6 December, Eddie Shackleton phoned from Victoria, where he happened to be visiting. He had hoped to see Harry, but Hilda had to tell him, regretfully, that this was not possible.[57] Nonetheless, this call from their old friend of over 40 years must have boosted her morale.

When Hilda went to the hospital on the morning of Christmas Day, she found Harry asleep or unconscious: "Could not recognize the framed picture I took him of the presentation of the Order of Canada by the Queen."[58] He died that evening, at the age of 81. Cause of death was recorded as atherosclerotic heart disease due to an aortic aneurysm.[59]

Harry's body was cremated, but his name was added to the tombstone on the grave of his brother Archibald in the churchyard at Ampney St. Mary, only a stone's throw from the Mill at Ampney Crucis where his brother Bill had lived. Their mother lies in the next grave and his brother Bill just beyond her.

Hilda had written to the Queen to inform her of Harry's death, and she subsequently received letters of sympathy from Buckingham Palace,[60] from Governor-General Jules Léger,[61] and from Eddie Shackleton, who was by then Baron Shackleton of Burley: "Betty joins me again in sending all kind

St. Mary's church, Ampney St. Mary, Gloucestershire, where Harry's name has been added to his brother's tombstone (one of graves at left).

thoughts & sympathy for the loss of a great & good man," he wrote at the end of the letter.[62] Eddie also wrote a sympathy letter to Bill Stallworthy:

> Although we had not seen much of one another in recent years, I had the highest regard for him, and it was very gratifying when he got the Canadian honour a few years ago for so much of his splendid work. He was a great Polar man—indeed perhaps one of the greatest Royal Canadian Mounted Police Arctic travellers.[63]

Eddie also wrote to Commissioner M.J. Nadon and his letter of tribute was published in the *RCMP Quarterly*. It is a fitting tribute to an old friend and fellow-traveller:

> Dear Commissioner,
> I was very sorry to learn of the death of Sergeant Harry Stallworthy, formerly of the Royal Canadian Mounted Police, and would like to pay tribute to him.

As the organiser, and now sole survivor of the Oxford University Ellesmere Land Expedition of 1934–35, I would like to say how much we all owed to Harry Stallworthy. This Expedition...owed a very great deal to the help of the Royal Canadian Mounted Police, and in particular to their attachment to us of Harry Stallworthy.

Harry Stallworthy...was one of the greatest of Arctic travellers. His journey searching for the lost German explorer, Dr. Krueger, north-west of Axel Heiberg, provided one of the epic sledge journeys....

It was our intention to winter in the North, but as none of us had Polar experience, it was of vital importance that we should find someone else for the expedition who had not only travelled and lived in the Arctic, but also had a good deal of knowledge of the methods of travel that were necessary in the country which we were aiming to visit.... Major-General Sir James MacBrien, of the Royal Canadian Mounted Police, very generously offered a great deal of valuable support to the expedition, including the loan of a really experienced "Mountie" who knew the Arctic regions.... We were very fortunate that the man who should have been chosen to go with us was Sergeant Stallworthy.... I could tell many anecdotes of Harry Stallworthy and of his contribution to the expedition. The fact that we achieved anything at all and indeed survived, owed so much to this remarkable Polar man. He taught us Eskimo; he taught us to drive dogs; he taught us everything about Arctic living, including how to make sour dough hot cakes—and I remember him with affection and admiration.[64]

Hilda lived without Harry in Comox for another eight years. Of his last months, during which Hilda visited him daily, she later wrote:

He could make me laugh, always—even in his last three months in hospital. One day I laughed and said, "Oh, Harry dear—you clown!" If I looked sad he didn't like it. One day he said "Smile, darling. You look beautiful when you smile." I knew that I must not show any of my grief. He helped me even when he knew he was leaving me behind. That was his only regret.

I sat with him day and night, even when he was asleep, because when he wakened he would say, "Are you there darling?" I would take his hand and he would tell me what he was thinking. He talked about his friends the Eskimo whom he admired, who had been his companions and friends on many difficult and hazardous patrols. They thought the same about him....

When he was dying in the last months of 1976 he said one day "How could I have been so lucky to find you in all the dozens of times I went in and out of the Arctic and home to England. Then I met you." I said: "I was lucky too. We were both two lucky people."[65]

NOTES

1 | HARRY STALLWORTHY'S LIFE OF ADVENTURE

1   Henry Webb Stallworthy, Patrol Report: Bache Peninsula Detachment to
     Head of Flagger River, Craig Harbour and Mackinson Inlet, Ellesmere Island,
     31 May 1931, Stallworthy Collection, Arctic Institute of North America,
     Calgary (hereafter cited as Stallworthy Collection); H. Stallworthy, "The
     loneliest journey," *Blue Book Magazine* 92, no. 2 (1950): 13–15.

2   Hilda Stallworthy to C. Richard Harrington, 5 February 1983, Stallworthy
     Collection.

3   Ibid.

4   Ibid.

1   Henry Webb Stallworthy, Service Register, Royal Canadian Mounted Police Archives, Ottawa (hereafter cited as Service Register).

2   Ibid.

3   Ibid.

4   Ibid.

5   "Four murdered near Whitehorse," *Dawson Daily News*, 30 September 1915.

6   "Full report of the trial of Gagoff—to hang March 10," *Dawson Daily News*, 11 November 1915.

7   Ibid.

8   Henry Webb Stallworthy, Service Register.

9   "Alex Gagoff dies on gallows without flinching," *Dawson Daily News*, 10 March 1916.

10 Ibid.

11 Department of the Interior, *The Yukon Territory* (Ottawa: King's Printer, 1916), 204.

12 Ibid., 232.

13 G.B. Jod to Henry Webb Stallworthy, 1 November 1917, Stallworthy Collection.

14 Henry Webb Stallworthy to O.C., Dawson, 23 February 1917, Stallworthy Collection.

15 R.S. Knight to Henry Webb Stallworthy, 6 March 1917, Stallworthy Collection.

16 Henry Webb Stallworthy to R.S. Knight, 10 May 1917, Stallworthy Collection.

17 R.S. Knight to Henry Webb Stallworthy, 19 May 1917, Stallworthy Collection.

18 "Returns get in from Mayo District. All returns now in," *Dawson Daily News*, 5 September 1916.

19 Henry Webb Stallworthy, Service Register, 1 June 1917; R.S. Knight to the Commissioner RNWMP, 30 May 1917, Henry Webb Stallworthy, Service File, f. 34, Royal Canadian Mounted Police Archives (hereafter cited as Service File).

20 T.E.G. Shaw, "Hanged by a shoe lace," *RCMP Quarterly* 28, no. 3 (1963): 189; "Mysterious murder near Dawson City," *Dawson Daily News*, 27 June 1917.

21 "Roy Yoshioka is held by authorities," *Dawson Daily News*, 28 June 1917.

22 Shaw, "Hanged," 190.

23 "Yoshioka is held for trial for murder," *Dawson Daily News*, 17 July 1917.

24 Shaw, "Hanged," 191; *Dawson Daily News*, 13 August 1917.

25 Shaw, "Hanged," 191; *Dawson Daily News*, 23 November 1917.

26 Henry Webb Stallworthy, Service Register; R.S. Knight to Commissioner RNWMP, 29 June 1917, Henry Webb Stallworthy, Service File, f. 36.

27 Henry Webb Stallworthy to R.S. Knight, 18 December 1917, Stallworthy Collection.

28 Henry Webb Stallworthy to R.S. Knight, 7 January 1918, Stallworthy Collection.

29 R.S. Knight to Henry Webb Stallworthy, 10 January 1918, Stallworthy Collection.

30 Henry Webb Stallworthy to R.S. Knight, 14 January 1918, Stallworthy Collection.

31 R.S. Knight to Henry Webb Stallworthy, 31 January 1918, Stallworthy Collection; Henry Webb Stallworthy to R.S. Knight, 2 February 1918, Stallworthy Collection.

32 R.S. Knight to Henry Webb Stallworthy, 14 March 1918, Stallworthy Collection.

33 R.S. Knight to Henry Webb Stallworthy, 25 March 1918, Stallworthy Collection; R.S. Knight to Henry Webb Stallworthy, 28 March 1918, Stallworthy Collection; R.S. Knight to Henry Webb Stallworthy, 9 April 1918, Stallworthy Collection; Henry Webb Stallworthy to R.S. Knight, 3 April 1918, Stallworthy Collection.

34 Henry Webb Stallworthy to R.S. Knight, 3 April 1918, Stallworthy Collection.

35 Henry Webb Stallworthy to R.S. Knight, 2 April 1918, Stallworthy Collection.

36 Henry Webb Stallworthy, Attestation Paper, Canadian Overseas Expeditionary Force, 9 May 1918, Henry Webb Stallworthy, Service File, ff. 39–40.

37 Elaine Mellor, personal communication, 2002.

38 I. Sheldon-Williams, and R.F. Lardy, *The Canadian Front in France and Flanders* (London: A. and C. Black, 1920); H. Steele, *The Canadians in France 1915–1918* (New York: E.P. Dutton and Co., 1919); D. Morton, and J.L. Granatstein, *Marching to Armageddon. Canadians and the Great War 1914–1919* (Toronto: Lester and Orpen Dennys, 1989).

39 Morton and Granatstein, *Marching to Armageddon*.

40 Henry Webb Stallworthy to O.C., Depot Division, Regina, 16 March 1919, Henry Webb Stallworthy, Service File, f. 44.

41 Henry Webb Stallworthy to O.C., Vancouver, B.C., 25 April 1919, Henry Webb Stallworthy, Service File, f. 47.

42 Henry Webb Stallworthy to O.C., Vancouver, B.C., 15 July 1919, Henry Webb Stallworthy, Service File, f. 48.

43 Henry Webb Stallworthy, *Patrol to Ross River*, 26 April 1920, Stallworthy Collection.

44 Ibid.

45 Ibid.

46 Elaine Mellor, personal communication, May 2004.

47 Henry Webb Stallworthy to William Stallworthy, 20 July 1920, Stallworthy Collection.

48 K.S. Coates, and W.R. Morrison, *Land of the midnight sun. A history of the Yukon* (Edmonton: Hurtig, 1988).

49   M. Zaslow, *The opening of the Canadian North 1870–1914* (Toronto: McClelland and Stewart, 1988).

50   Henry Webb Stallworthy to William Stallworthy, 10 October 1920, Stallworthy Collection.

51   Report from S/Sgt. W. J. D. Dempster on patrol to Hart River & return to cache supplies for Dawson-MacPherson Patrol, 22 December 1920, National Archives of Canada, Ottawa (hereafter cited as NAC), RG 18, Vol. 3157, File G1312–1.

52   D. North, *The lost patrol* (Anchorage: Alaska Northwest Publishing Company, 1978).

53   "Hit the long trail tomorrow for M'Pherson," *Dawson Daily News*, 5 January 1921.

54   North, *The lost patrol.*

55   "Four patrols met at Fort MacPherson," *Dawson Daily News*, 8 March 1921.

56   "Police patrol arrives," *Dawson Daily News*, 5 March 1921.

57   The weather had been bitterly cold on the outward trip, although not extreme by Yukon standards. The minimum temperature at Dawson on their second day on the trail (8 January) had been -37°F (-38°C) and it dropped to -47°F (-44°C) on the 15th and -45°F (-43°C) on the 17th, while on the day they reached Fort McPherson the temperature dropped to -42°F (-41°C). While the temperatures may not have been quite the same along the route of the patrol, these temperatures at Dawson give some idea of the conditions the patrol was facing. On the return trip temperatures were much milder. The lowest to which the temperature dropped at Dawson during their return was -36°F (-38°C) on both 16 and 17 February, while it was above zero for the entire latter part of their trip, from 22 February onwards, the low being only a balmy +16°F (-9°C) on the day they returned to Dawson. All these temperature data are derived from the daily weather reports in the *Dawson Daily News*.

58   Gray Campbell, draft of article entitled "Stallworthy," December 1961, Stallworthy Collection.

59   R. E. Tucker to Commissioner, R.C.M. Police, 7 January 1921, Henry Webb Stallworthy, Service File, f. 53.

60   Henry Webb Stallworthy to William Stallworthy, 2 May 1921, Stallworthy Collection.

61   H. M. Newson to O.C., "B" Division, 27 June 1921, Henry Webb Stallworthy, Service File, f. 56.

62   Henry Webb Stallworthy to Davies, 27 October 1931, Stallworthy Collection.

63   Coates and Morrison, *Land of the midnight sun*, 186.

64   Henry Webb Stallworthy to Davies, 27 October 1931, Stallworthy Collection.

65   Elaine Mellor, personal communication, May 2004.

1   Henry Webb Stallworthy to William Stallworthy, 15 October 1922,
    Stallworthy Collection.

2   Henry Webb Stallworthy to William Stallworthy, n.d (Fall), 1922, Stallworthy
    Collection.

3   Ibid.

4   Ibid.

5   Henry Webb Stallworthy to William Stallworthy, 31 December 1922,
    Stallworthy Collection.

6   Ibid.

7   Ibid.

8   Henry Webb Stallworthy to William Stallworthy, 20 May 1923, Stallworthy
    Collection; Henry Webb Stallworthy, partial letter to Florence Stallworthy,
    June 1923, Stallworthy Collection.

9   Henry Webb Stallworthy to Commissioner, R.C.M. Police, 5 May 1923,
    Stallworthy Collection.

10 Harry Webb Stallworthy to William Stallworthy, 20 May 1923, Stallworthy
    Collection.

11 Henry Webb Stallworthy to Florence Stallworthy, June 1923, Stallworthy
    Collection.

12 M.H. Vernon to Officer Commanding "N" Division, 11 June 1923, Henry
    Webb Stallworthy, Service File.

13 Telegram from M.H. Vernon to Officer Commanding, Montreal, 12 July 1923,
    Henry Webb Stallworthy, Service File.

14 Henry Webb Stallworthy, "Nowya was a primitive," unpublished manuscript,
    Stallworthy Collection.

15 Th. Mathiassen, "Report on the expedition," in *Report of the Fifth Thule
    Expedition 1921-24*, vol. 1, bk. 1 (Copenhagen: Gyldendallske Boghandel.
    Nordisk Forlag, 1945), 74-75.

16 Henry Webb Stallworthy to William Stallworthy, 28 October 1923,
    Stallworthy Collection.

17 Stallworthy, "Nowya."

18 Ibid.

19 Ibid.

20 Henry Webb Stallworthy to William Stallworthy, 11 November 1923,
    Stallworthy Collection.

21 Stallworthy, "Nowya," 9-16.

22 Henry Webb Stallworthy to William Stallworthy, 6 February 1924, Stallworthy
    Collection.

23 Henry Webb Stallworthy, Report: Patrol to Daly Bay and Cape Fullerton
    districts, 20 February 1924, Stallworthy Collection.

24 A. P. Low, *Report on the Dominion Government expedition to Hudson Bay and the Arctic Islands on board the D. G. S.* Neptune *1903–1904* (Ottawa: Government Printing Bureau, 1906).

25 Henry Webb Stallworthy to William Stallworthy, 6 February 1924, Stallworthy Collection.

26 Stallworthy, "Nowya," 22.

27 Henry Webb Stallworthy to William Stallworthy, 6 February 1924, Stallworthy Collection.

28 Henry Webb Stallworthy, Report: Hunting walrus for dog feed for the Chesterfield Inlet Detachment, 20 July 1924, Stallworthy Collection.

29 Henry Webb Stallworthy to William Stallworthy, 27 January 1925, Stallworthy Collection.

30 Ibid.

31 Henry Webb Stallworthy, Report: Patrol to Southampton Island, 1 September 1924, Stallworthy Collection; A. D. Copeland, *Coplalook, Chief Trader, Hudson's Bay Company* (Winnipeg: Watson and Dwyer, 1985).

32 Copeland, *Coplalook*.

33 Henry Webb Stallworthy, Report: Patrol to Repulse Bay, 1 September 1924, Stallworthy Collection.

34 K. Rasmussen, *Across Arctic America. Narrative of the Fifth Thule Expedition* (New York: G. P. Putnam's Sons, 1927).

35 Henry Webb Stallworthy, "Maggie Clay," unpublished manuscript, Stallworthy Collection.

36 Ibid., 3–4.

37 Ibid., 5.

38 Ibid., 6.

39 Ibid., 7.

40 Ibid., 8–9.

41 Ibid., 9.

42 Ibid., 10.

43 Elaine Mellor, personal communication, May 2004.

44 Stallworthy, "Maggie Clay," 10.

45 Ibid., 11.

46 Henry Webb Stallworthy to William Stallworthy, 27 January 1925, Stallworthy Collection.

47 William Stallworthy to Inspector M. H. Vernon, 1 December 1924, Henry Webb Stallworthy, Service File.

48 M. H. Vernon to William Stallworthy, 12 December 1924, Henry Webb Stallworthy Service File.

49 Henry Webb Stallworthy, Report on Patrol from Chesterfield Inlet to Baker Lake District, 1 May 1925, Stallworthy Collection.

50 Henry Webb Stallworthy to William Stallworthy, 28 August 1925, Stallworthy Collection.

51 Ibid.

52 Henry Webb Stallworthy to Florence Stallworthy, 8 September 1925, Stallworthy Collection.

53 W.D. Warner to Henry Stallworthy, n.d., Stallworthy Collection.

54 J. Wade, Report: Re: Memorial to Late Mrs. S.G. Clay, 28 June 1926, Stallworthy Collection.

4 | FROM A NEAR-DEATH EXPERIENCE TO JASPER

1   Royal Canadian Mounted Police Archives (hereafter cited as RCMPA), Henry Webb Stallworthy, Record of Service.

2   Henry Webb Stallworthy to Officer Commanding, Headquarters Division, 15 September 1925, Henry Webb Stallworthy, Service File, f. 110.

3   Telegram, R.Y. Douglas to Officer Commanding, Edmonton, 17 September 1925, Henry Webb Stallworthy, Service File, f. 114.

4   Personal communication, Mrs. Barbara Stallworthy, 2002.

5   Henry Webb Stallworthy to William Stallworthy, 30 October 1925, Stallworthy Family Collection, Cirenchester, Great Britain (hereafter Stallworthy Family Collection).

6   David C. Jones, *Empire of dust. Settling and abandoning the prairie dry belt* (Edmonton: The University of Alberta Press, 1987).

7   Ibid.

8   This is almost certainly a reference to the town of Carlstadt (later renamed Alderson) south of Jenner and northwest of Suffield, which was known as the "Star of the Prairies" and had a population of 460 in 1912 (Jones, *Empire of dust*). Like Jenner, it went into a rapid decline after 1917 and at present no longer exists.

9   Henry Webb Stallworthy to William Stallworthy, 30 October 1925, Stallworthy Family Collection.

10 Henry Webb Stallworthy to William Stallworthy, 28 September 1925, Stallworthy Collection.

11 Henry Webb Stallworthy to William Stallworthy, 30 October 1925, Stallworthy Collection.

12 J. Ritchie to Commissioner, RCMP, 10 December 1925, Henry Webb Stallworthy, Service File, f. 121.

13 Henry Webb Stallworthy to William Stallworthy, 15 December 1925, Stallworthy Collection. One example of such a report is: Henry Webb Stallworthy, Report re: Lawrence Morris, Applicant for naturalization, 23 November 1925.

14 Henry Webb Stallworthy, Crime report re: Henry Cardinal (Indian), Cold Lake Reserve, Alta. Indian Act, 15 January 1926, Stallworthy Collection.

15 Henry Webb Stallworthy, Crime report re: Joshua Shirt (Treaty Indian), Saddle Lake, Alta., common assault, 14 January 1926, Stallworthy Collection.

16 Henry Webb Stallworthy, Crime report re: Paul Breast (Treaty Indian), Goodfish Lake, Alta., Indian Act, 13 January 1926, Stallworthy Collection.

17 Henry Webb Stallworthy, Crime report re: Martin Koproske (Russian), Spedden, Alta., Indian Act, 13 January 1926, Stallworthy Collection.

18 Henry Webb Stallworthy, Crime report re: Andrew Owczar, Dalmuir, Alta. Possession of illicit still. Excise Act, 5 January 1926, Stallworthy Collection.

19 Henry Webb Stallworthy to William Stallworthy, 7 March 1926, Stallworthy Collection.

20 Ibid.

21 "Agreement of partnership," 13 March 1926, Stallworthy Collection.

22 Henry Webb Stallworthy to William Stallworthy, 13 March 1926, Stallworthy Collection.

23 J. Ritchie to Commissioner, RCMP, 31 March 1926, Henry Webb Stallworthy, Service File, f. 128; Henry Webb Stallworthy, Medical File, RCMPA, Ottawa (hereafter cited as Medical File), f. 48.

24 J. Ritchie to Commissioner, RCMP, 11 April 1926, Henry Webb Stallworthy, Service File, f. 129; Medical File, f. 47.

25 Telegram, C. Starnes to Mrs. F. Stallworthy, 12 April 1926, Henry Webb Stallworthy, Service File, f. 131.

26 J. Bridgeman to William Stallworthy, 18 April 1926, Stallworthy Collection.

27 J. Ritchie to Commissioner, RCMP, 25 April 1926, Henry Webb Stallworthy, Service File, f. 135.

28 E.A. Braithwaite to J. Ritchie, 30 April 1926, Henry Webb Stallworthy, Service File, f. 136.

29 J. Ritchie to Commissioner C. Starnes, 30 April 1926, Henry Webb Stallworthy, Service File, f. 137; Medical File, ff. 43-4.

30 J. Ritchie to Commissioner C. Starnes, 1 May 1926, Henry Webb Stallworthy, Service File, f. 138; Medical File, f. 42.

31 E. A. Braithwaite to J. Ritchie, 7 May 1926, Henry Webb Stallworthy, Service File, f. 139; Medical File, f. 41.

32 J. Ritchie to Commissioner C. Starnes, 13 May 1926, Henry Webb Stallworthy, Service File, f. 141; Medical File, f. 40.

33 E.A. Braithwaite to J. Ritchie, 20 May 1926, Henry Webb Stallworthy, Service File, f. 142.

34 Henry Webb Stallworthy to Mrs. Florence Stallworthy, 19 May 1926, Stallworthy Collection.

35 J. Ritchie to Commissioner C. Starnes, 26 May 1926, Henry Webb Stallworthy, Service File, f. 144.

36 E. L. Pope to E. A. Braithwaite, 9 June 1926 (misdated 9 January), Henry Webb Stallworthy, Service File, f. 125; Medical File, f. 35.

37 J. Ritchie to Commissioner C. Starnes, 4 June 1926, Henry Webb Stallworthy, Service File, f. 146.

38 J. Bridgeman to William Stallworthy, 28 June 1926, Stallworthy Collection.

39 E. A. Braithwaite to J. Ritchie, 20 October 1926, Henry Webb Stallworthy, Service File, f. 183.

40 E. A. Braithwaite to J. Ritchie, 9 June 1926, Henry Webb Stallworthy, Service File, f. 148; Medical File, f. 34.

41 E. A. Braithwaite to J. Ritchie, 23 June 1926, Henry Webb Stallworthy, Service File, f. 154; Medical File, f. 33.

42 E. A. Braithwaite to J. Ritchie, 13 July 1926, Henry Webb Stallworthy, Service File, f. 156; Medical File, f. 32.

43 Henry Webb Stallworthy to Mrs. Florence Stallworthy, 4 August 1926, Stallworthy Collection.

44 F. Spriggs to William Stallworthy, 28 November 1926, Stallworthy Collection.

45 Ibid.

46 J. Ritchie to Commissioner C. Starnes, 2 November 1926, Henry Webb Stallworthy, Service File, f. 192.

47 J. Ritchie to Commissioner C. Starnes, 6 August 1926, Henry Webb Stallworthy, Service File, f. 163.

48 Telegram, C. Starnes to Harry Webb Stallworthy, 22 September 1926, Henry Webb Stallworthy, Service File, f. 176.

49 Henry Webb Stallworthy to Mrs. Florence Stallworthy, 16 August 1927, Stallworthy Collection.

50 Henry Webb Stallworthy to Davies, 27 October 1931, Stallworthy Collection.

51 C. Starnes to J. Ritchie, 9 November 1926, Henry Webb Stallworthy, Service File, f. 192.

52 Henry Webb Stallworthy to William Stallworthy, 21 February 1927, Stallworthy Collection.

53 Henry Webb Stallworthy to Mrs. Florence Stallworthy, 16 August 1927, Stallworthy Collection.

54 Henry Webb Stallworthy to William Stallworthy, 9 October 1927, Stallworthy Collection.

55 Ibid.

56 Henry Webb Stallworthy to William Stallworthy, 21 February 1927, Stallworthy Collection.

57 Henry Webb Stallworthy to Mrs. Florence Stallworthy, 12 April 1927, Stallworthy Collection.

58 J. Ritchie to Commissioner C. Starnes, 9 December 1926, Henry Webb Stallworthy, Service File f. 196.

59   Henry Webb Stallworthy to Mrs. Florence Stallworthy, July 1927, Stallworthy
     Collection.

60   Henry Webb Stallworthy to William Stallworthy, 26 April 1927, Stallworthy
     Collection; Henry Webb Stallworthy to Mrs. Florence Stallworthy, 12 April
     1927, Stallworthy Collection.

61   Henry Webb Stallworthy to Mrs. Stallworthy, 18 September 1927, Stallworthy
     Collection; Henry Webb Stallworthy to William Stallworthy, 9 October 1927,
     Stallworthy Collection.

62   Ibid.

63   Henry Webb Stallworthy to William Stallworthy, 21 February 1927,
     Stallworthy Collection.

64   Henry Webb Stallworthy to William Stallworthy, 6 November 1927,
     Stallworthy Collection.

65   Henry Webb Stallworthy to William Stallworthy, 19 February 1928,
     Stallworthy Collection.

66   Henry Webb Stallworthy to William Stallworthy, 6 November 1927,
     Stallworthy Collection.

67   Henry Webb Stallworthy to William Stallworthy, 9 October 1927, Stallworthy
     Collection.

68   Henry Webb Stallworthy to Mrs. Florence Stallworthy, 18 September 1927,
     Stallworthy Collection.

69   Elaine Mellor, personal communication, May 2004.

70   Hilda Stallworthy, "One start on Harry's story," unfinished manuscript, p. 1,
     Stallworthy Collection.

71   Henry Webb Stallworthy to Mrs. Florence Stallworthy, 18 September 1927,
     Stallworthy Collection.

72   Henry Webb Stallworthy to William Stallworthy, 9 October 1927, Stallworthy
     Collection.

73   Hilda Stallworthy, "One start," p. 3.

74   Henry Webb Stallworthy to Mrs. Florence Stallworthy, 30 October 1927,
     Stallworthy Collection.

75   Henry Webb Stallworthy to William Stallworthy, n.d., quoted in Hilda
     Stallworthy, "One start," p. 2.

76   Henry Webb Stallworthy to William Stallworthy, 12 April 1928, Stallworthy
     Collection. Harry has got his facts wrong: Elaine was the youngest, Hilda was
     the middle sister, and Ethelind was the eldest.

77   Hilda Stallworthy, "One start," p. 2.

78   Ibid., p. 3.

79   Henry Webb Stallworthy to J. Ritchie, 14 January 1927, Henry Webb
     Stallworthy, Service File, f. 200.

80   Ibid.

81 Henry Webb Stallworthy to William Stallworthy, 26 April 1927, Stallworthy
Collection.

82 Hilda Stallworthy, "One start," p. 2.

83 Henry Webb Stallworthy to Davies, 27 October 1931, Stallworthy Collection.

84 C. Starnes to J. Ritchie, 17 February 1928, Henry Webb Stallworthy, Service
File, f. 222.

85 Henry Webb Stallworthy to William Stallworthy, 19 February 1928,
Stallworthy Collection.

5 | STONY RAPIDS, 1928–1930

1 Henry Webb Stallworthy, Requisition for stores for detachment to be
stationed at "Fond du Lac" Saskatchewan, 1928, Stallworthy Collection.

2 Henry Webb Stallworthy to William Stallworthy, 28 May 1928, Stallworthy
Collection.

3 Henry Webb Stallworthy to William Stallworthy, 12 April 1928, Stallworthy
Collection.

4 Ibid.

5 Henry Webb Stallworthy to William Stallworthy, 10 June 1928, Stallworthy
Collection.

6 Henry Webb Stallworthy, Report re: Establishment of Stony Rapids
Detachment, Saskatchewan, 29 September 1928, p. 1, Stallworthy Collection.

7 Henry Webb Stallworthy to William Stallworthy, 10 June 1928, Stallworthy
Collection.

8 Henry Webb Stallworthy, Report re: Establishment, p. 1.

9 Ibid., p. 1.

10 Ibid.

11 Ibid., p. 2.

12 Ibid.

13 Henry Webb Stallworthy to William Stallworthy, 15 August 1928, Stallworthy
Collection.

14 Ibid.

15 Henry Webb Stallworthy to William Stallworthy, 28 September 1928,
Stallworthy Collection.

16 Ibid.

17 Henry Webb Stallworthy, Report re: radio reception, Stony Rapids
Detachment, 31 December 1928, Stallworthy Collection.

18 Henry Webb Stallworthy to William Stallworthy, 9 January 1929, Stallworthy
Collection.

19 Ibid.

20 Henry Webb Stallworthy, Report re: Establishment, p. 2.

21 Henry Webb Stallworthy to William Stallworthy, 9 January 1929, Stallworthy
Collection.

22 K.M. Molson, *Pioneering in Canadian air transport* (Winnipeg: J. Richardson, 1974).

23 Ibid.

24 Henry Webb Stallworthy, Report re: Establishment, p. 2.

25 Henry Webb Stallworthy, Report re: Patrol by airplane from Stony Rapids to Wholdaia Lake, N.W.T. and return, 29 September 1928, Stallworthy Collection.

26 Ibid.

27 Henry Webb Stallworthy to William Stallworthy, 6 September 1928, Stallworthy Collection.

28 Henry Webb Stallworthy to J. Ritchie, 1 February 1929, Henry Webb Stallworthy, Service File, f. 231.

29 J. Ritchie to Commissioner C. Starnes, 8 April 1929, Henry Webb Stallworthy, Service File, f. 232.

30 Ibid., p. 1.

31 Henry Webb Stallworthy, Patrol report, Stony Rapids Detachment, Saskatchewan, to Nueltin Lake district, NWT and return, 10 May 1929, Stallworthy Collection.

32 Henry Webb Stallworthy, Copy of patrol diary, Stony Rapids to Nueltin Lake and return, 4 May 1929, p. 1, Stallworthy Collection.

33 Ibid., p. 2.

34 Ibid., p. 3.

35 Henry Webb Stallworthy, Patrol report, Stony Rapids, p. 3, Stallworthy Collection.

36 Henry Webb Stallworthy, Copy of patrol diary, p. 4, Stallworthy Collection.

37 J. Ritchie to Commissioner C. Starnes, 3 September 1929, Henry Webb Stallworthy, Service File, f. 239.

38 A.J. Cawdron to J. Ritchie, 10 September 1929, Henry Webb Stallworthy, Service File, f. 240.

39 Henry Webb Stallworthy to J. Ritchie, 31 December 1929, Henry Webb Stallworthy, Service File, f. 241.

40 M.H. Vernon to J. Ritchie, 3 March 1930, Henry Webb Stallworthy, Service File, f. 242.

41 Henry Webb Stallworthy to William Stallworthy, 13 July 1930, Stallworthy Collection.

6 | BACHE PENINSULA

1 Henry Webb Stallworthy to William Stallworthy, 13 July 1930, Stallworthy Collection.

2 Henry Webb Stallworthy to William Stallworthy and Mrs. Florence Stallworthy, 30 July 1930, Stallworthy Collection.

3   Hilda Stallworthy to Ethelind and Elaine Mellor, 23 January 1978, Stallworthy Collection.

4   M. Zaslow, *A century of Canada's arctic islands* (Ottawa: Royal Society of Canada, 1981).

5   O. Sverdrup, *New land: four years in the arctic regions* (London and New York: Longmans, Green, 1903).

6   D.B. Macmillan, *Four years in the white North* (New York and London: Harper and Bros., 1918).

7   W. Barr, *Back from the brink. The road to muskox conservation in the Northwest Territories*, Komatik Series 3 (Calgary: Arctic Institute of North America, 1991).

8   J.B. Harkin to W.W. Cory, 16 June 1920, NAC, RG 85, Vol. 1203, f. 401-3.

9   Dr. Trevor Lloyd, personal communication, 1988.

10   Knud Rasmussen to the Administration of the Colonies in Greenland, NAC, RG 85, Vol. 1203, f. 401-3.

11   J.B. Harkin to W.W. Cory, 16 June 1920, NAC, RG 85, vol. 1203, f. 401-3.

12   Ibid.

13   H.P. Lee, *Policing the top of the world* (London: John Lane The Bodley Head Ltd., 1928); W.R. Morrison, *Showing the flag. The Mounted Police and Canadian sovereignty in the North* (Vancouver: University of British Columbia Press, 1985); L. Dick, *Muskox Land. Ellesmere Island in the age of contact* (Calgary: University of Calgary Press, 2001).

14   Henry Webb Stallworthy to Mrs. Florence Stallworthy, 16 July 1930, Stallworthy Collection.

15   Henry Webb Stallworthy, Annual report, Bache Peninsula Detachment, 2 August 1931, Stallworthy Collection; also held at NAC, RG 18 Vol. 3012.

16   Henry Webb Stallworthy to William Stallworthy, 5 August 1930, Stallworthy Collection.

17   Ibid.

18   Ibid.

19   Ibid.

20   Ibid.

21   Ibid.

22   Henry Webb Stallworthy to William Stallworthy, 30 July 1930, Stallworthy Collection.

23   Henry Webb Stallworthy to William Stallworthy, 10 August 1930, Stallworthy Collection.

24   Henry Webb Stallworthy to William Stallworthy, 11 January 1931, Stallworthy Collection; Henry Webb Stallworthy, Annual report, p. 1.

25   Henry Webb Stallworthy to William Stallworthy, 11 January 1931, Stallworthy Collection.

26   C.R. Harrington, "Nookapingwa (1893-1956)," *Arctic* 42, no. 2 (1989): 163-65.

27   Ibid.; Henry Webb Stallworthy, Annual report, p. 1.

28 Ibid.

29 Henry Webb Stallworthy to William Stallworthy, 11 January 1931, Stallworthy Collection.

30 Henry Webb Stallworthy, Annual report, p. 4.

31 Henry Webb Stallworthy to William Stallworthy, 25 January 1931, Stallworthy Collection.

32 Henry Webb Stallworthy, Annual report, p. 2.

33 Henry Webb Stallworthy to William Stallworthy, 11 January 1931, Stallworthy Collection.

34 W. Barr, "Otto Sverdrup (1854–1930)," *Arctic* 37, no. 1 (1984): 72–73.

35 Henry Webb Stallworthy, Annual report, p. 4.

36 Ibid., p. 5.

37 Henry Webb Stallworthy to William Stallworthy, 25 January 1931, Stallworthy Collection.

38 W. Barr, "The career and disappearance of Hans K. E. Krüger, Arctic geologist, 1886–1930," *Polar Record* 29, no. 171 (1993): 277–304.

39 Ibid., 278.

40 F. de Laguna, *Voyage to Greenland. A personal initiation into anthropology* (New York: W. Norton and Co., 1977), 45.

41 Barr, "The career and disappearance," 290.

42 Ibid., 290.

43 Ibid.; Henry Webb Stallworthy, Patrol report: Bache Peninsula Detachment to Head of Flagger River, Craig Harbour and Mackinson Inlet, Ellesmere Island, 31 May 1931, p. 1, Stallworthy Collection.

44 Ibid.

45 Ibid.

46 Henry Webb Stallworthy to William Stallworthy, 28 July 1931, Stallworthy Collection.

47 Henry Webb Stallworthy, Patrol report: Bache Peninsula, p. 2.

48 Henry Webb Stallworthy to William Stallworthy, 28 July 1931, Stallworthy Collection.

49 Henry Webb Stallworthy, Patrol report: Bache Peninsula, p. 4; H. Stallworthy, "The loneliest journey," *Blue Book Magazine* 92, no. 2 (1950): 13–15.

50 Henry Webb Stallworthy, Patrol report: Bache Peninsula, p. 4; marginal note in Stallworthy's hand writing: "This is not correct. I had more than 1 drink."

51 Henry Webb Stallworthy, "The loneliest journey."

52 Henry Webb Stallworthy to William Stallworthy, 28 July 1931, Stallworthy Collection.

53 Henry Webb Stallworthy to William Stallworthy, 1 August 1931, Stallworthy Collection.

54 Ibid.

55 Henry Webb Stallworthy to Davies, 27 October 1931, Stallworthy Collection.

56   Henry Webb Stallworthy to O.C., Headquarters Division, 1 August 1931,
      Henry Webb Stallworthy, Service File, f. 264.
57   H. E. Hume, "Report of the Chairman, Dominion Lands Branch," in *Annual
      Report of the Department of the Interior for the fiscal year ended March 31, 1932*
      (Ottawa: F. Acland, 1932), 25–50; R.W. Hamilton, unpublished manuscript;
      D.S. Robertson, *To the Arctic with the Mounties* (Toronto: Macmillan Co. of
      Canada, 1934), 10.
58   Roberston, *To the Arctic*, 69.
59   Henry Webb Stallworthy, Annual report, Bache Peninsula Detachment,
      1931–32, p. 1, Stallworthy Collection; Hamilton, unpublished manuscript.
60   Robertson, *To the Arctic*, 85–87.
61   Telegram, T. Burwash to O.S. Finnie, August 1931, NAC, RG 85, Vol. 756, f.
      4275, Pt. 1; Telegram, A. H. Joy to J. H. MacBrien, 13 August 1931, NAC, RG
      85, Vol. 756, f. 4275, Pt. 1.
62   A. H. Joy to Commissioner, RCMP, 25 September 1931, NAC, RG 18, Acc. No.
      85-86/048, Vol. 33, File G804-9, Pt. 1:73.
63   Hamilton, unpublished manuscript.
64   Henry Webb Stallworthy, Annual report 1931–32, p. 3.
65   Ibid.
66   Henry Webb Stallworthy, Report re: German Arctic Expedition—missing.
      Search patrol from Bache Peninsula Detachment to Axel Heiberg Island, 25
      June 1932, p. 2, Stallworthy Collection.
67   W. Barr, *Back from the brink*.
68   Henry Webb Stallworthy, *Annual report, 1931–32*, p. 2.
69   Ibid., p. 3.
70   Ibid., p. 2.
71   Henry Webb Stallworthy, Report, Re: German Arctic Expedition, p. 2.

7 | SEARCHING FOR KRÜGER, 1932

1   R.W. Hamilton, R.W., unpublished autobiography.
2   Henry Webb Stallworthy, Re: German Arctic Expedition—missing. Search
     patrol from Bache Peninsula Detachment to Axel Heiberg Island, 25 June
     1932, p. 3, Stallworthy Collection; also available at NAC, RG 85, Vol. 756, f.
     4275, Pt. 1.
3   E. Anstead, personal communication 1988, In R. Osczevski, "The hunt for
     marine reptile fossils on western Ellesmere Island," *Polar Record* 28, no. 165
     (1992): 109.
4   Henry Webb Stallworthy, Re: German Arctic Expedition, p. 4.
5   Ibid., p. 5.
6   Ibid., p. 7.

7   R.E. Peary, *Nearest the Pole: a narrative of the polar expedition of the Peary Arctic Club in the SS Roosevelt, 1905–1906* (London: Hutchinson & Co., 1907).

8   W. Barr, "The career and disappearance of Hans K.E. Krüger, arctic geologist," *Polar Record* 29, no. 171 (1993): 295.

9   Henry Webb Stallworthy, Re: German Arctic Expedition, p. 9.

10   Henry Webb Stallworthy to Dr. Ray Thorsteinsson, 12 December 1957, Stallworthy Collection.

11   Elaine Mellor, interviewed by Ole Gjerstad, 2003.

12   Henry Webb Stallworthy, Re: German Arctic Expedition, p. 11.

13   C. Vibe, *Langthen og nordpaa. Skildringer fra "Den Danske Thule- og Ellesmereland-ekspedition 1939–40"* (København: Gylendal, 1948).

14   Henry Webb Stallworthy, Re: German Arctic Expedition, p. 12.

15   Ibid., p. 14.

16   Ibid., p. 14.

17   Ibid., p. 14.

18   Ibid., p. 14.

19   R.W. Hamilton, Report re: Patrol to Cornwall Island and return via Makinson Inlet, 12 July 1932, Stallworthy Collection; also available at NAC, RG 85, Vol. 756, f. 4275, Pt. 1.

20   Ibid.

21   R.W. Hamilton, unpublished autobiography.

22   Ibid.

23   R.W. Hamilton, Report: Cornwall Island, p. 2.

24   R.W. Hamilton, unpublished autobiography.

25   R.W. Hamilton, Report: Cornwall Island, p. 3.

26   Ibid., p. 3.

27   R.W. Hamilton, unpublished autobiography.

28   Sally Hamilton, personal communication, 2002, as recounted by her late father.

29   R.W. Hamilton, unpublished autobiography.

30   Ibid.

31   Ibid.

32   Henry Webb Stallworthy, Re: German Arctic Expedition, p. 16.

33   Ibid.

34   Ibid.

35   R.W. Hamilton, Report: Cornwall Island, p. 5.

36   P. Dersch, Report on sledge trip in search of missing expedition, 6 April 1932, NAC, RG 18, Acc. No. 85–86/048, Vol. 33, File G 804–9, Pt. 1.

37   G. Hattersley-Smith, personal communication, March 1990.

38   G. Hattersley-Smith, and other members of the expedition, "Northern Ellesmere Island, 1953 and 1954," *Arctic* 8, no. 1 (1955): 16.

39   R. Thorsteinsson, "The history and geology of Meighen Island, Arctic Archipelago," *Geological Survey of Canada Bulletin* 75 (1961): 1–19.

40 V. Stefansson, *The friendly Arctic: the story of five years in polar regions* (New York: Macmillan, 1921).

41 Thorsteinsson, "The history and geology," p. 5.

42 Ibid.

43 Ray Thorsteinsson to Henry Webb Stallworthy, 5 November 1957, British Columbia Archives (hereafter BCA), ED St1c.

44 Henry Webb Stallworthy to Ray Thorsteinsson, 12 December 1957, Stallworthy Collection.

45 J. Kobalenko, *The horizontal Everest. Extreme journeys on Ellesmere Island* (Toronto: Penguin/Viking, 2002).

46 R.C. Brooks, J.H. England, A.S. Dyke and J. Savelle, "Krüger's final camp in Arctic Canada?" *Arctic* 57, no. 2 (2004): 225–29.

8 | MOVING TO CRAIG HARBOUR

1 Henry Webb Stallworthy, Annual Report, Bache Peninsula Detachment 1931–1932, Bache Peninsula, p. 5, Stallworthy Collection; R.W. Hamilton, unpublished autobiography.

2 Hilda Stallworthy to Ethelind and Elaine Mellor, 23 January 1978, Stallworthy Collection.

3 Hamilton, unpublished autobiography.

4 Henry Webb Stallworthy, Annual Report, 1932–33, Bache Peninsula, p. 1.

5 Hamilton, unpublished autobiography.

6 Henry Webb Stallworthy, Annual report, 1932–33, p. 1.

7 J.H. MacBrien to William Stallworthy, 7 November 1932, Stallworthy Family Collection.

8 William Stallworthy to Commissioner J.H. MacBrien, 3 December 1932, Henry Webb Stallworthy, Service File, f. 293.

9 Radio message, William Stallworthy to Henry Webb Stallworthy, Henry Webb Stallworthy, Service File, f. 295.

10 William Stallworthy to Commissioner J.H. MacBrien, 13 December 1932, Henry Webb Stallworthy, Service File, f. 301; J.H. MacBrien to William Stallworthy, 29 December 1932, Henry Webb Stallworthy, Service File f. 299.

11 J.H. MacBrien to the Manager, CKY Winnipeg and to G.A.Wendt, 17 December 1932, Henry Webb Stallworthy, Service File, ff. 297 and 298.

12 H.E. Hume, "Report of the Chairman, Dominion Lands Branch," in *Annual report of the Department of the Interior for the fiscal year ended March 31, 1933* (Ottawa: O. Patenaude, 1933), 27.

13 Henry Webb Stallworthy, Annual report: Bache Peninsula, 1932–33, p. 2; Hamilton, unpublished autobiography.

14 Elaine Mellor, personal communication, May 2004.

15 Hamilton, unpublished autobiography.

16   Henry Webb Stallworthy, Annual report, Bache Peninsula, 1932–33, p. 2.

17   Henry Webb Stallworthy, Telegram to Commissioner, RCMP, Ottawa, 4 May 1933, NAC, RG 18, Acc. No. 85–86/048, Vol. 33, File G 804–9, Pt. 1, p. 2; also available in Henry Webb Stallworthy, Service File, f. 304.

18   J.W. Spalding to William Stallworthy, 8 May 1933, Henry Webb Stallworthy, Service File, f. 307.

19   William Stallworthy to Commissioner J.H. MacBrien, 7 June 1933, Henry Webb Stallworthy, Service File, f. 312.

20   Henry Webb Stallworthy, Annual report, Bache Peninsula, 1932–33, p. 4.

21   Ibid., p. 4; Hamilton, unpublished autobiography.

22   Hamilton, unpublished autobiography.

23   Ibid.

24   Ibid.

25   Henry Webb Stallworthy, Patrol report: Craig Harbour to Dundas Harbour and return, 1933, NAC, RG 18, Vol. 3663, G 567–25: 83–84.

26   Ibid., p. 84.

27   Hamilton, unpublished autobiography.

28   A.H. Joy, Patrol report: Craig Harbour to Dundas Harbour and return, 1926, NAC, RG 18, Vol. 3663, G 567–25, pp. 20–25.

29   P. Dersch, Patrol report: Patrol from Dundas Harbour to Jones Sound, 1932, NAC, RG 18, Vol. 3663, G 569–29, pp. 34–35.

30   H. Kearney, Patrol report: Attempted patrol—Craig Harbour to Dundas Harbour 1935, NAC, RG 18, Vol. 3663, G 567–25, pp. 93–97.

31   H.M. MacLeod, Patrol report: Patrol from Dundas Harbour, N.W.T. to Craig Harbour, N.W.T. and return, 1946, NAC, RG 18, Vol. 3663, G 569–29, pp. 43–47.

32   Henry Webb Stallworthy, Patrol report: Craig Harbour, p. 84.

33   Henry Webb Stallworthy, Patrol report: Patrol to Coburg Island—hunting, 15 June 1933, Stallworthy Collection.

34   William Stallworthy to Commissioner MacBrien, 7 June 1933, Henry Webb Stallworthy, Service File, f. 313.

35   J.W. Spalding to G.A. Wendt, Canadian Westinghouse, 19 June 1933, Henry Webb Stallworthy, Service File, f. 316.

36   Henry Webb Stallworthy, Annual Report, 1932–33, Bache Peninsula, p. 5.

37   Hamilton, unpublished autobiography.

38   Henry Webb Stallworthy to William Stallworthy, 29 September 1933, Stallworthy Collection.

39   Hamilton, unpublished autobiography.

40   Elaine Mellor, interviewed by Ole Gjerstad, 2003.

41   Henry Webb Stallworthy to William Stallworthy, 29 September 1933, Stallworthy Collection; Henry Webb Stallworthy to Hilda Austin, September 1933, Stallworthy Collection.

42 Henry Webb Stallworthy to Hilda Austin, August 1933, Stallworthy Collection.

43 V.A.M. Kemp to O.C. "O" Division, 2 June 1933, Service File, f. 310.

44 Henry Webb Stallworthy to Hilda Austin, September 1933, Sunday, Stallworthy Collection.

45 Hamilton, unpublished autobiography.

46 Ibid.

9 | MARRIAGE AND HONEYMOON

1 Henry Webb Stallworthy to Hilda Austin, August 1933, Stallworthy Collection.

2 Henry Webb Stallworthy to Hilda Austin, September 1933, Sunday, Stallworthy Collection.

3 V.A.M. Kemp to O.C., "C" Division, 18 July 1933, Henry Webb Stallworthy, Service File, f. 321.

4 Ibid.

5 Ibid.

6 D.A. Whitton, M.D. to J.M. Tupper, 25 October 1933, Henry Webb Stallworthy Service File, f. 336.

7 Henry Webb Stallworthy, Medical File, Case History Sheet, ff. 27-29, Royal Canadian Mounted Police Archives, Ottawa.

8 Henry Webb Stallworthy to William Stallworthy, 9 November 1933, Stallworthy Collection.

9 Henry Webb Stallworthy to J.M. Tupper, 30 October, 1933, Henry Webb Stallworthy, Service File, f. 339.

10 V.A.M. Kemp to J.M. Tupper, 2 November 1933, Henry Webb Stallworthy, Service File, f. 340.

11 Nancy Pierce, Geographical names/Toponymes, Natural Resources Canada, personal communication, May 2004.

12 Hilda Austin, Diary, 29 October 1933, Stallworthy Collection.

13 Ibid., 16 November 1933.

14 Ibid., 20 November 1933.

15 Ibid., 22 November 1933.

16 J. MacBrien to the Honourable the Minister in Control of the Royal Canadian Mounted Police, 5 November 1933, Henry Webb Stallworthy, Service File, ff. 341-2; J. MacBrien to the Under Secretary of State, 8 November 1933, Henry Webb Stallworthy, Service File, f. 346.

17 L. Kempff to O.D. Skelton, 26 January 1934, NAC, RG 85, Acc. No. 85-86/048, Vol. 33, File G 804-9: 202.

18 Hilda Stallworthy, Diary, 5 December 1933, Stallworthy Collection.

19 Ibid., 6 December 1933.

20   E. Shackleton, *Arctic journeys. The story of the Oxford University Ellesmere Land Expedition 1934–5* (London: Hodder and Stoughton, 1937), 20–21.

21   H.H. Rowatt to Edward Shackleton, 19 September 1933, Stallworthy Collection.

22   Oldendaw, Grønlands Styrelse to Edward Shackleton, 5 July 1933, Stallworthy Collection.

23   Edward Shackleton, Confidential report: Proposed expedition to Ellesmere Land, 23 October 1933, Stallworthy Collection.

24   J.H. MacBrien, to OC "N" Division, 13 November 1933, Stallworthy Collection.

25   Henry Webb Stallworthy to OC "N" Division, 17 November 1933, Stallworthy Collection.

26   Ibid.

27   Hilda Stallworthy, Diary, 8 December 1933, Stallworthy Collection.

28   Ibid., 15 December, 1933.

29   Ibid., 25 December 1933.

30   Ibid., 26 December 1933.

31   Elaine Mellor, personal communication, 2001.

32   *Wilts and Gloucestershire Standard*, 7 January 1934.

33   Hilda Stallworthy to Mr. & Mrs. William Stallworthy, 8 February 1934, Stallworthy Collection.

34   Hilda Stallworthy, Diary, 20 February, 1934, Stallworthy Collection.

35   Henry Webb Stallworthy, Report re: Expedition of Mr. E.E.A. Shackleton to Ellesmere Island, N.W.T., 20 February 1934, Henry Webb Stallworthy, Service File, f. 360.

36   Ibid., f. 361.

37   Henry Webb Stallworthy to William Stallworthy, 5 March 1934, Stallworthy Collection.

38   Hilda Stallworthy, Diary, 21 February 1934, Stallworthy Collection.

39   Hilda Stallworthy, Diary, 7 March 1934, Stallworthy Collection.

40   Henry Webb Stallworthy to William Stallworthy, 5 March 1934, Stallworthy Collection.

41   Hilda Stallworthy, Diary, 13 March 1934, Stallworthy Collection.

42   Ibid., 14 March 1934.

43   Ibid.

44   Henry Webb Stallworthy to William Stallworthy, 18 March 1934, Stallworthy Collection.

45   Edward Shackleton to Henry Webb Stallworthy, 28 February 1934, Stallworthy Collection.

46   J. MacBrien to Superintendent T.H. Irvine, 17 May 1934, Stallworthy Collection; also available at; Henry Webb Stallworthy, Service File, f. 380.

47   J. L. Turner, to Superintendent T. H. Irvine, 18 May 1934, Stallworthy Collection; also available at: Henry Webb Stallworthy, Service File, f. 381.

48   Telegram, Secretary of State for External Affairs to Canadian High Commissioner, London, 22 May 1934, Stallworthy Collection; also available at: Henry Webb Stallworthy, Service File, f. 385.

49   Edward Shackleton to General J. MacBrien, 28 May 1934, Stallworthy Collection.

50   H. Stallworthy, "Winter patrols in the Arctic," *Royal Canadian Mounted Police Quarterly* 2, no. 2 (1935): 17–25.

51   Hilda Stallworthy, Diary, 6 May 1934, Stallworthy Collection.

52   Henry Webb Stallworthy to William Stallworthy, 15 May 1934, Stallworthy Collection.

53   Hilda Stallworthy, Diary, 31 May 1934, Stallworthy Collection.

54   Ibid., 7 June 1934.

55   Henry Webb Stallworthy to Supt. T. H. Irvine, 28 May (3 letters), Stallworthy Collection.

56   Henry Webb Stallworthy to Supt. T. H. Irvine, 23 May 1934, Stallworthy Collection; Henry Webb Stallworthy to William Stallworthy, 15 May 1934, Stallworthy Collection.

57   Elaine Mellor, personal communication, May 2004.

58   Hilda Stallworthy, Diary, 13 June 1934, Stallworthy Collection.

59   Ibid.

60   T. H. Irvine to Henry Webb Stallworthy, 14 June 1934, Stallworthy Collection; also available at: Henry Webb Stallworthy, Service File, f. 392.

61   Telegram, J. MacBrien to Henry Webb Stallworthy, 15 June 1934, Stallworthy Collection; also available at: Henry Webb Stallworthy, Service File, f. 391.

10 | THE OXFORD UNIVERSITY ELLESMERE LAND EXPEDITION 1934–35

1   Hilda Stallworthy, Diary, 23 June 1934, Stallworthy Collection.

2   Ibid., 30 June 1934.

3   Shackleton, *Arctic journeys*, 37.

4   Hilda Stallworthy, Diary, 7 July 1934, Stallworthy Collection.

5   Ibid.

6   Ibid., 4 July 1934.

7   Ibid., 5 July 1934.

8   Telegram, MacBrien to Henry Webb Stallworthy, 8 July 1934, Stallworthy Collection.

9   Hilda Stallworthy, Diary, 15 July 1934, Stallworthy Collection.

10   Henry Webb Stallworthy, Report re: Oxford University Ellesmere Land Expedition, 15 November 1935, NAC, RG 18, Accn. 85–86/048, Vol. 43, File G–804–44, p. 2.

11   Hilda Stallworthy, Diary, 16 July 1934, Stallworthy Collection.

12 Henry Webb Stallworthy to William Stallworthy, 15 July 1934, Stallworthy Collection.

13 Stallworthy, Report re: Oxford, p. 3.

14 *Daily Express* and *Daily Telegraph*, 18 July 1934.

15 Hilda Stallworthy, Diary, 17 July 1934, Stallworthy Collection.

16 Stallworthy, Report re: Oxford, p. 4.

17 Ibid., p. 5.

18 Ibid.; H.W. Stallworthy, "An Arctic expedition," *Royal Canadian Mounted Police Quarterly*, 3, no. 3 (1936): 150.

19 Stallworthy, Report re: Oxford, p. 7.

20 Ibid., p. 8; Stallworthy, "An Arctic expedition," 152.

21 Shackleton, *Arctic journeys*, 62.

22 Ibid., p. 63.

23 Stallworthy, Report re: Oxford, p. 9.

24 Stallworthy, "An arctic expedition," 152.

25 Stallworthy, Report re: Oxford, p. 10.

26 Shackleton, *Arctic journeys*, 66.

27 Henry Webb Stallworthy to William Stallworthy, 15 August 1934, Stallworthy Collection.

28 Hilda Stallworthy, Diary, 19 September 1934, Stallworthy Collection.

29 Rudolf Sand to Hans Nielsen, 27 August 1934, Shackleton Papers, Scott Polar Research Institute, Cambridge, England (hereafter SPRI).

30 Hans Nielsen to Edward Shackleton, 26 November 1934, Shackleton Papers, Scott Polar Research Institute, Cambridge, England (hereafter cited as SPRI).

31 D.B. Macmillan, *Four years in the white North* (Boston: The Medici Society of America, 1925).

32 Stallworthy, Report re: Oxford, p. 12.

33 Ibid.; Stallworthy, "An arctic expedition," 153; Shackleton, *Arctic journeys*, 74.

34 Stallworthy, Report re: Oxford, p. 13.

35 Shackleton, *Arctic journeys*, 82.

36 Ibid., pp. 86–87; Stallworthy, Report re: Oxford, pp. 14–15; Stallworthy, "An arctic expedition," 153–54.

37 Stallworthy, Report re: Oxford, p. 16.

38 Ibid.

39 Shackleton, *Arctic journeys*, 106.

40 Stallworthy, Report re: Oxford, p. 17.

41 Shackleton, *Arctic journeys*, 107.

42 Stallworthy, Report re: Oxford, p. 18.

43 Hilda Stallworthy, Diary, 3 October 1934, Stallworthy Collection.

44 Stallworthy, Report re: Oxford, p. 18.

45 Hilda Stallworthy, Diary, 30 October 1934, Stallworthy Collection.

46 Stallworthy, Report re: Oxford, p. 18.

47   Shackleton, *Arctic journeys*, 114.

48   Ibid., 127; Stallworthy, Report re: Oxford, p. 22.

49   Hilda Stallworthy, Diary, 8 November 1934, Stallworthy Collection.

50   Ibid., 20 November.

51   Hilda Stallworthy to Station KDKA, Pittsburgh, 20 November 1934, Stallworthy Collection.

52   Shackleton, *Arctic journeys*, 118.

53   Ibid., 125.

54   Stallworthy, Report re: Oxford, p. 23; Stallworthy, "An arctic expedition," 157.

55   Shackleton, *Arctic journeys*, 43.

56   J. MacBrien to the Under Secretary of State, 7 January 1935, Henry Webb Stallworthy, Service File, f. 397.

57   J. MacBrien to the Under Secretary of State, 8 May 1935, Henry Webb Stallworthy, Service File, f. 398.

58   Stallworthy, Report re: Oxford, p. 22.

59   Ibid., p. 26.

60   *The regulations for the protection of game and wild fowl contained in the laws of the Cape York Station, Thule, of 7 June 1929, given by Knud Rasmussen, Ph.D. and sanctioned by the Ministry of Shipping and Fisheries* (Copenhagen: Gylendals Forlagstrykkeri, 1931).

61   Stallworthy, Report re: Oxford, p. 24.

62   Ibid.; Shackleton, *Arctic journeys*, 159.

63   Stallworthy, Report re: Oxford, p. 26.

64   Ibid.

65   Ibid.

66   Shackleton, *Arctic journeys*, 164.

67   Stallworthy, Report re: Oxford, p. 28.

68   Ibid.

69   Ibid., p. 31.

70   Shackleton, *Arctic journeys*, p. 167.

71   Ibid., 168; R. Bentham, n.d. "Comments on manuscript of 'Arctic journeys,'" Shackleton Collection, SPRI.

72   Ibid., p. 169; Stallworthy, Report re: Oxford, p. 32.

73   Ibid., p. 32.

74   Shackleton, *Arctic journeys*, 171.

11 | NORTH TO LAKE HAZEN, SPRING 1935

1   Shackleton, *Arctic journeys*, 171; Stallworthy, Report re: Oxford, p. 33.

2   Stallworthy, Report re: Oxford, p. 34

3   Shackleton, *Arctic journeys*, 237; Henry Webb Stallworthy, Diary, 3 April 1935, Stallworthy Collection.

4   Stallworthy, Report re: Oxford, p. 35.

5   Henry Webb Stallworthy, Diary, 3 April 1935, Stallworthy Collection.

6   Ibid., 7 April 1935.

7   Ibid.; Stallworthy, Report re: Oxford, p. 38.

8   Henry Webb Stallworthy, Diary, 11 April 1935, Stallworthy Collection.

9   Stallworthy, Report re: Oxford, p. 39; Shackleton, *Arctic journeys*, 242.

10   L. Koch, "The geology of the south coast of Washington Land," *Meddelelser om Grønland* 73, no. 1 (1929), 39 pp.

11   Stallworthy, Report re: Oxford, p. 40; Henry Webb Stallworthy, Diary, 14 April, 1935, Stallworthy Collection.

12   Shackleton, *Arctic journeys*, 245.

13   A.W. Greely, *Three years of Arctic service. An account of the Lady Franklin Bay expedition of 1881–84 and the attainment of the farthest north* (New York: Charles Scribner's Sons, 1886).

14   R.E. Peary, "Four years' Arctic exploration, 1898–1902," *Geographical Journal* 22 (1903): 646–72; Dick, *Muskox Land*, 358–60; L. Dick, "The Fort Conger shelters and vernacular adaptation to the High Arctic," *Society for the Study of Architecture in Canada Bulletin* 16, no. 1 (1991): 13–23.

15   Dick, *Muskox Land*, 359–60. Peary lived in a reinforced tent, of which little evidence remains.

16   G.S. Nares, *Narrative of a voyage to the polar sea during 1875–6 in H.M. ships "Alert" and "Discovery"* (London: Sampson Low, 1878).

17   G. Hansen, "Den tredje Thuleekspedition; Norges depotekspedition til Roald Amundsen," in R.E.G. Amundsen, *Nordostpassagen. Maudfaerden langs Asiens kyst 1918–1920* (Kristiania: Gylendal, 1921), 437–62.

18   Shackleton, *Arctic journeys*, 267.

19   Henry Webb Stallworthy, Diary, 23 April 1935, Stallworthy Collection.

20   Stallworthy, Report re: Oxford, p. 44.

21   Henry Webb Stallworthy, Diary, 27 April 1935, Stallworthy Collection.

22   Ibid., 30 April 1935; Stallworthy, Report re: Oxford, p. 46.

23   Shackleton, *Arctic journeys*, p. 249.

24   Stallworthy, Report re: Oxford, p. 46.

25   Ibid., p. 48.

26   Shackleton, *Arctic journeys*, 251.

27   Stallworthy, Report re: Oxford, p. 49.

28   Shackleton, *Arctic journey*, 253.

29   Henry Webb Stallworthy, Diary, 8 May 1935, Stallworthy Collection.

30   Stallworthy, Report re: Oxford, p. 51.

31   Henry Webb Stallworthy, Diary, 17 May 1935, Stallworthy Collection.

32   Stallworthy, Report re: Oxford, p. 53.

33   Shackleton, *Arctic journeys*, 262.

34   Ibid., 263.

35   Stallworthy, Report re: Oxford, p. 54.

36 E.K. Kane, *Arctic explorations; the second Grinnell expedition in search of Sir John Franklin, 1853, '54, '55* (Philadelphia: Childs & Peterson, 1856).

37 Shackleton, *Arctic journeys*, 265.

38 Ibid., 178.

39 N. Humphreys, E. Shackleton and A.W. Moore, "Oxford University Ellesmere Land Expedition," *Geographical Journal* 87, no. 5 (1936): 405, fn. 1.

40 Shackleton, *Arctic journeys*, 195.

41 Ibid., 203.

42 Ibid., 236.

43 Ibid., 270–73; Stallworthy, Report re: Oxford, pp. 56–58.

44 Shackleton, *Arctic journeys*, 272.

45 Stallworthy, Report re: Oxford, p. 58.

46 Shackleton, *Arctic journeys*, 275.

47 Ibid., 291.

48 Ibid., 308.

49 Stallworthy, Report re: Oxford, p. 60.

50 Henry Webb Stallworthy to Hilda Stallworthy, 7 October 1935, Stallworthy Collection.

51 Ibid.

52 Telegram, Henry Webb Stallworthy to Commissioner J. MacBrien, 14 October 1935, Henry Webb Stallworthy, Service File, f. 400; Telegram J.H. MacBrien to Harry Webb Stallworthy, 15 October 1935, Henry Webb Stallworthy, Service File, f. 403.

53 Henry Webb Stallworthy to Edward Shackleton, 22 October 1935, Stallworthy Collection.

54 Cecily Shackleton to Edward Shackleton, 3 June 1935, Shackleton Papers, SPRI; Cecily Shackleton to Edward Shackleton, 27 June 1935, Shackleton Papers, SPRI.

55 Signed affidavit by members of Oxford University Ellesmere Land Expedition, 31 October 1935, Shackleton Papers, SPRI.

56 Edward Shackleton to J.H. MacBrien, Henry Webb Stallworthy, Service File, f. 406.

57 Governor-General George Vanier to J.H. MacBrien, 24 November 1935, Stallworthy Collection.

58 Henry Webb Stallworthy to William Stallworthy, 3 November 1935, Stallworthy Collection.

12 | SOUTHERN MOUNTIE

1 Henry Webb Stallworthy to William Stallworthy, 3 November 1935, Stallworthy Collection.

2 Ibid.

3   Henry Webb Stallworthy to William Stallworthy, 17 November, 1935, Stallworthy Collection.

4   Ibid.

5   T. H. Irvine to Commissioner J. MacBrien, 15 November 1935, Henry Webb Stallworthy, Service File, f. 409.

6   V. A. M. Kemp to T. H. Irvine, 20 November 1935, Henry Webb Stallworthy, Service File, f. 411.

7   Statement of account with C. M. Lampson, 26 November 1935, Stallworthy Collection.

8   Henry Webb Stallworthy to William Stallworthy, 3 November 1935, Stallworthy Collection.

9   Henry Webb Stallworthy to William Stallworthy, 17 November 1935, Stallworthy Collection.

10   Henry Webb Stallworthy to Edward Shackleton, 11 January 1936, Stallworthy Collection.

11   Hilda Stallworthy, Manuscript draft of introduction to a biography of Henry Webb Stallworthy, n.d., p. 10, Stallworthy Collection.

12   W. L. Sclater to Henry Webb Stallworthy, 18 November 1935, Henry Webb Stallworthy, Service File, f. 416.

13   Edward Shackleton to Henry Webb Stallworthy, 21 November 1935, Stallworthy Collection.

14   Royal Canadian Mounted Police, General Orders, Part One, week ending 22 February 1936, Stallworthy Collection.

15   Henry Webb Stallworthy to William Stallworthy, 21 March 1936, Stallworthy Collection.

16   "Career Summary," Henry Webb Stallworthy, Service File, f. 1.

17   H. Stallworthy, "An Arctic expedition," *Royal Canadian Mounted Police Quarterly* 3, no. 3 (1936): 149–72, reprinted in William H. Kelly, *The Mounties: as they saw themselves* (Ottawa: The Golden Dog Press, 1996), 126–53.

18   Henry Webb Stallworthy to William Stallworthy, 2 February, 1936, Stallworthy Collection.

19   S. T. Wood to Commissioner J. MacBrien, 22 April 1936, Henry Webb Stallworthy, Service File, f. 443.

20   Henry Webb Stallworthy to William Stallworthy, 2 February 1936, Stallworthy Collection.

21   "Plans for expedition to Canadian Arctic," submitted to Sir James MacBrien, 31 January 1936, NAC, RG 85, Vol. 872, File No. 7022, Pt. 2.

22   Dick, *Muskox Land*, 312–14.

23   Edward Shackleton to Henry Webb Stallworthy, 29 January 1936, Stallworthy Collection.

24   Henry Webb Stallworthy to William Stallworthy, 2 February 1936, Stallworthy Collection.

25 Henry Webb Stallworthy to Edward Shackleton (draft), 6 June 1936, Stallworthy Collection.

26 Dick, *Muskox Land*, 314.

27 T. H. Irvine to Commissioner J. MacBrien, 2 May 1936, Henry Webb Stallworthy, Service File, ff. 438–443; Operation record, Medical file, ff. 20–23.

28 T. H. Irvine to E. P. C. Salt, 4 May 1936, Henry Webb Stallworthy, Service File, f. 445.

29 D. Ryan, Memorandum of instructions—Coast Guard Service, Season 1936, 14 May 1936, Stallworthy Collection.

30 Henry Webb Stallworthy to Edward Shackleton (Draft), 6 June 1936, Stallworthy Collection.

31 Robert Bentham to Henry Webb Stallworthy, 12 August 1936, Stallworthy Collection.

32 Julian Baber to Henry Webb Stallworthy, 20 and 26 August 1936, Stallworthy Collection.

33 F. A. Blake to E. C. P. Salt, 23 September 1936, Henry Webb Stallworthy, Service File, f. 450.

34 Henry Webb Stallworthy to Superintendent Sandys-Wunsch, 10 October 1936, Stallworthy Collection.

35 Superintendent Sandys-Wunsch to Henry Webb Stallworthy, 22 October 1936, Stallworthy Collection.

36 Henry Webb Stallworthy to William Stallworthy, undated draft, Moncton, N. B., Stallworthy Collection

37 Ibid.

38 Henry Webb Stallworthy to William Stallworthy, 8 December 1936, Stallworthy Collection.

39 T. H. Irvine to W. V. Bruce, 15 March 1937, Stallworthy Collection; R. A. Gibson to Commissioner James H. MacBrien, 5 March 1937, Stallworthy Collection.

40 Arthur R. Hinks to George P. Vanier, 1 February 1937, Stallworthy Collection.

41 Henry Webb Stallworthy, "Re: Mr. Haig-Thomas' proposed expedition to Ellesmere Island—1938," March 1937, Stallworthy Collection.

42 David Haig-Thomas to Henry Webb Stallworthy, 8 May 1936, Stallworthy Collection.

43 Ibid.

44 D. Haig-Thomas, *Tracks in the snow* (London: Hodder and Stoughton, 1939), 20.

45 Ibid., 21.

46 Ibid.; D. Haig-Thomas, "Expedition to Ellesmere Island, 1937–38," *Geographical Journal* 95, no. 4 (1940): 265–77.

47 Paddy Hamilton to Henry Webb Stallworthy, 26 December 1938, Stallworthy Collection.

48 J. Wright, "South-east Ellesmere Island," *Geographical Journal* 95, no. 4 (1940): 278–91; J. Wright, "Account of the spring survey in Ellesmere Land, 1938," in D. Haig-Thomas, *Tracks in the snow* (London: Hodder and Stoughton, 1939), 280–88.

49 Henry Webb Stallworthy to William Stallworthy, undated draft, Moncton, N.B., Stallworthy Collection.

50 Invoice made out to H.W. Stallworthy from The Lounsbury Co., Moncton, 30 July 1937, Stallworthy Collection.

51 W.V. Bruce to J.D. Bird, 21 May 1937, Stallworthy Collection.

52 Henry Webb Stallworthy To O/C, R.C.M. Police, Moncton, N.B., 24 April 1939, Stallworthy Collection.

53 Henry Webb Stallworthy to George T. Hann, 20 October 1938, Stallworthy Collection.

54 George Hann to Henry Webb Stallworthy, 25 October 1938, Stallworthy Collection.

55 Application for RCMP Long Service Medal, 10 April 1937, Henry Webb Stallworthy, Service File, f. 452.

56 Memo from G.L. Jennings, 18 June 1937, Henry Webb Stallworthy, Service File, f. 456.

57 Memo, V.A.M. Kemp to O/C, "J" Division, 8 September 1937, Stallworthy Collection; also available at: Henry Webb Stallworthy, Service File, f. 457.

58 Hilda Stallworthy, Note attached to memo, V.A.M. Kemp to O.C., "J" Division, 8 September 1937, 30 January 1984, Stallworthy Collection.

59 Memo from F.A. Blake, 29 February 1940, Henry Webb Stallworthy, Service File, f. 487.

60 Henry Webb Stallworthy to W.V. Bruce, 28 January 1939 and 28 February 1939, Henry Webb Stallworthy, Service File, ff. 461 and 472.

61 Adjutant F.A. Blake to Henry Webb Stallworthy, 16 February, 1939, Stallworthy Collection.

62 J.G. McConnell, "The Fort Smith area 1780 to 1961: an historical geography," (Master's Thesis, Department of Geography, University of Toronto, 1965).

63 Adjutant F.A. Blake to W.V. Bruce, Superintendent Commanding "J" Division, 4 May 1939, Henry Webb Stallworthy, Service File, f. 476; T.B. Caulkin to Commissioner, 2 May 1939, Henry Webb Stallworthy, Service File, f. 476.

64 Inspector D.J. Martin to Commissioner, 7 November 1940, Henry Webb Stallworthy, Service File, ff. 490–492.

65 Henry Webb Stallworthy to William Stallworthy, 3 December 1940, Stallworthy Collection.

66 Hilda Stallworthy to Jimmy and Edie, 7 February 1940, Stallworthy Collection.

67 Hilda Stallworthy, Diary notes, 15 October 1939, Stallworthy Collection.

68 Ibid.

69   Ibid., 5 November 1939.

70   Ibid., 29 October 1939.

71   Ibid., 28 November 1939.

72   Ibid.

73   Ibid., 3 December 1939

74   Ibid., 5 November, 1939.

75   Hilda Stallworthy to Jimmy and Edie, 7 February 1940, Stallworthy Collection.

76   R. Bettaney to D.J. Martin, 3 April 1941, Henry Webb Stallworthy, Service File, f. 494.

77   D.J. Martin to Commissioner, 26 April, 1941, Henry Webb Stallworthy, Service File, f. 496.

78   R. Bettaney to Inspector D.J. Martin, 29 April 1941, Henry Webb Stallworthy, Service File, f. 494.

79   Hilda Stallworthy, Memo, 30 January 1984, Stallworthy Collection.

80   "Butter and sugar from Canada," *Canada's Weekly*, 27 June 1941, Henry Webb Stallworthy, Service File, f. 498.

81   J.A. Urquhart, Memo re: Sergeant Stallworthy, 22 November 1941, Henry Webb Stallworthy, Medical File, ff. 12–14.

82   Henry Webb Stallworthy to D.J. Martin, 12 February 1942, Henry Webb Stallworthy, Service File, f. 503.

83   D.J. Martin to Commissioner, RCMP, 12 February 1942, Henry Webb Stallworthy, Service File, f. 503.

84   Henry Webb Stallworthy to D.J. Martin, 19 March 1942, Henry Webb Stallworthy, Service File, f. 506.

85   R.C. Bowen to Commissioner, RCMP, 3 June 1942, Henry Webb Stallworthy, Service File, f. 514.

86   Henry Webb Stallworthy to William Stallworthy, 21 July 1946, Stallworthy Collection.

87   F.A. Blake to R.C. Bowen, 8 June 1942, Henry Webb Stallworthy, Service File, f. 521.

88   Telegram, Commissioner RCMP to O.C., Edmonton, 13 June 1942, Stallworthy Collection.

89   Supt. F.A. Blake to O.C., "E" division, Vancouver, 15 June 1942, Stallworthy Collection; also available at: Henry Webb Stallworthy, Service File, f. 525.

90   F.A. Blake to O.C., "E" Division, Vancouver, 17 July 1942, Henry Webb Stallworthy, Service File, f. 529.

91   V.A.M. Kemp to Commissioner, RCMP, 30 March 1942, Henry Webb Stallworthy, Service File, f. 508.

92   V.A.M. Kemp to Commissioner, RCMP, 17 August 1942, Henry Webb Stallworthy, Service File, ff. 533 and 534.

93   Henry Webb Stallworthy to William Stallworthy, 26 August 1943, Stallworthy
      Collection.

94   Henry Webb Stallworthy to O.C., "O" Division, Toronto, 14 and 17 October
      1942, Stallworthy Collection.

95   Henry Webb Stallworthy to William Stallworthy, 21 July 1946, Stallworthy
      Collection.

96   Henry Webb Stallworthy to William Stallworthy, 29 November 1944,
      Stallworthy Collection.

97   Henry Webb Stallworthy to William Stallworthy, 17 July 1945, Sault Ste.
      Marie, Stallworthy Collection.

98   F. A. Blake to Commissioner F.W. Schutz, 10 October 1944, Henry Webb
      Stallworthy, Service File, f. 553.

99   Vilhjalmur Stefansson to Hilda Stallworthy, 6 December 1943, Stallworthy
      Collection.

100   Vilhjalmur Stefansson to Lt.-Col. W. Hurst Brown, 13 March 1944,
      Stallworthy Collection.

101   Henry Webb Stallworthy to William Stallworthy, 29 November 1944,
      Stallworthy Collection.

102   Henry Webb Stallworthy to William Stallworthy, 20 May 1946, Stallworthy
      Collection.

103   Henry Webb Stallworthy to Hilda Stallworthy, 16 September 1944,
      Stallworthy Collection.

104   Henry Webb Stallworthy to William Stallworthy, 21 July 1946, Stallworthy
      Collection.

105   F. N. Hughes to Commissioner F.W. Schutz, 24 August 1944, Henry Webb
      Stallworthy, Service File, f. 552.

106   Henry Webb Stallworthy to William Stallworthy, 31 May 1945, Stallworthy
      Collection; also available at: Henry Webb Stallworthy, Medical File, Hospital
      Record and Case History Sheet, RCMPA.

107   A. Blake to Commissioner F.W. Schutz, 9 May 1945, Henry Webb Stallworthy,
      Service File, f. 551.

108   D.C. Saul to F.A. Blake, 12 May 1945, Henry Webb Stallworthy, Service File,
      f. 558.

109   Henry Webb Stallworthy to William Stallworthy, 29 November 1944,
      Stallworthy Collection.

110   Henry Webb Stallworthy to William Stallworthy, 31 May 1945, Stallworthy
      Collection.

13 | TIMBERLANE

1   Adjutant D.C. Saul to O.C., "O" Division, 5 December, 1945, copy forwarded
      to Sergeant Major Stallworthy, Stallworthy Collection.

2   Henry Webb Stallworthy to William Stallworthy, 21 July 1946, Stallworthy Collection; Henry Webb Stallworthy to O.C. "O" Division, 24 December 1945, Stallworthy Collection.

3   Henry Webb Stallworthy to William Stallworthy, 9 January 1946, Stallworthy Collection.

4   Henry Webb Stallworthy to William Stallworthy, 20 May 1946, Stallworthy Collection.

5   Henry Webb Stallworthy to William Stallworthy, 21 July 1946, Stallworthy Collection.

6   Henry Webb Stallworthy to William Stallworthy, 3 May 1947, Stallworthy Collection.

7   Elaine Mellor, personal communication, May 2004.

8   Henry Webb Stallworthy to Mrs. Florence Stallworthy, 4 October 1948, Stallworthy Collection; Hilda Stallworthy to Mrs. Stallworthy, 4 October 1948, Stallworthy Collection.

9   Gray Campbell, "Stallworthy" (typescript of article dated 1961), p. 11, Stallworthy Collection.

10   Hilda Stallworthy to Bruce Carruthers, 30 June 1949, Stallworthy Collection.

11   Ibid.

12   Pierre Berton, *Hollywood's Canada. The Americanization of our national image* (Toronto: McClelland and Stewart, 1975), 139–46.

13   Bruce Carruthers to Henry Webb Stallworthy, 11 November 1937, Stallworthy Collection.

14   Bruce Carruthers to Henry Webb Stallworthy, 30 May 1937, Stallworthy Collection.

15   Ibid.

16   Bruce Carruthers to Henry Webb Stallworthy, 18 August 1949, Stallworthy Collection.

17   Bruce Carruthers to Henry Webb Stallworthy, 25 January 1950, Stallworthy Collection.

18   Henry Webb Stallworthy to William Stallworthy, 20 October 1952, Stallworthy Collection.

19   Hilda Stallworthy, Diary, 17 and 19 November 1953, Stallworthy Collection.

20   Personal communication, Elaine Mellor, summer 2001.

21   Hilda Stallworthy, Diary, 25 and 26 March 1954, Stallworthy Collection.

22   Elaine Mellor, personal communication, 2004.

23   Ibid.

24   Ibid.

25   Henry Webb Stallworthy to William Stallworthy, 4 May 1952, Stallworthy Collection.

26   Hilda Stallworthy, Diary, 23 January 1954, Stallworthy Collection.

27 George McClellan to Henry Webb Stallworthy, 3 July 1956, Stallworthy Collection.

28 Hilda Stallworthy, Diary, 28 and 29 June 1956, Stallworthy Collection.

29 Thomas Lawrence to Henry Webb Stallworthy, 2 August 1956, Stallworthy Collection.

30 H.M. Frediani to Henry Webb Stallworthy, 2 August 1956, Stallworthy Collection.

31 Hilda Stallworthy, Diary, 6 August 1956, Stallworthy Collection.

32 T.E. Lawrence to Henry Webb Stallworthy, 17 September 1956, Stallworthy Collection.

33 Hilda Stallworthy, Diary, 18 August 1956, Stallworthy Collection.

34 Ibid., 19 August 1956.

35 Ibid., 5 October 1956.

36 Ibid., 7 and 9 October 1956.

37 Henry Webb Stallworthy to Ben Siverts, 22 December 1956, Stallworthy Collection.

38 Hilda Stallworthy, Diary, 18 February 1957, Stallworthy Collection.

39 Ibid., 21 March 1957.

40 Henry Webb Stallworthy to Frank (?), Foundation Company of Canada, Montreal, 3 September 1957, Stallworthy Collection.

41 Henry Webb Stallworthy to Frank (?), 3 September 1957, Stallworthy Collection.

42 Ibid.

43 Hilda Stallworthy, Diary, 10 September 1957, Stallworthy Collection.

44 Elaine Mellor, personal communication, May 2004.

45 Hilda Stallworthy, Diary, 6 December 1957, Stallworthy Collection.

46 Hilda Stallworthy to Ethelind Mellor, 27 July 1977, Stallworthy Collection.

47 Ibid.

48 Elaine Mellor, personal communication, May 2004.

49 Ibid.

50 Ibid.

51 Hilda Stallworthy, Diary, 11–15 September 1973, Stallworthy Collection.

52 Ibid., 16 September 1973.

53 Elaine Mellor, personal communication, May 2004.

54 C. Lochnan to Henry Webb Stallworthy, 26 April 1973, Stallworthy Collection; E. Butler to Henry Webb Stallworthy, 19 June, 1973, Stallworthy Collection.

55 Hilda Stallworthy to Ethelind Mellor, 18 February 1977, Stallworthy Collection.

56 *RCMP Veterans' Association, Victoria Division, Bulletin*, October 1977, Stallworthy Collection.

57 Hilda Stallworthy, Diary, 6 December 1976, Stallworthy Collection.

58 Hilda Stallworthy, Diary, 25 December 1976, Stallworthy Collection.

59 Registration of death, Henry Webb Stallworthy, Department of Health, Division of Vital Statistics, British Columbia, Registration No. 76-09-019297, BCA.

60 Philip More? or Thom? to Hilda Stallworthy, 4 February 1977, Stallworthy Collection.

61 Jules Léger to Hilda Stallworthy, 26 January 1977, Stallworthy Collection.

62 Edward Shackleton to Hilda Stallworthy, 17 January 1977, Stallworthy Collection.

63 Edward Shackleton to William Stallworthy, 14 January 1977, Shackleton Papers, SPRI.

64 Edward Shackleton to Commissioner M.J. Nadon, 17 January 1977, in *RCMP Quarterly* 42, no. 2 (1977): 4–5.

65 Hilda Stallworthy, Introduction to unfinished manuscript biography of Henry Webb Stallworthy, Stallworthy Collection.

BIBLIOGRAPHY

Anonymous. *The regulations for the protection of game and wildfowl contained in the laws of the Cape York Station, Thule, of 7 June 1929, given by Knud Rasmussen, Ph.D., and sanctioned by the Ministry of Shipping and Fisheries*. Copenhagen: Gylendals Forlagstrykkeri, 1931.

Barr, W. "Otto Sverdrup (1854–1930)." *Arctic* 37, no. 1 (1984): 72–73.

———. *Back from the brink. The road to muskox conservation in the Northwest Territories*. Komatik Series 3. Calgary: Arctic Institute of North America, 1991.

———. "The career and disappearance of Hans K.E. Krüger, Arctic geologist." *Polar Record* 29, no. 171 (1993): 277–304.

Berton, P. *Hollywood's Canada. The Americanization of our national image*. Toronto: McClelland and Stewart, 1975.

Brooks, R.C., J.H. England, A.S. Dyke and J. Savelle. "Krüger's final camp in Arctic Canada." *Arctic* 57, no. 2 (2004): 225–29.

Coates, K.S. and W.R. Morrison. *Land of the midnight sun. A history of the Yukon.* Edmonton: Hurtig, 1988.

Copeland, A.D. *Coplalook, Chief Trader, Hudson's Bay Company.* Winnipeg: Watson and Dwyer, 1985.

De Laguna, Frederica. *Voyage to Greenland. A personal initiation into Anthropology.* New York: W. Norton and Co., 1977.

Department of the Interior. *The Yukon Territory.* Ottawa: King's Printer, 1916.

Dick, L. *Muskox Land. Ellesmere Island in the age of contact.* Calgary: University of Calgary Press, 2001.

Haig-Thomas, D. *Tracks in the snow.* London: Hodder and Stoughton, 1939.

———. "Expedition to Ellesmere Island, 1937–38." *Geographical Journal* 95, no. 4 (1940): 265–77.

Hattersley-Smith, G., et al. "Northern Ellesmere Island, 1953 and 1954." *Arctic* 8, no. 1 (1955): 3–36.

Hume, H.E. "Report of the Chairman, Dominion Lands Branch." In *Annual Report of the Department of the Interior for the fiscal year ended March 31, 1932.* Ottawa: F. Acland, 1932.

———. "Report of the Chairman, Dominion Lands Branch." In *Annual Report of the Department of the Interior for the fiscal year ended March 31, 1933.* Ottawa: O. Patenaude, 1933.

Jones, D.C. *Empire of dust. Settling and abandoning the prairie dry belt.* Edmonton: The University of Alberta Press, 1987.

Kelly, W. *The Mounties: as they saw themselves.* Ottawa: The Golden Dog Press, 1996.

Kobalenko, J. *The horizontal Everest. Extreme journeys on Ellesmere Island.* Toronto: Penguin/Viking, 2002.

Lee, H.P. *Policing the top of the world.* London: John Lane/The Bodley Head, 1928.

Low, A.P. *Report on the Dominion Government expedition to Hudson Bay and the Arctic Islands on board the D.G.S. Neptune 1903–1904.* Ottawa: Government Printing Bureau, 1906.

Macmillan, D.B. *Four years in the white North.* New York and London: Harper and Brothers, 1918.

Mathiassen, Th. "Report on the expedition." In *Report of the Fifth Thule Expedition 1921–24,* Vol. 1, bk. 1. Copenhagen: Gyldendallske Boghandel. Nordisk Forlag, 1945.

McConnell, J. "The Fort Smith area 1780 to 1961: an historical geography." Master's Thesis, Department of Geography, University of Toronto, 1965.

Molson, K.M. *Pioneering in Canadian air transport.* Winnipeg: J. Richardson, 1974.

Morrison, W.R. *Showing the flag. The Mounted Police and Canadian sovereignty in the North.* Vancouver: University of British Columbia Press, 1985.

Morton, D. and J.L. Granatstein. *Marching to Armageddon. Canadians and the Great War 1914–1919.* Toronto: Lester and Orpen Dennys, 1989.

North, D. *The lost patrol.* Anchorage: Alaska Northwest Publishing Co., 1978.

Osczevski, R. "The hunt for marine reptile fossils on western Ellesmere Island." *Polar Record* 28, no. 165 (1992): 105–12.

Peary, R. E. *Nearest the Pole: a narrative of the polar expedition of the Peary Arctic Club in the S. S. Roosevelt, 1905–1906.* London: Hutchinson and Co., 1907.

Rasmussen, K. *Across Arctic America. Narrative of the Fifth Thule Expedition.* New York: G. Putnam's Sons, 1927.

Robertson, D. S. *To the Arctic with the Mounties.* Toronto: Macmillan Co. of Canada, 1934.

Shackleton, E. *Arctic journeys. The story of the Oxford University Ellesmere Land Expedition 1934–5.* London: Hodder and Stoughton, 1937.

Shaw, T. E. G. "Hanged by a shoe lace." *Royal Canadian Mounted Police Quarterly* 28, no. 3 (1963): 187–91.

Stallworthy, H.W. "Winter patrols in the Arctic." *Royal Canadian Mounted Police Quarterly* 2, no. 2 (1935): 17–25.

———. "An arctic expedition." *Royal Canadian Mounted Police Quarterly* 3, no. 3 (1936): 149–72.

———. "The loneliest journey." *The Blue Book* 92, no. 2 (1950): 13–15.

Steele, H. *The Canadians in France 1915–1918.* New York: E. P. Dutton and Co., 1919.

Stefansson, V. *The friendly Arctic: the story of five years in the polar regions.* New York: Macmillan, 1921.

Sverdrup, O. *New land; four years in the arctic regions.* London and New York: Longmans, Green, 1904.

Thorsteinsson, R. "The history and geology of Meighen Island, Arctic Archipelago." *Geological Survey of Canada Bulletin* 75 (1961): 19 pp.

Vibe, C. *Langthen og nordpaa. Skildringer fra "Den Danske Thule-og Ellesmereland-ekspedition 1939–1940."* København: Gylendal, 1948.

Wright, J. "Account of the spring survey in Ellesmere Land." In *Tracks in the snow*, D. Haig-Thomas, 280–88. London: Hodder and Stoughton, 1939.

———. "South-east Ellesmere Island." *Geographical Journal* 95, no. 4 (1940): 278–91.

Zaslow, M. *The opening of the Canadian North 1870–1914.* Toronto/Montreal: McClelland and Stewart, 1971.

———. *A century of Canada's Arctic islands, 1880–1980.* Ottawa: Royal Society of Canada, 1981.

INDEX

63; extent of injuries, 62–63; funeral for, 66–67; leg amputated, 64; memorials to, 71; previous northern experience, 62

Clay, S.G., 60, 62–64, 68, 70; reaction to wife's death, 67

Clements Markham Inlet, 252

Cleveland, George, 60, 62

C.M. Lampson and Co., 274

coal, 245, 254

Coast Range, 306

Coates Island, 61

Coburg Island, 129, 184–85

Cochrane River, 106

Cocked Hat Island, 138, 176

Comox, British Columbia, 317, 319–22

Conibear, Barbara, 291–92

Cook, Frederick, falsifies photo of North Pole, 150

Cook, Henry, 13–14

Cook Peninsula, 258

Copeland, Dudley, 60–61

Copenhagen, Denmark, 199, 226, 246

Copes Bay, 257

Coral Harbour, NWT, 60–61

corals, 244, 255

Cornwall Island, 145, 151–52, 158–59, 178

Coronation Gulf, 76

Cotswold Hills, 4

Craig Harbour Detachment, 1, 119, 126, 129, 133, 136–37, 283; advantages of, 172; butchering walrus, 119–20; buildings spruced up, 185; detachment moved to, 179–80; establishment of, 115; Harry's visit to, 129–30; site of, 142 (map), 180

cricket, 212

"Crocker Land", 147

Croker Bay, 165

"Crossed Revolvers", 84

cryolite, 266

Cumberland Sound, 189

Cumming Inlet, 165

Cummings, Ross, 103–4, 106

Cunningham Mountains, 181

curling, 84

Currie, Arthur W., 22

Currie, J.B., 164

Daly Bay, 55–56

Daly Peninsula, 261

Danish Government, 113

Danish Island, 44, 62

Danish Thule and Ellesmere Island Expedition, 153

Dannebrog, 219, 264–65; delayed at Castlebay, 266–67; experiences rough crossing, 266

Dapp, Alberta, 76

Darmstadt, Germany, 125

Dawson City, Yukon, 7, 11, 15–16, 36, 133, 294; conditions at, 17, 25; population, 25; temperatures at, 330 n. 57

Dedrick, T.S., 246

De Laguna, Frederica, opinion of Krüger, 125

Dempster, W.J.D., vii, 7, 27, 30, *31*

Denain, France, 22

Department of the Interior, 114, 213; subsidizes OUELE, 206

Depot Island, 54–55, 59–61

Depot Point, 126, 146

Dersch, P., 183; mounts patrol to Craig Harbour, 180–81; searches for Krüger, 164–65

Devon Island, 108, 130, 132, 142 (map), 164, 199; Ice Cap, 181–83

Devonshire, Lord, 113

DEW-Line, 6 (map), 313–17

Dickins, C.H. (Punch), 100, 109

Discovery, 246

Discovery Harbour, 246